OTHER BOOKS BY TOM AINSLIE

The Compleat Horseplayer
Handicapper's Handbook
Ainslie's Complete Guide to Harness Racing
Ainslie on Jockeys
Ainslie's Complete Hoyle

Ainslie's
COMPLETE
GUIDE TO
Thoroughbred
Racing

THIRD EDITION

by TOM AINSLIE

SIMON AND SCHUSTER
New York

Published by Simon and Schuster
A Division of Simon & Schuster, Inc.
Simon & Schuster Building
Rockefeller Center
1230 Avenue of the Americas
New York, New York 10020

SIMON AND SCHUSTER and colophon are registered trademarks of Simon &
Schuster, Inc.

Designed by Stanley S. Drate/Folio Graphics Co. Inc.

Manufactured in the United States of America

10 9 8 7 6 5 4 3 2 1

Library of Congress Cataloging in Publication Data

Ainslie, Tom.
    Ainslie's complete guide to thoroughbred racing.

    Includes index.
    1. Horse race betting.   2. Horse race betting—
United States.   3. Horse-racing.   4. Horse-racing—
United States.   I. Title.   II. Title: Complete guide
to thoroughbred racing.
SF331.A48   1986   798.4'01'0973   86-3879

ISBN: 0-671-62414-8

CONTENTS

FOREWORD
TO THE THIRD EDITION

In Thoroughbred racing as in most other sectors of modern life, technology has quickened the tempo of change.

The first edition of this book was published in 1968. It was an earnest and comprehensive attempt to summarize the realities of our great game, as I perceived them at that time. Change rendered the book obsolete by 1979, when a second version appeared. Now, after a briefer interval marked by dramatically accelerated and truly fundamental change, here comes a third edition. And none too soon.

Electronics and veterinary medicine have affected aspects of racing enough to make them unrecognizable to someone whose knowledge of the game stopped growing in 1979.

Consider the proliferating computer. Computerized pari-mutuel wagering systems now enable racetracks to offer exotic bets in unprecedented variety, inviting the eager innocent to risk the farm in numerous different ways on a single race. During the pre-race betting periods, video monitors display the probable payoffs on each combination of horses involved in some of the least complex of these gimmick bets. This information allows mathematically adept players to exploit the blunders of the helpless crowd.

After each race, instant video replays now provide an advantage to handicappers who have learned to watch races with great care, noting the losers that had legitimate excuses, and discounting apparently better performances attributable more to happenstance than to superior ability. These handicappers can see a race several times, first on the track and then on the monitors.

I mentioned medicine. Veterinarians now can heal injuries that formerly ended a Thoroughbred's career. These accomplishments, plus lenient anti-drugging rules and even more lenient enforcement thereof in most racing jurisdictions, have brought drastic revision to certain traditions of Thoroughbred training and therefore to the realities of handicapping. Horses now can race more frequently, with fewer and shorter sick leaves. And with a little help from a friendly pharmacologist, a trainer can bring horses back in winning form after lengthy absences.

Now that racing itself has become so much more sophisticated than at any time in its checkered history, the game of trying to pick winners demands a corresponding increase in knowledge and technique.

For more than two decades I have been scolding the racing industry about its bubble-headed inability (or reluctance) to help its own customers become good handicappers. That defect remains essentially unchanged. Today, as in 1968 or 1979, the likeliest way to keep pace with developments in handicapping is to read books.

I hope you enjoy this one.

TOM AINSLIE
Millwood, New York
January 1986

PREFACE:
IN WHICH WE
NAME THE GAME

This book seeks to fill an enormous void in the literature of American Thoroughbred racing.

Other volumes celebrate the romance of the turf, the feats of champions, the distinctiveness of the breed, the exploits of horsemen dead and gone. This one occupies different territory. It is an encyclopedic review of handicapping theory and technique—the first such work in the long history of the game. Its sole concerns are (1) the competition among horsemen for purse winnings and (2) the competition among horsemen and fans for pari-mutuel winnings. Its goal is to help the fan by revealing the strategy and tactics that lead to the winner's circle and the mutuel cashier's window.

Racing is unique in sport. Its paying customers are more than spectators. They are participants. They go to the track not only to see something but to do something. Specifically, they go to bet. In these pages I propose to enhance their pleasure in the game by helping them to become good at it.

I hasten to concede that one need not be a winning bettor to enjoy an occasional outing at the track. Horse races are incomparably exciting. Moreover, these are prosperous times. Millions of men and women can afford the very minor misfortunes with which racing penalizes innocence. Unless the racegoer gambles insanely, a losing excursion to the track costs no more than a night on the town.

Nevertheless, it is more fun to win than to lose. Nobody with normal emotions can possibly be indifferent to the outcome of races and bets. I therefore find it preposterous that no serious effort has been made (until now) to undress, dissect and analyze this multibillion-dollar pastime for those whose wagers are its main source of revenue.

Rank-and-file players should know the percentages and probabilities of the game. They should know how horsemen decide what to do with their animals, and when, and why. They should know the criteria on which professional handicappers and successful bettors base their judgments. They should, in other words, be made privy to the what's what, who's who and how come of the game they play.

Inasmuch as human beings tend to concentrate on pastimes in which they are skilled and to avoid those in which they take a thumping, one might fairly ask why racing has been so remiss about educating its own clientele. Why the huge omissions from the tons of literature issued by the racing industry and its able publicists? Has Thoroughbred racing's eminence as our largest "spectator" sport blinded it to the fact that most of it customers, however enthusiastic they may be, are transients? And that, aside from a small minority of neurotically compulsive losers, persons who attend racing regularly do so only because they have learned how to avoid serious financial loss? And that the way to increase the popularity of any game, no matter how popular it may be to begin with, is to teach people how to play it?

The reason that racing fails to grasp such opportunities is that it is afraid to. The fear is understandable. It derives from the sport's checkered past.

Not more than three generations ago, it was taken for granted that the only reputable persons at the track were the high-society types who owned the best horses. Their excuse for having all that fun was that they were perpetuating the glorious traditions of their class, improving the breed. They all bet, of course. But any commoner who went to the track to bet was a practitioner of evil. It surprised nobody when he turned out to be the black sheep of someone's family, or an absconding bookkeeper, or a stage-door johnny, or a degenerate gambler, or she a madam. The tracks were overrun with pickpockets and bunco steerers. Anyone with half a brain knew that many races were fixed. Victorian moral standards, or the instinct of self-preservation, or both, discouraged ordinary folk from entering such an environment. The sport was too seamy to mess with.

Great changes have occurred. Victorian morality has all but vanished. People no longer equate excitement with sin. Racing, an excitement if ever there was one, has responded by tidying its house. It now draws customers by the millions from the arts, the sciences, the professions and the upper reaches of the country's business and political establishments. The clientele of racing has become a representative cross section of the American public, as respectable as any other. And the act of going to the track to bet has achieved social acceptance. This is not quite as comfortable as social approval, but is a lap ahead of social toleration. In my opinion, the game will cross the threshold of approval as soon as it recognizes that it deserves to. It has become an industry of immense importance.

Every year, tens of millions of racing enthusiasts deposit more than $8 billion in the pari-mutuel betting pools at North American tracks. Thoroughbred tracks remit over $450 million to government treasuries, which get another $200 million from harness and quarter-horse racing.

To put it mildly, the state and local governments welcome these tax contributions. They also enjoy the political jobs made possible by establishment and expansion of commissions charged with supervision of the sport. And they seem to appreciate the highly moral flavor of racing's communications with the voting public. The owners and managers of the game are careful to thwart anti-vice elements and other moralizers by playing down the lure of betting. So that neither they nor their political protectors will be mauled for "encouraging gambling," the tracks promote the spectator aspects of their business. They pretend that the pari-mutuel machines are not the main attraction in the store.

Which returns me to the original point. A major book explaining the game of racing to the bettor might have come from the industry itself, as a goodwill effort to educate the customers toward wiser, less costly betting. Yet one searches in vain for printed matter in which racing officials or active horsemen emit so much as a hint about the art of selecting winners.

So sensitive is the industry to the hostility of anti-gambling fanatics that it even discourges the use of words like "horseplayer." The purple-necked gentleman tearing up a fistful of losing mutuel tickets and bawling abuse at the jockey is not to be called "horseplayer." He is a "racing fan." If it is bad taste to call a horseplayer a horseplayer, what shall we call a poker player?

Let us grant that the sport's modest garb, woven of 100 percent pure, virgin fig leaves, shields it from charges that it promotes vice. Let us applaud anything that frustrates the bluenoses who oppose racing. But let us question whether it is necessary any longer to appease the bluenoses. And let us recognize that the timid failure of racing experts to explain the art of handicapping actually encourages gambling. Their secretiveness is a primary reason why millions of floundering fans waste money on unintelligent bets!

The viewpoint of this book is that few racegoers are emotionally crippled gamblers, hell-bent to make themselves miserable by squandering the milk money. Most horseplayers are capable of learning how to function more effectively at the track—if someone would only do them the honor of showing them how.

How Experts Get That Way

From long experience in a variety of games, I feel qualified to make a most unusual but absolutely valid statement about the handicapping of horse races: It demands no less mental prowess than bridge, poker or chess. The skills of the expert handicapper are, in fact, closely comparable to those of the good bridge, poker or chess player. In any such competition, players who depend on instinct, trial-and-error, inexpert advice, superstition or reckless guesses are at a disadvantage. They cannot hope to hold their own against persons who have acquired an understanding of the game as a whole.

The bedside table or living-room bookcase of every serious bridge player holds encyclopedic volumes by Charles Goren, Alfred Sheinwold and Louis Watson. Chess players make endless use of comprehensive texts by Reuben Fine, Emanuel Lasker, Fred Reinfeld and Bobby Fischer. Mediocre poker players become tough propositions after studying Oswald Jacoby, Herbert O. Yardley and Irwin Steig. But horseplayers are not accustomed to help of such quality and abundance.

Armed only with unreliable tips, insubstantial systems and hope, most horseplayers take a cruel battering in a game that really is not all that tough. Not, that is, for the few players lucky enough to know its theory and technique.

In response to the racing enthusiast's need, this book offers a comprehensive review of handicapping theory and technique. It dismantles the barriers that traditionally separate the paying customer from the professional horseman and professional handicapper. It presents the entire story, the full range of possibilities. Truths about Thoroughbreds and the humans who race them are revealed here for the first time. These truths are the essence of sound handicapping, sound wagering.

Above all, the book equips its reader with standards with which to judge the relevance of the dizzyingly diverse items of coded technical information which are the handicapper's stock in trade. Believe it or not (and, if you have been going to the races for a while, you will believe it), most players consciously avoid that information, because they don't know what to make of it. Which is like trying to navigate without looking at the map.

The Importance of Predictability

Apart from its neglect of handicapping, published information about Thoroughbred racing is abundant, detailed and accurate. A superb daily newspaper, several magazines and yearly encyclopedias offer to horsemen, officials and fans a range of news, statistics and commentary unsurpassed in any sport.

These easily available materials are more than merely interesting. They are essential to the orderly conduct of the game. They help the horseman make decisions about horses. They help the expert fan make decisions about bets. For both individuals the name of the game is prediction. And published information is the raw material from which prediction is made. Moreover, it provides the background against which errors in prediction may be diagnosed and corrected.

Certain patterns have become well established in centuries of Thoroughbred racing. The running condition of horses improves and declines in cycles familiar enough to make sudden reversals of form both noticeable and suspect. The class, or quality, of horses is also patterned, as is their ability to cope with high weights or unfamiliar distances, or with races in which the early stages are run at unusually fast or slow speeds. For these reasons and many others, race results themselves follow what might be termed a pattern of reasonable predictability.

A limitation on predictability is the unalterable fact that the race is a contest among mute animals of impermanent quality and unstable temperament. Nobody can interview a horse. The creature reveals the truth about itself only after the race has begun and the bets have become irrevocable. Moreover, its ability to do its best is affected by the handling it gets from humans of varying competence and integrity—trainers, grooms, stablehands and jockeys. These circumstances explain why any player able to win 40 percent of the bets made in a year is probably a genuine expert. And a marvel of self-discipline. Winners pick their spots with great care. Only a rare day allows more than three bets.

Another aspect of racing's predictability is more melancholy, and is closely linked to what I have just said. Anyone who tries to pick a winner in every race will be unable to predict the outcome of more than three races in ten if he persists in the practice for a year.

A third aspect is that racetrack crowds do better than that. The crowds function on a blend of hunch, horoscope, hot tip, individual handicapping, the motley forecasts of newspapers and tip sheets (which somehow name almost every horse in most races) and the dubious predictions of innumerable selection systems. Yet the crowds pick the winner of one race in every three. That statistic, which holds up year after year, is, of course, the percentage of victories by betting favorites. The public's consistency is one of the inexplicable mysteries of the sport.

If these aspects of predictability seem to impose a ceiling on success at the track, they also suggest the possibility of a floor under failure. The racing industry recognizes this. It understands all too clearly that its hold on public confidence would become infirm if race results were to depart from the established patterns of reasonable predictability. The industry expends much money and a good deal of ingenuity to prevent and/or punish hanky-panky.

Here again, published information is vital. In deciding whether a suspect race was honestly contested, officials have access to videotapes of it and of previous races involving the same horses and riders. They also avail themselves of the published record about those past races. They do so knowing that the expert fan uses the same information. His ability to interpret the information is a spur to the authorities. The penalty for official laxness is public indignation—a first step toward desertion.

Horsemen, Handicappers and Information

For an example of how horsemen use public information, let us consider a trainer. He has a pretty nice kind of four-year-old sprinter which he regards as ready to win a race for $20,000 animals at three quarters of a mile. But his arch rival, the wily Trainer Doe, has just imported a large, bright-eyed colt from Illinois. If our horseman had to wait and see Doe's colt in a race or two before learning anything about him, his ability to manage the affairs of his own horse would be seriously impaired. Indeed, such a plight would mean that he and Doe and everyone else in racing had been transported, science-fiction style, to the beginning of the century, when published information was sparse and horsemen resolved their problems by collusion, chicanery and simple assault.

Our modern horseman can learn a great deal about Doe's import without budging from his desk. Microfilmed results charts and printed past-performance records offer an almost photographic profile of the creature. Its quality, its running style, its favorite distances, its ability to carry high weight, its liking for wet or muddy running surfaces and even its capacity for retaining top form after a long journey are all there in the records. If the colt was losing to $15,000 horses in Illinois it had better not jump up and beat $50,000 ones in its debut here or Doe may find himself in a jam. Such reversals of form were common in the bad old days and are scarcely unheard of now, but as suggested earlier, fans and officials are equipped to recognize most of them. Although racing officials are not celebrated for their crusading vigor, they usually find ways to discourage and even to penalize gross misconduct.

Good handicappers may disagree about individual races or individual horses, but as a class they make remarkably accurate appraisals of most. With exceptions that we shall discuss in full detail later, they can tell which entrants are likely to be in contention and which have only negligible chances. The minutely specific information contained in result charts and past-performance records is a foundation of such judgment. Supplemental data appears in published tabulations that include the winning averages of trainers, jockeys, owners and breeders. The racing press also contains useful news of breeding transactions, livestock sales, personnel shifts, owners' and trainers' plans, and equine injury and illness.

Their regular presence at the track and the large amounts of money they bet suggest that published information works for the horsefolk and expert customers who are the mainstays of the pari-mutuel handle. Each takes pride in possession of private or personal information garnered through close observation of horses and their handlers, but few could survive without the printed matter.

All these experts may not be big winners, but it is evident that even the least expert of them manage to hold losses to an endurable level. And make no mistake: Thousands of fans combine intelligence, knowledge and self-control in proportions adequate to win money for themselves year after year and even season after season or month after month. Week after week and day after day are entirely beyond human reach, but things work out nicely in the long run. And even for the fan whose pleasure in the game outweighs the effect of small but inevitable losses it can be seen that Thoroughbred racing is reasonably predictable.

Yet of the persons who buy 55 million tickets of admission to North American tracks and bet their hard-earned $8 billion or so during a typical year in the mid-80s, I doubt that one in five hundred qualifies as an expert. I doubt, in short, that more than a tiny percentage exploit the predictability of racing by putting available information to profitable use. But their numbers can increase.

Confessions of an Author

My own interest in racing arose more than half a century ago. I was fascinated by the commotion of the break from the starting barrier, the skill of the jockeying on the turns, the tension and suspense of the sprint down the homestretch. But I was a serious-minded type, with a thin billfold. I saw no profit in betting on something about which I knew nothing. I decided to buy some books.

No such thing was to be had. I was appalled. Nostalgic volumes about the history of the turf were available for nine cents on the remainder counter of every bookshop, but a book about the art of picking winners was available at no price.

"The reason they don't publish books for horseplayers," explained one merchant, "is that horseplayers can't read."

Certain magazines contained fragmentary articles extolling the un-demonstrated advantages of various handicapping angles or outlining equally unsubstantiated selection systems. Advertisements in the same periodicals hawked pamphlets revealing alleged "secrets" of successful "turf speculation." The pamphlets were similar in quality and substance to the magazine pieces. They offered a glimmering of what might have been wisdom, but nothing remotely like a comprehensive view of the overall problem with which they purported to deal. Also, the mail-order promoters who published these tracts invariably turned out to be tipsters and touts who kept one's mailbox cluttered with promises of riches beyond belief—for a $5 bill. I was young and naive, but it never occurred to me to patronize the touts. I wondered uneasily about the age and worldliness of those who did.

The *Daily Racing Form* published, as it still does, full instructions on how to decipher the notations in results charts and past-performance records. This was helpful. But mastery of the cipher left one with the fundamental problem of how to *interpret* the decoded information. What was important? What was not? Which end was up?

I remained interested in racing for years, without betting a nickel on any race. In spare time I tested various systems on paper, much as a would-be stock investor might attempt dry runs with theories of market analysis. A few bookmakers and several professional horsemen supplied some lore, guiding me toward a beginning grasp of the game. In time, by dint of lonesome, laborious study of a sort so dedicated as to raise questions about the mental hygiene of anyone willing to undertake it, I reached a point where I could go to the track without fear of losing my shirt. It had taken me fifteen years of intermittent study to learn what a decent book could have taught me in a few weeks.

When racing entered its boom period of expansion after World War II, volumes of advice to horseplayers began to materialize in the bookshops. Persons who had never gone near a track now began dropping around to try the daily double. The books were an understandable effort to grab this new market. They continue to appear. I have at least eighty of them and am sure that twenty more must have escaped my attention. With few exceptions, the ones I have seen pose very little challenge to the theory that "horseplayers can't read."

Most of them are unreadable, whether one be a horseplayer or not. The worst are not only unreadable but fraudulent. The best, including the very few that have been written by authentic experts, outline systematic methods of prediction. They are serviceable in the limited sense that any more-or-less sound method is superior to no method at all. Their chief weakness is that they leave the reader in the dark about the multitudinous possibilities untouched by their systems. Lacking the time, space, knowledge or willingness to do otherwise, their authors seek to imprison the reader in procedures which, while of some use in special situations, neglect the infinite variety of the game. Also, no single system is likely to be compatible with the temperament, mentality and bankroll of the individual player.

Fond of racing and offended by the book-length material offered to my companions in the audience, I finally decided to write books of my own.

In 1966, *The Compleat Horseplayer** explained a handicapping method based on a more than ordinarily comprehensive view of the total problem. Its illustrative examples were the records of, and reasoning behind, wagers made during a successful week at Monmouth Park, New Jersey. In 1967 came *Ainslie's Jockey Book*† (later reissued as *Ainslie on Jockeys*), another version of the same method, emphasizing certain previously unpublicized truths about the relationship of the rider to the winning or losing of the race.

These books quickly became the best-selling handicapping manuals in the history of the pastime. They met with unprecedented praise from professional horsemen and other racing experts. But, in my opinion and in that of insiders whose views I respect, both books were too fragmentary to fill the void.

What the racing follower needs is not someone else's method of handicapping, but his own. A book containing a procedure highly esteemed by Tom Ainslie is only a partial help. The chances are that its value derives less from its explanation of Ainslie's method than from what Ainslie discloses about the nature of the game itself.

To evaluate a handicapping procedure, whether he finds it in print or dreams it up himself, the player must understand what the other possibilities are. What other procedures exist? What fundamental principles must be taken into account in the development of any sound approach? Having reviewed the entire array, the individual is well situated to determine his preferences, test them at his leisure and amend them as events and his own developing knowledge may dictate.

To make that possible for its readers is the business of this book.

Anyone who has ever spent a precious summer Saturday afternoon watching his five "best bets" run out of the money will agree, I think, that it's high time.

Beginners are also welcome. Anything one might need to launch oneself into the fascinating game of racing will be found in these pages.

How We're Going to Operate

The book begins with a description and explanation of the materials necessary, or useful, to development and maintenance of expert skill.

We then take a good look at the physical layout of racetracks. One should know more than the location of one's seat, the finish line, the mutuel windows, the frankfurter stand, the bathroom and the parking lot.

Next we analyze the arithmetic of racing. We start with the percentages of the game—figures with which every expert reckons. We proceed

---

*(Simon and Schuster, New York, 1966.)
†(Simon and Schuster, New York, 1967.)

to the pari-mutuel system and how its deductions from winnings affect expert methods of play. We then examine the economics of the industry itself, a kind of arithmetic which has much to do with the outcome of races. We conclude the section with some of the most important arithmetic of all—the cost of the hobby, and how this influences the size of the bet.

We come now to the horse itself. We strip breeding of the hocus-pocus that has mystified and confused generations of players. We discuss the size, weight and appearance of the Thoroughbred, explaining what he should look like, and why.

The central section of the book explores the arts of handicapping. After a summary review of the accepted schools of thought, we describe and analyze each fundamental of theory and method. Under appropriate headings, the reader will find concrete information about factors such as distance, form, class, age, sex, consistency, weight, footing, speed, pace, racing luck, post position, the owner, the trainer, the jockey. And ways to recognize playable-beatable races. And the secrets of the paddock and post parade. And a huge array of supplementary "angles" or "plus factors." And the strategic differences among tracks; professional speed formulas; methods of calculating daily track-speed variants; pace-rating procedures; the principles of class handicapping, form or trip handicapping, speed handicapping and pace handicapping; the form cycle and how to recognize improvement or deterioration; the usefulness of workouts; the truth about the drugging and "stiffing" of horses; the leading trainers; the leading riders; the leading owners and breeders; methods of recognizing sore, dull or unwilling Thoroughbreds before betting on them. And much more, with explicit instructions at every turn.

After all that comes something that I have not tried before and have never seen in print before. It carries the logic of the book a step further than usual by showing the reader how to build an individualized system of handicapping from principles and procedures described in previous chapters. In that effort, we trot out supplementary handicapping techniques—known in the game as angles. Many of these have been peddled to unwary horseplayers for as much as $300 each. Used in the proper context, with due attention to the fundamentals of handicapping, they become legitimately useful adjuncts to expert analysis of races. I believe that many readers will find this chapter a source of entertaining exercise that narrows the gap between theory and practice, hastening the development of polished skills.

The book then presents *Daily Racing Form*'s own explanations of the numbers, abbreviations and symbols contained in its past-performance tables. Finally I offer a full glossary of racing terms.

Acknowledgments

I am indebted to Triangle Publications, Inc., for permission to reproduce copyrighted materials from *Daily Racing Form, American Racing Manual* and from booklets explaining result charts and past-performance records.

Howard A. Rowe, editor-in-chief of *American Turf Monthly,* and one of the most astute journalists in the field, has given me numerous invaluable suggestions. I thank him warmly and hasten to absolve him of responsibility for the content or tone of the book.

Because much of the information in these pages has never been made public before, the reader will deduce that I have been interviewing jockeys, trainers and other experts. That is true, in a sense. The book's insights are the fruit of many years of observation, conversation and successful play. I doubt it would be a kindness to name any of the professional horsemen who, during the years, have contributed (usually unwittingly) to the development of those insights.

Ainslie's
COMPLETE
GUIDE TO
Thoroughbred
Racing

1

THE TOOLS
OF THE TRADE

Most thoroughbred races are at distances of three quarters of a mile or more, around at least one turn, from a standing start. The margin of victory often is narrow enough to be measurable in inches or hundredths of a second. The best horse usually wins, but not always. Bad luck and human error are factors in the running of every race. They can make an abject loser of an animal that should have won easily. Considering the influence of luck and error in a game of inches and split seconds, it is remarkable that the best horse wins as often as it does.

The horse may be of distinctly higher quality than its rivals. It may also be in peak physical condition. But it may lose its race in the paddock, before it ever gets to the starting gate. A clumsy trainer or groom may fasten the saddle too tightly, or not tightly enough, causing sufficient discomfort to throw the animal hopelessly out of sorts. Or the horse may be upset by the nervousness of another horse, or the sudden roar of a low-flying airplane, or the frightening whiteness of a windblown news-paper. If the handlers misunderstand this and react with more harshness or less firmness than the situation demands, the ensuing fracas can deplete the horse of its winning energy.

If the horse is not familiar with its rider, or does not like that person, or if the rider is not attuned to the animal, the race can be lost during the post parade. Some horses resent being busted with a whip during a pre-race warm-up. In trying to get away from the whip, such a horse may get more exercise than is good for him.

If he is a fast-breaking, front-running animal, eager for action, he may lose the race in the starting gate. The start may be delayed by the sulkiness or unruliness of other entrants, or by this horse's own high-strung behavior. When the bell finally sounds, it may catch him standing cross-legged. Or his jockey may have lapsed into a daydream. The effort of recovering the lost ground may empty the horse of the stamina it needs for the homestretch.

Another nervous type, whose disposition has suffered in the paddock, post parade or gate, may express himself by running rankly, frantically, uncontrollably, exhausting himself in the first half-mile.

A horse may break nicely from the gate and be jarred off stride by a careening neighbor. Bumps and brushes can cost precious split seconds of running time at any stage of a race, especially on the turns. Or an animal's new shoes may fit improperly, throwing his gait into imbalance and crippling him as soon as he attempts to lengthen stride.

Saving ground on the rail, a jockey may find himself without running room in the stretch, hemmed in by horses fore, aft and starboard. If daylight appears, the rider's hesitation for only a fraction of a second may prevent the mount from seizing an opportunity to run to the wire. Or the jockey may ride into a blind switch, swinging a few widths to the inside or outside for room on the turn—and racing straight into the pocket. Or the rider may be forced to check the animal's stride to avoid a pile-up with tiring horses that are backing up to him. Or it may be a timid rider, or a fatigued rider, or a rider weakened by dieting and dehydration, and unable to muster the whoop-de-doo necessary to get the horse's head up at the finish. Or the rider may use the whip too soon and too much, or too late and not enough. Or the horse may stumble on a clod of earth or a hoofprint.

The list of mishaps and errors could be prolonged for pages but need not be. The message is clear: The best horse can be beaten in a multitude of ways. Which is one of the reasons why sages declare, "You can't beat the races." Other sages modify this. "You can beat a race," they say, "but you can't beat the races." A more precise description of the situation is that some players beat the races, and most do not. For those who do not, the chief problem is a lack of know-how. Yet some persons with know-how are insufficiently motivated to use the knowledge. They'd rather eat hot dogs and drink beer and have fun in the sun and lose a few hundred dollars a year than expend the effort necessary to catch the extra few winners that would put their accounts into the black. It is their sovereign right. They'd rather cream you on the golf course, or beat you at the poker or bridge table. It's all a matter of taste.

Persons who beat the races are, on the very face of it, knowledgeable players, motivated to use the knowledge. They enjoy winning so much that they are willing to work at it. Yet they may be unable to understand why an expert poker player will lie in ambush at the table for two and a half hours before sandbagging his companions. Again, it's a matter of taste.

As far as I know, horseplayers who win more money than they lose are almost invariably persons who have learned to be expert handicappers. To be sure, a medical friend of mine, who does not know which end kicks or which end bites, financed the establishment of his practice with $60,000 he won on hot tips. He was an intern at the time. The tips came from underworld characters who were grateful for a kindness he had rendered one of their relatives. The horses all won. Every month or two would come a tip on a horse at some small track. And every tip paid off— $60,000 worth in two or three years. It can be assumed that the mob continues to rig a few races at various minor-league tracks and that anyone with access to the information can beat such races. The rest of us are obliged to work for our winnings. We are obliged to learn how to handicap.

Some of the most consistent losers at any track are insiders, or friends of insiders, who depend on stable information. It is nice to know for certain that a certain stable plans to "go" with its horse, and is not simply sending the animal out for exercise. Unfortunately, three or four other stables are also likely to be all-out to win the same race, and may have the horseflesh to do it with. Which is why the player who knows how to handicap does not need stable information or, if he gets it, will not be misled by it.

As a class, professional horsemen are much better handicappers than the paying customers are. But an individual customer can be as effective a handicapper as any horseman. The expert customer's judgment is free of the pressures that result from loyalty to a stable owner or enthusiasm about a particular horse. A handicapper learns to mistrust and avoid all enthusiasms except the delight of lining up at the cashier's window to collect the rewards of good judgment.

By the same token, the accomplished player resists the emotional squalls that might be induced by ill fortune. You learn that you can't win every bet. You expect to lose more than half of them. Like the competitive golfer, the homicidal poker player and the expert bridge player—all of whom you resemble in many other particulars—you take reverses in stride. There will be other races today, or the next time. And every now and then, as you know full well, you will bet on a horse, discover during the running of the race that it is not the best horse after all, and will cash the bet anyhow, racing luck or human fallibility having made a loser into a winner.

Knowledge, motivation to use the knowledge, self-control and composed self-confidence. These, then, are the primary attributes of the good player. Anyone who begins with the motivation, and enjoys maintaining it, can develop the knowledge, the self-control and the confidence. The latter two qualities are products of experience—successful experience based on knowledge.

In acquiring the necessary experience, the readers probably will use this volume as home base, a primary source of essential knowledge. But they will want additional materials with which to check and test this knowledge and entrench it firmly. Still other materials will help replenish and expand existing knowledge in light of new developments in the game.

Such materials are the tools of the handicapper's trade. Some are indispensable. Others can be omitted, depending on the amount of effort the player is willing to give to his pastime.

Here are the materials most useful to the hobby of handicapping Thoroughbreds:

"Daily Racing Form" [INDISPENSABLE]

It is impossible to handicap a field of horses without this newspaper. Most players rely exclusively on the individual past-performance records which the paper publishes every racing day. Some also keep files of the official result charts which appear in the paper. The charts are far more detailed than past-performance records. They are especially useful in establishing the actual class of competition against which a horse has been competing. As shall be demonstrated later in this book, among three or four horses that have been winning in $5,000 claiming races, one may actually have been defeating animals of decisively superior quality. The result charts show this—and much else that we shall notice in due course.

Because the hobbyist is likely to be an infrequent visitor to the track, he may find the acquisition of official result charts a greater chore and expense than he wants to incur. Rather than buy the *Form* every day to get the charts, he may prefer to rely on the past-performance records available on the day he goes to the track. Many winning players survive this way, although it must be assumed that they would win somewhat more if they had access to a file of charts.

Another sort of file is almost mandatory, however. To test the concepts and procedures and selection systems found in this book or elsewhere, the player must have a file of *Form*s. A month of back issues would be good. Six months would be twenty times as good. An angle might show a profit in a month's trial simply by accident. But if it holds up well over a six months' trial, it may be worth trying in real life with real money. Back issues are obtainable from *Form* offices or from mail-order firms that advertise in racing magazines.

"The American Racing Manual" [IMPORTANT]

Every year this magnificent encyclopedic by-product of the *Form* gives last year's record of every horse, rider, owner, trainer and breeder. Plus track and world speed records; charts of the principal races; lengthy articles summarizing and analyzing the chief developments and accomplishments of the year; tabulations showing who did best in every department of the game; other tabulations showing how often the betting favorites won at every track, and how much purse money was paid out at every track. And several hundred other items, all of keen interest to handicappers.

Magazines [USEFUL]

The most useful are these:

"American Turf Monthly," 505 Eighth Avenue, New York, 10018. Frankly addressed to horseplayers, with liberal helpings of the pie-in-the-sky that nourish their hopes, this monthly contains more handicapping advice than other racing periodicals. Its best column, "Increase Your Horsepower," offers timely inside information about the maneuverings of trainers. Articles cover a wide range of angles and techniques. Every issue contains three or four selection systems, some of which are ingenious enough to merit experimental self-educational study by the budding player.

"The Blood-Horse," P.O. Box 4038, Lexington, Kentucky 40504. A splendid weekly that views the game through the eyes of the breeder and will fascinate the player.

"The Thoroughbred Record," P.O. Box 4240, Lexington, Kentucky, 40544. Breeding, training, economics, who's doing what. Another well-edited weekly, worth keeping up with.

"Turf and Sport Digest," 511–513 Oakland Avenue, Baltimore, 21212. Feature articles about riders and other horsemen, and an occasional selection system, usually with adequate documentation of results. Well worth subscribing to.

Microfiche [USEFUL]

The official result charts of all races on all American tracks, in convenient filmstrip form. Available from Triangle Publications, Inc., 731 Plymouth Court, Chicago, 60605. Triangle is the parent corporation of *Daily Racing Form.*

Computer Software [NOT YET]

Good handicapping is too subtle and varied a process for incorporation into the oversimplified kinds of computer programs that lend themselves to mass marketing. The handicapper makes a racing selection much more quickly without a computer than with. If the computer program is elaborate enough to encompass the complexities of good handicapping, it will take the handicapper too long to feed the necessary information into the machine.

At this writing, and as far as the near future may be concerned, computers are useful adjuncts to the work of careful handicappers, who may choose to use them for storage and retrieval of special information privately accumulated. For example, a sharp race-watcher can compile computer records of performance patterns which, when subject to statistical analysis by the machine, may reveal valuable information about the methods of various trainers. Some trainers do better in certain kinds of races than in others. Some follow unique patterns of switches in class and/or distance and/or footing and/or jockey when bringing a horse to a winning effort.

Optical scanners such as those used at supermarket checkout counters to read prices and other data printed on packages can also read words and numbers and convey them to computer memory for analysis. In time, and probably sooner than later, these gadgets will be available at prices reasonable enough to commend them to serious handicappers. You will run the result charts into the scanner, which will relay all the information to your computer. Your enormously advanced program will rate each horse. And every morning you will feed the day's entries and the conditions of each race to the scanner. Out will come your printed selections. If your computer program is as good at handicapping as you are, you will have transported yourself into an electronic Shangri-la, complete with push-button winners. It sounds good, but I bet there will be clinkers in it.

Notebooks [ESSENTIAL]

Written records are the only reliable means of telling whether one's handicapping is good or not. Notebooks provide a continuous record of what you do and how it works. Some players, as we shall see, use notebooks to record daily track variants, or the actual class of every race, or to keep tabs on horses whose imminent improvement has been noticed in the result charts or at the track.

Local Newspapers [USEFUL]

Few papers ever mention handicapping, much less discuss any of its ramifications, but racing columnists often give significant news of horses and horsemen.

Gadgets [DOUBTFUL]

Advertisers peddle a stupefying variety of metal, cardboard and laminated plastic devices guaranteed to relieve the player of the need to use his own brain. None is a substitute for handicapping. Most are hand-held electronic calculators or variants of the slide-rule principle, highly simplified to include the two or three or four factors built into the inventor's system. Those that calculate a horse's percentage of winning or in-the-money races may save enough arithmetical effort to seem worthwhile.

Binoculars [IMPORTANT]

Most players sit or stand where they can see the track. But few see much of the race except the finish. A good pair of seven- or eight-power binoculars with a wide field enables a well-positioned player to see the entire race. This is fun. It also is informative, because it helps the player to approach the full truth about how the selections run and how their jockeys ride. To that extent, binoculars improve handicapping.

Leisure [INDISPENSABLE]

Some experts can learn all they want to know about a day's program of races in less than half an hour with the *Form*. Others use more elaborate methods which require as much as an hour of careful study per playable race. No matter where one may stand between these extremes, it is safe to assert that only a player of enormous skill and long experience can do his handicapping in the hustle and bustle of the track. The place to figure the horses is in private, on the morning of the race, or—if the racing paper is available—on the previous night. Even with basic handicapping completed before the trip to the track, the player finds plenty to do while there. Eleventh-hour jockey changes, last-minute scratches, unforeseen changes in weights, and the player's all-important visits to the paddock, plus careful viewing of odds displays and post-race video replays provide more than enough activity.

Daily Track Program [INDISPENSABLE]

Not more than eight out of ten persons at the track buy the program, which costs about half a dollar. Many of those who save the money can be seen forking over a couple of dollars for tip sheets. Anybody who cares to be his own master at the track will want a program. It gives all but the final scratches and jockey changes, offers the track's official guess as to what the odds may be (a guess which influences the odds considerably) and lists the leading trainers and jockeys at the current meeting. Expert players do a good deal of pencil work on their programs. To be at the track without one is like playing golf without a putter.

And now some items that every horseplayer should try to do without.

Bookies

Where bookmaking is legal, or otherwise secure from the cops, a player unable to get to the track may sometimes feel like taking a flyer on a horse. The likelihood that the horse will win is somewhat smaller than if the player were at the track. For one thing, no bet is as sound as it should be until the player has seen the horse and has evaluated its readiness. Animals that look great on paper often look awful in the paddock.

But the main problem with bookies is that they usually are on the lam from the law. The day you hit them for $700 is the day they vanish over the state line to avoid arrest. I use the sum of $700 because it happened to me many years ago. The guy was not running out on his debt to me. He was literally running from arrest. I suppose he could have mailed me the money, but this obviously was too much to expect.

In more recent years I have had other problems with bookies. They have refused to take my action after discovering that I was a consistent winner with whom they could not catch up. Others have limited the size of my bets, apparently for the same reason. It is posssible that old-time gentleman bookies still exist, accepting wagers from anyone with good credit and settling accounts once a week. Such operatives used to welcome the trade of a winner. In the first place, they had good and sufficient reason to expect that he might turn out in time to be a loser. Secondly, his success was a nice advertisement for the game. It provided incentive to other players, losers all.

I no longer fool with bookies. The ones I meet nowadays smell of penitentiary. I'd sooner travel seventy-five miles to the nearest track, or stay home and read a book.

Legal Bookies

The legalized off-track betting shops established in New York and later in Connecticut may have spread west by the time the reader comes across these words. Conceivably, but by no means inevitably, the off-track customer will be able to see a video picture of the odds board and paddock before betting, and of the race itself afterward. No more inevitably, the customer who bets on a winner will be paid off at track odds. As these words are written, the New York OTB customer collects much less on winning tickets than would be paid at the track.

Until OTB mimics Australia and provides the visual aids with which a customer can avoid betting on an unseen horse at unfair odds, the track is the place to go, just as it always has been. Incidentally, none of these words should be interpreted as hostile to OTB. I have long favored it. I think that the off-track establishment should be an outpost of the track itself. If the video facilities were adequate and the odds other than punitively low, many tracks would become outdoor television studios and, therefore, much more pleasant and less congested places to go. Track managements that collected a fair percentage of off-track betting proceeds would not mind the new arrangement at all.

A highly promising development has been the video simulcasting of races from one track to another, with pari-mutuel proceeds being shared by the two places. Known as ITW (Intertrack Wagering) or OTW (Other Track Wagering), the innovation has brought the usual political scrimmaging for control but has benefited participating tracks and their patrons and can be expected to achieve a firm foothold before too long. Some industry leaders fear that satellite video plus ITW might kill the racing at lesser tracks, converting their grandstands into mere TV viewing and betting centers. The fear runs particularly high among large breeders, who tremble at the prospect of ringing up fewer sales of inferior livestock if the number of active tracks diminishes. As a handicapper, I vote for anything that improves the quality of the racing on which handicappers bet. Three cheers for evolution.

Public Selectors

Although they need to make their final selections on the day before the races, unsure of the condition of the racing strip or of late scratches and jockey shifts, and with no opportunity to see the horses before committing themselves, some newspaper handicappers do remarkably well. The best I have ever known, Russ Harris of the *Daily News* in New York, picks about 30 percent of all the winners, a remarkable achievement for someone tackling every race on every program in circumstances so difficult. Jim Bannon, who puts out the *Racing Guide* at the tracks of the Ontario Jockey Club in Canada, does equally well and affords his customers an unusual luxury—detailed analysis of each horse's chances.

Most selections found in newspapers and tip sheets are no better than any normally motivated handicapper can achieve after a few months of experience. But a player who discovers that some local selector maintains a high average can take advantage of the situation by obtaining the particular newspaper or tip sheet.

Many Eastern professionals would not dream of concluding the day's handicapping without checking the selections of Russ Harris. When he gives high marks to a horse that I have dismissed, I take another careful look at the record of that horse. When in doubt, however, I stick with my own selections, because one's personal judgment is the indispensable basis of this particular pastime.

Which reminds me that in many racing centers the selections printed in the multicolored tip sheets are nearly useless, mainly because they name too many horses in each race but partly because the handicapping is mediocre. Honorable exceptions include New York sheets like *Clocker Lawton, The Beard* and *Centaur,* whose opinions are routinely checked by many professional players of my acquaintance.

And no racegoer in Southern California should fail to obtain *Today's Racing Digest,* an unbelievably advanced booklet that contains selections along with specific handicapping details of a sophistication unequalled elsewhere. Also available and useful on that racing circuit is *Bob's Card,* a first-rate tip sheet produced by the hard-working Sam Giller and Bob Byram.

Touts

Although pickpockets have been eliminated from most tracks, touts have not. Many trainers, grooms, stable boys, jockeys, jockeys' agents and track employees supplement their incomes by promoting what are known in the trade as "clients"—persons willing to bet substantial sums for them on horses they recommend. All this hustling of hot information (three quarters of which turns cold after the results are posted) heightens the conspiratorial atmosphere at the track.

Most touts are good enough handicappers to know which four or five horses in a race have the best chances. They "give" one horse to each of four or five tourists. After the race they find the winning sucker and demand the proceeds of a $5 or $10 bet.

Although the small-time tout who buttonholes you at the sandwich stand claims to have intimate stable connections, he almost never does. Even if he did, his information would be of small use, because stable information is not often profitable. Furthermore, while many persons with stable connections supplement their incomes through touting, few would dare to tout a stranger. He might turn out to be a private detective in the pay of the Thoroughbred Racing Associations. At major tracks, the penalty for touting is exile.

A kind of "help" as insidious as that of the tout is the advice given by one's companion at the track. If the player has done his homework and is satisfied, on the basis of past experience, that his selections are as good as anyone else's he should stick with them. If his companion disagrees, the debate should be resolved by a 25-cent side bet on the race. Occasionally, of course, a trusted friend with superior knowledge and experience can point out a flaw in one's handicapping. That's different.

2

KNOW THE TRACK

A good handicapper knows something about the performance patterns of horses. A superior handicapper is intimately familiar with the ways of horses, trainers and riders. And he knows his track. On first visit to a strange track, a smart player is likely to turn up hours before the start of the first race, to get the lay of the land.

Here are some of the things worth knowing about:

Paddock and Walking Ring

As one race ends, the entrants in the next race are led to their covered paddock stalls for final grooming and saddling. They then go to the walking ring, or parade ring. In nice weather they usually parade around the ring twice with their grooms. After the riders mount (in response to the order "Riders up!"), the horses walk the ring once or twice more and then amble to the track for another parade in front of the stands, followed by pre-race warm-ups which take them to the starting gate.

The design and location of paddock and walking ring are important to the expert player. You need to see the animals in their paddock stalls. You also need to see how they look in the walking ring. At most establishments, paddock and walking rings are behind the stands, necessitating a hike. The player is used to this. In a day at the races, pilgrimages from your seat to various other facilities and points of interest will take you at least six furlongs, some of it at a trot. It's the nature of the game.

If paddock and walking ring are behind the stands, they may be rather widely separated. It is most unusual to find a single spot that commands an unobstructed view of both. On a first visit, the provident player takes such problems into account, planning to watch the paddock proceedings and then take the most direct route to a point of vantage at the walking-ring rail. Expert players may sometimes be fat, but they're nimble. More about paddock activities in Chapter 17.

Among other concerns during the minutes between races is the trend of betting, as reflected in the shifting odds. Some tracks put electric odds boards or video monitors where they can be seen from the walking ring. If a player is sufficiently dubious about the condition of a horse to want to see how it moves during the pre-race warm-ups, there may be no opportunity to study the odds until the warm-up is over, two or three minutes before the race starts. This is ample time. Odds can be mulled while standing on line at the mutuel window, where odds boards are always visible. I mention this only to demonstrate that a player eager to win and willing to work at it is likely to become quite busy during the period immediately preceding a playable race. Knowing where things are helps you to organize your time and motion profitably.

Seats

The expert cases the joint to find out where the best seats are. There is no such thing as a good seat at a racetrack, but some seats are better than others. In general, the best possible seat is high enough to afford a clear view of the entire race, and close enough to the finish line to permit an accurate guess as to which nose arrived first. At many tracks the very best seats are in the private boxes of the upper crust. If the regular occupants don't show up, the player can sometimes gain admittance by slipping the usher a couple of dollars. First, of course, you must get into the clubhouse, a ticket to which usually costs two or three dollars more than the general admission to the grandstand.

For some reason, the reserved sections of the grandstand are often in better locations than any but the choicest private clubhouse boxes. And unreserved grandstand seats are often closer to the finish line than unreserved clubhouse ones. A player who does not mind the low-rent district is far better off in most grandstands than in most clubhouses. Nowadays, when the benefits of astute race-watching are being exploited by so-called trip handicappers and are becoming more evident to hobbyists, the clear view of the finish line becomes less important than it used to be. Race-watching yields maximum rewards when the watcher can see everything that happens as the horses and their riders negotiate the final turn into the homestretch. At a conventionally designed track, this means sitting in the grandstand—or even standing at its topmost level.

The main advantage of the clubhouse (except on summer Saturdays and holidays) is extra elbowroom. Another advantage is the presence of professional horsemen and other sophisticated regulars, who tend to be quieter and more civil than ordinary players. Still another advantage is the comfort of clubhouse dining rooms and bars. But the grandstand has no worse food at better prices. And, unless you happen to sit next to a maniac, you usually have more privacy in the grandstand. They don't know you. You don't know them. They leave you alone to study your figures. In the clubhouse, where you probably know somebody, you talk. The more you talk, the more you miss.

Racing Secretary's Office

Most horseplayers have never been near the place. But the expert locates it as soon as possible and makes regular visits thereafter. Here, without cost, are the condition books in which the racing secretary prescribes the terms of entry for every race on every program. A player with a complete file of condition books published during the current season is not quite as well off as a player with a complete file of result charts. But the books tell with certainty the quality of opposition today's horses faced in their previous starts at the track. The condition book also helps one decide whether to come back next Wednesday, or whenever. The book tells exactly what kind of races will be held on each day. You need not wait until the entries are published in the newspaper.

Other useful information published in some condition books includes the names and riding weights of all active jockeys on the grounds; the track's rules; the proportions in which purses are divided among winners and runners-up; track records; and the dates of forthcoming major races.

At or near this office most tracks have a bulletin board on which items of interest are posted. On a Monday, the board contains the names of horses that worked out on Sunday, and the distances they ran, and the speeds at which they were clocked. Because Monday's racing papers are published on Sunday, they cannot report these workouts. The presence or absence of a horse's name on the Sunday list can be a matter of great significance to the player, as we shall explain in a later chapter.

Shoe Board

At modern tracks, a panel on the infield totalisator board tells what kind of shoes each horse is wearing. Elsewhere, the board may be found tucked away near the paddock, or the racing secretary's office, or under the stands. The expert needs this information, and makes sure to find it.

Tracks in General

The diagram on page 41 represents a typical Thoroughbred track, one mile in circumference. From a seat in the grandstand, to the left of the finish wire, the fan sees the tote board. It is the electric sign that shows the amounts bet on each horse for win, place and show, and the approximate odds on each horse to win. The first odds posted, before any money is bet, are those printed in the track program. They comprise "the morning line"—the track handicapper's estimate of what the final odds will be. The estimate is never anything to bank on. The horse named as favorite may or may not become the favorite and may or may not deserve to. But the morning line influences many bettors, some of whom actually believe that the horse listed as favorite is the horse to bet, regardless of where his odds finally roost.

The tote board flashes new betting totals, and revised odds, every ninety seconds until post-time. It also shows the time of day, the number of minutes remaining until post-time, and the condition of the running surface (fast or sloppy or muddy or slow or good or heavy). During the race it shows the times in which early stages of the running are clocked. At the end it gives the final time, the program numbers of the leading horses and, at last, the mutuel prices they paid.

The finish line is not a line. It is an overhead wire. The various poles on the infield rail are named in accordance with the distance between each of them and the finish line. For example, horses run three quarters of a mile (six furlongs) from the three-quarter pole to the finish line. Races are run counterclockwise, of course, which means that they pass the stands from left to right on the homestretch and from right to left on the backstretch.

At a one-mile track, the first pole encountered in a mile race is the fifteen-sixteenths pole—seven and a half furlongs to the wire. Next comes the seven-eighths pole, followed by the six-and-a-half furlong pole. That pole might as well be called the thirteen-sixteenths pole, but it isn't. Similarly, the three-quarter pole is never referred to as the six-furlong pole. But the pole situated five eighths of a mile from the finish is called, as the diagram shows, the five-furlong pole! And the four-furlong pole is never, but never, alluded to as the four-furlong pole. It's the *half-mile* pole.

The chute in the lower right corner, near the five-and-a-half-furlong and three-quarter poles, is where races of six, six and a half and seven furlongs start. The long straightaway is easier for the horses, permitting them to settle into stride before having to negotiate turns. The chute at the head of the homestretch is where races of a mile and a quarter start.

Nowadays, the better tracks are offering more races on grass (turf races) than ever before. The turf course is always situated on the inner

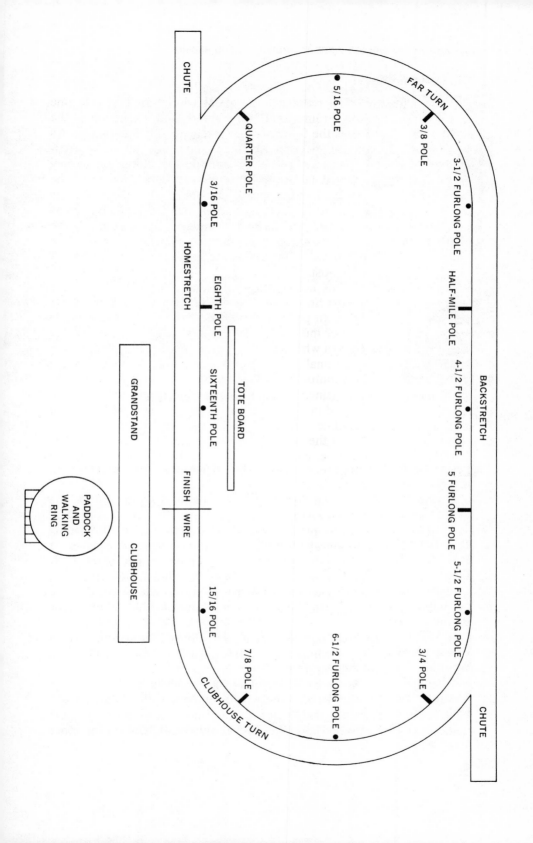

Start of the Futurity in 1902 at Sheepshead Bay. JAMES HOLMES

perimeter of the main racing strip. This means that the turf course is always shorter, with sharper turns.

If your track is on the following list, it is a mile track and looks very much like the diagram on page 41:

Ak-Sar-Ben, Albuquerque, Aqueduct (inner track), Bay Meadows, Bowie, Calder, Caliente, Churchill Downs, Darby Downs, Delaware Park, Del Mar, Detroit, El Comandante, Fair Grounds, Fairmount Park, Finger Lakes, Fort Erie, Fresno, Garden State, Golden State, Gulfstream, Hawthorne, Latonia, Longacres, Louisiana Downs, Meadowlands, Monmouth Park, Oaklawn, Penn National, Philadelphia Park, Pimlico, Pleasanton, Portland Meadows, River Downs, Rockingham Park, Sacramento, Santa Anita, Santa Fe Downs, Stockton, Suffolk Downs, Sunland Park, Tampa Bay Downs, Thistledown, Turf Paradise, Woodbine and Yakima Meadows.

The following tracks are a mile and an eighth in length:

Aqueduct, Arlington Park, Atlantic City, James C. Ellis Park, Hialeah, Hollywood Park, Laurel, Saratoga.

Belmont Park is a majestic mile and a half, Keeneland a mile and a sixteenth.

The Bull Rings

The major tracks in the United States are those that attract the best stables and jockeys by paying the largest purses. All major American tracks are at least a mile in length. Some minor tracks are also a mile or more in length, but most are shorter. The short ones are known to horsemen as "bull rings," because of the sharpness of their turns. Some offer more comfortable seating, more courteous service and better food than one finds at most major tracks. Although the quality of their horse-flesh is inferior, the better minor tracks offer races as formal and honest as can be found anywhere. A good handicapper can keep body and soul together at a half-mile oval. An indifferent handicapper is in trouble wherever he goes.

3

THE ARITHMETIC
OF RACING

The handicapper attempts to unravel a multitude of factors. Some are clear, some obscure. But each relates to all the others in ways that vary from horse to horse, race to race and day to day.

Because the raw materials are numerous, changeable and deceptive, handicapping is a highly personal kind of approximation, closer to an art than to an exact science. Which is why the predictions of experts coincide only part of the time.

Two good handicappers may often play the same horse in the same race. Both may refrain from betting on certain other races. Some races find one of them betting and the other with wallet buttoned. And, without fail, they frequently bet against each other—picking different horses in the same race. Even if they try to employ identical methods, they reach less than identical conclusions. Differences of this kind are, of course, the fascinating hallmark of any great game.

I enjoyed a demonstration of handicapping's personal aspects after people began reading *The Compleat Horseplayer*. Letters of thanks arrived from racing enthusiasts throughout the United States. Many claimed to have achieved unprecedented success, for which they credited the book. Some of their feats made me drool. Longshots! A Chicagoan gave *The Compleat Horseplayer* full marks for a winner that had paid him more than $90 on a $2 mutuel ticket. I was almost tempted to inquire how he had done it. I had never picked a $90 winner in my life.

Obviously the procedure so painstakingly described in *The Compleat*

Horseplayer had been modified by the individual mentality. Some readers had become capable of turning up bonanzas of a magnitude quite beyond my own grasp. No doubt the same readers had also been backing more losers than I could possibly tolerate.

I make these observations about the personal, non-scientific nature of handicapping for several reasons. The first and most urgent is that the reader should harbor no illusions. No matter what theory of handicapping may seem most plausible, the handicapper will be attempting to predict the future by interpreting past events of uncertain character and inexact significance. Yet survival at the track will demand predictions of considerable accuracy.

Beating the Percentages

If certainty about the past is so limited, must not certainty about the future be terribly slight? How can anyone wrench a profit from such confusion? .

By dealing in probabilities. Or, as they say at the track, working *with* the percentages instead of against them.

It so happens that the old saw "You can beat a race, but you can't beat the races" is quite wrong. It turns reality upside down. The truth is that nobody can be sure of beating an individual race, but lots of people win more money than they lose in a season's activity at the track. There is nothing unusual about this. In any game worth playing, the outcome of any one play (any one race) is rarely a matter of absolute certainty. But someone who plays well finishes ahead in the long run.

Take poker as an example. No matter how expert the player, nothing short of a royal flush guarantees a winning bet. The expert is lucky to hold one royal flush in forty years of play. In other words, he can't necessarily beat the race. But an expert beats the game.

Let us suppose that our poker expert competes with six others in a game of jackpots. After he has been at the table with these sharpers a few times he knows a great deal about their courage, wiles and weaknesses. He undoubtedly knows more about them than any handicapper can know about a field of horses. The usefulness of this knowledge varies from session to session, of course. In poker, last week's tabby is this week's tiger, his mood having modified his style for the time being. A further limitation on the expert's success is that his opponents also are experts and know a good deal about *his* style.

In the end, therefore, the poker expert's main armor against all uncertainties is knowledge of the game itself—more particularly, knowledge of the *percentages* that give the game its central character. As long as he is faithful to the laws—the probabilities—embodied in these percentages, he seldom loses. And when he combines knowledge of the probabilities with accurate guesses about the tactics of his opponents, he becomes a big winner.

Allow me to pursue the matter further. By reminding you how the percentages are used in poker, I hope to whet your appetite for discussion of the less familiar, but equally important percentages of racing.

A 52-card poker deck contains slightly less than 2.6 million five-card hands. The exact probability of drawing any specific hand is a matter of established mathematical knowledge. So is the exact probability of improving any hand on the draw. If the expert has a chance to convert a hand into a straight by discarding one card and drawing either a nine or an ace, will he bet the money required for the gamble? It all depends.

He knows that the odds against drawing either an ace or nine are 5 to 1. He may draw the right card and lose the pot to someone who holds a flush or a full house. But he will win in the long run on hands of this kind if he respects the percentages of the game. He will win in the long run if he stays with such a hand *only* when the pot promises to pay *at least* five times the money he bets. If he draws to this kind of straight on occasions when the pot pays less than a 5 to 1 gamble should, he eventually will lose. Winning one such hand in every six or seven he plays, he will take in less money than he spends on the losing ones.

Identical principles apply to horseplaying. Certain percentages are as cut-and-dried in racing as in cards, and deserve comparable respect. They occur with astonishing uniformity, year after year. They affect the handicapper's choice of horse. They affect the size and frequency of bets.

What is more, racing is so patterned that a handicapper's own methods are certain to embody percentages of their own. If his methods are consistent (regardless of whether they are profitable or not), they turn up winning horses at a rate that fluctuates hardly at all from one year to the next. Likewise, his annual rate of profit or loss on each invested dollar varies but slightly from year to year. He may encounter long losing streaks and incredible strings of winners, but in the end his handicapping settles at its own percentage level. When he knows this percentage, and the accompanying rate of profit or loss, he is able to judge the efficiency of his methods. He remains uncertain about the outcome of any individual bet, but he knows with considerable certainty that, in due course, he can expect to win a predictable minimum percentage of bets, with a predictable minimum profit or loss per invested dollar.

A life insurance company does the same kind of thing on an incomparably larger scale. It hitches its treasury to the laws of probability. It does not have the vaguest idea when you will die. But it knows, within the practical limits of earthly certainty, the percentage of people your age who will die this year, or next, or twelve years from now. It designs its premium rates accordingly. In the long run its books show a predictable percentage of "winners" and a predictable rate of profit.

Although good handicappers are respectfully attentive to the established percentages of the game, and to the percentages achieved by their own methods, handicapping is not necessarily a mathematical pastime. Some of the best handicappers use pencil and paper only to cross out the names of horses they think will lose. Other good handicappers do simple arithmetic, but not much of it. Still others devise rather elaborate arithmetical formulas in an attempt to introduce reassuring order into the hodgepodge of information with which they deal. Whatever style is most appealing to the individual, no mathematical skill is required beyond the ability to add, subtract, multiply and divide.

Even the numbers contained in this chapter need not be committed to memory. Far more important than the numbers are the conclusions they permit about the nature of the game.

The Magic Number

Anybody who bets $1,000 on the races and emerges from the experience with less than $800 is doing something dreadfully wrong. A $2 bettor who selected horses with a hatpin, or by using numerology, or by consulting tea leaves, would seldom lose much more than $200 in a series of 500 bets—an investment of $1,000.

It is, of course, more than theoretically possible to go broke at the track. Desperate gamblers do it every day. And victims of inefficient selection methods or wasteful betting systems also manage to run out of cash long before they should.

The shortest route to disaster is to bet too much of one's money at a time. The person with a $1,000 bankroll who plays it all on one horse has a splendid chance of losing it all. The one who bets the $1,000 in five installments of $200 each also risks extinction: In any given series of five bets, no handicapper on earth can be sure of winning so much as one!

How, then, can a less-than-expert player expect to have $800 left after betting $1,000?

The magic number is 20.

Without knowing the slightest thing about horses, and betting entirely at random, the player's long-term losses should not exceed 20 percent of the total amount wagered. To limit losses to that extent, one need only bet in amounts small enough to assure a large, representative number of bets.

It works like this. Of all money bet on any race, most tracks deduct approximately 18.5 percent for taxes and their own revenue. The remaining 81.5 percent is disbursed to the holders of winning mutuel tickets.

This means that, regardless of how the individual player fares with a bet, the crowd as a whole loses 18.5 percent of its wagered dollar on every race, every day, every week, every year. A random bettor, playing horses at random, should do no worse. A selection system employing daisy petals or playing cards or dice or something else entirely unrelated to handicapping should leave the bettor with close to 80 percent of the original capital after a series of 500 or more bets.

Any handicapping procedure that results in seasonal losses as high as 20 percent of all money wagered is, therefore, no better than the hatpin method. And anyone who loses more than 18.5 cents of every dollar wagered in a season is—whether he realizes it or not—going out of the way to find trouble.

The high-percentage "take" of racetracks has been compared unfavorably with the smaller levies imposed by gambling houses. A roulette player, for instance, should lose only slightly more than a nickel of each dollar bet, assuming that the computation is made after a long, representative series of plays. The difference between roulette and racing is, however, a considerable one. The wheel spins every few seconds, all night. The roulette fanatic makes hundreds of bets in one session. The house "take" of 5 percent-plus nibbles away at his capital, and he finally has nothing left.

But the horseplayer encounters only nine races a day, a daily double, some exactas (perfectas), a trifecta or two and perhaps a pic six. If he confines his wagering to the smallest possible fraction of betting capital, he might play for months or years before emptying his pocket.

It follows that anything useful that a player learns about the horses should help to begin reducing the percentage of loss. In this chapter we shall see how to reduce that percentage merely by learning some of the probabilities of the game, and without learning a thing about horses themselves!

Betting on Favorites

An infallible guide to the reliability or intelligence, or both, of a racing expert is his attitude toward persons who bet on favorites. All experts know that, in a representatively large sample of races, one of every three will be won by the betting favorite—the horse on which the most money is bet. The conclusions various writers achieve in light of this statistic are a dead giveaway to their knowledge of probabilities. Anyone ignorant of probabilities is not only unable to evaluate his own chances at the track but hopelessly unqualified to advise anyone else.

It is fashionable to sneer at "chalk players"—the conservative types who play nothing but favorites. Observing that favorites win only one third of the time, many sages proclaim, with flawless arithmetic, that the crowd is wrong two thirds of the time. They insist that the secret of success at the track is to part company with the crowd, avoid favorites and, presumably, begin winning a lion's share of the two races in three which find the crowd wrong. Such advice is crude nonsense. Whatever truth it contains is strictly coincidental.

Any child will understand the reason for this, after a few facts are set forth. At major tracks, the typical race involves nine horses. This means that about eighty horses go to the post on a representative day. The crowd picks nine of these animals as betting favorites. Three of the nine win. Anyone who thinks it easier to find winners among 71 non-favorites than among nine favorites is thinking backwards.

The fact that non-favorites win two thirds of all races does not mean that non-favorites have twice as good a chance of winning as favorites do. Quite the contrary. Until we handicap the entire field and see which horse is probably the best of the lot (a task few players can perform), we know nothing about the non-favorite except that it is one of eight non-favorites in the race. But we know more than that about the favorite. We know that it wins one race in three. This means that the "natural" odds against it are 2 to 1. But the "natural" odds against a random non-favorite in a nine-horse race are 11 to 1! (This figure is obtained by the statistical process of dividing the number of races that non-favorites win [⅔] by the number of non-favorites [8].)

We now have established that it is foolish to reject a horse simply because it is the favorite, or to stab at another horse simply because it is a non-favorite. We therefore are in better position to appreciate some interesting statistics. We begin with a blazer:

To cut the magic number of 20 just about in half and bring one's losses within striking distance of the break-even point, one need only confine one's bets to horses that are the favorites in their races!

Many years ago, the resourceful Robert V. Rowe studied a series of 7,301 races. He reported in *American Turf Monthly* that a bet on each of the favorites would have produced a loss of 8.4 percent for each dollar wagered. More recently, Burton P. Fabricand studied 10,035 races and came up with a closely similar figure. In a highly original book—*Horse Sense,** proposing a mathematical approach to the game—Fabricand writes that a flat bet on each favorite would have lost the player nine cents per dollar. The house take from mutuel pools was lower in those days. The loss nowadays might be about 14 cents in some places.

Many selection systems, including Fabricand's and several that I describe later in this book, attempt to convert the loss into a profit by applying handicapping principles to the past-performance records of favorites. Because the starting point of such systems finds the player only a hop and a skip from profit's promised land, they are among the best possible procedures for persons unacquainted with the game.

Fabricand found that bets on favorites paying extremely short prices (1 to 2 or less) resulted in a small profit. On such wagers, it would seem that the magic number is reduced to zero or thereabouts before a bit of actual handicapping has been undertaken.

In Praise of the Crowd

I have just said some harsh things about experts who base their theories on disdain for the judgment of the crowd. I have showed that the crowd as a whole does a better job of conserving its money than is likely to be done by someone who refuses in any circumstances to agree with the crowd. The object of this book is, nevertheless, to equip the player to surpass the crowd by means of expert handicapping.

The next step in that direction is to analyze a second accomplishment of the crowd. Insiders have long known that, even though the crowd loses 18.5 cents on the dollar, it does a rather remarkable job of handicapping. If it bets in such proportions as to make a horse a 3 to 1 shot, that horse is more likely to win than the animal that goes off at 4 to 1. Putting it another way, any long series of 5 to 2 shots will win a higher percentage of races for the bettor than a comparable series of horses that run at higher odds.

Fabricand's study of more than 10,000 races included 93,011 horses. Classifying the animals according to the mutuel prices at which they ran, he found the following percentages of winners:

Mutuel Price Range	Percentage of Starts Won	Mutuel Price Range	Percentage of Starts Won
Up to 3.10	71.3	10.00–10.90	16.1
3.20–3.50	55.3	11.00–11.90	15.5
3.60–3.90	51.3	12.00–13.90	12.3
4.00–4.30	47.0	14.00–15.90	11.0
4.40–4.70	40.3	16.00–17.90	9.9
4.80–5.10	37.9	18.00–19.90	8.2
5.20–5.50	35.5	20.00–21.90	8.2
5.60–5.90	30.9	22.00–31.90	6.0
6.00–6.90	28.9	32.00–41.90	4.0
7.00–7.90	23.0	42.00 up	1.4
8.00–8.90	20.9		
9.00–9.90	18.6		

The lower the odds, the greater the likelihood that the horse will win.

Fabricand also demonstrates that it is impossible to turn a profit by playing *all* horses in a given odds range. The very shortest-priced horses on his list earned an insignificant profit when played in that way. But all other odds ranges showed a loss.

However, some important lessons are to be learned from the percentages of loss in each odds range:

1. The largest single group of horses on the list were the 25,044 animals that went off at odds of 20 to 1 or more (mutuel prices of $42 and up). A bet on each of those longshots would have meant a loss of 54 cents on every wagered dollar, even though 340 winning tickets would have been cashed!

2. The odds ranges below 5 to 2 (mutuel prices below $7) yielded losses that clustered around 6 percent of the wagered dollar.

3. Only on horses at 5 to 1 and higher did the percentage losses exceed the normal track take.

4. These results, mind you, were based on uncritical wagering without recourse to handicapping. The sole basis for the paper bet was the odds at which the horse left the starting gate.

It now is possible to modify an earlier statement about the quality of a handicapping procedure that loses as much as 20 percent. A player not only would do far better to play all favorites indiscriminately, but would do still better by picking an odds range below 2 to 1 and playing all horses that fell into that range! He would be betting on about half of all races, and would lose 10 or 11 percent of capital in the long run.

If he took the trouble to learn handicapping, he could then move in one of two directions. He could become more sensibly selective about the horses in his pet odds range. Or he could become more selective about horses in general, betting on apparently promising horses regardless of their odds. The test of his method would now be whether or not his bets yielded a loss smaller than 10 percent. His glee at cashing an occasional longshot ticket would remain provisional until he had balanced his books for the season. To hit the dreamed-of longshot or two and end with a loss of 21 cents on the dollar, as many players do, is to carry enjoyment past the point of diminishing returns. For anyone but a person with unlimited means and an uncontrollable yen to gamble, a procedure of that kind is downright foolish.

What Kind of Favorites?

Numerous players believe that certain kinds of races are more formful than others. That is, they believe that the favorites win a substantially higher percentage of one kind of race than of another, producing smaller dollar losses. Statistical surveys that appear to demonstrate the truth of such theories are all based on inadequate studies. More extensive samplings, such as Fabricand's and Robert Rowe's, show that the percentage of winning favorites remains essentially the same in all types of races, and that the profit or loss in each odds range does not vary significantly according to the quality of the race itself.

To show how inflexible the percentages of the game really are, I surveyed the results of all U.S. and Canadian races in 1984 that either paid purses of $200,000 and higher or were rated Grade I by the industry's ranking committee. Of those 176 top-level races, the favorites won 75, or 42.6 percent. A $2 bet on each favorite would have netted the player a loss of 10.9 percent on the wagered dollar. Which is just about where we came in.

Extra Ways to Lower the Magic Number

Here are some other well-established statistics that enable a player unacquainted with handicapping to keep long-term losses below 18 percent:

1. *Favorites at even money or less produce losses of about 5 percent when bet to win.*

2. Odds-on-favorites cost about 1 percent when bet to show.

3. All favorites to place cost about 5 percent.

4. Odds-on favorites in major handicaps, stakes races and featured allowance races at major tracks throw off a *profit* of almost 5 percent when bet to place. This exception to all other rules occurs too infrequently to mean very much in the way of riches, but is worth knowing about. It happens because the horses involved are animals of the highest grade, and seldom run worse than second.

And here is something borne in mind by expert players. It may induce non-experts to brush up on their handicapping: If a handicapper's methods customarily yield about one winner in every three attempts, the "natural" odds against any single one of his selections are about 2 to 1. Therefore, when his handicapping points out a horse running at odds higher than that, he is in an enviable situation. The percentages of the game are with him. His position is comparable to that of the poker player who draws to a bobtail straight when he knows that the pot will pay more than the necessary 5 to 1 odds.

The word "overlay" is heard constantly at the tracks. It describes an animal that runs at higher odds than its winning chances would seem to call for. The very best kind of overlay is the horse we have just discussed—picked by the methods of a competent handicapper, and running at odds more than sufficient to repay the handicapper for the losing bets he makes. Those of us who win at the track do so with overlays.

Attainable Results

A successful handicapper with a prejudice against betting on favorites is forced to refrain from betting until there appears a race in which the favorite seems undeserving. Then the handicapper must be able to find a non-favorite that seems clearly superior to the other entrants.

Another successful handicapper, with no prejudice against favorites, must avoid betting on too many favorites that lose, and must bet on a certain number of winning non-favorites, or there will be no profit.

Regardless of the individual's handicapping style, the percentages of the game govern results. Generally speaking, the more bets on longshots, the fewer wins. And the more bets on low-priced horses, the more wins. But the rate of profit—the only meaningful index to success—depends on wins at prices high enough to compensate for losses.

It has long been taken for granted in racing that a first-class handicapper can win about four bets in ten by being extremely conservative, betting on relatively few races, and favoring horses whose odds average about 2 to 1. Such a level of play brings a profit of about 20 cents for every dollar in bets, increasing capital at a tremendous rate. For example, if your capital is $2,000 and you make an average of two $100 bets a day for 200 racing days (spread over a period of years, perhaps), your operations return a profit of $8,000, enlarging your capital to $10,000.

A great deal of garbage is published about the 100 percent profits allegedly yielded by one or another winning system. In every instance, the high profits were earned (if indeed they were earned at all) over periods of time too short for significance. During the week of success at Monmouth Park that I recorded in *The Compleat Horseplayer,* my rate of profit was 92 cents on the invested dollar. Profits of that magnitude are entirely beyond reach over the long haul. If I had stayed at Monmouth for the following week I might well have suffered a shellacking.

My usual rate of profit over a period of years has been closer to 30 percent. I employ the word "usual" in a loose sense. Since most of my excursions to the track are for recreation and do not involve grimly serious handicapping, the records on which I base the 30 percent statistic are the records of days such as those at Monmouth Park, when the sole object was to win dough. When I go to the track to laugh and play and get a sunburned nose, I consider myself extremely lucky to break even.

Be that as it may, the percentages of the game and the limits of human capability seem to limit long-range profits to something like 40 cents on the dollar. A more easily attainable rate would be about 20.

Some handicappers hint that through careful selection of their spots they manage to win half of all their bets. I suppose this is possible, but whether it is possible to turn a good profit by doing it is another matter. A far more realistic objective for the handicapper is a bet-winning average in the range of 30 to 40 percent, with mutuel prices high enough for profit.

The reader will be rewarded by a few moments with the following figures.

To earn a rate of profit of 20 cents on the wagered dollar, a handicapper must:

1. Win half of all his bets, at average odds not lower than 7 to 5, or
2. Win 40 percent of his bets, at average odds of 2 to 1, or
3. Win a third of his bets, at average odds of 13 to 5, or
4. Win 30 percent of his bets, at average odds of 3 to 1.

Anyone who hopes to do twice that well, earning profits at the rate of 40 cents on the wagered dollar, must:

1. Win half of all his bets, at average odds of 9 to 5, or
2. Win 40 percent of all his bets, at average odds of 5 to 2, or
3. Win a third of his bets, at average odds of more than 3 to 1, or
4. Win 30 percent of his bets, at average odds exceeding 7 to 2.

Any of the formulas in those two lists is at least theoretically attainable. But the practicalities of the game, and of human self-control, suggest that the beginning handicapper deserves a medal if he can achieve results in the neighborhood of items 2 and 3 on the first of the lists. If he does that well, he will be able to buy his own medal.

Beware the Law of Averages

Statisticians and others acquainted with the laws of probability try, wherever possible, to measure situations in precise terms. They know that averages are misleading. The classic example is of the man who needs to cross a river. Having learned that the average depth is only five feet, and being six feet tall, he tries to wade across. In midstream he sinks like a stone and drowns. A river can be 12 feet deep at midstream and still have an average depth of only five.

Or take the following series of numbers: 1, 2, 3, 4, 5, 6, 7, 8, 9, 75. The average of those numbers is 12. But if the numbers represent the results of something or other—like the odds paid by a series of racing selections—the average distorts reality. Nine of the ten horses ran at odds of 9 or less, yet the striker of averages stumbles around under the delusion that he can expect an "average" return of about 12 on his next series of ten winners. Unless the horse that returned 75—and threw the average out of whack—was a normal, predictable, usual selection, a statistician would prefer to say that the *median* of the series was between 5 and 6. In other words, he would look for the point that falls midway in the series. Five of the numbers in this series were 6 or more. The other five were 5 or less. The median is, therefore, around 5.5. Which ain't 12.

In the handicapping of Thoroughbred horses it is essential to remember the illusory nature of averages. To give an extreme example, the player sometimes encounters a horse that has won over $100,000 in twenty starts—an average of about $5,000 per race. No other animal in the race may show winnings close to that average. To decide that the $100,000 horse is the classiest in the race might be a mistake. It might have won most of its $100,000 in one race last year and have won not a dime since. Indeed, it might have won only two races in its entire career. Another horse in today's race, with average earnings of only $3,000, might have an enormous edge in current class and condition.

Knowing that averages can never be more than rough yardsticks, the good handicapper makes them work for him. He looks beyond them.

Above all, he pays no heed whatsoever to the racetrack superstition known as "the law of averages."

Example: If favorites win one of every three races, and nine races in succession have been won by non-favorites, it is incorrect to suppose that the favorite in the tenth race has a better than ordinary chance to win. The favorite is *not* "due." Aside from what the handicapper may think of the animal's quality, which is quite another matter, its status as a favorite tells only one thing about its winning chances. That one thing is a generality: In the long run, favorites win one race out of three.

But the long run is often a *long* one. Persons who base their play on the inevitability of victory by favorites sometimes increase the amount of their bets after every loss. They lose more than they should. In fact, if they go the route of doubling their bets after each loss, they end in ruin. It is not unusual for favorites to lose ten races in succession. At Aqueduct during 1985, there was a losing series of 14. At other tracks the losing streaks ran as high as twenty. The man who bets $2 on a favorite, loses it, bets $4 on the next, and $8 on the next and continues to double up in hope that the favorite is "due" will have parted with $1,022 after nine successive losses. He will be required to bet another $1,024 on the next race, if he has it. His bet might drive the odds down from the usual 3 to 2 to something like even money. If the horse wins, which is by no means inevitable, the bettor emerges with a profit of $2 on an investment of $2,046.

The law of averages is equally meaningless in connection with the performances of jockeys. Chris McCarron and Pat Day may win more than 20 percent of their starts every year, but they also lose as many as thirty races in succession while doing it.

Similarly, the handicapper's carefully recorded knowledge that his selections win almost twice in every five attempts is poor grounds for an assumption that seven losers in a row will be followed by an immediate winner. Or that seven winners in a row make the next selection a sure loser.

Another even more harmful product of this kind of misunderstanding occurs at every track every day. A longshot wins a race. A disappointed bettor consults his *Form* and discovers that the longshot had been timed at 36 seconds in a breezing three-furlong workout a couple of days ago. No other horse in the race had worked so rapidly so recently. Powie! A new system is born! The player now loses eight bets in a row on horses whose records contain that particular workout angle.

Or a player reads a system that seems plausible, tries it on paper for a week and discovers to his delight that it picks eight winners in sixteen attempts for a profit of $1.45 on every hypothetical dollar bet. So he takes it to the track and it hits one winner in the next sixteen races, for a monumental loss. He now discards it. But it might actually be a good system. His first mistake was to assume that it was good without sufficient evidence. His second mistake was to risk money on it. His third was to discard it without sufficient evidence.

To summarize, it is not possible to determine probabilities without a large, representative series of cases. One robin doesn't make a spring. And, even after the probabilities are determined, they remain nothing but long-range probabilities. In no way do they guarantee the outcome of a single isolated event. Nor do they guarantee the outcome of any short series of events. The feeblest handicapper enjoys winning days and winning weeks. The only inevitability in his situation is that he will end as a heavy loser if he persists in his usual methods. And the best handicapper suffers losing days and weeks, but recovers the ground if his methods remain sensible and he plays in his usual style.

As I have insisted before, and as may seem more agreeable by this time, you can't necessarily beat a race, but you may be able to beat the races. To do so you will have to overcome the unfavorable percentages of the game. You will have to confine your play to situations in which (1) your handicapping knowledge tells you that an animal has an especially good chance to win and (2) the gross returns on your winning bets are more than sufficient to repair your losses.

The House Percentage

Our poker player holds four diamonds and a spade. Among the unseen 47 cards not in his hand, there are 9 diamonds. He has 9 chances in 47 to draw a diamond, or odds of 38 to 9 against—very close to 4 to 1. If it has cost $1 to stay in the game until now, and will cost another $1 to discard the spade and draw a new card, he will do so, provided that the total pot contains at least $10. If he succeeds in getting his flush, it probably will win the pot. And the pot—at least $4 of their money to every $1 of his—will more than compensate for the risk.

Suppose, however, that every time the player won a pot, the owner of the card table extracted a cut of about 20 percent of the money? The odds against drawing the flush would remain 4 to 1. But the player no longer would be able to break even on such gambles unless the pots offered at least 5 to 1.

Chances are the player would look elsewhere for a poker game. Or, if this was the only game in town, he would revise his methods. He would play much more conservatively. He would incur fewer risks. Where winning probabilities decrease, losses become more costly, more difficult to overcome.

This is exactly what has happened in Thoroughbred racing. Notwithstanding the unfragrance of old-time racing, when pari-mutuel machines were unheard of, a good handicapper enjoyed idyllic advantages. For instance, he often could get 5 to 2 from a track bookmaker on a horse that finally went off at 9 to 5. Nowadays, he would get no more than 3 to 2 on the same horse, because the house keeps a lot of the money for itself. The arithmetic is worth noting; certain bets on which the player used to make $5 in profit now yield him only $3. His profit on a bet of that kind has been reduced by 40 percent. Or, looking at it another way, that profit used to be 67 percent higher than it is now. He therefore plays much more conservatively now. He has to. The house cuts every pot with a cleaver.

The principle of pari-mutuel betting is eminently fair. The odds paid by the winning horse are—in principle—the ratio between the amount of money bet on it and the amount bet on all the losers.

Theoretically, if members of the crowd bet $30,000 on Horse "A" and other players bet a total of $60,000 on all other horses in the race, "A" is a 2 to 1 shot (60 to 30). The mutuel price should be $6, representing the bettor's original $2 plus a $4 profit. In actuality, "A" pays nothing like $6. At most tracks in the year 1986 it pays only $4.80, having been cut from 2 to 1 by the house and the state.

The house deductions are called take and breakage. They finance track operations and provide tax revenues to the state and other governments. Tracks need funds with which to pay purses, hire employees and keep themselves spruce. Governments are undoubtedly entitled to a slice, too. During the 1960s, '70s and '80s, unfortunately, state legislatures carried this principle beyond the borders of reason, increasing government's share of racetrack betting pools so remorselessly that tens of thousands of devoted horseplayers no longer could afford to go to the races as frequently as in the past. Many of these worthies took up other pastimes and stopped going to the races at all. And for newcomers unable to handicap horses, the track admission gates became revolving doors. Sensible persons who found themselves losing too much money simply gave up the game before becoming seriously involved in it.

What had formerly been a combined track-state deduction of 10 percent from the betting pools rose to a standard 17, with some states increasing the bite to as much as 25 percent on trifecta pools. As already observed, these increases meant lower profits for winning bettors, making the game more difficult than ever. The following chart shows how drastically the proceeds of winning bets are affected by apparently small increases in takeout.

The Tote Board and the Price

This table shows the mutuel prices represented by the figures posted on racetrack odds boards. Horses posted at 4 to 5 or higher may pay more than the minimum mutuel price, but they never pay less. The computations are revised at frequent intervals until post-time.

Odds	Price	Odds	Price	Odds	Price
1-9	$2.20	2-1	$6.00	18-1	$38.00
1-8	2.20	5-2	7.00	19-1	40.00
1-7	2.20	3-1	8.00	20-1	42.00
1-6	2.20	7-2	9.00	21-1	44.00
1-5	2.40	4-1	10.00	22-1	46.00
1-4	2.40	9-2	11.00	23-1	48.00
1-3	2.60	5-1	12.00	24-1	50.00
2-5	2.80	6-1	14.00	25-1	52.00
1-2	3.00	7-1	16.00	30-1	62.00
3-5	3.20	8-1	18.00	35-1	72.00
3-4	3.40	9-1	20.00	40-1	82.00
4-5	3.60	10-1	22.00	45-1	92.00
1-1	4.00	11-1	24.00	50-1	102.00
6-5	4.40	12-1	26.00	60-1	122.00
7-5	4.80	13-1	28.00	75-1	152.00
3-2	5.00	14-1	30.00	99-1	200.00
8-5	5.20	15-1	32.00		
9-5	5.60	16-1	34.00		
		17-1	36.00		

Natural Odds	Natural Mutuel Payoff	Payoff With 10% Take	Payoff With 14% Take	Payoff With 17% Take
6-1	$14.00	$12.60	$12.00	$11.60
5-1	12.00	10.00	10.20	9.80
4-1	10.00	9.00	8.60	8.20
3-1	8.00	7.20	6.80	6.60
2-1	6.00	5.40	5.00	4.80
1-1	4.00	3.60	3.40	3.20
4-5	3.60	3.20	3.00	2.60

By "natural odds" of 4 to 1, please remember, the chart refers to a situation in which the bets on the horse amount to one fifth of the betting pool. That is, with $1,000 bet on the horse and $4,000 on its opponents, we have a natural 4 to 1 shot. However, before the payoff to winning bettors, the legislated take is subtracted from the pool, severely reducing the profits awarded to winning bettors. The final column of the chart is the gasser. It shows that someone who bet on a natural 2 to 1 horse at the typical track during the early and mid-1970s collected only $4.80 when the horse won. The natural profit of $4 had been cut to $2.80, a reduction of 30 percent. And the player who collected $2.60 on a natural 4 to 5 shot had been deprived of 62.5 percent, which was outright confiscation.

The Truth About Dime Breakage

Let us now return to Horse "A," on which $30,000 has been bet. The other horses in the race have attracted a total of $60,000. The mutuel pool is $90,000.

The first thing that happens is that the track lifts $15,300 from the pool—representing the 17 percent take provided by law in most states at this writing.

After the take, $74,700 remains in the pool, including the $30,000 bet on the winning horse. The remainder of $44,700 is supposed to be the profit for winning bettors, but is not. Here is what happens:

$$30,000 \enspace \big| \enspace \frac{44,700.00}{1.49}$$

The $30,000 has been divided into the $44,700 to see how much money in profit is due per dollar bet on "A." Another way of saying it is that the division gives the dollar odds on "A."

Inasmuch as nobody can bet $1 at a track, mutuel prices are always stated in terms of a $2 bet. Therefore, the next step should be to multiply 1.49 by 2. The product, 2.98, would be the profit on a $2 bet—the odds in terms of $2. To compute the actual mutuel payoff, one then would add the bettor's original $2 to the $2.98, giving a mutuel price of $4.98 on "A."

But it is not done that way.

Instead, the dollar odds of 1.49 are reduced to 1.40. If the odds had been 1.41 or anything else up to and including 1.49, they also would have been cut to 1.40. This is known as "dime breakage." Unless dollar odds turn out all by themselves to end in a string of zeros, they are always cut to the next lower dime. Track and state pocket the leftover pennies—millions of dollars a year.

Back again now to Horse "A" and the poor soul who bet on him to win. Now that the dollar odds are only 1.40, the odds on the $2 bet are $2.80 to 2.00 and the mutuel price becomes $4.80.

There is no logic in the procedure, except as a pretext for raising taxes without seeming to. This legalized pilferage began years ago, when mutuel prices were computed by a slightly different method. Instead of dividing the amount bet on the *winner* into the amount bet on all the *losers,* and coming up with the basic dollar odds, the tracks worked in terms of $2 units. They divided the amount of the entire betting pool by a figure representing *the number of $2 tickets* sold on the winner. The answer was the winner's mutuel price. This is worth exploring further, since it shows how breakage has developed into the larceny that it now is. Let us therefore take another look at Horse "A," this time using the old-fashioned method of calculating his mutuel price.

The $30,000 bet on him represents 15,000 mutuel tickets. The pool, after take, is $74,700. The arithmetic:

$$\begin{array}{c|c} 15,000 & 74,700.00 \\ \hline & 4.98 \end{array}$$

Under this old method, the track would have paid $4.90 to any holder of a winning $2 ticket on "A." In those days, furthermore, the track take was no higher than 10 percent, so the mutuel would have been $5.40. But that's another story.

Breakage arose because few mutuel prices came out in neat round figures. The correct payoff on "A" might have been $5.12. Rather than bother their mutuel clerks with the chore of making chicken-feed change, the tracks adopted dime breakage, reducing the $5.12 to $5.10. As I have now shown, dime breakage under the old method was less costly to the player than dime breakage as currently practiced. Under the old method, the winning player collected a higher mutuel on "A" than he does now.

At some point, a procedure called nickel breakage came into vogue. Odds were computed at the dollar level. If a ticket on "A" was worth 1.45 to 1.00, the mutuel remained $4.90. If the ticket was worth 1.49 to 1.00, the odds were cut to 1.45 and the mutuel stayed at $4.90. Dollar odds were always reduced to the next lower nickel.

Which paved the way for dime breakage calculated in terms of the dollar odds. A whopping increase over old-style dime breakage. Take a horse whose dollar odds are 2.19 to 1.00. Under nickel breakage the odds became 2.15 to 1.00 and the mutuel price was $6.30. But the new, unreasonable dime breakage reduces dollar odds of 2.19 to 2.10. The horse pays only $6.20. Breakage that used to be 8 cents has become 18 cents.

Consider what this means to the holder of a ticket on a short-priced horse. If the dollar odds turn out to be .99, they are reduced to .90 and the animal pays 18 cents less on the dollar than it should have. For a horse in the even-money range this means *a profit diminution of about 18 percent on every winning ticket!*

In New York, breakage of that kind adds slightly more than one full percentage point to the total take. At Aqueduct, Belmont Park and Saratoga during 1975, breakage approached $7 million, of which the state got almost 70 percent. The basic take at the three tracks gave the state another $68 million. Which brings us to the percentages that affect place and show betting.

Place and Show Lunacy

As most players—but not all—understand, the holder of a show ticket collects a profit if the horse wins or runs second or third. A place ticket wins if the horse finishes first or second. A win ticket *loses* unless the horse wins the race.

Obviously, the best horse in the race has a better chance of running second or third than of winning. Some excellent handicappers try to capitalize on this theory. They bet only for place or show. The profits on a successful place or show bet are low, but the players hope to compensate by winning many more bets than they lose.

The profits are low in place betting because the money lost on unsuccessful bets must be divided between two groups of winners—those who hold place tickets on the animal that won the race, and those who backed the horse that ran second. The profits are even lower in show betting because the profits must be divided three ways.

The arithmetical facts are sobering:

1. To win money on horses that pay $2.20, it is necessary to cash 91 of every 100 bets.

2. To win money on horses that pay $2.40, it is necessary to cash more than 83 of every 100 bets.

3. To win money on horses that pay $2.60, it is necessary to cash more than 77 of every 100 bets.

4. To win money on horses that pay $3.00, it is necessary to cash more than 66 of every 100 bets.

Those are large orders.

The following statements about place and show betting can be accepted as absolute maxims. They derive not from my own prejudices but from the facts of racetrack life, the patterns and percentages of the game:

1. It is harder to make money by betting horses for place and show than by betting on them to win.

2. The number of correct predictions necessary to produce a profit in any representative series of place or show bets is unattainable by any but a supremely expert, supremely patient handicapper.

3. The relatively low natural profits on place and show winnings are drastically reduced by take and breakage, making the task of the place or show bettor even more difficult.

4. The guaranteed profits from place bets on odds-on favorites in high-class races are too low and the betting opportunities too infrequent to alter the overall situation.

5. Anyone able to show a profit from a long series of place or show bets has the ability to make important money on straight betting—betting to win.

6. The only sensible reason to make place bets (other than those on an occasional odds-on favorite) is the attempt to cushion one's bankroll and psyche against the after-effects of loss. Some years ago, I started betting to win and place on all selections that went off at 7 to 2 or better and found the results salutary. When the horse won, the place price was a bonus. When the horse lost but finished second, the place payoff often was more than $4, thereby supplying a profit on a losing horse. But let the reader remember that a handicapper able to show a profit on win bets can only enlarge that profit by resisting the temptations of place and show, using the money where it does the most good—to win.

Calculating Place and Show Odds

The place pool consists of all the money bet on all the horses for place. Like the win pool, it is subject to take and breakage.

Unlike the win pool, it is divided (after take and breakage) between two groups of bettors. Those who bet on the winning horse for place share the profits with those who bet on the runner-up for place. Here is an example which takes the liberty of assuming that the take is only 15 percent, which it well may become in many places where the 17 percent toll has been driving customers away.

> Total amount in place pool: $48,000
> Remainder after 15 percent take: $40,800
> Total bet on "A" to place: $20,000
> Total bet on "B" to place: $12,000

The total profit to be returned to the successful place bettors on this race is $8,800. That figure is obtained by subtracting from the net pool of $40,800 the $32,000 that was bet on "A" and "B." The remainder is what the losing bettors have lost to the winning bettors.

The $8,800 is now divided in half, leaving $4,400 in profits for distribution to the backers of "A" and $4,400 for those who bet on "B."

We'll take "A" first:

$$20,000 \mid \frac{4,400.00}{.22}$$

The correct dollar odds in "A" to place are .22 to 1.00. Breakage transforms this to 20 cents on the dollar, making "A" a 1 to 5 shot for place. The mutuel is $2.40.

If there were no such things as take and breakage, the mutuel would be $2.80. Take and breakage reduce the natural profits on "A" by a full 50 percent!

Now let us see what happens with "B":

$$\frac{12,000 \quad | \quad 4,400.00 \text{ plus}}{.36 \text{ plus}}$$

Breakage reduces the dollar odds to .30 to 1.00 and makes "B's" mutuel price $2.60 for place. But the natural mutuel, without take and breakage, would be $3.33. The profits have been cut by 55 percent.

The difficulties of place and show betting are even more pronounced than these examples indicate. Most notably, the purchaser of a place or show ticket buys a pig in a poke. He may have reason for confidence in the horse's ability to finish second or third, but he cannot begin to know what the place or show ticket will be worth until after the race is over. If he must share the profits with holders of place tickets on an odds-on favorite, his own ticket will be worth little. If his horse wins the race and a longshot finishes second—or vice versa—the place ticket will be worth more. Thus, his position is comparable to that of a poker player with a bobtail straight who agrees to buy a card without knowing how much money is in the pot. He might as well play a slot machine.

To make this clear, let us now see what happens to the place price on the well-backed "A" if Longshot "C" wins the race or finishes second. The pool remains $40,800, after deduction of the take. The crowd has bet $5,000 on "C" to place. That amount, plus the $20,000 bet on "A," is now deducted from the pool, leaving $15,800 for distribution. Holders of tickets on "A" will get $7,900. So will the supporters of "C." Compute the odds on "A":

$$\frac{20,000 \quad | \quad 7,900.00}{.39}$$

The correct dollar odds on "A" are slashed to .30 to 1.00 by breakage, making the mutuel price $2.60. This is more than "A" paid when the pool was shared with backers of the fairly well supported "B." But now that "B" has failed to finish first or second, the $12,000 bet on him for place has been lost, and the losses have increased the profits available for distribution to owners of cashable place tickets.

I doubt that it is necessary to work out the computations on a show pool. After the take, the amounts bet on all three horses are subtracted from the pool. The remainder is divided into three equal parts, and the show price on each horse is then calculated in the usual way.

Since the place or show price on a horse depends only partly on how much has been bet on it for place or show, but depends also on how well other in-the-money horses were supported, a sensible rule can be suggested:

A time to consider betting on a horse for place is when it is an odds-on favorite and all, repeat all, other likely contenders are longshots. In such circumstances, the horse might pay only $2.40 to win but could pay almost that much—and sometimes more— to place or show. When Roman Brother won the Jockey Club Gold Cup in 1965, he paid $2.40 to win and $2.40 to place. In the Spinaway Stakes that year, Moccasin paid $2.60 to win and $2.60 to place.

Betting More than One Horse to Win

Jule Fink and his celebrated "Speed Boys" attracted national attention years ago with their practice of betting two and three horses to win the same race. As far as I know, Fink and other successful players still make money that way. It is a perfectly reasonable approach for any good handicapper with plenty of capital. If you can narrow the contention in a race to two or three or four animals, and the odds on each are high enough to assure a net profit, such betting makes sense.

Booking Percentages

Before the advent of mutuel machines, a hustler could shop among the trackside bookmakers for the best odds. Good handicappers made money that way by betting on every horse in a race except rank outsiders, overrated favorites and other animals that figured to lose.

The practice was known as "dutching," supposedly in honor of its originator, a player known as Dutch. Its basis was the bookmaker's scale of percentages, which showed how odds varied according to the fraction of the betting pool represented by the total money bet on each horse. For an easy example, if the player felt that an even-money choice could not win, he would operate as if half the betting pool—the proportion represented by the bets on that horse—were up for grabs. Simply by betting on every other horse in the race in amounts equal or proportionate to their booking percentages, he would win a substantial amount.

I understand that some players try to do the same thing at the mutuel machines. Knowing that the mutuel pool adds up to about 118 percent (the extra 18 being take and breakage), they try to eliminate horses whose odds represent 30 or 40 percent of the pool. Then, by betting the remaining horses in proportions indicated by the table of booking percentages, they beat the race.

It is easier in theory than in real life. Bets must be made at the last possible moment, in amounts that require lightning calculation. Enormous capital and outstanding ability as a handicapper are needed.

I do not say that mutuel dutching is impossible. But it requires capital of such magnitude, and handicapping talent so well developed that the rare person able to carry it off would probably do better by betting on two or three good horses a day.

The Percentages

Odds	Percentage	Odds	Percentage	Odds	Percentage
1-9	90.00	8-5	38.46	13-1	7.14
1-8	88.89	9-5	35.71	14-1	6.66
1-7	87.50	2-1	33.33	15-1	6.25
1-6	85.68	5-2	28.57	16-1	5.88
1-5	83.33	3-1	25.00	17-1	5.55
1-4	80.00	7-2	22.23	18-1	5.26
1-3	75.00	4-1	20.00	19-1	5.00
2-5	71.42	9-2	18.19	20-1	4.76
1-2	66.67	5-1	16.67	25-1	3.85
3-5	62.50	6-1	14.29	30-1	3.23
3-4	57.14	7-1	12.50	40-1	2.44
4-5	55.55	8-1	11.11	50-1	1.96
1-1	50.00	9-1	10.00	60-1	1.64
6-5	45.45	10-1	9.09	75-1	1.32
7-5	41.67	11-1	8.33	99-1	.99
3-2	40.00	12-1	7.69		

Simplifying the Booking Percentages

Persons able to narrow the contention in a race to three or four horses can use the following table to guarantee a profit. By betting on each of the contending horses in the precise proportions called for by the odds, the player wins, no matter which of the horses wins. Naturally, if some other horse wins, the entire amount is lost. The only limit on this adaptation of the old-fashioned booking-percentage table is that the total amount wagered may not exceed $42. Of course, if the player wants to double or triple or quadruple the prescribed amounts, his possible outlay increases to the chosen multiple of $42. Note also that the method is not usable with extremely short-priced horses.

Odds at Post-Time	Bet	Odds at Post-Time	Bet	Odds at Post-Time	Bet
8-5	$19	7-2	$11	7-1	$6
9-5	18	4-1	10	8-1	6
2-1	16	9-2	9	9-1	5
5-2	14	5-1	8	10-1	5
3-1	12	6-1	7	11-1 and up	4

Progressive and System Betting

Most betting systems are poison. They require the player to increase the bet after every losing attempt. Their theory is that the player is "due" to win at some point, and that the increased bet will return enough to make up for prior losses. We have already noted the disaster that awaits anyone who, relying on a "law" of averages, doubles his bet after every loss on a favorite, or on a top jockey. One need not double the bets, of course. Modifications of the double-up method are frequently used. But they only modify the player's losses. They cannot produce profits except briefly and accidentally. Also, they require investment outlays out of all proportion to the returns.

A pet method of some players is known as "due-column betting." The racegoer decides that the track owes him a daily stipend—say, $100. He therefore bets as much on each of his selections as will produce the desired return. Let us say that he likes a horse in the first race. Shortly before post-time, the odds board holds the animal at 4 to 1. The player bets $25. If the horse wins, the player has his $100 and goes home. If the horse loses, the player now must win $125 to make his $100 net profit.

The most evident flaw in that procedure is the underlying supposition that anyone can make a profit at any track on any given day. Or in any given week. Due-column betting thus multiplies the player's losses during a losing streak, requiring him to increase the size of his losing bets. Few players can afford it.

A far more sensible arrangement is to abandon "due-columns" and allocate a fixed percentage of betting capital for each transaction. As the capital increases, so does the size of each bet. As the capital decreases, so does each bet, enabling the player to withstand a long succession of losses, if he has to.

The notion that a player should invest more when winning and less when losing is accepted as wisdom in every game. Players who bet according to that principle make more money—or lose less—than players who defy the principle. Indeed, if two handicappers are capable of turning a 20 percent profit, and each of them starts with a bankroll of $100, the player who bets 5 percent of capital on each of his selections will end the year with far more money than the player who goes in for due-column betting or progressive betting or other upside-down methods that violate the percentages of the game, the principles of sound investment and, last but not least, the tenets of common sense.

The player who bets 5 percent of his capital can stay in business at the track for months, without winning a dime. If he goes there with $100 and loses from the beginning, he will have $45 left even if he encounters twenty successive losses before hitting a single winner. Assuming that he is the kind who can actually make the 20 percent profit we have mentioned so often, he probably will go for years without a series of losers as grievous as that.

The due-column or progressive bettor would put himself out of business in such circumstances, even though he might be just as good a handicapper as the other guy. By the same token, neither the due-column bettor nor the slave of progressive betting systems makes as much money in a series of winning bets as the man who bets a fixed fraction of capital.

By way of demonstrating this, let us analyze the occasional but inevitable blessing of five winners in succession. For the sake of argument, we can assume that each horse pays 5 to 2. The due-column bettor has a bankroll of $400 and wants to make $50 per race. He bets $20 on each of these winners, netting $250 in profits and raising his bankroll to $650. He is happy as a clam.

The adherent of progressive betting also has a $400 bankroll. He bets $20 on the first horse, planning to apply his magic formula in such a way as to require a larger bet on the second horse, if the first one loses. But the first one wins, and so do the next four. He ends by making $250 on the series of bets. His bankroll is also $650, and he is perfectly satisfied.

The man who bets 5 percent of capital also has a $400 bankroll. His first bet nets $50, making the capital $450.

His second bet is $22, netting $55. Bankroll is now $505.

His third bet is $25, netting $62.50. Bankroll: $567.50.

His fourth bet is $28, netting $70. Bankroll: $637.50.

His fifth bet is $32, netting $80. Bankroll: $717.50.

He has done better than the others. Even when his next two horses lose, he will remain in better shape.

He will bet $36 on the first loser, reducing his capital to $681.50.

He will bet $34 on the second loser, reducing his capital to $647.50.

The due-column bettor will lose $20 on the first losing bet and, assuming we are still dealing with 5 to 2 shots, will be trying to win $70 on the second bet. He therefore will wager, and lose, $28. His bankroll is now down to $602.

The progressive bettor, no matter how conservative his system, will lose at least $50 on the two bets, reducing his bankroll to $600 or less.

Other Money-Management Ideas

Most seasoned handicappers agree that it is easier to pick winners than to make money at it. Part of the reason is that you may pick a winner but decide not to bet on the race. A larger part of the reason is that many of us have a propensity for plunging on losers and making miserly bets on winners. No wonder that wagering formulas (usually described in our literature as money management) are dependably popular, even when they not only fail to work but actually hasten the downfall of those who use them.

By far the best money-management plan I have ever encountered has been around for many years but is not yet as well known as it deserves to be. It was devised by James N. Selvidge, a Western author and lecturer with a devoted following.*

To test an approach to handicapping, or simply to test developing skills, and finally to begin augmenting the bankroll, Selvidge recommends that your base bet be the smallest amount accepted at the local windows. Let us call it $2, which is most likely in most places. You set aside $30, enough for fifteen bets.

Each bet is the base bet plus the square root of any profit that may have been netted along the way. The worst that happens is that you lose your $30, and return to your studies of handicapping before risking any more money. But if you are successful, adding the square root of profit to the base bet has a powerful growth effect.

In time, a successful practitioner of this idea will notice that the bets, though much larger than the base amount, have become a tiny percentage of bankroll, and that a much larger percentage could be risked to great advantage. Selvidge's response is that such a player should undertake "parallel flows," modifying the formula to a larger number of base bets—say five. He urges that the player continue to calculate in terms of a single base bet plus square root of the profit earned on that base bet, and then multiply by five. It works out better mathematically than would the more obvious procedure of simply adopting a new base bet five times the original size and working with the square root of the total profit.

A fairly well publicized but much less useful formula is called the Kelly Criterion, named after a Bell Laboratories engineer who wrote many years ago that bets should be sized in direct relation to the player's advantage over the game. For example, if betting on a sure thing, such as a fixed race, with a 100 percent advantage over the game, you should bet all your money. Otherwise you would not be taking full advantage of the situation.

The modern version of Kelly is that the handicapper should calculate a personal "advantage over the game" based on percentage of winners and average mutuels. I have already mentioned that idea in another connection and I approve of it, but I doubt that one handicapper in a thousand would do it, and I doubt that one in ten of those who did it would do it properly. For example, I think that very few handicappers who won 42 percent of their bets at an average mutuel price of $7.80 during a one-month period would have the slightest right to expect such results in the future, much less decide that their bets should be as large as those that might be more suitable for someone capable of maintaining a 42 percent average for years at a time.

*(Hold Your Horses, Jacada Publications, Las Vegas, Nevada.)

Trifectas and Other Lotteries

The pooh-bahs of racing have no bias against common gambling so long as they can cut each pot. Indeed, with the passage of time and the emergence of competition from state lotteries, casinos and unobstructed illegal gambling on baseball, football and basketball, the racing industry has struck back by imitating the competition. The similarities between a pic six and keno are greater than the differences.

In recent years most tracks (but by no means all) have redeemed themselves to some extent by finally eliminating the lottery characteristics that once distinguished daily doubles, exactas (perfectas) and quinellas. Television monitors now offer pre-race displays of possible payoffs on the various combinations offered in those bets. Until that happened, persons who bet on the double or exacta were betting in the blind, which deterred few of them but should have.

One of the appeals of race betting and the handicapping that precedes it is the possibility of restricting the role of sheer chance while maximizing the role of skill. Why would a handicapper ever bet on a pig in the poke such as a trifecta or pic six, neither of which ever is presented with pre-race postings of possible payoffs? Well, the bet is fun. No harm in a little fun. Another answer is that some handicappers are also compulsive gamblers and bet on those grab bags because they cannot resist doing so. Sometimes they reap huge payoffs as lucky members of trifecta or pic-six syndicates. But at the end of the chapter, they have won less per wagered dollar than any competent recreational handicapper does steadily and quietly as a matter of course.

Well all right, it is likely that a few specialists in the dreary art of pic-six syndication have done quite well from time to time by holding their fire until the bet had gone unwon for several days and the prize had enlarged to a hundred thousand or two or more. At that point, a syndicate with $100,000 to bet can often buy the pool, betting on virtually all possible combinations and ending with a profit in the neighborhood of even money, but a profit in six figures none the less.

Dear reader, enlarge and enjoy your skills through study and successful win betting. Tinker with doubles and exactas if you wish. Pay close attention to the possible payoffs. Always be sure to have a win bet on that horse you like in the daily double or exacta. And be sure that your bets are chosen to assure you a substantial profit if one of the combinations you choose should win. Otherwise, why bother?

Another valid complaint against the multiple bets is that they encourage and reward dishonesty. Scandalous revelations about the activities of twin-double betting syndicates at harness-racing tracks made that particular wrinkle unfashionable in major Thoroughbred racing. The trifecta is not much better. In 1977, a researcher helped me to establish that the percentage of winning favorites in trifecta races was substantially lower than in other kinds of races. Worse, the favorites ran entirely out of the money far more often than normal. The peculiarly low payoffs in occasional trifecta races won by longshot combinations demonstrate that fixers and other participants in betting coups send heavy money to the trifecta windows.

The well-accepted daily double opens the way to skulduggery of its own. A horseman can stiff his animal with high profit and relative impunity in a daily-double race. If the horse is a short-priced favorite, the horseman is able to enrich himself simply by preventing it from winning, after purchasing daily-double tickets on the other contenders. For a modest outlay, and without confiding in another living soul, he can make more money that way than by collecting the short odds and the wretchedly small winner's share of the purse at the cheap tracks he frequents.

The Economics of Racing

Among the most joyful recollections of any veteran horseman is the time he caught everyone napping and saddled a 70 to 1 shot that romped by four lengths at New Orleans, laughing all the way. Sometimes it was 20 to 1 or 50 to 1 at Empire City or Havre de Grace or Latonia or Havana. It happened over and over again.

"That colt had the tenderest mouth I ever saw," says the old-timer. "Couldn't stand the bit. When I bought him for $200 he hadn't won any part of a purse in more than a year. Soon as he'd feel the bit he'd sulk. Wouldn't run an inch. So I got him down to Hover de Graw and entered him in a $1,500 race and told the boy, 'Keep a stout hold on him all the way. Don't let him run off with you. He needs a lot of rating. Save his run for the stretch.' They break and the boy takes a tight wrap and the horse feels the bit and props and damned near throws the boy and they get beat by sixty lengths. So the next week I put the horse in a $2,500 race and tell the boy, 'Now boy, all I want you to do is sit there and let them reins hang loose. Let the horse do all the work.' Horse win all by hisself. I got almost a hundred bucks down on the race, all I had in the world. One book give me ninety to one and another give eighty-five and another eighty. I sell the horse for two grand and go to Europe for a year on my winnings."

Times have changed, but not completely. Now, as in the old days, the dream of every journeyman trainer is to find the hole card, the magic formula that converts a losing horse into a winner. The horseman needs to win a purse. He also needs to win some bets. The ideal situation is when the magic formula presents itself after the horse has run out of the money repeatedly, without showing any signs of improvement. The horse wins. The mutuel price looks like the registration number on a freight car. The stewards call in the trainer, to inquire about the miraculous reversal of form.

"The horse was off his feed for months," says the trainer truthfully. "But the other day a kitten wandered into his stall and the bugger perked up. I guess he was lonesome, or something. Him and that kitten are thick as thieves. Horse is real frisky all a of sudden."

Hoof, tail and muzzle, the economics of horse racing are tied to the pari-mutuel machines. The purse money comes from the mutuel betting pools. The funds with which struggling horsemen eke out their purses are earned at the betting windows. The horseman's prime object is to win races with his livestock, but he will go to any permissible length to conceal a horse's true form in hope of getting 5 to 1 on a natural 2 to 1 shot. He has to. He needs the dough.

Let it be agreed that certain leading trainers do not rely on bets for any part of their livelihood. Neither do certain glamorous owners. Many jockeys do not bet. But almost everyone else does, from the candy butchers and tip-sheet hawkers and ushers and sweepers and mutuel clerks to the occupants of the nice boxes in the upper tier.

The player may own a desk full of super-scientific speed charts. He may be able to recite Buckpasser's pedigree all the way back to

Goats and dogs are standard items in Thoroughbred barns. Race horses love company. ARLINGTON PARK PHOTO

Tregonwell's Natural Barb. He may know at a glance that yonder filly has bad knees. But his handicapping will be a game of blindman's buff unless he appreciates the significance of the winning bet in the life of the average horseman. The following facts are basic:

1. It costs at least $25,000 a year to feed, house, groom, shoe, doctor and train a Thoroughbred in the big leagues of racing. In lesser environments the cost may fall below $8,000, but not by much.

2. Transportation, jockey fees, entry fees, workmen's compensation insurance, equine mortality insurance and accident insurance increase the costs by thousands of dollars a year per active runner.

3. During a typical year in the mid-1980s, about 80,000 Thoroughbreds competed at tracks in the United States, Canada and Mexico. They earned about $600 million in purses, an average of $7,500 per animal—not enough to support a horse at a major track. Worse, as we find necessary to observe from to time, averages can be terribly misleading. Read on.

4. The year's top 35 money-winning horses listed in *Daily Racing Form*'s annual review of these matters (about ½₅ of 1 percent of all the runners) usually account for a whopping 5 percent of the purse money. Another 1,500 or so stakes-winning animals (3 percent of all) carry off an additional 25 percent.

This leaves an average of perhaps $5,500 apiece for the other 77,000 runners. But averages being what they are, many thousands of these animals bring home no earnings whatsoever. The brilliantly detailed and comprehensive studies of racing economics published each year in *The Thoroughbred Record* by Dr. Robert G. Lawrence of the University of Maryland showed that half of all racing Thoroughbreds were earning less than $2,400 a year during this period. The horse that actually pays its way is unusual.

5. Accordingly, an estimated 98 percent of racing stables lose money each year. Their deficits are compounded not only of high costs and low income, but of other expenses on which no return is realized—the cost of buying (or breeding) and feeding and training and doctoring animals that suffer injury or illness and never run in a race.

6. Some stable owners do not mind. An indeterminate number—far fewer than the losing 98 percent—are sports without financial worries, able to deduct their racing losses from personal or corporate taxes. More typical owners are recent recruits to racing, business persons seeking glamour, publicity, tax shelters or a combination thereof, and likely to disappear after a few losing seasons.

7. Most stable owners bet with both hands, hoping to augment purses with mutuel winnings when their horses seem ready. Naturally, all welcome an extra point or two in the odds.

8. The 35 top trainers of a year are likely to accumulate purse winnings of more than $80 million, which translates into an average of better than $225,000 each from the 10 percent purse bonuses usually given to trainers. The remaining 99.6 percent of trainers scramble and scuffle. Some make good livings, many eke things out by trying to wangle a commission for buying or selling a horse. Most try to get horses of their own, or to be part owners of horses that run in the names of others. A full partner's 50 percent share of a purse is five times the trainer's time-honored 10 percent. As the reader can readily understand, the needful trainer who does not bet on the stable's ready horses is a rare bird indeed. And many a betting trainer manipulates horses in ways that promote higher odds when the horses finally win.

9. The top 35 jockeys win purses upward of $170 million in a representative year. Translation: About 1 percent of jockeys capture 28 percent of the purses! Most riders have a harder time. They do not make a living in competition, but depend on other employment, such as exercising horses in the morning. Racing law forbids jockeys to bet against themselves, so that does not happen much. But the non-betting rider is as rare as the non-betting trainer or owner, and any jockey welcomes the pre-race news that the horse is ready to go and the owner has bet a hundred or two for the little person in the saddle.

It must now be evident that desire for a winning ticket is as avid in the barns and paddocks as in the grandstand. In time, handicappers learn to recognize stables whose methods put more than ordinary emphasis on betting. To overlook the phenomenon is to interpret certain past-performance records naively. Which is not smart handicapping.

The maneuvering that results in higher odds—the maneuvering that enables many horsemen to remain in the game—is so widespread that it affects the outcome of an overwhelming majority of races.

Do I imply that racing is dishonest, fixed, rigged? Do I suggest that the best horse in the race is pulled or drugged to build the odds for his next outing?

Not really. In big-time racing, when a horse is in shape to win and is entered against animals it can beat, the stable goes all out for the purse and the bet, regardless of odds. Few horses retain winning form long enough for the kind of odds-building shenanigans that require a ready animal to lose. Next time, when the odds are "right," it may no longer be able to win.

But something else is done. Every day, horses are entered in races that they cannot win except by sheer accident. They are outclassed, or at the wrong distance, or off their feed, or sore-legged, or short of wind. Two interrelated reasons account for their presence on the track:

1. Tracks have to fill nine or ten or as many as twelve races a day. Fields of fewer than eight horses are unpopular, but there are not enough fit and ready horses to go around. The tracks therefore expect (to put it mildly) every horseman to keep his stock active. A trainer who refuses to run as frequently as possible finds that the track would rather give the stall space to a more cooperative stable. Under these pressures, only the stables owned by the big names of racing are permitted to train horses in the proper way—racing them when ready to run at their best, and not before.

2. Most trainers have adapted to these economic and political realities. They now race their stock into shape. They no longer rely on the workouts, the patient nurture and careful doctoring that are the bases of sound training methods. They ruin numerous horses this way, but they have become used to it. They can't fight city hall. As a matter of fact, they have learned to turn the racing of unready horses to their own advantage. Chiefly, they use it to darken an animal's form. They deliberately seek out races in which the horse will look bad, even though its condition actually may be improving. When it finally is ready to win, the crowd may not recognize this in sufficient numbers to make the horse a favorite. It therefore pays gratifying odds, bailing out the horseman for the time being.

Man O' War sets world record for mile in 1920 Withers. UPI PHOTO

Fortunately, competent handicappers can usually tell when a horse's condition is improving. The result charts and past-performance records contain all the necessary information. Thus, the modern betting coup, in which the stable and its friends bet thousands of dollars, most often finds the horse romping in at modest odds. Members of the paying audience who happen to be good handicappers frequently get in on the coup, and help bring the odds down, by recognizing omens in the past-performance records, or picking up inside information about the scheme.

The Cost of the Hobby

There is such a thing as a professional horseplayer. Unless he lives across the street from the track and has a tax-free pass to the place, he must include transportation and admission among the costs of doing business. The hobbyist is well advised to do the same thing. Few players can buy their racing paper, get to the track, pay their way in, eat some lunch, and get home on less than $20.

If he goes to the track twenty times a year, the player's expenses, without betting, are at least $400. I do not regard this as exorbitant. Twenty decent dinners and movies cost much more. Twenty baseball games can also cost as much, depending on the location of the ballpark.

One of the pleasures of handicapping is the opportunity to recover the cost of the pastime. There is no need to be grim about it. In fact, being too grim spoils the fun. Yet there she sits, a $400 outlay for twenty afternoons at the track. How do we get it back?

We do *not* get it back with $2 bets. If the player has reached the stage of earning about 20 cents on every dollar he bets, he is likely to make not more than sixty bets in the twenty days. At $2 a bet, the sixty bets are an investment of $120. The profit will be about $24, not enough to pay expenses.

Bets of $20 are far more sensible.

Yet not everyone can afford to bet $20 on a horse.

There would seem to be a contradiction here.

The contradiction is resolved by betting *not one penny* on horses until the results of numerous paper bets demonstrate reasonable handicapping ability. It is as unintelligent to waste money in $2 bets as in $20 bets. Readers of this book will do themselves a great favor by risking no money on its teachings until a series of dry runs has shown that the lessons work.

After achieving that plateau, the player should make the transition to actual betting. But he should bet no money that will be missed after it is lost. Perhaps he will make bets of $2 or $5. If he is a talented handicapper with exceptional self-control, he may discover that he does as well with real money in the hurly-burly of the track as on paper at home. If he is less exceptional, it may take a while before he becomes accustomed to the difference between dry run and actual battle.

When his results finally warrant confidence, the player should begin betting in units of not less than $20, which would require investment capital of at least $400. If he does not have the $400, he should wait until he has saved it.

If it costs him $20 a day to go to the track, he may have to make bets of $30 or $40 to retrieve his "overhead."

It's fun to do it. And, depending on the individual personality, well worth the effort.

THE MYSTERY
OF BREEDING

Thoroughbreds are a separate, registered breed of horse, as distinctive in purpose and appearance as Percherons, Clydesdales or Appaloosas.

The breed originated in England, where racing has been an aristocratic pastime for about 1000 years. Late in the seventeenth century, during the reign of Charles II, numerous Middle Eastern stallions were imported to invigorate the tired blood of native British stock. Efforts to obtain prize specimens continued into the next century. Some of the imports were outstanding. Three of the stallions were so good that their descendants now monopolize the backstretch stalls and breeding barns of the world.

Although it is barely two centuries since the genetic superiority of the three imported stallions became evident in British racing, every single one of today's hundreds of thousands of Thoroughbreds descends in tail male (from sire to paternal grandsire and so on through the male line) from one of the three.

Their names were the Darley Arabian, the Byerly Turk and the Godolphin Barb. The Arabian, foaled in Syria, was held to be one of the foremost specimens of his breed ever seen in England. The Turk had been a military charger. The Godolphin was reputed to have been found in Paris, pulling a water cart. His ancestry was unknown, but he looked like the Moroccan (Barbary Coast) type known as a Barb.

The Darley Arabian's great-great-grandson, Eclipse, foaled in 1764, was probably the greatest runner of his century. He then became a great progenitor. Other Darley Arabian lines have vanished. But from Eclipse come all but a few of the Thoroughbreds that win major races in the United States.

Among the notables whose lineage traces to Eclipse in tail male have been Affirmed, Alibhai, Alsab, Alydar, Arts and Letters, Blenheim II, Bold Ruler, Buckpasser, Bull Lea, Citation, Colin, Count Fleet, Damascus, Dr. Fager, Equipoise, Exclusive Native, Foolish Pleasure, Forego, Graustark, Hail to Reason, Halo, Heliopolis, Hoist the Flag, Hyperion, John Henry, Kelso, Key to the Mint, Le Fabuleux, Lyphard, Majestic Prince, Menow, Minnesota Mac, Nashua, Nasrullah, Native Dancer, Never Bend, Nijinsky II, Northern Dancer, Polynesian, Princequillo, Prince John, Raise a Native, Ribot, Roberto, Round Table, Secretariat, Seattle Slew, Sir Gaylord, Spectacular Bid, Stage Door Johnny, Teddy, Tom Fool, Tom Rolfe and Vaguely Noble.

Descendants of the Godolphin Barb via his 1748 grandson, Matchem, have not won nearly as many American races, but it is hard to imagine the sport without the best of them: Man O'War. Also Seabiscuit, Busher, Discovery, War Admiral, Intentionally, In Reality, Full Pocket, Olden Times, Tentam and all their popular kith and kin.

From the Byerly Turk's 1758 great-great-grandson, Herod, we have had Ambiorix, Ambehaving, First Fiddle, Porter's Cap, Whiskery, Royal Minstrel, Epinard, The Tetrarch, Crozier and My Babu. The line accounts for an infinitesimal proportion of American stakes winners, but its blood flows in many more than that. Cross breeding among the three main strains of Thoroughbred is unavoidable and necessary. A typical descendant of Eclipse is sure to have numerous Matchems and Herods in its pedigree. Kelso, for example, descended in tail male from Eclipse, but his maternal granddam. Maidoduntreath, was a Man O'War mare, from Matchem.

As one might imagine, efforts to breed horses to go farther and faster began on a trial-and-error basis. To a large extent, the work is still largely a matter of by-guess-and-by-gosh. Scientific eugenics are standard in the breeding of cattle, hogs and poultry, but not in the breeding of Thoroughbreds. One reason is that Thoroughbreds are not cattle. They are not something to eat. Their value is not measurable in poundage, but in speed, courage and endurance. Accordingly, a breeder's mistakes and triumphs may not come into clear focus for years—when the foals have grown and raced and ended their careers and begun to produce tested runners or proven washouts of their own.

None of this necessarily rules out scientific study and experimentation, but the keenly competitive, high-pressure economics of racing and breeding are serious obstacles. If given an opportunity, a scientist might be able to argue that a mating of Stud "A" and Mare "B" could produce a promising foal. But the breeder knows that Stud "C" is more fashionable. The progeny of "C" is worth far more on the market. He therefore goes to "C." If the mating turns out poorly and the foal shows little promise, it can always be unloaded at yearling sales, and often for a fancy price, thanks to its glamorous pedigree. So many races are run every day at so many tracks that it is possible to make good money selling horses that would not have been allowed on a track thirty years ago. Moreover, such horses finally win a race or two, after they are entered against animals of their own feeble ability.

Sire vs. Dam

Thoroughbred breeding is so remote from science that completely contradictory theories are practiced without arousing more than mild controversy. Colonel E. R. Bradley used to declaim that 65 percent of a Thoroughbred's quality came from the dam. John E. Madden, breeder of five Derby winners, thought that the *sire* contributed 75 percent of the quality.

The chances are that both were wrong. Do human beings inherit intelligence from fathers or mothers? Obviously, from both. Horses, like all other living creatures, abide by Mendel's Law.

One of the few qualified persons ever to study Thoroughbred breeding was Dr. Dewey G. Steele, Professor of Genetics at the University of Kentucky. He wrote:

"Pedigrees must be judged primarily on the basis of ancestors in the first and second generation, and individuals beyond the third generation may for all practical purposes be ignored.

"There is no evidence that the tail-female line or any other line exercises a hereditary influence greater than would be expected on a purely chance basis."

Old Colonel Bradley, believing that the "class is in the dam," sought classy dams and got a percentage of classy horses. John Madden, looking at things the other way, used classy sires and got a percentage of classy horses. Why not?

The Unscience of Breeding

Breeders no longer are quite so innocent of genetic rules as they used to be. They formerly tended to evaluate horses in Mayflower terms, poring over pedigrees to see how many champions appeared on remote branches of the family tree. Bitter experience finally taught them that the best index to an animal's possible class was the class of its parents and grandparents, as demonstrated on the track and in the breeding stall. It made no sense to cherish a man solely because one of his ancestors had been an archduke. The same was true of a horse.

To add a touch of stamina to a line that seemed short of that quality, breeders used to look for "doses" of staying power several generations back, and breed their stock accordingly. Sometimes it worked, more often it did not. Some of them persist in a variation of this, looking for "nicks"—previously successful combinations of bloodlines that might be repeated with equal success.

The simple arithmetic of genetics frustrates most maneuvers of that kind. Any single ancestor five generations removed was, after all, but one of 32 great-great-great-grandparents. The hereditary influence of such an ancestor is modified, for good or ill, by the contributions of the 61 other recent ancestors whose blood combines in the new foal.

Nowadays, the best breeders try to mate the classiest possible stallion with the classiest possible mare. Extensive research by the late Joseph A. Estes, distinguished editor of *The Blood-Horse,* and his successor, Kent Hollingsworth, has demonstrated that the stallions and mares most likely to produce topnotch runners are animals who themselves were winners of major stakes races.

In general, today's expensive, fashionably bred yearling is the offspring of champions or near-champions or, of course, sires and dams that have already proved themselves capable of yielding good racers. By the same token, the cheap, unfashionably bred yearling is from parents and grandparents that were below the first flight as runners and have done nothing to redeem themselves in the boudoir. But Nature runs a lottery. Every now and then, an expensive yearling proves to be a throwback to the worst of its ancestors. And every season, several runners of unpromising pedigree turn out to be reincarnations of great-great-grandpa, the champ.

One of the most extreme examples of this kind of thing became noticeable on October 3, 1960, when a highly unfashionable two-year-old colt named Carry Back caught Globemaster in the stretch of the seven-furlong Cowdin Stakes at Belmont Park and won by a length and a half, going away. He paid $14.60.

The opinion makers of racing were unimpressed. Carry Back's sire was Saggy, who had beaten Citation at six furlongs in the mud on a day in 1948 when the great horse was out of condition. Saggy had done nothing else to distinguish himself as a racer and had begotten no outstanding foals in several years of trying. Carry Back's dam was a $150 mare, Joppy. The breeder, Jack A. Price, served also as trainer. Nobody had nominated him for any known Hall of Fame.

A few days after the Cowdin, Carry Back was left at the post and lost the Champagne Stakes. The very notion of Price getting anything much with this beast was so unacceptable that Carry Back paid $18.40 when he sauntered to an easy victory in the Garden State Stakes on October 29. For romping the mile and a sixteenth over a sloppy track, he earned $172,782. All of a sudden the game had a Cinderella horse.

In 1961, Carry Back won seven races, including the Kentucky Derby and Preakness. He earned more purse money that year—$556,874—than any other Thoroughbred and was everyone's choice as champion three-year-old.

Experts who studied Carry Back's pedigree were unable to find any excuse for his championship stamina, speed and soundness. The sire's dam, Chantress, was by the celebrated Hyperion but had such dreadful-looking feet that her owners, the Greentree Stud (Whitney), had un-loaded her. The paternal grandsire, Swing and Sway, another Greentree cull, had won some purses without reminding anyone of his daddy, Equipoise. And Equipoise, while a good runner, had suffered from hoof trouble and had been transmitting it to his get. Another blemish in Carry Back's pedigree was the maternal grandsire, Star Blen, which had shown a touch of speed but not a trace of stamina.

By any standards, Carry Back was a freak. He inherited none of the shortcomings to which his immediate ancestry should have condemned him. He was the accidential reincarnation of distinguished forebears. But all Thoroughbreds, even the worst, have distinguished forebears. Nature is fickle. "Breed the best to the best and hope for the best," shrug horsemen.

It would be silly to suggest that any scientist could have foreseen a Derby winner by Saggy out of Joppy. Science ain't all that wise. But under present non-scientific auspices, surprises are bred with almost comic frequency. One must assume that the horsemen are running several laps behind Nature. They hope for the best, but are not necessarily able to recognize it when it arrives.

Thousands of examples come to mind. Here are a few notable ones. The capable Sunny Jim Fitzsimmons sold mighty Seabiscuit for $7,500 to C. S. Howard, for whom the colt earned over $400,000 and became 1938 horse of the year. Alsab, two-year-old champion in 1941 and three-year-old champion in 1942, was a $700 purchase. Stymie, eventually to become handicap champion of 1945, was so hard to handle that Max Hirsch, a great trainer, entered him in a $1,500 claiming race. Hirsch Jacobs claimed the rogue and made $918,485 with him.

Ballydam had run in $1,500 claimers. Celestial Blue was a cheap mare. Their coupling yielded a foal that went for $5,000 in the yearling sales. It was Bally Ache, Preakness winner which shared 1960 Horse-of-the-Year honors with Kelso, earned $758,522, and was sold to a syndicate for $1.25 million.

During the 1970s, the auction prices of well-bred yearlings rose to unprecedented heights, which became paltry by comparison with ex-cesses committed during the 1980s. To convey the sheer grossness of it all, let me recall that in 1968 a new all-time high price was established with the $405,000 paid for Reine Enchanteur, a filly by the celebrated

French stallion Sea-Bird. But in 1978, no fewer than nine yearlings each sold for $400,000 or more at the Kenneland, Kentucky, summer auctions. The sales topper was $1.3 million, for which a British group obtained a colt by Northern Dancer, leading sire in both North America and England. The price fell $200,000 short of the then-record amount spent in 1977 by a Canadian combine for a Secretariat colt which they named Canadian Bound

In *The Thoroughbred Record* of July 20, 1985, Anne Scott showed that no fewer than 115 yearlings had brought $1 million or more apiece at North American auctions from 1976 through 1984. As of the article's publication date, the record price had become the $10.2 million spent in 1983 for Snaafi Dancer, by Northern Dancer. The animal, who turned three on January 1, 1985, had trained in England but never raced and finally retired to stud in 1986.

And on July 23, 1985, with the ink of Ms. Scott's article barely dry, a British combine paid $13.1 million at Keeneland for a yearling colt by Nijinsky II out of My Charmer, dam of Seattle Slew.

Among the aforementioned $115 million-plus yearlings, five had actually become seasonal champions (all in Europe). This was a percentage of success far higher than is found in the Thoroughbred population at large. But most of the expensive purchases never came close to success of any kind in racing.

Fantastic auction prices attested partly to economic inflation in the United States and the declining international value of the dollar. As well, the prices demonstrated the growing prosperity of world racing, the importance of American bloodstock and the widespread belief that money expended on a prize yearling could be regained manyfold, either on the racetrack or at the breeding farm.

While all that was going on, bargain purchases continued to produce jackpots. Canonero II, bought in 1969 for $1,200, won the Kentucky Derby and Preakness. Bold Forbes, three-year-old champion of 1976, was bought for only $15,200. Seattle Slew, in 1977 the first undefeated runner to win the U.S. Triple Crown, had been knocked down for a mere $17,500 as a 1975 yearling. That was the year in which disappointments like Elegant Prince cost a record $715,000, Brahms went for $500,000, Four Ten for $410,000, Transworld for $375,000 and I shall not continue with this. The point is made. Big-ticket breeding is a tremendous gamble in itself, and the purchase of expensive yearlings is a bigger one.

Training Beats Breeding

Anybody who pays big money for a yearling Thoroughbred does so on expert advice. The horse's breeding seems to warrant the investment. Similarly, not much is thought of the potentialities of a horse sold for small change or entered in a cheap claiming race. And then the surprises begin. Jack Price, operator of Carry Back, used to argue that the reason cheap horses run cheap is that they are treated cheap. He said that there was no surprise about Carry Back. The dam and foal had been treated properly.

Price was not suggesting that good handling can make a silk purse of a sow's you-know. He was just trying to remind everyone that he was a good handler. In so doing he raised a point often overlooked by the pedigree-conscious: Breeding determines the horse's potential, but training and the luck of the game determine whether the horse will have a chance to achieve its potential.

With luck, a good trainer can get more from a mediocre horse than a lesser trainer can from a potential champion. Buckpasser, by Tom Fool out of Busanda, by War Admiral, was a potential champion on paper. Bill Winfrey, who developed him, and Eddie Neloy, who guided him to greatness, provided the nurture without which nature goes awry. Hundreds of trainers could have ruined Buckpasser, and probably would have. The list of potential Triple Crown contenders sabotaged by stupid,

Stymie *(second from left)* **pours it on in home turn of 1947 International Gold Cup at Belmont Park. Assault** *(far left)* **finished third. Natchez** *(on rail)* **was second.** UPI PHOTO

greedy mismanagement in their two- or three-year-old seasons would fill this chapter.

Whether making his own mistakes, or doing what his employer demands, the trainer is vital to the career of the horse. So vital that breeding eventually becomes secondary. All Thoroughbreds descend from champions, as we have seen. The humble parents of a Carry Back or Bally Ache may not have been so humble, after all. Their inability to do much as racers may have been a matter of ill fortune or misdirection.

As a two-year-old, Stymie was frantic. He would resist going to the post. He would break tardily from the gate, losing all chance at the very beginning of his races. When Hirsch Jacobs, one of the greatest connoisseurs of Thoroughbred quality in the history of racing, bought Stymie for $1,500, he treated him like a million-dollar horse. He correctly assumed that the poor thing was afraid of people. He spent hours with Stymie, calming him down. He worked the horse by leading him with a rope instead of saddling him with exercise riders. In due course, Stymie acquired the composure that was his birthright and went on to greatness.

More recently, an unattractive weanling colt of nondescript pedigree was sold for $1,100. Later, as an ill-tempered handful named John Henry, the gelding was sold again for $25,000 and proceeded to become the leading purse earner in racing history (the total reached $6,597,947 before a training injury forced the marvelous runner's retirement in 1985 at age ten). The credit for recognizing and developing this rogue's extraordinary ability goes to Victor J. (Lefty) Nickerson, who trained him in New York, and Ron McAnally, who took over when John Henry's home base became California.

To be fair about it, similar tales could be told about all other leading trainers. All have been able to find the magic formula with horses that have defied the best efforts of other trainers. And all have had failures to match such successes. The purpose at this time is not to compare trainers with each other. We shall do that in the chapter reserved for that pastime. For now, it is important to agree that the horse that runs nowhere for Trainer "A" is the same horse that breaks track records for Trainer "B." His pedigree has not changed.

Moreover, if he is a fractious horse, the kind that exhausts itself in the paddock before getting onto the track, little purpose is served by saying, "He got that from the male line. All Nasrullahs have the tendency." It is impossible to deny that temperamental differences are discernible among the various strains of Thoroughbred, just as size and weight differences and hoof differences and color differences are. But a more essential truth is that any Thoroughbred, regardless of pedigree, can develop a ruinous disposition unless handled intelligently. And a companion truth is that 99.9 percent of every thousand horses with good pedigrees are susceptible to intelligent handling. Some rogues are born, but most rogues are made. Horses that loaf or sulk or hate the starting gate or refuse to run on the rail or stop as soon as they reach the lead or quit when whipped were born with the potential to develop evil traits of that sort. But their handlers deserve full blame for the intensification and perpetuation of the traits.

Where does that leave the racing fan? How can he use a knowledge of breeding in his efforts to pick winning horses? Here are some useful facts to bear in mind:

1. Good handicappers are aware of the by-guess-and-by-gosh character of Thoroughbred breeding, the haphazard results achieved by breeders and the variable influences of trainers on their horses. For those reasons, they refer to pedigrees only in special situations where past-performance records are too brief to tell a persuasive story.

2. These special situations are non-claiming maiden and allowance races for lightly raced two- or three-year-olds.

3. Except for an occasional selection in a turf-course race (with which we shall deal presently), pedigrees are generally useless when handicapping claiming races. In claiming races the physically impaired or badly mismanaged offspring of champions are regularly defeated by better-conditioned animals of equal or lesser pedigree. With rarest exception, claiming races run on dirt tracks are handicapped exclusively in terms of past performances.

4. As we shall see below, a particular kind of breeding analysis is dependable in helping winnow out the likely losers when trying to pick winners of the Kentucky Derby and Belmont Stakes and, to a lesser extent, other grueling stakes races for lightly raced horses. Otherwise, the past-performance records are the best indicator of a Thoroughbred's ability to win at longer distances—the names of sire and dam and broodmare sire to the contrary notwithstanding.

When the most promising new two-year-olds race each other at five and five and a half furlongs in the spring and early summer, it often is possible to pick winners by handicapping the parents. After the youngsters have competed a few times, their records usually tell more than might be deduced from their genealogy. But with first-time starters in maiden-special-weights races or with other entrants in maiden or allowance races that have competed too sparingly to offer a clear picture, the player looks for the following:

1. A sire listed among the nation's or region's leaders
2. A maternal grandsire similarly listed
3. A leading breeder
4. A leading stable.

Carry Back, the lowborn aristocrat, struts onto the running surface at Aqueduct, with Johnny Sellers up. UPI PHOTO

Carry Back *(far left)* **outgames Crozier** *(second from left)* **to win 1961 Florida Derby. Johnny Sellers rode the "Cinderella Horse." Bill Hartack was on Crozier.** UPI PHOTO

Leading Sires

In the mid-1980s, the following stallions were outstanding among sires of North American runners. Their offspring included unusually consistent winners in competition of the highest class. Handicappers who check pedigrees against this list and those that follow will have useful information about the potential class of lightly raced animals entered in maiden races or allowance races for limited winners at major tracks.

ACK ACK
ALLEGED
ALYDAR
BLUSHING GROOM
CARO
CLEVER TRICK
COX'S RIDGE
DAMASCUS
DANZIG
EXCLUSIVE NATIVE
FAPPIANO
GRAUSTARK
GREEN DANCER
GUMMO
HALO
HIS MAJESTY
ICECAPADE
IN REALITY
KEY TO THE MINT
LYPHARD
LYPHEOR
MAJESTIC LIGHT
MISWAKI
MR. LEADER

MR. PROSPECTOR
NIJINSKY II
NODOUBLE
NORTHERN DANCER
NUREYEV
RICH CREAM
RIVERMAN
ROBERTO
SEATTLE SLEW
SECRETARIAT
SHAM
SHARPEN UP
SIR IVOR
SOVEREIGN DANCER
SPECTACULAR BID
STAR DE NASKRA
STATE DINNER
STOP THE MUSIC
STORM BIRD
THE MINSTREL
VAGUELY NOBLE
VALID APPEAL
VICE REGENT
VIGORS

Leading Broodmare Sires

A lightly raced Thoroughbred whose dam was sired by one of the following stallions (or by one found on the preceding list) has at least a potential advantage over competitors of lesser lineage. Note that this list includes names of some all-time great runners, some of whom are dead, and all of whom qualified for years as top sires of other runners. Some of their female offspring remain leading producers of Thoroughbreds and will continue producing for a while.

BOLDNESIAN	IN REALITY
BUCKPASSER	MAJESTIC PRINCE
CHIEFTAIN	NASHUA
CORNISH PRINCE	NEVER BEND
CRIMSON SATAN	NORTHERN DANCER
CROZIER	OLDEN TIMES
DR. FAGER	PRINCE JOHN
DOUBLE JAY	RAISE A NATIVE
FLEET NASRULLAH	ROUND TABLE
FORLI	SIR GAYLORD
GALLANT MAN	THE AXE II
GRAUSTARK	T.V. LARK
GREY DAWN	VAGUELY NOBLE
HAIL TO REASON	VERTEX

Leading Breeders

The following breeders have been producing the best stock. They appear on this list because they breed horses that not only earn a lot of money but win with reasonable consistency.

PETER M. BRANT	BRERETON C. JONES
CLAIBORNE FARM	W. S. KARUTZ
ELMENDORF	KINGHAVEN
FARNSWORTH FARM	LASATER FARM
PETER FULLER	H. T. MANGURIAN JR.
FRANCES A. GENTER	PAUL MELLON
TOM GENTRY	JOHN A. NERUD
GOLDEN CHANCE FARM	OCALA STUD
GREENTREE STUD	NUCKOLS BROS.
HARBOR VIEW	SPENDTHRIFT FARM
W. R. HAWN	TARTAN FARMS
FRED W. HOOPER	E. P. TAYLOR
NELSON B. HUNT	

The Rewards of Study

On May 29, 1985, one of the three-year-old maiden colts entered in the fifth race at Belmont Park (see pp. 92–93) was Dual Honor, a previously unraced son of Seattle Slew out of L'Extravagante, whose own sire was the powerful Le Fabuleux. The owner was Tayhill Stable, one of the racing stables of the folks who owned Seattle Slew in his running days and retained a major interest in his career at stud. They had bred many of his offspring themselves, but were willing to buy others at auction.

Dual Honor had been purchased that way, as handicappers could surmise after noting that his breeder was Joseph Allen and not Wooden Horse, which is the breeding arm of the Slew empire. (Readers who do not know about things of this kind can rest assured that all names and functions become familiar in time. They become familiar most rapidly to handicappers studious enough to read *Daily Racing Form, The Thoroughbred Record* and *The Blood-Horse*. But back to Dual Honor).

The 1984 auction supplement of *The Blood-Horse* showed that Tayhill had paid $360,000 for the yearling at the glamorous Saratoga auctions in August 1983. That's no tremendous sum to pay for a Seattle Slew colt but it represents a certain amount of enthusiasm, considering that the purchasers were hardly suffering from a shortage of Seattle Slews.

Dual Honor did not race at two, but looked ready at three on this day at Belmont Park. His workouts had been the long, frequent ones of a horse being prepared to run well at seven eighths of a mile. His jockey, Angel Cordero, rarely rode horses that were simply out for educational exercise. This was one of the reasons that he was New York's leading rider for years on end. Nothing else in the field looked as strong as Dual Honor.

The favorite, Jazz Festival, had been exercising nicely and deserved respect, but was not bred as sturdily and had not been working for endurance as the Slew colt had. Harley C. and Air Wing seemed unlikely to be comfortable until the races got a lot longer in late summer.

Best of all, and quite a surprise, Dual Honor went off at almost 8 to 1. Students of auction reports and other breeding news find opportunities of this kind many times a year.

Readers mystified by any of the foregoing will enjoy returning for another attempt after reading a few more chapters and achieving some ease about matters like distance and current condition. For now, it may stimulate them to know that they someday will be glad to have acquired a grasp of such things.

Breeding Procedures

The breeding season runs from mid-February to the end of May. Breeders try to get the job done as early as possible, so that the foals will arrive at the beginning of the following year. Under the rules of racing, every foal becomes a yearling on the New Year's Day after its birth, and has a birthday every New Year's thereafter. A horse foaled in late spring or summer is at a disadvantage as a two-, three- and four-year-old, having to run against more mature animals. Northern Dancer, the great little Canadian horse who later became the world's leading sire, overcame that disadvantage. Foaled on May 27, 1961, he was not yet three years old when he won the 1964 Kentucky Derby.

A broodmare is ready for breeding about a week and a half after dropping a foal. The mare's tail is bound up and she goes to the stall of an unfortunate stallion known in the trade as a "teaser." His job is to make sure that the mare is ready for breeding. If she is not in season yet, the valuable stud with whom she is to mate is spared the frustration of an unsuccessful attempt.

If she proves to be ready, she is hauled away from the eager teaser and led to the big shot's stall. There she is held in position with leg straps. After the stallion is finished, the mare returns to her foal. Three weeks later she is brought back to the teaser. If she is now in foal, she will be indifferent to his advances. If she displays interest it means that the previous "cover" or "service" did not work, and she returns to the court of her mate for another attempt.

Breeding for Mud and Grass

Years ago, when muddy tracks were more common than they now are, handicappers and horsemen could often tell by an animal's pedigree whether it would run well in the heavy gumbo. Reigh Count, a great performer on off-tracks, transmitted the talent to Count Fleet and his other progeny, some of whom relayed it to their own. Man O' War, Petee-Wrack, Challedon and Sailor were other good mudders which begat good mudders. Yet every muddy racing day found horses winning in spite of pedigrees that offered no indication of such ability.

Modern tracks are well drained and contain a great deal of sand. Most of them rarely stay muddy for long. The sandiest and best drained ones, like Aqueduct, are sometimes slowest when drying out and labeled "fast" or "good." When covered with water and called "sloppy" they often are faster than when the tote board says, "Track Fast."

Some tracks do get muddy, of course. Those that don't become really gooey nevertheless acquire what horsemen call a "holding" quality while drying out after a rain. When the track is "muddy" or "slow" or "good" or otherwise sticky enough to hold back the horses, the player can be fairly certain that animals that have run badly over similar surfaces in the past will run badly again.

A sore-legged creature that has been having trouble on hard, fast tracks sometimes runs in (wins surprisingly) on a softer footing. Horses with small hooves also seem to move ahead by several lengths on a deep, muddy track. Questions of this kind are best settled by looking at the past-performance records and examining the animals in the walking ring. Increasing numbers of successful players inspect the feet of every horse at it goes to the saddling enclosure, noting those with the small, upright

5 BELMONT

7 FURLONGS
BELMONT PARK

7 FURLONGS. (1.20⅖) MAIDEN SPECIAL WEIGHT. Purse $22,000. 3-year-olds. Weights, 122 lbs.

Harley C. — B. c. 3, by Lyphard—Hasty Dawn, by Pronto — Lifetime 1 0 0 0 $140 — 1985 1 M 0 0 $140; 1984 0 M 0 0
Own.—Hickory Tree Farm — Br.—Oxley J T (Ky) — Tr.—Stephens Woodford C — 122
4Feb85- 3GP fst 6f :22 :45⅘ 1:11⅗ Md Sp Wt 10 10 10¹⁶ 9¹² 76¾ 77 Bailey J D 122 *2.70 74-18 Medieval Road 122¾ Prince Jebb 122¾ No Draw 122³ Off slowly 10
LATEST WORKOUTS May 25 Bel 5f fst 1:01 h May 21 Bel 6f fst 1:15 h May 17 Bel 6f fst 1:16 b May 13 Bel 6f fst 1:14⅕ h

Mount Reality — B. c. 3, by Mount Hagen—Tentative Date, by Tentam — Lifetime 4 0 0 2 $11,268 — 1984 4 M 0 2 $11,268
Own.—Berry M — Br.—Berry M (Ky) — Tr.—Casse Mark — 122
25Aug84- 6Sar fst 6f :22⅕ :45⅖ 1:10⅗ Md Sp Wt 3 5 33½ 46½ 615 822½ MacBeth D b 118 5.60 64-18 Herat 1187¼ Another Reef 118½ Testimonial 118¾ Tired 11
8Jly84- 8Bel fst 6f :22⅕ :45⅘ 1:12⅕ Tremont 3 2 23½ 34 33 36 MacBeth D 113 8.00 75-15 BetMDddy1134¾LordCrlos1171½MountRlity11315¾ Lacked fin. bid 4
8Jly84-Grade III
25Jun84- 4Bel fst 5f :22 :45⅗ :58⅕ Md Sp Wt 3 5 54 53½ 53 43½ MacBeth D 118 11.50 92-16 Don's Choice 1181½ Herat 1181½ Nickel Back 1181 In close st. 8
13Jun84- 4Bel fst 5f :22⅘ :46⅖ :58⅘ Md Sp Wt 6 7 67 45 36½ 38½ MacBeth D 118 22.30 85-18 Don'tFoolWithM118⁸Attrbut118ⁿᵏMountRlty1183¼ Bothered early 8
LATEST WORKOUTS May 24 Bel 6f fst 1:14 h May 16 Bel 5f fst 1:01⅕ h May 11 Bel 4f fst :48⅘ h

Belleau Wood — Ro. c. 3, by Sawbones—Raise A Belle, by Raise A Native — Lifetime 3 0 1 0 $4,845 — 1985 3 M 1 0 $4,845; 1984 0 M 0 0
Own.—Hobeau Farm — Br.—Hobeau Farm Inc (Ky) — Tr.—Jerkens H Allen — 115⁷
21Apr85- 3Aqu fst 6f :22⅗ :46⅕ 1:11 3↑Md 75000 3 5 52¼ 42½ 53½ 48¼ Deegan J C b 112 4.50 78-21 Area Rug 107¾ Lucky Belief1121¾IfIHadAHammer1125¾ No factor 7
14Apr85- 3Aqu fst 1 :47⅗ 1:13⅗ 1:39 3↑Md 70000 3 3 21½ 21½ 3½ 22½ Deegan J C 111 6.60 68-22 Sovereign'sMsk1062½BelleuWood1111½Bruciefruit1124¾ Ducked in 6
30Mar85- 5Key fst 6f :23 :46⅖ 1:11⅗ Md Sp Wt 2 7 42¾ 53¾ 58½ 513½ Ruane J 122 *1.10 70-17 Tall & Light 122ⁿᵏ Full Caper 1228½ Arabian Lite 1222 Tired 7
LATEST WORKOUTS May 21 Bel 3f fst :34⅖ h May 11 Bel 4f fst :52 b May 1 Bel 5f fst 1:03 b Apr 10 Bel 5f fst 1:05⅗ b

Air Wing — Ch. c. 3, by His Majesty—Beating Wings, by Bold Lad — Lifetime 1 0 0 1 $2,640 — 1985 1 M 0 1 $2,640; 1984 0 M 0 0
Own.—Darby Dan Farm — Br.—Darby Dan Farm (Ky) — Tr.—Veitch John M — 122
9May85- 6Bel fst 6f :22⅘ :46⅕ 1:11⅕ 3↑Md Sp Wt 3 5 68½ 48 37½ 34¾ Maple E 113 *1.80 81-25 Available Power 113ʰᵈ Wicked Wike 1134¾ Air Wing1136¾ Rallied 6
LATEST WORKOUTS May 28 Bel 3f fst :35⅘ b May 24 Bel 4f fst :49⅖ b May 18 Bel 4f gd :48⅗ h May 7 Bel 4f fst :48 h

Dual Honor — Dk. b. or br. c. 3, by Seattle Slew—L'Extravagante, by Le Fabuleux — Lifetime 0 0 0 0 — 1984 0 M 0 0
Own.—Tayhill Stable — Br.—Allen Joseph & Jones Jr (Ky) — Tr.—Hertler John O — 122
LATEST WORKOUTS May 24 Bel 5f fst 1:00⅕ hg May 19 Bel 5f fst 1:03 b May 14 Bel 6f fst 1:14⅘ h May 10 Bel 5f fst 1:04 b

Ok Fine — Dk. b. or br. c. 3, by J O Tobin—Fine Prospect, by Mr Prospector — Lifetime 0 0 0 0 — 1985 0 M 0 0; 1984 0 M 0 0
Own.—Stonewall Farm — Br.—Matthews Carla C (Ky) — Tr.—Jerkens Steven T — 122
LATEST WORKOUTS May 28 Bel 3f fst :35⅖ b Apr 27 Bel 7f fst 1:31⅗ b Apr 19 Bel 4f fst :49 h Apr 9 Bel 6f fst 1:18⅘ b

Jazz Festival — B. c. 3, by Stop The Music—Quick Cure, by Dr Fager — Lifetime 0 0 0 0 — 1985 0 M 0 0; 1984 0 M 0 0
Own.—Firestone B R — Br.—Firestone Mr-Mrs B R (Va) — Tr.—Watters Sidney Jr — 122
LATEST WORKOUTS May 27 Bel 3f fst :36⅘ bg May 23 Bel 4f fst :49⅖ bg May 17 Bel 3f fst :39 bg ●May 12 Bel 6f fst 1:12⅖ h

hooves and visible heels of mud runners and those who have inherited the wide, flat feet (the less heel the better) of good grass runners. Where wet-track racing is involved, this is more fruitful than mere reliance on pedigree. For grass racing, the presence of a turf foot supplements pedigree.

Leon Rasmussen, whose penetrating articles about breeding are a regular feature of *Daily Racing Form,* writes, "Several years ago I indulged in some research on the winners of off-track races throughout the United States. Hundreds of races were studied and the breeding of the winners duly recorded. When I was all through with my analysis, no definite pattern had exposed itself. That is, no particular male line manifested itself, and neither did any particular stallion."

Some horses run well on grass but not on dirt. Some run well on dirt but not on grass. In 1975, Dr. William L. Quirin, of the mathematics faculty at Adelphi University, Garden City, New York, produced a large statistical study which demonstrated beyond possibility of doubt that animals of certain bloodlines are more likely than others to perform successfully on turf courses. Indeed, the study showed that anyone who bet on such animals in their first and second starts on grass would reap substantial profits, ignoring the horses' previously rotten performances on dirt tracks. The leading sire line was that of the European stud Prince Rose, via Princequillo, Prince Bio and Prince Chevalier. Among grass

---

FIFTH RACE **7 FURLONGS. (1.20⅗) MAIDEN SPECIAL WEIGHT. Purse $22,000. 3-year-olds. Weights, 122 lbs.**

Belmont

MAY 29, 1985

Value of race $22,000; value to winner $13,200; second $4,840; third $2,640; fourth $1,320. Mutuel pool $105,435, OTB pool $77,055. Exacta Pool $209,296. OTB Exacta Pool $157,779.

Last Raced	Horse	Eqt.	A.	Wt	PP	St	¼	½	Str	Fin	Jockey	Odds $1
	Dual Honor		3	122	5	1	$1^{\frac{1}{2}}$	2^{2}	1^{5}	$1^{3\frac{3}{4}}$	Cordero A Jr	7.80
9May85 ^{6}Bel^{3}	Air Wing		3	122	4	5	6^{8}	6^{5}	$2^{\frac{1}{2}}$	$2^{3\frac{3}{4}}$	Maple E	1.10
4Feb85 ^{3}GP^{7}	Harley C.		3	122	1	7	7	7	6^{2}	$3^{\frac{3}{4}}$	MacBeth D	9.60
21Apr85 ^{3}Aqu^{4}	Belleau Wood	b	3	115	3	4	4^{hd}	5^{2}	$3^{\frac{1}{2}}$	$4^{\frac{3}{4}}$	Wynter N A^{7}	12.50
25Aug84 ^{6}Sar^{8}	Mount Reality	b	3	122	2	3	$3^{1\frac{1}{2}}$	3^{2}	$4^{1\frac{1}{2}}$	$5^{4\frac{1}{2}}$	Migliore R	17.80
	Ok Fine		3	122	6	2	5^{3}	4^{1}	7	$6^{3\frac{1}{2}}$	Bailey J D	20.40
	Jazz Festival		3	122	7	6	$2^{\frac{1}{2}}$	1^{hd}	$5^{\frac{1}{2}}$	7	Vasquez J	1.80

OFF AT 3:09 Start good for all but HARLEY C. Won ridden out. Time, :22⅖, :45⅕, 1:10⅕, 1:23⅕ Track fast.

$2 Mutuel Prices:			
6-(F)-DUAL HONOR	17.60	4.80	3.60
5-(E)-AIR WING		3.00	2.60
1-(A)-HARLEY C.			4.20

$2 EXACTA 6-5 PAID $52.80.

Dk. b. or br. c, by Seattle Slew—L'Extravagante, by Le Fabuleux. Trainer Hertler John O. Bred by Allen Joseph & Jones Jr (Ky).

DUAL HONOR saved ground while vying for the lead to the stretch, drew off quickly and was riddenout to hold sway. AIR WING angled out while moving entering the stretch and was going well at the finish. HARLEY C. dwelt at the start, then finished with good energy. BELLEAU WOOD saved ground to no avail. MOUNT REALITY raced forwardly until near the stretch and gave way. OK FINE tired badly. JAZZ FESTIVAL rushed into contention from the outside on the backstretch, remained prominent until near the stretch and stopped suddenly. BELLEAU WOOD raced with mud caulks.

Owners— 1, Tayhill Stable; 2, Darby Dan Farm; 3, Hickory Tree Farm; 4, Hobeau Farm; 5, Berry M; 6, Stonewall Farm; 7, Firestone B R.

Trainers— 1, Hertler John O; 2, Veitch John M; 3, Stephens Woodford C; 4, Jerkens H Allen; 5, Casse Mark; 6, Jerkens Steven T; 7, Watters Sidney Jr.

sires of that and other lines most prominent at this writing were Advocator, Ambernash, Big Spruce, Blushing Groom, Busted, Caro, Diplomat Way, Empery, Exclusive Native, Fifth Marine, Halo, His Majesty, Hoist the Flag, Icecapade, Key to the Mint, Le Fabuleux, Little Current, London Company, Lyphard, Lypheor, MacDiarmida, Majestic Light, Mill Reef, Minnesota Mac, Mr. Leader, Naskra, Nijinsky II, Nodouble, Northern Dancer, Nureyev, One for All, Our Native, Proud Clarion, Riverman, Roberto, Seattle Slew, Sir Gaylord, Stage Door Johnny, Star Envoy, Stop the Music, TV Commercial, Verbatim and Vigors. If one of these is the sire or even the broodmare sire of a newcomer to grass racing, the chances are better than even that the animal will like the footing. And if this kind of blood is on both sides of the immediate ancestry, as shown in the *Daily Racing Form* past-performance record, the chances multiply.

Dr. Quirin publishes updated studies from time to time, as in *Thoroughbred Handicapping—State of the Art,* issued in 1984 by William Morrow and Company, New York. You also can update your list by spending a couple of hours a year with the pedigrees and other records of active stallions that appear in the annual *Stallion Register* and *Stakes Winners* supplements of *The Blood-Horse* and the equally useful *Thoroughbred Record Sire Book.*

Dr. Roman: Breeding for the Classics

At the turn of the century, one Lieutenant Colonel J. J. Vuillier of the French cavalry propounded the notion of *chefs de race,* a relatively few Thoroughbred stallions whose names kept appearing in the pedigrees of the very best runners. He believed that sound breeding practices demanded matings designed to combine the blood of *chefs* in standardized proportions, which he called "dosages."

An Italian named Franco Varola carried the idea further by classifying the various *chefs* according to the racing aptitudes most prominent in the offspring and later descendants of each. The number of categories has fluctuated over the years and recently has settled down to five, ranging from Brilliant (for stallions whose descendants are noted for speed) to Professional (the heirs and heiresses of which don't show much in sprints but can run all day).

Steven A. Roman, Ph.D., of the United States, gained serious attention from students of breeding during the 1980s when his statistical approach to dosage produced remarkably accurate ratings of horses entered in the Kentucky Derby, differentiating those that had no chance from those that did.

Assigning 16 points to a *chef de race* sire, 8 to a grandsire, 4 to a great-grandsire, and 2 to a properly qualified great-great-grandsire, Roman finds the *chefs* in each generation of the pedigree and then totals the points under each of the five dosage categories—Brilliant, Intermediate, Classic, Solid and Professional (which might be represented, respectively, by Raise a Native, Nashua, Buckpasser, Man O' War and Le Fabuleux). The resultant numbers are the Dosage Profile, which shows the proportions of speed dosages to those more predictive of stoutness or stamina.

From the numbers in the Profile, Roman calculates the ratio of speed aptitude to stamina aptitude. That number is the Dosage Index. Since 1940, no Thoroughbred with a DI above 4.00 has won the Kentucky Derby and only three (Damascus, Conquistador Cielo and Creme Fraiche) have won the Belmont Stakes.

Moreover, the Roman analyses have helped allay confusion about many sires and their descendants. For example, I believe that Raise a Native was the best two-year-old I have ever seen. I was distressed that injury retired him before he even had a chance to race as far as six furlongs. So I was delighted when he became a great sire of racehorses and of other outstanding sires. Yet his popularity as a stallion was not easily achieved: Because he had only run in short dashes, many horse-folk took for granted that he lacked stamina and would transmit that defect to his progeny. Steven Roman shows that Raise a Native had a dosage index of 1.57 and would therefore have been a legitimate Derby contender. Contender? He would have won it all.

Roman writes occasional articles in the racing press and collaborates with *Daily Racing Form*'s breeding expert, Leon Rasmussen, in analyses that appear in the *Form* before important races. Anybody who bets on a Kentucky Derby entrant with a Dosage Index above 4.00 deserves to lose.

Run-of-the-Mill Breeders

With scores of tracks demanding seventy or eighty ambulatory Thoroughbreds with which to fill nine or more races a day, the quality of the breed has declined seriously. The woods now are full of industrialized breeding establishments, the products of which have nondescript pedigrees, misshapen limbs, and no more class than is needed to stagger three quarters of a mile. In bygone days, animals as disadvantaged as this never got to the track. They could not compete with real racehorses. But they now are found in profusion—even at major tracks, where the horse shortage is as severe as anywhere else.

Unable to infuse any real class into this stock, the breeders concentrate on speed. Sometimes a cheap mare from a family that has been showing more staying power than speed is mated with a stud from a line of front-runners. All too often, in the words of the late Charles Hatton, the result is a horse that "has the speed of the stayer and the stamina of the sprinter." Errors of that kind also occur at fancier breeding farms.

5

THOROUGHBRED CONFORMATION

When buying a yearling or trying to decide whether to get rid of one, horsemen attach major importance to the animal's physical appearance. The pedigree may be splendid, but if the conformation departs from normal in any major respect, horsemen turn thumbs down.

Yet the test of the Thoroughbred is performance on the racetrack. Every year, horses with dubious pedigrees or unfortunate conformation, or both, finish first in important races. The saying goes that any horse looks good in the winner's circle. Another saying is that there is no such thing as a perfect-looking horse. By the time a horse is two or three and has been to the post a dozen times, earlier judgments of his looks are subject to drastic revision.

Kelso, horse of the year five times in succession, and one of the biggest earners in the history of the sport (almost $2 million), was castrated as a yearling because he was a runt. The theory was that undersized geldings grow more satisfactorily than undersized colts. Sometimes they do. Kelso became a full-sized horse. But Roman Brother, another gelded runt, remained small, ran off with almost $1 million in purses and succeeded Kelso as horse of the year in 1965. Nobody will ever know whether Kelso would have been a great racer if he had not been gelded. All that can be known is that he would have been available for breeding purposes.

No horse in history ever looked better in the winner's circle than Kelso, and he had the bankroll to prove it. But his hocks stuck out farther

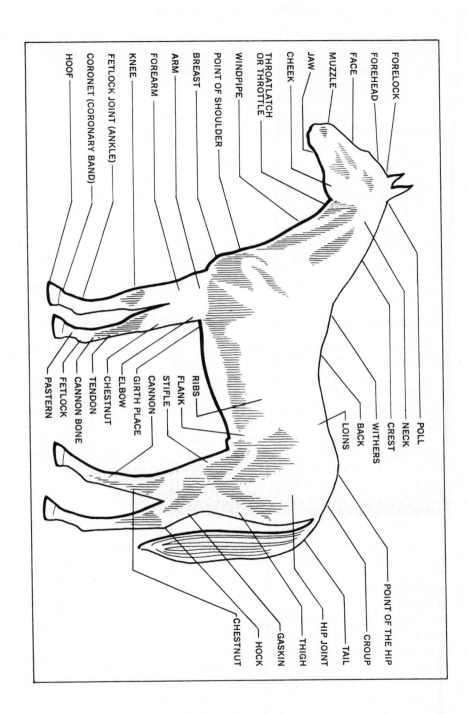

FORELOCK
FOREHEAD
FACE
MUZZLE
JAW
CHEEK
THROATLATCH OR THROTTLE
WINDPIPE
POINT OF SHOULDER
BREAST
ARM
FOREARM
KNEE
FETLOCK JOINT (ANKLE)
CORONET (CORONARY BAND)
HOOF

RIBS
FLANK
STIFLE
CANNON
GIRTH PLACE
ELBOW
CHESTNUT
TENDON
CANNON BONE
FETLOCK
PASTERN

POLL
NECK
CREST
WITHERS
BACK
LOINS
CROUP
TAIL
HIP JOINT
THIGH
GASKIN
HOCK
CHESTNUT
POINT OF THE HIP

97

than is proper. He seemed susceptible to sore stifles. Also, his hooves were delicate. With less discerning care than that of Carl Hanford, his trainer, he might never have won a dollar. His hooves might have cracked if he had been shod less carefully.

Roman Brother had a crooked knee, his pasterns were somewhat too long and he had hoof troubles. In fact these difficulties finally made it impossible for him to withstand training and he had to be retired. After earning $1 million.

Buckpasser's knees aroused criticism. Cracked hooves kept him out of races worth hundreds of thousands of dollars. Bold Lad's near (left) foreknee never looked too good to the experts. Gun Bow's hooves were a constant headache for his handlers. The great two-year-old Hail to Reason had a curby (suspiciously swollen) hock, which did not prevent him from running like one of the best of all time. His racing career ended accidentally, when he broke a sesamoid (a small bone above the fetlock). He then became a world-class sire. Tom Rolfe was faulted for prominent hocks and cannon bones longer than the ideal. Truly, the perfect horse is never seen.

Conformation is important to the racing fan for several reasons:

1. It is fun to appraise the physique of unraced two-year-olds when they come to the paddock and walking ring.

2. It occasionally is possible to pick the winner of a maiden-special-weights race on grounds of conformation—especially when the best-looking horse in the walking ring has a fine pedigree and hails from a leading barn.

3. If you don't know the difference between a hock and a pastern you won't know what horsemen are talking about. You therefore will get less than your money's worth from your racing papers and your days at the track.

Feet and Ankles

We have already noted the difference between the small, upright foot generally associated with ability to run in mud, and the wide, flat foot of the grass runner. Those indicators are quite reliable, although the usual exceptions obtain. The great grass runner and sire of grass runners Round Table lacked a typical grass foot. Moreover, the tendency of some horseplayers and trainers to lump both sloppy and muddy tracks under the heading of "off-tracks" often obscures the fact that a horse with the flat grass foot usually handles the splashing water and hard base of a sloppy track, but not the splashing mud and soft base of muddy one.

Good judges of horseflesh begin their inspection of a Thoroughbred at the ground and work their way up. They are quite choosy about hooves, and it makes sense. The Thoroughbred weighs in the neighborhood of

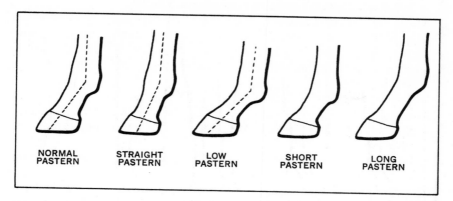

| NORMAL PASTERN | STRAIGHT PASTERN | LOW PASTERN | SHORT PASTERN | LONG PASTERN |

half a ton. When traveling at full speed—about forty miles an hour—the entire weight lands on one hoof at a time. If the hoof is too narrow, the foot has to absorb too many pounds of impact per square inch of surface. On today's hard, fast tracks, this is more than the bony structure can bear. Narrow-footed horses go lame more rapidly than horses with wider hooves. They are more susceptible to tendon troubles in the knee region, more susceptible to broken ankle bones and cracked hooves.

Hoofprints are important. If a horse is slightly pigeon-toed he may be a perfectly good runner. But if he toes in considerably, or toes out more than a bit, horsemen downgrade him. The best legs are those with hooves that point straight ahead, leaving hoofprints almost exactly parallel to each other.

As much attention is paid to pasterns as to feet. The pastern should slope at an angle of 45 degrees from fetlock to hoof. If it is more upright than that, it is less springy than it should be. It transmits concussion to the fetlock and knee, which eventually go bad. On the other hand, a pastern with too low a slope flexes more than it should. Such a horse "runs down"—scrapes its fetlocks on the ground while running, and strains tendons and ligaments as well. Furthermore, short pasterns are preferred to long ones. Horses with long pasterns on the forelegs tend to cut their own elbows with their hooves while running. Also, the long pasterns exert undesirable strain on tendons.

On the hind pasterns, a lower slope is accepted. The hind legs provide the horse's forward propulsion and are subjected to less concussion than the forelegs, the vaulting poles of the horse's stride. Therefore, the tendon troubles attributable to faulty pasterns are found often in front and rarely in the rear.

Cannon, Knee and Hock

Horsemen like to see short, sturdy cannon bones, for a longer upper leg and longer stride. Some animals have incredibly fragile-looking cannons. Their legs immediately below the knee are so slender that they look, in the language of the trade, "tied in." Horses with forelegs of that kind are

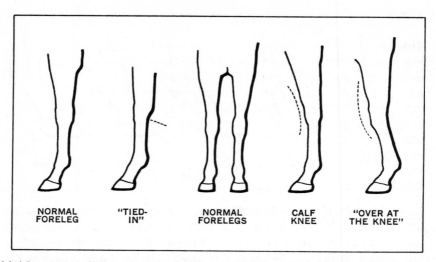

NORMAL FORELEG   "TIED-IN"   NORMAL FORELEGS   CALF KNEE   "OVER AT THE KNEE"

highly susceptible to permanently disabling tendon troubles. The tendons that run down the bone from behind the knee are displaced to begin with and cannot stand the strain of racing.

The knees of the Thoroughbred are located in his forelegs only. The corresponding joint in the hind leg is called the hock. The knee contains seven or eight bones (the number varies from horse to horse and seems to make no difference). These bones help to disperse the concussion of running. Accordingly, Nature intends the normal knee to be situated plumb below the horse's elbow. In other words, straight up and down.

Horses whose forelegs bend somewhat backward at the knee are called "calf-kneed" or "back at the knee." They are not good candidates for long careers. Their tendons suffer, just as if they had straight pasterns. Horses whose knees protrude forward are called "over at the knee." Many topnotch runners suffer from this blemish. In fact, not many horsemen regard it as a flaw at all, unless it occurs in extreme form.

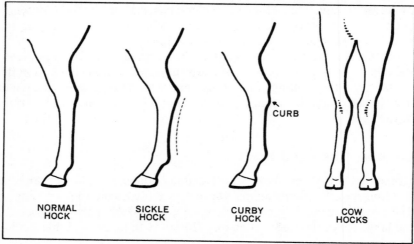

NORMAL HOCK   SICKLE HOCK   CURB   CURBY HOCK   COW HOCKS

Horsemen prefer Thoroughbreds whose hind legs drop almost straight down from the hocks. If the hoof is noticeably forward of the hock, the animal is charged with a sickle hock. Pronounced cases lead to curby hocks, swellings of the tendon that often end in serious lameness. Also, it is agreed by one and all that an animal with normal hocks can stride forward more easily, covering extra ground in each jump. However, so many other factors affect the performance of a Thoroughbred (including human factors) that a mild case of sickle hocks is not necessarily calamitous. Kelso did all right on imperfect rear legs, and so have hundreds of other stakes winners.

Cow hocks are another matter. The horse looks knock-kneed from the rear. When he runs, his hooves fly in odd directions, which is no way to get to the finish line in a hurry. Horses with this structural defect can be counted on to develop tendon trouble. Also, they "interfere"—banging their legs together in midair or hitting and cutting one leg with the hoof of the other.

Bandy-legged horses are almost as unpopular. Their hocks bow outward, and the rear hooves are pigeon-toed. The leverage for strong forward propulsion is lacking, the gait is unrhythmical and, as if that were not enough, the animals are odds-on to cut themselves with their own hooves while trying to run.

Shoulders, Hips and Barrel

Long, sloping shoulders are attributes of the horse that runs fast and far. They are associated with short cannons, long forearms and a consequently long, easy, powerful stride. Horses with short, straight shoulders often have short, straight pasterns—the "stilty" look that means a cramped stride.

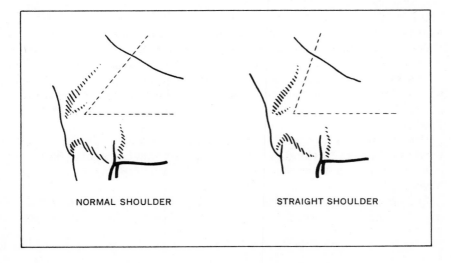

NORMAL SHOULDER   STRAIGHT SHOULDER

The chest should be deep, the ribs well sprung rather than straight and flat. Conformation of that kind suggests plenty of lung capacity and stamina. The withers should be fairly prominent, indicating the long spinal muscles of the good strider. The muscles of the loin should also be evident. They tie the horse's rear to his front, creating the "close-coupled" appearance of well-coordinated runners. If "light over the kidney" or "wasp-waisted"—slender-loined and slack in the coupling—a horse has trouble transmitting power from rear to front.

Broad, muscular, rounded (but not fat) hindquarters and close coupling are signs of speed. Narrower rumps and rangy, loose coupling suggest weakness.

Head and Neck

Short-necked horses usually lack balance and stamina. Their strides are too short, and they seldom can be counted on for anything more than a burst of early speed.

Horsemen want the neck to be relatively long and limber, with a slight convexity from withers to poll. The horse with a concave neck, which curves down from the withers and then up to the poll, is called a "ewe-neck." He is not pretty but he runs as well as any other horse.

Much attention is paid to the head, ears and facial expression of the young Thoroughbred. A broad, open forehead and large, clear, dark hazel eyes are taken as signs of kindly, manageable intelligence. Ears that seldom move are a warning of sluggishness. But ears constantly twitching bespeak a nervous disposition.

Size and Weight

It is said that a good big horse can always beat a good little horse. On the other hand, little horses are forever beating big horses. Round Table, a leading money winner, was small. So were Roman Brother and Northern Dancer. Tom Rolfe was no giant. Forego was. Gallant Fox was good and big at 1,100 pounds. Northern Dancer was good and little at 900.

The height of the horse is measured from the withers in "hands"—units of four inches each. A big horse is 16 or 17 hands high, a little horse about 15. If the measurement is 15 hands, 2 inches, it is given as 15.2, or "fifteen-two."

Horsemen work themselves into lathers about the relative merits of big and little horses. Handicappers keep calm. They are guided by past performances and what they see in the paddock just before the race begins.

In trying to differentiate one new two-year-old from another, it seldom pays to prefer the big horse to the smaller. A compact, well-knit juvenile usually learns how to run in a straight line more easily than a bigger, more awkward specimen. The big ones tend to need extra racing and extra training before they settle into winning form. On the other hand, if someone like Woody Stephens sends out a big youngster for its first start in mid-summer, the player can be sure that most of the green un-gainliness has already been ironed out and the horse is ready.

Possibly because they are a bit more nimble, small horses sometimes seem to have an extra edge in races on grass or in mud. They are especially good at picking their way through the traffic jams on the turn for home, finding holes that larger floundering animals cannot always take advantage of.

None of this constitutes a recommendation to bet on horses because of their stature. The intent is simply to reinforce the observation that the little horse is the best bet in the race if its record is best.

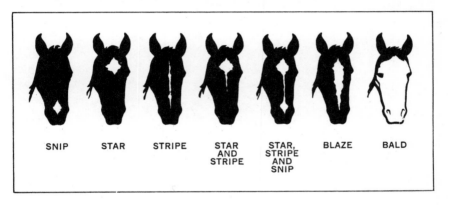

Color and Markings

The official colors:

1. Bay. About half of all Thoroughbreds have the brownish body and the black "points" (black mane, tail and lower legs) that classify them as bay. The body color may be anything from a yellowish tan to a deep, reddish mahogany or a dark brown.

2. Dark Bay or Brown. If the hairs on muzzle or flank are tan or brown, the horse is in this category.

3. Chestnut. The bodies vary from a dark liver to reddish gold, copper and light yellows. Mane and tail are brown or flaxen, never black—although a few black hairs may be prsent.

4. Black. Sometimes these are unmistakably black. Occasionally they look dark brown, but are distinguishable by the fine black hairs on the muzzle.

5. Gray. A mixture of white and black hairs.

6. Roan. A mixture of black, white and yellow hairs, or black, white and red.

Because the patches known as "markings" are always white, they never are referred to by color.

A *snip* is a small patch of bare skin or white hairs on lip or nose.

A *star* is a small patch of white on the forehead.

A *stripe* is a narrow mark running down the face to the nose or lower.

A *blaze* is a larger patch. When it covers the entire face, the horse is called white-faced or bald-faced.

Markings also are found on the heels, the coronet of the hoof, the pasterns, ankles (half-ankle or full ankle), and above, where they are known as socks, half-stockings or stockings. Many horsemen distrust the bone structure of horses with white legs, ankles or pasterns.

6

HANDICAPPING THEORIES

Several years ago an animal named Embarrassed won the opening race on an Aqueduct program and paid more than $20. A jubilant lady in the queue outside the mutuel cashier's window explained to all within earshot that she had been dreadfully embarrassed that morning. Something to do with a shoulder strap breaking and her slip landing in a heap at her feet. As soon as she got the paper and saw that Embarrassed was running she knew she had a winner.

A man ahead of me on the line shook his head wryly. "She's some handicapper." He grinned. On impulse, I asked how he had come to play the horse.

"Easy," he said. "It was the only one in the race that ever did three quarters of a mile in less than one-ten."

Months earlier, Embarrassed had covered the first three quarters of a one-mile race in something like 1.09⅘. A lot of water had gone under the bridge since then, of course. The man evidently was a speed handicapper of some kind. He had not noticed, or had not cared, that Embarrassed's previous good clocking at three quarters of a mile had been achieved on the long straightaway which speeds up the early stages of all mile races at Aqueduct. He had seen the raw time figures and become content. Questions of pace, class, weight, condition and the like had troubled him not. And Embarrassed, the 10 or 11 to 1 shot, had rewarded his hasty judgment. If he could make one successful guess like that in every ten attempts, he could end any season with a profit. And if my aunt were constructed differently, she'd be my uncle.

An orator on the adjoining payoff line was jubilant about the jockey. "Give me Errico every time on a horse like this!" he yelled. Scamp Errico, an able rider of front-running horses, had mounted few winners in recent years. He had suffered several injuries and was out of fashion among the trainers. Anybody who bet on him "every time" would deserve an award for marathon optimism.

"Gee!" exulted a youngster to his companion on the line. "This is some system!" He was waving a booklet. "Bang-bang-bang!" he cried. "Half a minute and you've got a longshot!"

Bang-bang-bang. The miracle system. Half a minute and you've got a longshot. Half a season and you've got an eviction notice.

I returned to the cashier's window a couple of more times that afternoon. The hunch-playing lady, the speed theorist, Errico's loyal fan and the proprietor of the thirty-second longshot system were nowhere to be seen. But some familiar faces were. Faces become familiar at the track. Especially when you see them almost every time you cash a ticket. They are the faces of expert handicappers: Speed handicappers, pace handicappers, class-consistency handicappers and handicappers whose methods fit no particular label.

On the rare occasions when these people discuss handicapping theory with each other, they discover large areas of disagreement. And yet they have a great deal in common.

First and most prominent is their repeated presence in the payoff line. Ability to win bets is, after all, what identifies them as expert. No other credential counts.

Secondly, they are all "spot players." None attempts to bet on every race. Some go for days on end without betting at all. Many come to the track only when the racing paper's past-performance pages promise a few betting opportunities. Few bet on more than three or four races a day. It goes without saying that they bet only on races that strike them as especially favorable opportunities.

They arrive at these decisions by divergent routes. Some analyze every horse in every race, looking for animals that stand out from the crowd. Others don't bother with all that toil. They regard certain kinds of races and certain kinds of horses as less predictable than others. So they refuse to bet on two-year-olds. Or on females. Or on stakes or handicaps or allowance races. Or they shun maiden races. Or races on the turf course.

Some attach deep importance to handicapping angles, distinct from handicapping fundamentals. For example, some never play a horse that won or finished in the money in its last race. Others go to the opposite extreme, playing no horse *unless* it won its last race. Some bet only on consistent geldings that won—or did not win—their last races.

Some try to get on the side of the percentages by confining their speculation to favorites whose records can withstand severe scrutiny. Others turn a profit by looking for races in which the favorite is overrated by the crowd and a longer-priced horse has an outstandingly good chance.

Some play no horses that seem to be moving up in class. Others avoid horses moving down in class. Some give little time to a study of class as such, believing that the true quality of a horse is revealed in its ability to set or overcome a fast early pace and get to the finish wire in good time.

Some play no horse running today's distance for the first time. Others disdain such conservatism, making their selections on the basis of numbers contained in speed charts.

Some mistrust any horse running with substantially more weight than it has been able to carry to victory in the past. Others adjust their speed ratings to reflect pounds added or deducted from the horse's most recent imposts. Some pay no attention whatever to weight, unless it is especially high and the race especially long.

Some give extra credit to horses from favored barns or with leading jockeys. Others insist that the horse is the thing. They ignore trainer and jockey alike.

You Can't Win 'Em All

How contradictory can they get? How can methods so diverse produce long-term winnings in a game as difficult as this?

Answer: Nine races a day make a varied menu. During the height of the season on any major racing circuit, there is seldom a day in which an expert handicapper is unable to find one or more betting opportunities.

Moreover, the differences among successful handicapping methods are more apparent than real. In his own way, each expert takes heed of the fundamentals of the game. The winning player who emphasizes class and consistency may never look at a speed or pace chart but is careful to estimate how today's race will be run and whether its pace will suit the style of his horse. And the successful pace handicapper attends to class with numerical formulas which embody the relationship of class to early and late speed. At the same time, he hesitates to give a horse full credit for a fast race run in suspiciously cheap company.

The player who bets only on a horse that won its last race can win money by applying any handicapping method that encompasses the fundamentals of distance, form, class, age, sex, consistency, weight, speed, pace, jockey. So can the one who *refuses* to bet on horses that won their last races. Obviously, neither player encounters as many betting opportunities as each would if the method were less specialized. But both may own the unimpeachable certificate of the expert—the notebook-ledger that shows a long-range profit. The one who favors last-out winners to repeat probably wins a higher percentage of bets. But the other method very likely gets higher mutuel prices.

The player who specializes in bets on claiming races for older horses misses wagering opportunities available to someone with a more varied approach. Yet he may end each season with a higher rate of profit, depending on how well he knows his specialty and how intelligently he manages his money. He might increase his enjoyment and enlarge his profits if he were to learn how to handicap allowance races, and races for two-year-olds, and certain maiden races. But he may not feel like it. He may be getting all the action he wants.

Prescription for Success

We have now reconfirmed a previously emphasized truth: Handicapping is a highly personal pastime. For the 99.9 percent of readers who have not yet found a suitably comfortable and successful procedure, or want to improve the performance of a method that is not quite in the black, some general statements will be useful:

1. The fewest bets, the highest percentage of winners and the highest rate of profit await the player who has the time and patience to apply a method that embraces all handicapping fundamentals in full detail.

2. To the degree that standards relax and one or another fundamental is slighted, the number of bets increases and the percentage of winners decreases. But the median or average mutuel price tends to rise and the rate of profit may decline only slightly, if at all. This explains why some players are forever trying to simplify their own procedures. Some manage to do it quite successfully. In fact, readers who do not care for full-dress handicapping may be able to use this book's teachings to develop their own collections of spot-play systems. A player equipped with an arsenal of five or six such selection methods can "handicap" an entire program in a few minutes, find two or three plays a day and do about as well as the average burner of midnight oil.

3. Rate of profit is important, but it is not everything. In fifteen days at the track, a conservative player might make thirty bets and a less conservative one might make sixty. If the conservative player bets $20 on each horse and realizes profit at the rate of 25 cents per dollar, the net profit is $150. If the less conservative player also makes $20 bets and realizes profits of 15 cents on the dollar, that net is $180.

I have prepared the following twelve chapters with such possibilities in mind. Each of the chapters deals with one or more of the fundamentals of handicapping, fully explaining the relations of each to all others. Conservative methods of using each factor are made plain. Less conservative methods—and their possible consequences—also are explained.

7

FINDING THE
BEATABLE RACE

Most races are truly run. The best horse usually gets there first. Next week one of the losers might be in better form and beat him. But not today. Whether he won by a nose or a city block, his victory established certain truths:

1. He was in good enough condition to demonstrate his superiority over today's field.

2. The distance of the race suited him.

3. The weights suited him. (He did not carry high enough weight nor did any other entrant carry low enough weight to alter the outcome.)

4. The pace of the race and the condition of the racing strip were comfortable for him. (If he is a front-running type, nothing else was able to keep up with him in the early stages and he had plenty of energy left for the homestretch. If he prefers to run behind the early pace, he either outclassed the field decisively or was helped by the presence of two or more front-runners, which ran each other into the ground, clearing his path to the wire.)

5. His jockey was equal to the demands of the situation.

6. He was not outclassed. (If there were classier animals in the race they lacked the condition to prove it, or were unsuited to the distance or the weights or the pace, or were ridden by jockeys unable to get the best from them.)

It is easy to handicap a winner after the race is over. I have done it myself thousands of times, wondering how I could have failed to notice *before* the race what suddenly became so obvious afterward. The process of retracing one's steps in hope of diagnosing error is good exercise for the beginner. It encourages careful habits.

The grandstands at any racetrack are cluttered with people who know a great deal about the game but manage to defeat themselves with sloppy handicapping. Experts are careful. They have to be. The percentages provide no margin for careless error. Just as in poker or bridge, a single thoughtless move can convert profit to loss. Knowing this, the expert makes sure that he has a complete profile on every contending horse in any race on which he bets. He knows precisely why he thinks his own choice has an unusually good chance to win. He knows exactly which animals promise to challenge his choice at each stage of the running. When his horse loses—as it does more than half the time—he may re-handicap the field to see if he has made a boo-boo, but he seldom finds one. You never hear an expert say: "I shoulda had the winner but I didn't notice that fast workout he ran the other day." If an expert's choice loses, the reason is usually one or more of the following:

1. **Its condition was not as good as expected.**
2. **Some other horse was in surprisingly good condition.**
3. **The surprisingly good or bad condition of another horse affected the pace of the race, depriving the expert's choice of its predicted advantage.**
4. **The rider failed to exploit his opportunities, or lost unnecessary ground on the turns, or ran the animal into switches, or was victimized by bad racing luck.**

The Expert's Main Problem

That list is worth analyzing. It indicates that the expert's main difficulty is his effort to assess the current condition of horses. Matters like class, weight and distance were not listed, because the real expert rarely makes the kind of error that misleads him into selecting an outclassed or overweighted horse, or a horse unsuited to the distance of the race. As we shall see, there is no excuse for *anyone,* expert or beginner, to be misled in that way.

Observation of one simple rule will place the reader in position to save himself from outclassed, overweighted and outdistanced horses. The rule provides the best possible chance to determine the current condition and the pace preference of other horses. The rule:

Avoid playing any race in which the relative abilities of the horses are not clearly evident.

Among all reasons why the great majority of players lose, none is more basic than their violation of that rule. They insist on finding a bet in every race. They treat racing as if it were a roulette wheel. One of eight or ten horses has to win, so they take a flyer. They want action. They waste their money on races in which the past-performance records offer inadequate information about the entrants' class or condition or their distance and weight and pace preferences.

Experts call such races unplayable. A more precise term would be "unbeatable."

I have heard losers dispute this. "The favorite wins one out of three, whether it's a claiming race or a turf race or a race for first-time starters," they argue. "This means that one race is like another. No matter what kind of race it is and no matter how hot a handicapper you are, you wind up making a guess. If you don't have a clear picture of class or form or pace, you can find angles to handicap from. Everybody else is in the same boat. Every race is a chance to win. And a chance to lose."

Right. But some races offer a better chance to win, which is why experts concentrate on them.

It is impossible to deny that favorites win unplayable-unbeatable races as frequently as they win any other kind. It also is impossible to deny that an undiscriminating player of favorites winds up 12 or 13 percent behind the game. But the object of the game is to reduce losses to the vanishing point and make inroads into the black. This can only be done by avoiding unbeatable races and looking for beatable ones.

Here are the guideposts.

Seasons and Cycles

When the first edition of this book was written, Thoroughbred racing was a seasonal treat. The major Northern circuits of New York, New Jersey, Kentucky and Illinois opened in April or May and closed during the fall. The major Southern circuits of Florida and California operated during the winter. Maryland offered good racing in the warm months and marginal racing in the cold, modeling the year-around grind that has since become standard in most places.

New York, New Jersey, Illinois, Florida, Maryland and Southern California now function on a twelve-month basis. But the quality of racing continues to change with the seasons. The horses that compete on Aqueduct's winterized inner track or at the rival Meadowlands in New Jersey are inferior to those that run in warm weather—either in Florida or Southern California during the winter, or at Belmont Park, Saratoga and Aqueduct's main track and turf course during more clement periods of the Northeastern year. Now as in the past, the best stables rest their most important runners on Southern farms during the winter and race them only when the hazards of weather are at a minimum.

Horses that cannot get out of their own way at Belmont Park suddenly become tigers when the snow clouds gather over Aqueduct's inner track and superior animals head South. Horses that win everything in sight during the Calder summer meeting and the transitional Tropical Park-at-Calder session of December and January cannot be found at the finishes of Hialeah or Gulfstream races. August killers at Del Mar are January losers at Santa Anita.

Careful handicappers have learned to proceed with great caution when winning stables vacate their barns in the North or South and head for the more suitable weather and fatter purses that await them in the South or North. Each such migration ushers in a new season, a new cast of horses and riders, a whole new ball game. Handicapping becomes more difficult than usual. Every race includes horses whose present abilities are obscure. Some have not run in months. Will they benefit from the rest and win at first asking? Or will they need some actual competition before rounding into form? Some have traveled thousands of miles in vans or planes. Will they need a race or two before becoming acclimated? Or will their journeys agree with them?

Most of the jockeys are familiar enough to the fans, but some are newcomers. Weeks must pass before anyone can know whether the new rider is as good as a New England or Ohio or Illinois record implies—able to perform well with all kinds of horses or less versatile than that.

Watchful waiting and extremely conservative betting are essential during these periods of transition. Wait a couple of weeks until the newly arrived horses have had races over the track. To do this is to liberate oneself from the impossible task of trying to compare apples and pears. It is always easier to rate horses on the basis of what they have done in recent competition with each other at the present track or a nearby sister track.

When It Rains

Many successful players refuse to go to the track unless the weather is pleasant and they know that the running surface is dry. But patient, adaptable handicappers can find lucrative opportunities on off-tracks, just as they do on fast ones.

Several times in every season, the Weather Bureau touts everyone onto a loser. "Fair and warmer," the forecast says. But the morning sun gives way to clouds and the rain begins to fall at noon. By post-time for the first race the running surface is a mess. What to do? Some players go home. Others hunt for spots.

Official information about the condition of the track is posted on the tote board. Not infrequently, the board will pronounce the track "fast" even though everyone can see puddles gathering on it. The tote board is not exactly fibbing. It is doing the best it can. The distinction between a fast track and its immediate inferior, a "good" track, is a matter of judgment. Smart players are wary. They know that horses sometimes run seconds slower than expected and suffer serious losses of stamina on an officially "fast" track that is anything but.

The sandy scientifically drained running surfaces at most modern racing plants turn from "fast" to "good" to "sloppy" in a heavy rain. Unless the rain is exceptionally heavy, the track does not even get muddy. Sun and drainage soon combine to upgrade it from "sloppy" to "good" to "fast" in a single afternoon. Even if the surface gets actually muddy, the drying process seldom lingers at the stage known as "heavy," when the surface is as gooey as wet cement and horses' hooves sound like suction cups. Aqueduct dries from muddy to fast in a few hours of sunshine. The sequence is usually "muddy," "slow," "good," "fast."

Here is what the various terms mean, and what the handicapper does about them.

Fast: Dry. So dry that the maintenance crew waters it between races, to hold the dust down. The great majority of races are run on fast tracks. Hence, most horses are at their best on such tracks and have little experience on others. Speed figures recorded on a fast track stand up quite reliably whenever the same horses run again under the same conditions on the same ground.

Information about the running styles, preferred distances, weight-bearing abilities and class limitations of most horses is based on fast-track performances. The information is dependable as long as today's race is also on a fast track and the player has seen the watering trucks in action. Some track managements stretch the meaning of "fast" to cover a degree of wetness that might earn another label elsewhere. For example, on its way from legitimately fast and dry toward downright puddle-sloppy, many a track will produce increasingly fast times and be increasingly hospitable to horses with early speed. The infield board's proclamation of "fast" is more reliable in that situation than it may be after the rains, when the racing strip is drying out and the management hastens to replace the "muddy" and "good" signs with "fast." At a track where times become slower and longshots win more than their share of races on post-deluge "fast" tracks, wise handicappers learn to respect the difference between "fast" and "fast." In New York, for instance, it is not uncommon to hear otherwise sophisticated professionals berating one or another jockey for losing on a drying-out track when they should be spanking themselves for having bet. In some circumstances it is temporarily impossible to tell whether a particular running style is at the desired advantage or not. Until achieving clarity, the sensible tactic is to abstain from betting, or restrict one's action to nickels and dimes.

Sloppy: The track is covered with large puddles. The rain is still coming down or has ended recently. The drying process has scarcely begun.

When modern sandy tracks are sloppy, the horses run every bit as rapidly as when the surface is dry. Many players proceed with their handicapping as if the track were fast. This is a mistake. It is a mistake because front-running horses have an even better chance on a sloppy track (of the sandy sort) than on a fast track. They seem to hold their speed longer. Their come-from-behind rivals have more difficulty catching them.

It is agreed that the texture of a sloppy track favors the front-runner mainly because his position at the head of the stampede spares him the discomfort of having mud and slop kicked in his face. The horses behind him are obliged to run through a barrage of guck. Few of them appreciate it. It affects their spirit and saps their stamina. Many of them sulk or quit outright.

Therefore, when the handicapper's study shows that the best horse in the race is a front-runner, and that no other front-runner in the race has the speed to stay with him, the horse usually becomes a better bet on a sloppy track. If the horse's most formidable competitor is one that likes to come from off the pace but has done nothing in previous efforts on sloppy tracks, the front-runner becomes an even better bet.

The exception would be a front-runner that simply dislikes slop. A few of them do, and their records often show it.

A more difficult case arises when the best horse in the race is a come-from-out-of-it type. If it has already won in the slop by coming on in the stretch and overtaking the leaders, it may be a rugged sort. The player with access to old result charts would look up the animal's good race in the slop and see if the chart explains how it won. Perhaps it won because two front-runners perished in the stretch and it was the only other living thing in the vicinity of the finish wire. But if the horse ran with authentic gameness, or if today's front-runners seem likely to wear each other out—which can happen in the slop as easily as on a fast track—the player has found a good bet.

Lacking such evidence in result charts, the wise player remains skeptical about the winning chances of the come-from-behinder, even though it may have won in slop before. Unless the animal has a pronounced edge in all departments, and has never showed the slightest inclination to quit in the stretch, it may be wiser to pass the race. On the other hand, if it has won *more than one race* in the slop, it can be certified as a slop runner deserving of support.

As the reader can see, decisions of this kind depend on numerous variables. When in doubt, the expert abstains. It hurts to pass up a winner, but it costs no money. To pass up a loser saves money, and is gratifying in that respect.

Good: While getting drenched, the track passes from "fast" to "sloppy" via "good." While drying out, it progresses from "muddy" to "slow" to "fast" with a stopover at "good." A peculiarity of sandy tracks is that "good" refers to conditions not nearly as good as the innocent bystander might think. At Aqueduct, a so-called good track contains less moisture than a "slow" one and more than a "fast" one, but it often works havoc on the figures of an unsuspecting player. In the old days, a "good" track was only a bit slower than "fast," and had no marked effect on the running styles of most horses. But when the sandy track is on the slow side of "good" it holds horses back. Front-runners run out of gas sooner. Races are won by animals that come from off the pace to score victories that would not be likely on a fast track.

The safest approach to the modern track in a situation of this kind is to determine (if possible) how the early speedsters are being affected. If the situation is unclear, bet no horse unless it figured to win on a fast track and either has a clear edge in class or is the determined type that can be rated a few lengths behind the leaders before opening up in the stretch. If it has won in the past on "good," "slow" or "muddy" tracks, it becomes a better risk.

To repeat for emphasis, a pace-setting animal is a dubious choice on a holding track unless it is figured to romp on a fast track, has a decided class edge and has won on off-tracks in the past.

Slow: Very much the same standards apply to this moister surface. It is slow because it holds. It retards the animals. Front-runners have more difficulty.

Muddy: This kind of footing is wetter than anything but a sloppy track and often favors front-runners. The clods that fly from the front-runner's heels adhere to the rearward horses and jockeys like beauty-parlor facials. Hooves slip and slide. Horses become frightened of their unsure purchase on the ground. They sometimes quit running and look for the barn. So may a front-runner if the mud is particularly heavy and he tires in that going.

The only horse to bet in a race of this kind is one that not only should win if the track were fast but has already proved that it can win in mud. If it does not shape up as the best horse in the race, its previous victory in mud is no evidence that it will win today. Yet, if the mudder is the second- or third-best horse in the race, and the better two have already demonstrated a reluctance to run in mud, you may have something.

As often as not, the winner of a mud race turns out to be a sore-kneed varmint that never raced in mud before but appreciates the cool comfort of the stuff so much that it runs in at huge odds. I repeat, the nearest thing to a safe bet in mud, as on any off-track, is the horse with the double edge—the potential superiority on normal footing *plus* proven ability to cope with today's goo.

Heavy: A surface of this kind is rare at modern tracks. It occurs after a long siege of rain, when enough moisture has evaporated to leave the soil with a consistency comparable to the soft, damp clay used in nursery schools. A heavy track is slower than any other kind. The best hope of the player who tries to handicap races on such a surface is to take the best horse but *only* if it has won on heavy tracks in the past. To cash one such bet in four would be extremely lucky. The other three races will go to a variety of animals, including some that never have done well on off-tracks. As indicated above, the situation seldom arises at modern tracks, whose sandy racing strips and efficient draining systems do not become as sticky as the clay tracks of old.

Turf Courses: Heavy or protracted rainfall softens the turf. The infield board now calls the grass strip "good" or "yielding" or downright "soft" instead of the usual "firm." A firm course is just that—the grass itself cushioning the feet and supplying a resilience similar to that of a horse's natural habitat. Because most North American race meetings are lengthy, the tendency is to cancel turf racing (except for the most important stakes) on days when the grass course is wet. In such conditions, hooves tear up the sod, making for dangerous footing on the days that follow. But races on wet turf are not uncommon as meetings draw to a close. The best bets are horses that have performed well on softer footing. Especially good bets are animals imported from Europe that have raced in the much deeper going of French or Irish or English grass and may have had trouble on the rock-hard firmness of American courses. To race once again on a familiar footing often does those animals a world of good.

Bitter experience helps form the attitudes of most players toward rainfall and its consequences. If the past few pages seem to offer hope of success on days when the track is off, and the reader is emboldened to brave the elements instead of staying home, I urge caution. Like anything else in handicapping, wet-track predictions should be tested on paper before actual money travels from the wallet to the mutuel clerk.

The remainder of this chapter deals with the various types of Thoroughbred races, differentiating the less playable from the more so. Here again, a veteran racegoer may find nuggets that seem to promise success with kinds of races that previously have defied his best efforts. I urge once more that he proceed with care. If, for example, he has always avoided races for two-year-olds, having succumbed to the widespread superstition that young horses are unreliable, he should hesitate before deciding that the information in this chapter equips him to bet on a two-year-old. While hesitating, he should see what other chapters of this book can add to his understanding of two-year-olds. And he then should confine his activity to mental bets or paper bets until he has satisfied himself that he can beat such races.

We begin our review with claiming races. They not only are the most numerous races at most tracks, but offer the highest proportion of betting opportunities.

Claiming Races for Older Horses

Without claiming races there would be no racing at all. Owners would avoid the hazards of fair competition. Instead, they would enter their better animals in races against the sixth- and twelfth-raters that occupy most stalls at most tracks. The third-class horse might be unable to win a major race from one end of the year to the other, but would go undefeated in races against his inferiors. This would leave little or no purse money for the owners of cheap horses. The game would perish.

The claiming race changes all that. When he enters his animal in a race for $5,000 claiming horses, the owner literally puts it up for sale at that price. Any other owner can file a claim before the race and lead the beast away after the running. The original owner collects the horse's share of the purse, if it earned any, but he loses the horse at a fair price.

That is, he loses the horse at a fair price if it is a $5,000 horse. If it were a $10,000 horse, in a race for cheaper ones, the owner would get the purse and collect a large bet at odds of perhaps 1 to 10, but the horse would be bought by another barn at less than its true value.

Owners sell nothing at cut rates. Not on purpose. Which is why a $5,000 claiming race always matches horses whose value—a reflection of present class and soundness and estimated future earning capacity—is not much higher than $5,000. Their value may, in fact, be a good deal lower. At major tracks, claiming prices usually range from $15,000 to $100,000. Claiming races for $200,000 stock are seen occasionally.

The sophisticated racegoer likes to open his racing paper and find a claiming race at six furlongs for three-year-olds, or for three-year-olds and up. He knows that the race may provide his best bet of the day. That is not all he knows. He knows that the reason these horses are running at a claiming price is that they are unfit to run in better company. Some of them showed championship promise as yearlings or two-year-olds, but suffered injury from which they recovered only traces of their ability. Others may be jaded or partly crippled from too much training and racing, and may be on their way down the scale. Next year they'll be running at minor tracks, with $2,000 price tags. Others may be reliable enough animals in their present price bracket. Still others may be winners in a lower price bracket, but over their heads today.

There may be ten horses in the race, and members of the crowd may bet many thousands of dollars on each, but the handicapper usually finds that no more than three or four have a reasonably good chance to win. The rest are short of condition, short of class, running at the wrong distance, or facing animals that figure to cut out the wrong kind of pace for them. Or maybe their jockeys are outclassed.

The trainers of mature claiming horses manipulate the animals like puppets, darkening their form by entering them in races they can't win and then springing them for the money in races that suit them. Expert handicappers know all this, and how to recognize what's afoot. Strangely enough, although these claiming races lack real quality, the winner often turns out be a horse with a slight edge in class—provided, of course, that its physical condition allows it to demonstrate that inherent superiority. Where no significant class difference exists, the animal in best condition can be counted on to win, assuming that the distance and weights and pace and jockey suit him.

In the urgent effort to subsidize as many stables as possible by giving even the poorest three- and four-year-old and older horses a chance to win, the tracks are unable to rely solely on the class distinctions implied by claiming prices. Identical price tags notwithstanding, a group of $3,000 or $8,000 or $50,000 Thoroughbreds includes widely diversified talents. The tracks compensate for some of these differences by scheduling races at varying distances. But even this is not enough. The track must plan races for the least capable members of any claiming-price group and other races for the better.

In ascending order of quality, the more familiar of these claiming races are:

1. For maiden fillies. A race for four-year-olds of this description is inferior to one that includes three-year-olds or is exclusively for those younger, less shop-worn animals.

2. For maiden colts and geldings, or for both sexes. Again, the presence of three-year-olds suggests a better race.

3. For female non-winners of two races at any time. Once more, three-year-olds are generally the best animals in the category.

4. For male non-winners of two, or for both sexes. Three-year-olds are usually of higher quality than their elders.

5. For three-year-old non-winners of one or two or more races since a specified date. The larger the number of permissible previous victories and the more recent the date, the better the competition. Also, a race for males or both sexes is superior to one restricted to females.

6. For three-year-olds and up or four-year-olds and up, with other conditions as in the paragraph above. Among horses of proven winning ability, such as these, four- and five-year-olds usually enjoy clear superiority over three-year-olds of identical claiming price. This is especially true during the first half of the year and in longer races.

7. Open to all in the claiming bracket, aged three and up, or four and up. The best $7,500 animals on the grounds might be ineligible for certain of the races described in Paragraph 6, having won too often and too recently, but can get into this kind of gallop.

The racing secretaries, who plan track programs, resort to many ingenious variations on the foregoing themes. By the end of any representative season, winning opportunities will have been programmed for all but the very sorriest stock. Any trainer who doesn't find a spot for every animal in his barn has only himself—or them—to blame.

Although this is not the place for a discussion of the weight factor, it should be pointed out that the conditions of claiming races grant weight concessions to horses that have won fewer than a specified number of races within a specified time. Additional weight advantages sometimes are given to animals entered to be claimed at less than the maximum price. For instance, a race might be programmed for horses entered to be claimed for $4,500, $5,000 and $5,500. The ones entered at the lower prices would be allowed to carry three or five or seven pounds less than those entered at $5,500.

Older Claiming Maidens and Non-Winners of Two

Maiden claiming races for horses aged three or more are the saddest exhibitions on any card. Most of the entrants have had several opportunities as two-year-olds and have failed. They have done no better at age three. And some have reached four without a single win. The expert almost invariably writes off the four-year-old as hopeless in a maiden claimer. If it has lived this long without winning, there can be little expectation that it will win today.

Among three-year-old maidens entered to be claimed, the majority are equally hopeless. They have shown neither speed, stamina nor spirit. One that has been getting into the money frequently may attract the business of the crowd but is not necessarily a good bet. He very likely is a sucker horse, a chronic loser. His previous experiences have conditioned him to run as fast as is necessary to stay among the leaders, but he hates—and that's the word—to get out front, where he can't see any other horses. So he loses and loses and loses, although he often finishes second or third.

I have never known an expert who approached the maiden claiming race for older horses with any expectation of finding a good bet. Some do not bother to handicap such races at all. Others may bet on a three-year-old in a high-priced maiden claimer (about $50,000), if the animal has not yet proved itself a dud. For example, if it has had only a race or two or three in its previous career, has run at least one of them recently without disgrace, has been working out frequently and at respectable speed, and, above all, is from a leading barn, it may be superior to its rivals today. Perhaps the animal's previous race was a maiden-special-weights event, for the most valued non-winners in the place. If it did fairly well in that race and meets other standards, the maiden claiming race may be its dish of tea.

Or perhaps its last was a spirited race against $35,000 maidens and its surprised owner has decided to boost the ante. If the horse is the only thing in the field that looks like a horse, it may be a bet.

Claiming events for non-winners of two races are designed for animals only one step removed from the maiden category. These creatures often are no better than maidens. They prove it by never winning another race at a major track. The best of them is the lightly raced, well-trained three-year-old that wins a maiden race decisively. It has demonstrated an authentic edge in class over non-winners in this price range. The chances are excellent that it retains the advantage when facing non-winners-of-two in the same price bracket.

Another good bet is the occasional animal whose lone victory occurred not in a maiden claimer but in a straight claimer (a race for previous winners). A look at the result chart usually reveals that the race was for non-winners-of-two, but the horse deserves extra credit, especially if it showed any real speed.

Still another possibility is the horse that won a maiden-special-weights race, or has been finishing close to the winners in straight claimers of a value higher than today's. Example: a three-year-old that has been beating half or more of its field when racing against four- and five-year-old winners in a similar price range.

In trying to evaluate races for *female* maidens or non-winners of two races, the criteria remain the same. Certainly, any female that has shown the slightest spark of ability in a recent race against *males* can be assumed to have an extra something going for her when pitted against unpromising females at the same claiming-price level.

Bread and Butter

Straight claiming races for $3,000 to $100,000 horses with multiple victories are the bread and butter of the expert player. The fluctuations of the form cycle, the maneuvering of trainers and the relative unsoundness of much of the stock make it possible for the player to toss out most of the entrants as probable losers. The real contenders are quite easy to find. But things become stickier when claiming prices exceed $50,000. These higher-priced animals earn their substantial valuations by winning with fair consistency, or at least by indicating that they could do so if entered in suitable races. They are sounder and hold their winning form somewhat longer. Thus, a field of $75,000 Thoroughbreds often perplexes the handicapper with four or five animals that have done well enough in fairly fast company—and have done it recently enough—to qualify as contenders. The player's problem may be additionally complicated by the presence of horses dropping down to the claiming ranks after facing superior competition in allowance races.

A race of this kind, in which the handicapper is unable to separate the leading contenders, is every bit as unplayable-unbeatable as a race in which the present capabilities of the horses are unknown or in which no horse has demonstrated enough reliability to deserve a bet.

It is a grievous pain in the neck to spend time handicapping a race and end with two or three or four horses so evenly matched that decision seems impractical. Yet fortune sometimes smiles. One of the horses may be scratched. In the paddock and walking ring, two of the remaining contenders may seem grossly out of sorts. All of a sudden the fourth horse is an outstanding bet. More often than not he pays excellent odds, the crowd having pushed a good deal of its money onto the other prominent contenders.

Claiming races are the staple fare of the expert handicapper. I know none who avoid playing them. I know some who seldom play any other kind.

Races for Good Two-Year-Olds

Let it be asserted at the outset that the better two-year-olds at major tracks are among the most reliable Thoroughbreds anywhere. The prejudice of many players against two-year-olds is unwarranted. Anyone who knows what to look for in juvenile races can profit without nearly the expenditure of time and sweat that other kinds of handicapping demand.

The well-bred two-year-old that reacts well to training is handled like a potential champion. Its first run for money is against other highly regarded juvenile maidens at five or five and a half furlongs under uniform weights prescribed by the racing secretary of the track. Early in the season, most of the entrants in one of these maiden-special-weights affairs are likely to be first-time starters. One or more may be by Secretariat or Northern Dancer or Exclusive Native and trained by Laz Barrera, Jimmy Croll or other first-rate conditioners who specialize in winning with two-year-olds in the first attempt. What can the player do when confronted by so many attractive unknown quantities? Sit on his hands and wait.

As the season progresses, maiden-special-weights races crop up in which all but one or two of the horses have been to the post a time or three. A high-bred swifty from a good barn is entered. His past performances show that he has been trying, has been missing narrowly but

Official photo that established Tom Fool as winner of the 1953 Suburban Handicap. Royal Vale was second. UPI PHOTO

improving, and has been doing it all in excellent time. Frequently, he is the only animal of his description in the race. He is as good a bet as one ever finds.

The two-year-old may even be a good bet in its very first race. If all other entrants have had a few racing opportunities without demonstrating ability, the well-bred, well-trained youngster making its first start may well go to the post as a solid favorite.

Many players lose money on these sprints for potentially superior two-year-old maidens by overlooking an ancient tradition of the game. This tradition regards the form of a maiden as "the property of its owner." The horse can be sent out *not* to win but to acquire experience in actual competition. Inasmuch as the trainers do not notify the public of their intentions in that regard, a lot of money is wasted at the windows.

Before anyone calls the cops to report corruption, I should point out that no decent barn wants to lose any race. Yet no decent barn will permit a jockey to punish a green but expensive two-year-old in an effort to win. If it cannot win on its own raw talent and courage, it is allowed to lose. Treatment of that sort may be unkind to players, but is good for horses.

To avoid being entrapped into betting on a two-year-old maiden whose connections are not ready to shoot the works, the smart player simply reserves his support for animals that (1) have already tried to win and look like winners today or (2) regardless of prior performance or lack of it, seem to have a clear edge in quality over the zeros in today's field. The handicapping is done mainly in terms of speed, by means to be described in a later chapter. Other basic considerations are breeding, the identity of trainer and jockey and the swiftness of recent workouts. Class, weight and pace usually are irrelevant in these five-furlong sprints.

Winners of the maiden-special dashes proceed to allowance races, stepping-stones to the lucrative juvenile stakes. If the allowance race is at five or five and a half furlongs, and all entrants have already competed at the distance, the race can be analyzed entirely in terms of speed, with the usual edge to the best barns. If the distance is new to some of the horses, the race is harder to beat. It may even be unplayable, as we shall see in the next chapter.

At distances of six furlongs and up, under allowance or stakes conditions, the player often finds too many sound, evenly matched two-year-olds to choose among. Stickouts like Native Dancer turn up too infrequently to make the player's life simple. But when one does, the juvenile stakes are a joy. A Native Dancer, Citation, Secretariat, Seattle Slew, Graustark, Moccasin, Ruffian, Hail to Reason or Buckpasser pays miserly odds. But who cares? Animals of that kind figure to win big. Any race is playable in which a horse not only figures much the best but, in the manner of two-year-old champions, can be counted on to give it all he's got. The young champ loses now and then, but not often enough to throw the player's accounts out of joint.

Cheap Two-Year-Olds

Races for inferior two-year-olds are an entirely different matter. When a maiden juvenile is entered to be claimed, his proprietors announce, in effect, that he is a washout. They are so sure of his unsoundness or lack of innate talent that they do not even bother to protect him from sale. The races in which he runs are invariably the slowest at any track, and are not cheering to the eye.

Some players put their money on the supposed class of a glamorously bred two-year-old when it runs in company of this kind. But if the poor thing's breeding meant anything, it would be winning allowance races, not seeking its first win in the company of culls. Once in a great while, the player finds an entrant that has run faster in maiden-special-weights company than any of its competitors have run in their maiden claiming races. Unless the horse displayed that speed recently and has been working out at short, regular intervals, it can be assumed that it has deteriorated and will not equal the previous clocking today. The player who speculates on more than one of every five or six maiden claimers for two-year-olds is guilty of waste—especially at lower claiming-price levels.

Straight claimers for two-year-olds are as playable as other claiming events, but not early in the season. In late summer and fall, after the young horses have run often enough to sort themselves out a bit, the player approaches their claiming races with confidence. In spring, all he really knows about a field of two-year-old claimers is that the entrants have been good enough to win in the past but that something serious accounts for their inability to win in better company. A physical or temperamental flaw of that kind may not prevent the animal from going on to a long, honorable career. Indeed, it may move right out of the claiming ranks and become a stakes winner, like hundreds of underrated Thoroughbreds in the past. But the youngster's failings may be more serious. They may prevent him from ever repeating the swift previous victory that explains why the crowd has made him the favorite in today's race. In short, two-year-old claimers are among the least consistent of horses during the early months of the year, and deserve mistrust for that reason.

Although the horse with the fastest previous race at the distance is the likeliest contender in any two-year-old claiming sprint, the player is well advised to pass the race unless the horse has been active recently and has shown that it can *consistently* cover the ground in substantially faster time than any of its competitors. Even so, it may lose out to a beast that has been performing indifferently in allowance company but runs faster today than it has ever run before. These are tough races. I doubt that anyone beats them without extreme selectivity.

Allowance Races for Older Horses

The conditions of the allowance race resemble those of the claiming race, except that the horses are not for sale. Eligibility and weight allowances are prescribed in conditions written by the racing secretary. As in claiming races, the conditions usually tend to bar horses that are too good for the field, having won too many purses above a minimum value, or having won too often or too recently. On the other hand, the conditions permit a trainer to enter a horse that has not a prayer of winning, but needs the work.

Most players know that allowance races are designed to provide earnings for horses too good to be lost via the claiming route, but not good enough to beat stakes and handicap stars. But most players do not know that allowance races come in almost as many varieties as claiming races. To regard one allowance race as equal in quality to another is to invite losses. To search out those qualitative differences is to open the way to remarkable betting opportunities.

Let us suppose that two three-year-olds seem to be outstanding contenders in an allowance race. Each finished a fast-closing second in its previous start, after running close to the pace all the way. The past-performance records show that both horses have been entered in nothing but allowance races all year, and have been running successfully enough to inspire confidence.

Are they too closely matched? Not a bit of it. The player motivated to dig through the result charts discovers that the last race of Horse "A" was for three-year-olds that had not won a race with a purse as high as $15,000 on as many as three occasions in the previous six months. "A" was eligible for the race because his earnings had exceeded $15,000 in only two of his five victories. The horse that defeated him in the race was a three-year-old with credentials.

The records show that "B" has been facing animals of a different order. His last race was for three-year-olds and up. The purse was fatter than the purse in "A's" race. And the conditions of eligibility had permitted entry by several previous winners of handicap and stakes races. In running second, "B" outfooted several high-class animals older than he. A couple of his earlier victories had been against horses so good that they would not have been allowed into "A's" last race, and would not be allowed into today's race, either.

"B's" trainer has found a soft spot. For a change the horse is running against animals of his own age. They have never demonstrated that they can keep up with the kind of stock "B" has been beating. The player who knows what to look for has found a bonanza. Indeed, if "A" happens to have run his last couple of races in faster time than "B" and if the rider of "A" is the "hot" jockey on the grounds and if, as may be expected, a significant number of newspaper selectors and tip sheets pick "A," the player will collect a robust mutuel after "B" waltzes home in front.

The past-performance records in all editions of *Daily Racing Form* now include the purse values of allowance races. The recent history of a horse entered to compete for a $22,000 pot with other non-winners of three races may include appearances at the same track in allowance races that offered purses of $35,000. The higher purses are awarded to so-called classified allowance races, the eligibility conditions of which emphasize previous purse earnings during specific periods of time, often inviting participation by stakes winners whose much superior earnings may have been amassed during previous seasons, before the cut-off date.

When entered in a "conditioned" allowance race for non-winners or a race or two or three other than maiden or claiming races, a horse who has run well in classified competition deserves considerable respect.

Maiden-Specials for Older Horses

Many a well-bred horse goes through its entire two-year-old season without a single victory. Even after it has lost six or eight times, its owners refuse to enter it in claiming races. Perhaps they think that it may finally come to hand. Or they hope to use it for breeding purposes someday and don't want to lose it. Or the owner's wife loves its limpid hazel eyes and refuses to part with it in any circumstances.

All of a sudden January 1 arrives and the horse is a three-year-old maiden. Indeed, some otherwise successful barns harbor four-year-old maidens, still running in maiden-specials. The tracks are careful to arrange racing opportunities for the creatures. Needless to say, the majority are incurable losers. Some would have serious difficulty winning a $10,000 claimer at a minor track.

But the player misses some excellent bets by skipping past these maiden-specials without a glance at the past-performance records. Most of the four-year-olds are hopeless and can be ignored. But some of the threes *do* come to hand. They put together a couple of brisk races and some bright workouts and proceed to win like winners.

As a general rule of thumb, the likelihood that such an animal will wake up and win becomes smaller as his number of races increases. The fewer races in his record, the better his chances. The best plays of all are horses that did not start at age two, probably because they were late foals or slow developers or sick or hurt and their handlers decided not to overtax them. Occasionally, one of these three-year-old first-starters not only wins his race, but deserves betting support by the smart player. If his breeding is promising, his trainer outstanding, his workouts good, his rivals nondescript, and if he looks fit in the paddock, he's worth a chance.

More often, these good three-year-old maidens need a race or two before cracking down. They usually signal readiness by running more competently in their second outing than in their first.

It makes no sense to bypass maiden-specials for older horses. A highly satisfactory percentage of winners can be found in them by anyone who knows what to look for.

Turf Races

A grass race is likely to be playable if all the horses have already raced on that surface and one or more have demonstrated an affinity for it. *Daily Racing Form* past-performance records now differentiate turf from main-track races by including a "T" on the line that summarizes the particular past performance. Moreover, the paper summarizes each entrant's life-time grass-racing record, displaying the total number of starts, wins, seconds and thirds. All this helps.

Lucrative opportunities reward handicappers who take the trouble to learn the names of the sire bloodlines known for success on the turf (see pages 88–89), and supplement that fundamental knowledge with refer-ence works such as the annual *Statistical Review* and *Sire Book* published by *Thoroughbred Record,* and/or the annual *Stakes Winners* and *Stallion Register* volumes published by *The Blood-Horse,* and, for deeper digging, *Sires and Dams of Stakes Winners,* which lists all such Thoroughbreds from the year 1925 onward and is published by *The Blood-Horse.*

Stakes and Handicaps

Purists will be offended because I lump all handicap races and all the great stakes under one heading. I do so because I think that these aristocratic races offer relatively few betting opportunities. They are delightful to watch, of course. They bring together the best horses in the country, or the best horses at the particular track—animals so well matched that prediction is extra hazardous. In the year of a Secretariat, a Forego, a Kelso, a Count Fleet or a Citation, it is possible to make out nicely on some of the more important events. But most of the other name races simply are too close to bother with.

Overnight handicaps are not much better for the player. In these, top allowance-grade horses compete under handicap conditions—with the weights assigned by the racing secretary according to his evaluation of the entrants' recent performances. As might be expected, the problem is whether the class horse is in good enough condition to win at the particular weights and under the stress of the pace at which the procession is likely to go. Sometimes there is no way of telling whether one of the horses actually *does* have a class advantage. These are tough nuts to crack, and playing the favorite is no way out: It wins a third of the time but the player ends on the losing side of the ledger. Unless, of course, he plays odds-on favorites to place—risking dollars to win nickels.

Starter Handicaps

These are fascinating races. Eligibility is limited to horses that have started at a specified claiming price at some time during their careers, or during a fixed period of time. Weights are assigned by the racing secretary according to his estimate of the horses' abilities. Or the race might be called a "starter allowance," with weights prescribed according to number or value of recent victories.

In no other form of Thoroughbred racing do the maneuverings of trainers become more noticeable than in these regattas. The race may be limited to animals that have run in $10,000 claiming company, yet the field is sure to include several that usually bear price tags as high as $35,000, their $10,000 days long behind them. In fact, trainers have been known to enter expensive horses in cheap claiming races for no other reason than to make them eligible for subsequent starter handicaps and starter allowance races. (At some tracks, horses cannot be claimed on the first day of the season, enabling a barn to drop a decent horse into a bad race and qualify it for later starter handicaps without fear of losing it.)

Certain horses seem unable to win anything but these starter races. They lose when they run in straight claimers for lower purses, but they perk up when the bigger money is on the line. Many insiders with a nose for large mutuel prices take it as a rule of thumb that the best bet in a starter handicap is the horse that has won such a race in the past, regardless of how poorly he may have been doing in his most recent outings. It is a fact that such horses jump up and win these races—often winning two or three a season without accomplishing much in any other kind of race. Their success can be taken as evidence that their trainers know how to get them ready for a spot without advertising the readiness in the past-performance records.

Optional Claimers

In these races an animal may be entered to be claimed or not, depending on the preference of its management. If it wins when *not* entered to be claimed it is penalized by being declared ineligible for another optional race of the same grade at the same meeting, except if entered to be claimed. Also, the horse's eligibility for future allowance races is affected: The track usually credits its victory as having taken place in an allowance race! But if it *is* entered to be claimed in the optional affair that it wins, it is charged only with a victory in a claiming race.

By and large, these optional races are more difficult to handicap than straight claimers. But sometimes the class of the animals is apparent in the claiming prices and results of their recent efforts.

Jump Races

Hurdle races are run over low obstacles. Steeplechase races involve higher fences and water hazards. Both types are extremely dangerous for the horses and their riders and far too unpredictable for betting purposes. They are great fun to watch (except when some poor rider gets thrown onto his skull), but are absolute booby traps for the players. The reason should be obvious—the best horse in the race might meet with interference from a fallen horse, or might fall itself. Flat racing is tough enough. Jumps present the handicapper with an extra unknown factor. Only an incurable gambler risks important amounts of money in such circumstances.

Roll Up Your Sleeves

So much for playable-beatable races. Now for a detailed review of the methods whereby experts play them and beat them. In the remaining chapters we shall explore matters such as distance, current condition, class, age, sex, consistency, weight, speed, pace, the trainer, the rider, special handicapping angles, the paddock and post parade.

The chapters deal with these factors not in order of importance but in a sequence likely to be most convenient for the reader. Indeed, it is impossible to say which handicapping factor is most important of all. Importance varies according to the particular race and the particular horse. But no factor stands alone. Each affects the others, and must be considered with the others in mind.

8

THE DISTANCE FACTOR

The late Robert Saunders Dowst achieved prominence in the late thirties when his articles in *Esquire* and other magazines of mass circulation explained some of the rudiments of handicapping to the natives. Dowst enjoyed his fame but found that it had its price. Within a couple of years after he revealed to the general public that any dodo could make big money by betting on highly consistent horses, the system stopped winning.

It stopped winning mainly because the horses were yielding lower mutuel prices than ever. Dowst's grateful followers had not only been betting the boodle but spreading the word. Another reason why the system stopped winning was that a slightly lower percentage of the consistent horses was finishing first. As if their trainers were rebelling against the low odds and waiting for more lucrative opportunities.

Dowst himself denied, and rightly so, that any important number of trainers were deliberately stiffing the best, most consistent horses in racing rather than win at low odds. He mused that maybe the game was changing a little. It certainly was. His system had become public property when the sport was in transition to its present assembly-line state. The practice of racing Thoroughbreds into shape, long resisted by conscientious horsemen, was becoming more commonplace. Hence, an animal's record of consistency (an unusually high percentage of winning or in-the-money starts) could no longer be taken as absolute evidence that the creature was in condition to vie for the marbles every time it went to the post. The kind of horse that might have won a third of its starts in 1935 was unlikely to win more than a quarter of them in 1941, its handlers having discovered the boons and benefits of letting it get some of its training exercise in actual competition. While losing, that is.

From time to time during the years that have elapsed since Dowst's mild embarrassment, I have heard racetrackers cite his system as evidence that it doesn't pay to share the goodies of the game with members of the public. All that happens is that the odds go down, they say. And then, when the odds go down, the horsemen change their methods and the handicapping system or angle or theory becomes obsolete.

Could be. But I doubt it. I especially doubt it as far as the substance of the present chapter is concerned. What is revealed herein about the problem of a Thoroughbred's suitability to the distance of its race is unknown to most players of the game and neglected by many of the few who know it. If hundreds of thousands of players suddenly become aware of it, and begin betting accordingly, and boasting of the results, certain willing horses unquestionably will pay lower odds than before. But the game will not change as a result. The suitability of a Thoroughbred to the distance of its race is a product of heredity and training and cannot be turned on or off like a spigot.

The Law of the Yardstick

Most published material on the art of picking winners urges the reader to avoid betting on sprinters in route races and routers in sprints. The sprint is defined as a race of seven furlongs or less. All other distances are regarded as routes.

To classify an animal as a sprinter or a router, the player usually examines its record to see the kind of races in which it competes most often. More sophisticated analysts look for the kind of races in which it has won or finished close. Few players carry the investigation further. Which is a primary reason for the dismal regularity with which they lose.

Distance is a crucial factor in the training and racing of horses. Confronted with the problem of finding races that his livestock can win, the professional horseman takes pains to learn the *exact* distances best suited to their individual physiques, running styles and temperaments. The wise handicapper is no less painstaking about the distance preferences of the horses on which he bets.

The winning range of most horses is severely limited. If its trainer points at a four-year-old and declares that it can win at any distance in any company, you should remove your hat: You are in the presence of an all-time great Thoroughbred. The $25,000 gelding that beats its own kind every now and then at six furlongs may never be better than second best against the same company at seven furlongs. The slightly sturdier horse able to win at a mile and a sixteenth may lack the zip to beat a similar field at a mile, even though the half-furlong difference between the two races is only a matter of 110 yards. The run-of-the-mill Thoroughbred that steps out of its own distance category and wins either is the beneficiary of freakish good luck or enjoys a pronounced class advantage over the animals it beats at the new distance.

Many years ago, one of the world's foremost authorities on Thoroughbred racing and breeding, Peter Burrell, director of Britain's National Stud, summarized the facts:

"Races are run at all distances from five furlongs to two and a half miles, requiring different types of horse, the sprinter being as different from the stayer as a dairy cow from a beef cow.

"So high is the standard required today at each distance that the individual horse has become specialized for that particular distance, and we must regard the horse which is top class at all distances as something of a freak . . .

"It is not difficult to breed sprinters, but it is an undisputed fact that the more speed one breeds into a horse the less distance he stays, and with the stayers—also a type that breeds true—one can breed them to stay further, but they then begin to lack the turn of speed so essential to the final dash to the winning post.

"Our task would be much simpler if all two-year-old races were run at five to six furlongs and all races for older horses at a mile. After two hundred and fifty years we might and should have produced a definite type. Instead of which, we struggle to produce a sprinter with more stamina, a stayer with more speed, and in between find our classic horse—bred for more and more speed—failing to go the distance."

Because all that has been true for generations, its meaning has been incorporated into a maxim well known on the backstretch of any Thoroughbred track: "Every horse's best distance can be measured with a yardstick."

The player who accepts that truth and puts it to work for him has launched himself toward success at the races. *He stops betting on horses entered at unsuitable distances.* And he clears the air for himself in numerous other ways. Knowledge of the distance factor is essential to any workable understanding of other vital matters such as pace, current condition and the maneuverings of trainers.

How Trainers Use Distance

If you open any copy of *Daily Racing Form* it will take you only a few seconds to find a six-furlong horse. Chances are that its only victories have been at that exact distance. Several weeks ago, let us say, it won when entered to be claimed for $10,000. Seven days later, it ran against

$12,500 claimers at the same distance and lost, tiring in the stretch. It probably was slightly outclassed, and may also have lost its keen edge in the exertion of winning its previous race. Ten days later it was back in another $10,000 claimer at its favorite distance and finished a well-beaten fifth. Clearly, it had gone off form.

The trainer rested it for almost a month and brought it back against $12,000 stock at the usual distance. It led to the half-mile call, pooped out and staggered home seventh. Today it again is entered for $12,000, but in a mile race. What goes on?

The animal has run the mile before and has never had a thing left in the stretch. It has never even finished in the money at seven furlongs. Why is the trainer bothering to enter it at a mile today?

Two reasons. First and foremost, the brief layoff seems to have refreshed the horse. It showed a nice lick of early speed in its last race. It may soon be able to win, especially if it runs against its own kind—$10,000 horses—at its own distance. The trainer evidently believes that it needs another tune-up, a "tightener." To make that tightener a mile race may help the horse's condition by requiring it to gallop farther than it likes. Which brings us to the second reason for entering it at the unsuitable distance.

The trainer does not expect to win today's race and has no intention of taxing the horse with an all-out try. Obviously, he would be pleased if the horse took an early lead and managed to hold it all the way to the finish wire. Pleased? Astonished! But he would strangle the jockey with his bare hands if the boy whipped the horse into a state of exhaustion just to finish third or fourth. The trainer's principal interest is to prepare for a race scheduled to take place five or six days from now—a $10,000 claimer at three quarters of a mile. If the beast finishes seventh today, as expected, and loses the predictable six or eight lengths in the final stages, many members of the crowd will refuse to bet on it next week. The odds will be better. The trainer and his employer, the owner, will like that.

The trainer could have entered the horse in a six-furlong scamper on today's program. The race could have been an effective tightener. But the horse might have come close to winning. Its improving form would have been too apparent. When it went for the marbles next week, the odds would be anemic. The trainer and owner would not like that.

What I am getting at here is that the player who bets on a horse entered at an unsuitable distance must assume not only that the horse will violate its own nature and win, but that the trainer will violate *his* nature and go for broke. That is too much to assume.

In virtually every race, most of the entrants have negligible chances to win. Of these all-but-certain losers, some are entered at an uncomfortable distance. Their trainers are darkening their form while doing what they can to improve it. Stayers are encouraged to develop early speed by chasing fleet sprinters out of the starting gate. Sprinters develop needed stamina by chugging behind stayers in the final stages of route races.

How, then, do experts tell if a horse is entered at a suitable distance? Let's see.

The Right Distance

The conservative handicapper is more likely to win than his reckless companion. But it is possible to become too conservative. For example, it is possible to exaggerate the importance of the distance factor beyond all reasonable limits, refusing to bet on any horse that has not already *won* at today's exact distance. Certainly, if a horse has won several times at the distance, its qualifications in this department can be taken for granted. But to eliminate a horse only because it has never won at the distance may be costly.

To illustrate, let us compare the recent races of two animals entered in a $15,000 claimer at seven furlongs.

Horse "A"

6f	23$\frac{1}{5}$	46$\frac{3}{5}$	1.11$\frac{1}{5}$	Clm 15,000	4	8	7^5	6^5	5^4	3^4
6f	22$\frac{2}{5}$	46$\frac{1}{5}$	1.11$\frac{3}{5}$	Clm 15,000	2	9	8^7	8^6	5^4	3^3
7f	23$\frac{3}{5}$	46$\frac{2}{5}$	1.25	Clm 15,000	3	6	5^7	4^4	2^2	1$^{1/2}$

Horse "B"

6f	22$\frac{2}{5}$	45$\frac{3}{5}$	1.10$\frac{2}{5}$	Allowance	3	4	4^2	5^3	6^4	7^5
6f	22$\frac{2}{5}$	46	1.11$\frac{3}{5}$	Clm 16,500	1	1	1^2	1^4	1^3	1^{11}
7f	23	46$\frac{1}{5}$	1.24$\frac{1}{5}$	Clm 17,000	3	1	1^3	1$^{1/2}$	1no	4^3

Horse "B" is plainly the faster, classier animal. To discard it from consideration because it failed to carry its speed all the way in its only seven-furlong attempt would be a grave mistake. It set the pace in that race but was hooked at the quarter pole by another $17,000 horse (the result chart may show that the other horse was actually a $20,000 one), and continued gamely into the stretch before fading. In a six-furlong race, "B" would be odds-on against "A" on grounds of class, speed, pace, whatever. Its loss to allowance horses can undoubtedly be forgiven.

As to "A," it plainly qualifies for today's distance. Six furlongs apparently is too little ground for it, but it seems able to lumber into contention during the stretch run of a seven-furlong event. At least, it can do that when opposing $15,000 horses incapable of "B's" speed. If "B" is in shape today it should win in a walk over "A."

Problems of this kind are most perplexing early in the year, especially in races for three-year-olds. Many of them have not raced often enough to be ruled out on grounds of inability to win at the distance. The handicapper needs to develop criteria other than previous victories at the distance—unless he wants sorrow.

Later in the year, or in races for four-year-olds and older, the problem subsides. Unless the race is for what my friend Howard Rowe calls "giraffes," several entrants will already have won at the distance. And among the others that have run the distance without winning, several will have covered the ground swiftly enough, and against sufficiently good opposition, to qualify as contenders.

Make Your Own Guidelines

If a horse has already won a race of today's distance, its eligibility as a contender can be accepted. Other questions about its chances can be deferred until the player is ready to consider matters such as form, class, age, sex, consistency, weight, speed, pace.

Many handicappers work that way, one step at a time, systematizng their methods to avoid confusion. Others prefer to take larger bites. If the horse has won or run close-up in a race of today's distance, these players ask additional questions:

1. **Against what kind of animals did the horse do it?**
2. **When did he do it?**
3. **How authoritatively did he do it?**

In attending to such questions, the player recognizes the interrelationships between distance and class, form and pace, disposing immediately of chores that otherwise would have to be performed later. That gets the job done more quickly.

Your own approach will depend mainly on your personal tastes and partly on how much experience you have had with past-performance records. As long as you understand and apply the principles set forth in these pages, your eventual method will be as good as any other.

Before deciding *how* to analyze the distance factor, the reader might want to consider whether to dispose of it at the very beginning of the handicapping procedure.

Should Distance Come First?

The Compleat Horseplayer and *Ainslie on Jockeys* recommend a selection method in which the distance factor is handled before the other fundamentals. Excellent results may also be attained by starting with current condition, class, consistency, speed or pace. Since the fundamentals of handicapping are intertwined, the player who deals with one

Mrs. Richard C. DuPont goes to the Winner's Circle with her wonderful Kelso and a happy Arcaro after the 1960 Jockey Club Gold Cup. WIDE WORLD PHOTOS

Bold Ruler, a good middle-distance runner, beats General Duke in the 1957 Flamingo Stakes at Hialeah. Eddie Arcaro looks over his shoulder while hand riding the colt that later became one of the great sires of modern times. UPI PHOTO

of them must at least touch on some of the others at the same time. Furthermore, no matter where the handicapping process starts, it ends by covering the same ground.

I prefer to take up distance before all other factors because I have found that it saves time. Using fairly simple standards to determine horses' suitability to the distance of today's race, the player often is able to eliminate as many as half of the entrants. This sharply reduces the remaining work. To be sure, similar savings of time are achieved by starting with the factor of current condition. Many experts manage to attend to condition and distance with one sweep of the eye, having been in the game long enough to develop that kind of ease.

For readers who are not already set in their handicapping ways, I should like to propose that they plan to dispose of distance first. However, I shall describe the various methods in such a way that the reader may choose the ones he prefers, and fit them into any sequence he likes.

The Conservative Approach

Some experts refuse to bet on a slow or inconsistent horse, even when it seems to have a clear edge over the other nonentities in its race. These conservatives reason that it is bootless to try to pick the least unreliable animal in an unreliable field. In this same spirit, they bypass a race unless some entrant has already run the exact distance in respectable fashion.

What's more, they never bet that any horse, however good it may be, will be able to do something today that it has not managed to do in the past. They refuse, in other words, to risk their money on a horse running at an unfamiliar distance.

They have a point. They avoid many a loser that way. They also steer themselves off many a winner. More relaxed players do quite nicely with carefully selected bets on cheap races, horses that have never raced before, and horses running at new distances.

Which approach is best? A quick answer would be fraudulent. It all depends on the psyche and talent of the individual player. Those unwilling or unable to dig deeply and imaginatively into the records are best advised to work the conservative side of the street. This might also be the best plan for beginners. As experience accumulates, greater flexibility becomes possible and profitable.

Whether the expert be conservative or not, his study of the distance factor is the very keystone of the work he does on races for two-year-olds. The following review of the best approaches to that problem shows how some players win by playing relatively few such races, and how others win while playing many more.

Two-Year-Olds and Distance

The most cautious approach to the distance factor in juvenile races is this:

1. Consider no two-year-old for play unless (a) it and each of its rivals has already raced at today's distance and (b) the horse has managed to run within two seconds of the track record for the distance.

That rule restricts play to certain high-class allowance and stakes races and a very occasional maiden-special-weights affair. It bypasses the hazards of guessing how youngsters will perform at five and a half furlongs if they have never tried to race farther than five. It protects the player from the first-time starters that sometimes upset the dope and win at long prices. It forbids bets on other, more highly touted debutantes that go to the post as favorites and lose.

The rule requiring a previous speed rating of 90 or better (no worse than two seconds slower than the track record for the distance) guarantees that the player will risk money only on the best two-year-olds around.

If you should be attracted to that method you will bet on few two-year-olds and seldom will collect a large mutuel payoff. If the remainder of your handicapping procedure is in keeping with your approach to the distance factor, you will hit a high percentage of winners. But you will pass race after race in which other smart, slightly less cautious players find excellent wagers.

To increase betting opportunities without exposing yourself to accusations of recklessness, you might amend the procedure slightly:

2. After making sure that all horses in the race for two-year-olds have already run at today's exact distance, consider only those that have earned a speed rating of 85 or better at the distance.

You now will be able to play additional maiden and allowance sprints. But you will continue to detour races in which some of the horses are strangers to the distance.

A somewhat less conservative outlook permits many experts to cash a satisfactory percentage of bets on juvenile races in which some of the horses have not yet tried the distance:

3. Consider no two-year-old for play unless it has earned a speed rating of at least 87 at today's exact distance.

Observe that nothing is said about whether other horses in the race have run the distance. Yet the method is quite safe. At most tracks, any two-year-old that has traveled today's distance rapidly enough to earn a speed rating of 87 (2⅗ seconds short of the track record) is talented enough to be conceded an excellent chance against first-time starters or other animals which have never tackled the distance before. The horse not only is swift but has undoubtedly profited from the experience of testing its speed in an earlier race at the distance.

If the horse with the previous figure of 87 or better is being asked to face a well-publicized first-time starter from a leading barn and sired by Seattle Slew, the cautious player may choose to pass the race, depending on one's assessment of other factors.

A player who wants to cash in on some of the plausible betting opportunities presented by first-starters and other animals that have never tried today's distance must be prepared for more than occasional losses. If you are essentially a careful type, you may find the following approach comfortable:

4. A well-bred first-time starter from a leading barn qualifies for consideration if (a) it has been working out frequently and rapidly, (b) it is to be ridden by a leading jockey, and (c) none of its rivals has been able to earn a speed rating of 80 or better at today's distance.

In this case the player establishes that none of the horses that has tried the distance is any great shakes at it. The trainer of the high-priced newcomer seems to have found an ideal spot for its debut. Circumstances of this kind arise quite frequently in maiden-special-weights races. The first-starter usually goes to the post as favorite when facing animals that have shown no real speed. The favoritism is deserved.

5. A juvenile that has raced before but has not raced at today's distance qualifies for consideration if (a) no other animal in the race has demonstrated high-class speed at the distance and (b) the horse's races at a distance not more than half a furlong shorter than today's have indicated real ability.

This is not as elaborate as it may sound. If a two-year-old has never traveled six furlongs in competition, one would hesitate to back it against a competitor that has already shown authentic talent at the distance by earning a speed rating of 88 or thereabouts. But if no such speedster is in the race, the horse may be worth a closer look. If it ran at least as fast at five and a half furlongs as any other horse in today's race, it becomes quite interesting. And it qualifies for the most serious consideration if its record shows that it was able to stay fairly close to the pace of the shorter races before *gaining ground in the homestretch*. Whether it won or lost the races, it looks very much like an animal that will be comfortable at the extra sixteenth of a mile. If its own speed ratings at the shorter distance were genuinely high, it may be a splendid risk today.

Why Use Speed Ratings?

The use of speed ratings to determine a young Thoroughbred's aptitude is standard practice, even among many experts who deride speed handicapping and rely mainly on other analyses of class and form. Enthusiasts of speed handicapping go beyond speed ratings to the sophistication of speed *figures,* which are more difficult to come by but, as we shall see, are far more accurate indicators of ability. The alternative to speed ratings or speed figures is to require that the horse's history include a finish reasonably close to the winner in a race at today's distance against a field not seriously inferior to today's.

In handicapping races for two-year-olds, it is immensely difficult to solve the distance or the closely related class problem except in terms of speed. The only measure of the quality of a race for two-year-olds is the time in which it was run. The same is true of a juvenile allowance race. All that is known about the horses is that they are previous winners of maiden-specials or allowance affairs. The fastest are best. By the end of the season, the slower ones will be running in claimers.

And what about the distance factor in juvenile claiming races? Suppose the player is the less conservative kind who bets on some of the slower two-year-olds and wins at it? How is it done?

6. In any two-year-old race, if none of the entrants has run the distance rapidly enough to earn a speed rating of 80 or higher, consider betting on any animal that has earned a rating at least 2 points higher than that of any of its rivals.

Every day during the spring and summer, maiden-specials, maiden claimers and straight claimers for two-year-olds are won by horses whose best previous speed ratings have been in the 70s. It is possible to get a satisfactory percentage of winners in these slower races by confining one's action to entrants that have shown slightly more speed than their opponents. Naturally, the player has to be a shrewd analyst of current condition, trainers, jockeys and—as the season progresses—class. But the distance factor can be attended to by means of speed ratings. Later on, I shall discuss the computation of track variants, which modify running times or speed ratings to compensate for the effects of changes in the inherent speed of racing strips.

A survey of the foregoing information will provide you with all you need for your study of the distance factor in juvenile races. You can tighten or loosen any of the requirements, according to your own preferences and the results you achieve. During the early part of the year, before the youngsters are stretched out to six furlongs and beyond, you will find that your solution of the distance problem is almost all you have to do about handicapping the race. In these short sprints for two-year-olds, time—speed—is all-important. And time, of course, is what the player uses to decide whether any two-year-old is qualified to run the distance of its race.

Races for older horses are something else entirely. Class distinctions, current condition, weight and pace now become more important. Many experts refuse to look at speed ratings on older horses, even in connection with the distance factor. Others find the ratings convenient indicators of whether a horse can get today's distance in reasonably good time, quite apart from the effects of class, condition, pace and weight. Still others, as we shall see later, do *all* their handicapping in terms of speed.

Older Horses and Distance

In trying to decide whether an animal aged three or more is suited to the distance of his race, the most cautious players of the game often operate on the following line:

1. A horse qualifies if (a) it has won a race of this exact distance, or has finished close to the winner in respectable time and (b) the race took place this season.

Many practitioners of this theory add the further condition that the horse's good race should have been against animals not greatly inferior to those it faces today. In that way they manage to lop off obviously outclassed horses. I mention this merely to suggest that it can be done, but I ask the reader to go through the chapter on class before deciding whether to separate distance and class.

The phrase "close to the winner," as used in the above rule, usually means a finish not more than three lengths behind. Some experts prefer a finish within two lengths. Others, anxious to qualify more horses on the distance factor, ask only that the animal has run fourth or better. Still others want the horse to have come very close to winning in a cheaper race, but are lenient about its finishing position in a race of higher quality.

As to the term, "respectable time," the following speed ratings can be accepted as adequate, subject to slight variations which arise from unique conditions at the individual track:

90—Sprints for animals of handicap and stakes quality. (In weighing the distance factor in terms of speed, a sprint should be defined as any race run around no more than one turn. At some major tracks, this will include distances up to and including a mile. At others, where there is no mile chute at the head of the backstretch, the longest race run around one turn may be at six and a half or seven furlongs.)

88—High-grade allowance sprints.

85—Handicaps and stakes run around two turns. (If a race is at a mile and an eighth or longer, many experts disregard speed ratings entirely. They evaluate the horse's suitability in terms of the class and stamina it displayed in previous efforts at such distances.)

80—High-grade allowance routes, lesser allowance sprints and sprints for better claimers.

78—Cheap claiming sprints.

73—Route races for better claimers.

69—Route races for claimers valued at $10,000 or less.

A player who tosses out all horses that fail to meet those requirements is well on his way to sharing the success enjoyed by arch-conservative handicappers. He passes race after race. He frequently tosses out the eventual winner of an apparently playable race, but is so strict about other fundamentals of handicapping that he often saves his neck by eliminating the losers at later stages of the work, and passing the race altogether. If some losers qualify on the distance factor, they fail to meet his rigid requirements as to class, condition, consistency, weights, running styles, trainers or jockeys. He may get less action than he might, and far less than most players want, but a handicapper of this kind gets his kicks from winning. Action means nothing to him.

Here again, the handicapper who uses speed figures instead of ordinary *Form* speed ratings has wider latitude. But a flaw may remain. And that is the requirement that the horse's qualifying race be recent. A good race last year by no means guarantees a repeat performance this year. Injuries, illness and overwork have made many of last year's $50,000 horses into $5,000 ones long before now. Yet problems of that kind can be surmounted by a handicapper who wants to catch some of the winners that a more cautious player misses. For example:

2. A horse qualifies at today's distance if (a) it has ever finished as close as fourth, or within two lengths of a winner, in a race of today's exact distance at a major track, and (b) it has earned a respectable speed rating at the distance at some time within the past year at a major track, and (c) its record indicates that it may still be able to run well at the distance.

When handicapping horses aged four or more, the requirement of a mere close-up finish at the distance is terribly lenient. Any fully mature horse that cannot meet that requirement is undoubtedly entered at the wrong distance. For that matter, many mature horses that satisfy the rule are also at the wrong distance: a router sometimes produces sufficient steam in the stretch to finish close to the winner of a six-furlong race. But he is still a router, and hardly an ideal choice in a sprint. However, the two additional parts of the rule tend to weed out such duds. So, for that matter, does the common sense of the player. If one sees that most of the races and all of the victories listed in the past-performance record of a mature horse were at distances more than a furlong longer or shorter than today's race, one can be reasonably sure that the horse is out of its element today.

The loose requirement of a close-up finish is most helpful in handicapping lightly raced three-year-olds. Every season, scores of races are won at handsome odds by improving three-year-olds that have never won at the distance before. Their victories occur not only in claiming races but in allowance events for some of the snazzier young horses in the business. Part of the trick of catching these up-and-comers is to give them credit for even a mediocre previous race at the distance.

The notion that a horse can qualify for further attention if it logged good time at the distance within the past year could be dangerous, but need not be. For example, if the horse has declined very much in class since that ancient race, or if it has been running badly or infrequently since the race, the player has good reason to suspect that it has gone sour and therefore would disqualify it on grounds of form or class, either at this stage of the handicapping or later.

But the idea pays off at the mutuel windows in the late spring and early summer. At that time of year, a rigidly cautious player often discards an animal for failure to show a good recent race at the distance—even though it is perfectly ready to win today. It may be a nice little miler that has been campaigning at tracks where mile events are not programmed. Or it may have been resting for the winter. Its races this year may all have been at distances other than the mile. But if the horse's form has been improving (regardless of whether it has been winning or not), the trainer may be ready to crack down today.

If the approach embodied in this three-part rule is followed alertly, it can be counted on to qualify the ultimate winners of most playable races, and to disqualify a high proportion of the losers. It therefore clears the decks for concentrated study of the genuine contenders.

Older Horses at New Distances

At the beginning of each season and, to a lesser extent, throughout the remainder of the racing year, one encounters races in which three-year-olds attempt to run an altogether new distance. The safest approach is to bypass the race. Alternatively, one can handle the distance factor by methods similar to those employed in evaluating two-year-old races. Preference would go to horses with the best previous records and/or the most successful trainers and/or recent performances suggesting that the new distance might be comfortable for them.

Distance and Speed Charts

As readers of my earlier books are aware, I advocate pace handicapping, in the sense that I recommend inclusion of pace analysis in the player's methods. Some dyed-in-the-wool enthusiasts of pace and speed charts pay no attention to the distance factor, relying on the charted numbers to compensate for all unknowns. But others, whether they favor pace analyses or speed-weight formulas, may be interested in trying to profit from the distance factor. That is, they may want to experiment with the kind of pace handicapping or speed handicapping that applies pace or speed figures only to horses judged suitable to the distance of today's race.

To work in that fashion with pace or speed charts, it is highly advisable to use races that the horse has run at today's exact distance either on today's track or at a sister track on the same circuit. The only players able to profit by pace-rating races run at different tracks are the relatively few with access to sophisticated speed figures for all such tracks. Those numbers, when properly calculated (a rarity), are interchangeable from track to track and distance to distance. The handicapper without good speed figures for a large assortment of tracks is best advised to confine speed or pace analysis to performances recorded locally at today's exact distance and on days when the track was fast and the animals were producing reasonably typical running times. Races bypassed for lack of sufficient data of that kind are more than compensated for by a higher percentage of winning selections in authentically beatable races.

Naturally, more on speed and pace handicapping will appear in the appropriate chapters.

Sprinters in Route Races

Once in a while, a horse that has never run farther than six furlongs leads from wire to wire in a race at a mile and an eighth. A carefully observant player can sometimes forsee the possibility. It arises most often in route races among animals with no inclination to go to the front in the early stages. If the sprinter is the kind that has been taking the lead in its own shorter races and tiring in the stretch, if not earlier, it probably lacks the stamina to maintain the long, early lead it will enjoy today. But if it is the type that usually is fourth or fifth or sixth at the half-mile call in sprints and seldom quits in the stretch, it may be an excellent bet against today's plodders. Accustomed as it is to a much faster early pace than is characteristic in route races, it will undoubtedly take the lead immediately. If the jockey is good at rating horses to conserve their strength, and if the horse does not drop dead of surprise at being out in front so soon, it may last to the wire. You should not discard it on grounds that it fails to satisfy your distance requirements. Not, that is, unless you are sure that something else in the field has enough foot to catch the sprinter in the late stages.

Routers in Sprint Races

Every spring, last year's stakes and handicap champions begin tuning up for the season's big-money races. For many of them, the process includes entry in an allowance race at six furlongs. They usually lose. They lose because they are out for exercise and because they are unsuited to such short distances. Unless the confirmed distance runner entered in a sprint has shown pronounced early speed in its own good races, and unless its opponents in the tune-up are dismally inferior sprinters, the race is not worth a risk.

Among Thoroughbreds of less than championship quality, very much the same facts apply. An animal that wins at a mile and an eighth is odds-on to be out only for conditioning purposes any time it goes to the post in a sprint.

A Good Example

The essence of successfully opportunistic handicapping is the search for a horse whose record proclaims that today is the day. One particularly eloquent sign is the switch from unfavorable distances to the right distance. Another is a drop in class after reasonably good performances. Both occur in the following example, along with a third—an advantageous post position after a vigorous but losing performance out of a disadvantageous part of the starting gate.

Look at the records of the horses that started in the second race at Garden State on June 1, 1985. Among these three-year-olds entered to be claimed for $22,500 or $25,000, only one presents all the strengths mentioned above.

In each of his last four races, Gallant Passer has performed well before tiring. He has acted just like a horse that wants a shorter race. Today he gets it. Three races ago he ran just about as well in a higher-class claimer as at the $25,000 level. We can infer that he lost not because he was outclassed but because of distance and post position. And today, with that short run from the start to the first turn that you get when going a mile on a one-mile track, the colt draws the inside post position. He will be able to save ground and precious energy on the first turn.

Just Terrific is a sprinter unlikely to retain the lead after early duels with He's Coachable and Dedicated Hero. But He's Coachable looks a bit cheap to overcome Gallant Passer's advantages. He's probably outclassed. The same goes for Dedicated Hero. The outside post will not help the favorite, Makalite. I think that Gallant Passer should have been the betting favorite. See what you think.

2 GARDEN ST.

1 MILE
GARDEN STATE
START
FINISH

1 MILE. (1.35) CLAIMING. Purse $12,500. 3-year-olds. Weight, 121 lbs. Non-winners of two races at a mile or over since April 21 allowed 3 lbs.; one such race since then, 6 lbs. Claiming price $25,000; if for $22,500, 2 lbs. (Races where entered for $20,000 or less not considered.)

Gallant Passer

B. c. 3, by Fast Passer—Prevail, by Chop Chop
Own.—Asbell J — $25,000 — Br.—Howard F A (Va) — Tr.—Campo Salvatore — 115
Lifetime 18 3 6 2 $32,985 — 1985 9 2 2 2 $22,600 — 1984 9 1 4 0 $10,385

15May85- 7GS fst 170 :46⅕ 1:11⅕ 1:41⅘ Clm 25000 6 6 45 44½ 1½ 2hd Rocco J b 115 3.20 90-12 Major Setback 115hd Gallant Passer 115¹ Steal Steel118½ Gamely 10
27Apr85- 9GS fst 170 :47⅕ 1:12⅕ 1:42⅘ Clm 25000 2 3 52½ 32½ 3½ 33 Antley C W b 118 *2.00 82-15 Le Wigg 115½ Count Upwards 1132½ Gallant Passer 1181½ Wide 6
19Apr85- 9GS fst 170 :45⅘ 1:11⅗ 1:43⅕ Clm 32000 6 3 2hd 1½ 1hd 32 Lloyd J S b 116 3.90 — — Rand Bill 1161¾ Makalite 114nk Gallant Passer 1163½ Drifted out 6
2Apr85- 1GS fst 1¹⁄₁₆ :47⅘ 1:12⅕ 1:45 Clm 25000 3 1 11 2hd 21 22 Lloyd J S b 118 4.20 — — Ron Rivers 115² Gallant Passer 118² Makalite 115³ Gamely 7
23Mar85- 3Key sly 170 :47 1:12⅗ 1:45⅕ Clm 25000 7 2 2hd 1hd 1½ 1¾ Lloyd J S b 116 9.50 74-25 Gallant Passer 116¾ Say Gems 1181½ Son Of Pappa 1181½ Driving 7
22Feb85- 6Key fst 6f :22⅕ :45⅘ 1:11⅕ Clm 25000 5 8 62¾ 44 66½ 55½ Nied J Jr b 118 *1.90 80-21 Say Gems 116nk Satisfactory 1122½ Irv's Choice 1122½ No factor 9
18Feb85- 7Lrl fst 6f :22⅕ :45⅘ 1:12⅕ Alw 10000 7 4 45½ 68¾ 78 57¾ Lloyd J S b 115 13.70 74-20 RollDemBones1151¾AlongCameJones1143¾Ray'sBianchi115¾ Tired 8
24Jan85- 8Lrl fst 1 :46⅕ 1:11⅗ 1:37⅗ Alw 9500 6 1 1½ 3½ 21 57 Lloyd J S b 114 3.10 77-21 Little Bold John 1143½ Choix 117¾ Dubious Hands 114¹ Tired 8
14Jan85- 5Key fst 7f :22⅘ :45⅗ 1:23⅗ Clm 25000 2 2 1hd 2hd 1hd 1½ Antley C W b 119 3.70 89-19 GallantPasser119½JumpingJackFlsh112¾MkingWves1141¼ Driving 7
LATEST WORKOUTS May 30 GS 4f fst :48⅖ h May 11 GS 4f fst :49 b May 8 GS 4f fst :49 b Apr 17 GS 4f fst :48 h

Just Terrific

B. c. 3, by What Luck—Robin's Sprite, by First Landing
Own.—Delloso Betty A — $25,000 — Br.—Frasca & Zineman (Ky) — Tr.—Delloso Anthony J — 115
Lifetime 9 1 0 1 $6,910 — 1985 7 1 0 0 $5,700 — 1984 2 M 0 1 $1,210

24May85- 7Pim fst 6f :23⅕ :46⅕ 1:11⅕ Clm 25000 2 3 3½ 43 56½ 79¾ Maeda T b 119 3.10 80-13 DooleyDncer1142½StudentofDnce1091¼FullofFortun109nk Faltered 7
8May85- 8Pim fst 6f :23⅕ :46⅕ 1:11⅗ Alw 11000 3 6 31½ 33½ 44½ 64½ Maeda T b 114 22.00 83-18 Head Out 1152½ Don's Choice 114¾ Mr. V. Penny 115no Bore out 8
26Apr85- 3Pim fst 6f :23⅕ :46⅕ 1:11⅘ 3↑Md 30000 4 3 11 15 15 12 Maeda T b 112 *2.30 87-16 Just Terrific 112² Racing Ransom1123½MaidInMusic112nk Driving 8
20Apr85- 5Pim fst 6f :23⅕ :46⅗ 1:11⅕ 3↑Md Sp Wt 5 1 44 31 33½ 45¾ Maeda T b 112 22.20 84-12 Spring Laureate 1143½ Cyaneman 112nk Cywan 115² In close 12
8Apr85- 5Pim fst 6f :23 :46 1:11⅕ 3↑Md Sp Wt 7 1 32 34 46½ 411 Maeda T b 113 26.00 79-18 Alex'sGame115½SpringLaureate1144½RcingRnsom1166 Weakened 12
30Mar85- 6Pim sly 6f :23⅘ :47⅖ 1:12⅖ 3↑Md Sp Wt 5 2 2½ 44½ 56½ 79¾ Maeda T 112 8.40 74-16 Master Paul H. 1123¾ Nezami 114¾ Financial Minister 1121½ Tired 9
20Mar85- 5Pim fst 6f :23 :46⅗ 1:13⅖ 3↑Md Sp Wt 8 3 33 34 55½ 77½ Maeda T 112 6.80 71-22 Put Out The Fire 107¾LittleShecky1121½McCreaBridge122³ Tired 11
30Dec84- 7Aqu fst 6f ⊡:23 :46⅘ 1:11⅖ Md Sp Wt 7 5 52½ 76½ 79½ 69 Verge M E 118 25.30 78-15 IAmTheGm1184FirstConqust1131½HistoryRsponds118½ No mishap 11
18Dec84- 3Med fst 6f :23⅕ :47⅕ 1:12⅕ Md Sp Wt 6 3 51¾ 42½ 36 39 Melendez J D 118 1.70 72-21 My Rex 118⁷ Gold Quartz 118² Just Terrific 118⁵ No rally 7
LATEST WORKOUTS May 16 Pim 4f fst :48⅖ h May 4 Pim 3f fst :37⅗ b ●Apr 6 Pim 4f fst :47⅖ hg

He's Coachable

Ch. g. 3, by Roaring Spring—Aunt Lyd, by Limit To Reason
Own.—Golden Hill Stable — $25,000 — Br.—Grimsley C R (Va) — Tr.—Fallon Martin L — 115
Lifetime 15 3 2 4 $22,830 — 1985 7 1 2 2 $12,955 — 1984 8 2 0 2 $9,875

22May85- 7GS fst 6f :21⅘ :44⅗ 1:10 Clm 22500 3 6 34 35 34½ 33¾ Pizzo P S b 113 9.60 88-23 FirstAmbition1153¾RiverboatHero115noHe'sCoachble113⁴ Evenly 8
15May85- 7GS fst 170 :46⅕ 1:11⅕ 1:41⅘ Clm 25000 4 1 12 1½ 55½ 69 Pizzo P S b 115 4.30 81-12 Major Setback 115hd Gallant Passer 115¹ Steal Steel 118½ Tired 10
2May85- 3GS gd 6f :22⅖ :45⅗ 1:10⅗ Clm 22500 2 4 32 43½ 25 25½ Pizzo P S b 113 5.20 83-19 VibleProposition1155½H'sCochbl1132½JohnOnSix115⁵ Bobbled st. 5
5Apr85- 3GS fst 1¹⁄₁₆ :47⅗ 1:12 1:45⅖ Clm 16000 6 1 12 13½ 13 16 Gomez M A b 115 3.60 — — He's Coachable 115⁶EmergingGrowth118²Tigershark115¾ Driving 6
18Mar85- 6Key fst 6f :22⅗ :46⅗ 1:12⅘ Clm 14000 7 1 31½ 2hd 21 21 Pizzo P S b 116 3.60 76-24 NowW'vGotHm116¹H'sCochbl116noSonOfDplmt120³ Good effort 8
18Feb85- 6Key fst 170 :47⅖ 1:12⅖ 1:43⅕ Clm 14000 1 5 42 54½ 59 510¾ Pizzo P S b 110 5.40 73-22 MornngCsnv108nkBstdBdgt110⁷Hthrs'Myrrh114³ Broke in tangle 7
8Jan85- 5Key fst 170 :47⅗ 1:14⅗ 1:46⅗ Clm c-11000 5 10 10¹⁶ 61³ 410 313½ Black A S b 116 *.80 53-31 Road Atlas11612½Nisano116¹He'sCoachable116¾ Fractious pre-st. 10
26Dec84- 6Key fst 6f :22⅖ :46⅕ 1:12⅘ Clm 11000 8 4 35 44½ 37 34½ Black A S b 120 *2.60 74-25 Synchronize 1171¼ Terranian 1173¼ He's Coachable1203¾ Mild bid 10
15Dec84- 2Key fst 6½f :23⅗ :47⅗ 1:20⅘ Clm 11000 8 4 41 4nk 1½ 13 Black A S b 117 16.10 69-26 He's Coachable 117³ Big Upset 1162½ Sir Michael 120nk Driving 12
LATEST WORKOUTS May 12 GS 4f fst :53⅖ b Apr 29 GS 4f fst :50 b Apr 24 GS 6f fst 1:17 b Apr 19 GS 4f fst :50 b

Say Gems
Ch. c. 3, by Sadair—Jewel Talk, by Speak John
$25,000 Br.—Callaway V J (NMex)
Tr.—Kirk Jeffrey C
115
Lifetime 11 2 2 0 $18,220
1985 10 2 2 0 $18,010
1984 1 M 0 0 $210
Own.—Scarlett Farms

22May85- 7GS fst 6f :21⅘ :44⅗ 1:10 Clm 25000 6 4 78½ 69 49½ 47¾ Alligood M A b 115 *2.10 84-23 FirstAmbition1153¾RiverbotHero115noHe'sCochbl1134 No menace 8
4May85- 7GS fst 5f :21⅘ :45⅖ :58⅖ Alw 14000 2 6 613 612 45 42½ Alligood M A b 114 26.30 88-16 DARIBustr1141StrikUp120noDncingInThAr1141½ Broke sluggishly 7
24Apr85- 3GS fst 1 :47⅖ 1:12⅕ 1:38⅖ Clm c-20000 2 1 2hd 32 55 68 Vigliotti M J b 115 *1.80 75-13 Parma John 115no Major Setback 115no Lanier Place 1154½ Tired 7
12Apr85- 4GS fst 1 1/16 :47⅕ 1:12⅕ 1:44⅖ Clm 20000 4 2 2hd 1hd 1½ 22 Vigliotti M J b 115 6.30 — — Le Wigg 1152 Say Gems 115nk Count Upwards 1181 Game try 9
2Apr85- 1GS fst 1 1/16 :47⅖ 1:12⅕ 1:45 Clm 25000 5 3 53 66¼ 66¼ 58 Vigliotti M J b 115 4.80 — — Ron Rivers 1152 Gallant Passer 1182 Makalite 1153 Tired 7
23Mar85- 3Key sly 170 :47 1:12⅗ 1:45⅕ Clm 25000 4 3 44 44½ 43 2¾ Vigliotti M J b 118 3.30 73-25 Gallant Passer 116¾ Say Gems 1181½ Son Of Pappa 1181½ Rallied 7
13Mar85- 5Key fst 170 :47 1:12⅗ 1:43⅗ Clm 25000 1 5 44½ 68 57½ 410¼ Vigliotti M J b 120 *1.60 72-26 Henry John 1124 JupiterAccord1165SkinnyGeorge1181¼ No factor 6
22Feb85- 6Key fst 6f :22⅕ :45⅘ 1:11⅕ Clm 25000 1 6 31 54 32 1nk Vigliotti M J b 116 9.60 85-21 Say Gems 116nk Satisfactory 1122½ Irv's Choice 1122½ Driving 9
1Feb85- 1Key sly 6f :22⅗ :47⅕ 1:13⅖ Md 16000 8 2 1½ 11 15 18½ Vigliotti M J b 122 5.40 74-37 SayGems1228½SonOfDiplomat111noDedictedHero120½ Ridden out 12
LATEST WORKOUTS May 30 GS 4f fst :49⅘ b May 18 GS 4f sly :50 b Apr 9 GS 4f fst :50⅖ b

Command Break
Dk. b. or br. g. 3, by Dust Commander—Commerical Break, by Stevward
$22,500 Br.—Hill 'N' Dale Farms (Ont-C)
Tr.—Gross Mel W
113
Lifetime 11 1 3 1 $14,512
1985 9 1 3 1 $13,780
1984 2 M 0 0 $732
Own.—Hunt N B

22May85- 4GS fst 1 1/16 :47⅕ 1:12⅘ 1:45⅗ 3↑Md 20000 7 5 34 32 13 16¾ Antley C W b 113 *1.70 80-23 CommandBreak1136¾TylerFlls113nkMyLittleGllnt1113 Ridden out 9
15May85- 5GS fst 1 :47 1:11⅗ 1:37 3↑Md 35000 7 4 57 66½ 69½ 615½ Antley C W b 112 2.70 74-12 Waltzing Bandit 113½ Gate Hustler 1148 Petillo 1124 No factor 8
6May85- 1GS fst 1 :47 1:12⅕ 1:38⅖ 3↑Md 28000 1 2 32 21 2½ 2nk Antley C W b 112 *2.10 83-13 StelSteel114nkCommndBrek1122½GteHustlr11412 Brushed,drifted 7
26Apr85- 2Aqu fst 1⅛ :48⅘ 1:14⅕ 1:54 3↑Md 25000 8 4 52½ 54½ 53 42½ Moore D N5 b 107 *2.80 62-23 Handsomely120noBuckyBdger103noTillitfreezesover1102½ Late bid 12
3Apr85- 4Aqu fst 7f :22 :45⅘ 1:24⅖ 3↑Md 25000 1 11 118 87½ 52 21¼ Moore D N5 b 107 5.40 78-18 NwAdvntur1121¼CommndBrk107noNctoMtYo1052½ Sluggish early 13
22Mar85- 2Aqu fst 6f :23⅕ :47⅖ 1:14 Md 22500 7 3 42 52¾ 21½ 2nk Migliore R b 120 4.40 71-27 Patato 115nk Command Break 1201½ Vo Jangles 122½ Just missed 14
1Mar85- 2Aqu fst 6f ⊡:22⅘ :46⅖ 1:13⅖ Md 25000 2 7 88½ 812 57 46 Migliore R b 122 5.80 71-25 Blue Flack 1183 Sparkling State 1172¼ Patato 115¾ Sluggishly 11
18Jan85- 2Aqu fst 1 1/16 ⊡:48⅘ 1:14⅖ 1:48⅕ Md 30000 9 2 21½ 22 26 313½ Cordero A Jr b 118 *2.80 56-21 Uncompromsng11811½Flt'sHonr1221¾CmmndBrk118hd Weakened 9
7Jan85- 4Aqu fst 6f ⊡:23 :47⅖ 1:14⅕ Md 35000 2 12 61¾ 65 96¼ 97¼ Miceli M b 122 4.00 66-27 Soaring Romeo 118¾ Black Elk 118hd Rich Gift 1222¼ No factor 12
LATEST WORKOUTS May 4 GS 3f gd :37 b Apr 13 Bel tr.t 4f fst :49⅕ b

Dedicated Hero
Dk. b. or br. g. 3, by True Knight—Dronosian, by Drone
$25,000 Br.—Payson Virginia Kraft (Ky)
Tr.—Lopez Raimundo D Jr
115
Lifetime 13 2 4 1 $18,225
1985 8 2 3 1 $15,935
1984 5 M 1 0 $2,290
Own.—Garcia L O

26Apr85- 9GS fst 1 :46⅘ 1:11⅘ 1:38⅘ Clm 16000 6 2 3nk 11 13 13½ Alligood M A 115 15.90 81-14 Dedicated Hero 1153½ Viva Voce 1153 Tigershark 1151 Drifted in, 11
29Mar85- 3Key fst 6½f :22⅗ :45⅘ 1:18⅘ Clm 14000 4 2 41 43½ 33½ 21 Alligood M A 120 7.60 78-16 King Louie 1161 Dedicated Hero1202OntheMoneyRed1162 Rallied 7
19Mar85- 6Key fst 6f :22 :45⅘ 1:11 Clm 18000 1 5 42¾ 77¼ 66 510½ Pagan N 120 35.10 75-19 Satisfactory 1161 Josco Lad 1181½ Dashing Cut 1181 No factor 8
10Mar85- 4Key fst 6f :23 :46⅗ 1:13 Md 16000 8 1 1½ 12 12½ 1nk Pagan N 122 4.00 76-19 Dedicated Hero 122nk Subsidized 1221¼SprooseGoose1221 Driving 11
3Mar85- 4Key fst 6f :22⅘ :46⅕ 1:12⅖ Md 16000 10 3 31½ 46 58½ 57 Pagah N 122 *2.20 72-20 A. A. Special Kind 1223½ Dr.Rubinson117½DSpaceGame1222 Tired 11
3Mar85-Placed fourth through disqualification
17Feb85- 9Key fst 6½f :22⅗ :46⅕ 1:20 Md 16000 7 1 2½ 31 22 21½ Pagan N 122 4.40 71-23 RiverbotHero1221½DedictedHero1222PrincofthMint122nk 2nd best 12
1Feb85- 1Key sly 6f :22⅗ :47⅕ 1:13⅖ Md 15000 5 7 31 33½ 57½ 38½ Pagan N 120 *2.60 65-37 SayGems1228½SonOfDiplomat111noDedicatedHero120½ Weakened 12
14Jan85- 4Key fst 6f :22⅖ :46 1:12⅕ Md 15000 11 1 2½ 11 1½ 22 Pagan N 118 8.00 78-19 WhizzrooToo1202DedictedHero1183DHereditryRulr1165 Game try 12
22Dec84- 1Key my 6½f :23⅕ :47⅕ 1:21⅗ Md 15000 5 8 42½ 56½ 66 41½ Santiago J M 120 8.60 63-33 Dog'sMystcSd120hdDynstcChrmr120noSproosGs1181½ Closed gap 9
LATEST WORKOUTS May 28 Atl 7f fst 1:27 h Apr 19 Atl 6f fst 1:16⅗ b

Makalite — Own.—3 G's Stable

Ch. c. 3, by Tromos—Kapakahi, by Star Envoy — **$25,000** Br.—A I B A Inc Thoroughbreds & Carl (Cal) — Tr.—Henry Royston A — **115**

Lifetime 27 3 4 6 $38,825 — 1985 10 1 2 1 $17,060 — 1984 17 2 2 5 $21,765

16May85- 7GS	fst	1	:46⅗	1:11⅘	1:37⅘	Clm 35000	9	2	2^{2}	2½	1½	4^{1}	Thomas D B	b 112	10.00	87–10	GoldBombay116¾JumpingJackFlsh119^{hd}JettRink116^{hd}	Weakened	9
9May85- 3GS	fst	6f	:22	:44⅗	1:09⅗	Clm 35000	4	6	$7^{6\frac{1}{2}}$	6^{8}	5^{10}	$4^{11\frac{3}{4}}$	Vigliotti M J	b 112	11.10	83–11	SportsMdicin116$^{4\frac{1}{2}}$CoolNwYorkr112$^{6\frac{1}{2}}$PocktBndit116¾	Raced wide	7
27Apr85- 9GS	fst	1^{70}	:47⅕	1:12⅕	1:42⅘	Clm c-25000	1	1	2½	$6^{6\frac{1}{4}}$	5^{4}	$4^{4\frac{1}{2}}$	HampshireJFJr	b 115	3.40	80–15	Le Wigg 115½ Count Upwards 113$^{2\frac{1}{2}}$GallantPasser118$^{1\frac{1}{2}}$	No threat	6
19Apr85- 9GS	fst	1^{70}	:45⅘	1:11⅗	1:43⅕	Clm 28000	2	5	$4^{7\frac{1}{4}}$	4^{4}	3^{2}	$2^{1\frac{3}{4}}$	HampshireJFJr	b 114	2.60	— —	Rand Bill 116$^{1\frac{3}{4}}$ Makalite 114^{nk} Gallant Passer 116$^{3\frac{1}{2}}$	Rallied	6
2Apr85- 1GS	fst	$1\frac{1}{16}$	:47⅖	1:12⅕	1:45	Clm 25000	1	4	$4^{2\frac{1}{2}}$	$4^{3\frac{1}{2}}$	3^{4}	3^{4}	HampshireJFJr	b 115	*2.30	— —	Ron Rivers 115^{2} Gallant Passer 118^{2} Makalite 115^{3}	Lacked room	7
9Mar85- 7Key	fst	1^{70}	:46⅕	1:11⅗	1:42⅗	Alw 11500	5	3	3^{3}	$3^{1\frac{1}{2}}$	2^{hd}	1^{1}	HampshireJFJr	b 114	4.10	87–19	Makalite 114^{1} Le Wigg 113$^{2\frac{1}{2}}$ Son Of Pappa 112^{2}	Driving	8
1Mar85- 6Key	fst	1^{70}	:47⅗	1:11⅘	1:43	Alw 11500	1	5	4^{2}	4^{6}	4^{6}	$4^{3\frac{3}{4}}$	Nied D	117	7.60	81–19	Eloniche 117$^{2\frac{3}{4}}$ Le Wigg 113no Foxy Bud 112^{1}	Lacked fin. bid	7
17Feb85- 6Key	fst	6f	:22⅖	:46⅖	1:13⅗	Clm 18000	1	8	$8^{6\frac{3}{4}}$	$8^{5\frac{1}{2}}$	$7^{2\frac{1}{2}}$	2^{1}	Nied D	116	6.30	73–23	Emerging Growth 116^{1} Makalite 116$^{1\frac{1}{4}}$ Legsure 116^{1}	Rallied	8
23Jan85- 6Key	fst	6½f	:22⅘	:45⅗	1:18⅕	Clm 22500	7	7	$6^{3\frac{3}{4}}$	$8^{7\frac{1}{2}}$	$8^{6\frac{3}{4}}$	5^{7}	Nied D	113	13.50	75–21	TillRomBurns111½DungrvinPrincss113^{2}SkinnyGorg113½	No factor	8

LATEST WORKOUTS May 30 GS 4f fst :51⅕ b — May 25 GS 4f fst :50 b — Apr 12 GS 5f fst 1:00⅗ h

Infinite Domain — Own.—Daw & Russo

B. c. 3, by Nonparrell—Royal Ties. by Distinctive — **$22,500** Br.—Ocala Stud Farm & O'Farrell & Wiest (Fla) — Tr.—Camac Robert W — **116**

Lifetime 14 2 3 3 $19,795 — 1985 9 2 3 1 $18,170 — 1984 5 M 0 2 $1,625

25May85- 3GS	fst	1^{70}	:47⅕	1:12⅖	1:43⅖	Clm 22500	5	5	5^{4}	$4^{2\frac{1}{2}}$	1½	1½	Lovato F	b 113	9.30	82–12	Infinite Domain 113½ Dudley Eppel 113$^{1\frac{1}{2}}$ Steal Steel118^{7}	Driving	6
10May85- 3GS	fst	1^{70}	:47	1:12	1:43	3↑ Md 20000	5	5	$4^{2\frac{3}{4}}$	3^{1}	2½	2^{nk}	Lovato F	b 113	3.00	84–09	[D]WltnBndt106^{nk}InfntDmn113$^{2\frac{3}{4}}$NblClnsmn123^{no}	Jstld, forced out	7
10May85-Placed first through disqualification																			
27Apr85- 1GS	fst	1	:47⅗	1:13⅖	1:38⅘	3↑ Md 18000	4	5	$5^{2\frac{3}{4}}$	1^{2}	1^{1}	$2^{2\frac{1}{2}}$	Lovato F	b 112	2.40	78–15	DudlyEppl114$^{2\frac{1}{2}}$InfinitDomn112$^{5\frac{1}{4}}$JohnnyJffrson122$^{8\frac{1}{2}}$	Best of rest	11
17Apr85- 9GS	fst	1^{70}	:46⅗	1:11⅘	1:42⅖	3↑ Md 18000	8	9	9^{11}	3^{8}	$3^{7\frac{1}{2}}$	3^{6}	Lovato F	b 112	9.10	— —	Ziggy'sVision114^{6}WhatASlip113^{hd}InfiniteDomain112^{8}	Evenly late	11
15Mar85- 2Key	fst	1^{70}	:47	1:14	1:45⅘	Md 16000	6	8	8^{15}	9^{18}	8^{16}	$8^{18\frac{1}{4}}$	Lovato F	b 122	*2.10	53–26	Granbury 122$^{1\frac{1}{4}}$ Landing Creek 118^{5} Pahokee 122½	Outrun	10
4Mar85- 5Key	fst	1^{70}	:47⅗	1:13⅕	1:44⅘	Md 20000	5	5	4^{7}	4^{6}	$6^{9\frac{1}{2}}$	$6^{10\frac{3}{4}}$	Lovato F	b 118	*1.20	65–25	RockinRodny122$^{2\frac{1}{2}}$Ziggy'sVision118^{4}PrincofthMint122¾	No factor	7
22Feb85- 1Key	fst	1^{70}	:47⅖	1:12⅘	1:44⅕	Md 16000	12	3	3½	$3^{1\frac{1}{2}}$	2^{1}	2¾	HampshireJFJr	b 122	7.20	78–21	ToughCruise118¾InfiniteDomin122^{6}OverdueExpress122$^{1\frac{1}{2}}$	Gamely	12
1Feb85- 1Key	sly	6f	:22⅗	:47⅕	1:13⅖	Md 16000	3	9	$9^{5\frac{1}{4}}$	$10^{8\frac{1}{4}}$	$7^{9\frac{1}{2}}$	4^{9}	Lovato F	122	7.20	65–37	Say Gems 122$^{8\frac{1}{2}}$SonOfDiplomat111^{no}DedicatedHero120½	Steadied	12
1Jan85- 1Key	fst	7f	:22⅕	:45⅖	1:25⅕	Md 15000	6	10	9^{11}	$8^{9\frac{3}{4}}$	4^{8}	$2^{10\frac{1}{2}}$	Lovato F	b 119	9.30	70–24	Foxy Bud 115$^{10\frac{1}{2}}$ Infinite Domain 119$^{1\frac{1}{4}}$RiverBattle119¾	Game try	12

LATEST WORKOUTS May 20 GS 5f fst 1:01 h — May 8 GS 3f fst :37 b — Apr 16 GS 3f fst :37 b — Apr 9 GS 4f fst :49 b

SECOND RACE 1 MILE. (1.35) CLAIMING. Purse $12,500. 3-year-olds. Weight, 121 lbs. Non-winners of two races at a mile or over since April 21 allowed 3 lbs.; one such race since then, 6 lbs. Claiming price $25,000; if for $22,500, 2 lbs. (Races where entered for $20,000 or less not considered.)

Garden State

JUNE 1, 1985

Value of race $12,500; value to winner $7,500; second $2,500; third $1,375; fourth $750; fifth $375. Mutuel pool $59,389.
Exacta Pool $59,465.

Last Raced	Horse	Eqt.	A.	Wt	PP	St	¼	½	¾	Str	Fin	Jockey	Cl'g Pr	Odds $1
15May85 7GS2	Gallant Passer	b	3	115	1	4	3hd	21	24	24	1½	Nied J Jr	25000	2.30
22May85 7GS3	He's Coachable	b	3	115	3	2	11½	14	11	11	28	Pizzo P S	25000	7.90
26Apr85 9GS1	Dedicated Hero		3	115	6	1	43	41½	33	33¼	3no	Alligood M A	25000	10.00
22May85 7GS4	Say Gems	b	3	115	4	7	64	62	4½	52	4hd	Murphy D J	25000	8.20
22May85 4GS1	Command Break	b	3	113	5	8	8	8	5hd	4hd	53	Miceli M	22500	10.70
25May85 3GS1	Infinite Domain	b	3	116	8	6	7½	73	8	61	62	Lovato F	22500	7.20
16May85 7GS4	Makalite	b	3	115	7	5	5hd	5½	64	74	78	Thomas D B	25000	2.10
24May85 7Pim7	Just Terrific	b	3	115	2	3	22	3hd	7½	8	8	Thornburg B	25000	12.50

OFF AT 8:24 Start good, Won driving. Time, :23, :46½, 1:11½, 1:38% Track fast.

$2 Mutuel Prices:			
1—GALLANT PASSER	6.60	3.40	2.80
3—HE'S COACHABLE		6.20	4.60
6—DEDICATED HERO			7.60

$2 EXACTA 1-3 PAID $42.20.

B. c, by Fast Passer—Prevail, by Chop Chop. Trainer Campo Salvatore. Bred by Howard F A (Va).

GALLANT PASSER closed to the pace, wore down HE'S COACHABLE outside in a long drive under strong handling. The latter opened a clear margin on the backstretch and gave way stubbornly in the drive. DEDICATED HERO never far back outside, lacked the needed closing bid while drifting in through the lane. SAY GEMS was no factor inside. MAKALITE was wide. JUST TERRIFIC tired steadily.

Owners— 1, Asbell J; 2, Golden Hill Stable; 3, Garcia L O; 4, Scarlett Farms; 5, Hunt N B; 6, Daw & Russo; 7, 3 G's Stable; 8, Delloso Betty A.

Trainers— 1, Campo Salvatore; 2, Fallon Martin L; 3, Lopez Raimundo D Jr; 4, Kirk Jeffrey C; 5, Gross Mel W; 6, Camac Robert W; 7, Henry Royston A; 8, Delloso Anthony J.

9

THE CONDITION
FACTOR

Of all handicapping problems, none is more challenging than the riddle of condition—the form or fitness or sharpness or readiness of Thoroughbreds. In a representative field of nine horses, three or four may be in such dull form that even a novice can see the signs in their records. But the other entrants are likely to be a puzzlement.

Is the class horse in good enough shape to stand off its sharper, cheaper rivals? Can last week's victor do it again, or did the winning effort blunt its edge? Should one expect improvement from the animal that has been running closer and closer to the pace, or is it past the peak of its form cycle? Can Trainer Doe's gelding return from its six-week layoff and get the job done on workouts alone? Will the speed horse from Santa Anita show its California form in this, its first Maryland race?

The process of attempting to answer such questions is indispensable to success at the track. Knowledge of form prevents the astute player from betting on certain false favorites whose recent good races fool the rest of the crowd. The same knowledge enables him to back animals that win at long prices after apparently poor recent races. Yet, no matter how astute he may be, the subtle complications of the condition factor continue to challenge his best efforts. For every bet he loses through racing luck or a misjudged ride or an error in evaluating the class of a horse, he can expect to lose two because of surprises in the form department.

Most of these surprises derive from the very nature of the Thoroughbred. Contrary to the wishes of every loser, horses are not machines. They are highly sensitive beings, very much alive. Each is an individual, responsive in its own special way to changes in the weather, delays in feeding or watering, the moods of its handlers, the tensions of other horses, the commotion of the racetrack audience, the discomfort of an aching joint or muscle, the sight, sound or impact of the whip.

A horse's record may proclaim him the class of his field and sharp as a knife. He may breeze through his last pre-race workout in smashing time, without drawing a deep breath. He may eat everything in sight. His coat may shine with the deep gloss of health. But he may take it into his head not to race. His reluctance may be so evident in the paddock and walking ring that sophisticated players immediately cancel any plans they may have had to bet on him. Or his mood may sour when he steps on a sandwich wrapper while trotting to the post, or when one of the assistant starters grabs him too unceremoniously, or when an adjoining horse brushes or bumps him.

Or he may go the post as spry as can be, and run his race, and be beaten to the wire by a crippled old hide whose chronic disabilities vanish for a minute or two in the warmth of the afternoon and the heat of competition.

Hidden Form

Other reversals of form are more apparent than real. They have less to do with the nature of the Thoroughbred than with the nature of man. From time immemorial, most trainers have regarded it as their sacred duty to conceal or obscure the improving form of a horse. In the old days, when the sport was unsupervised, the object was exclusively to fool everybody and collect big odds. Nowadays, when racing is relatively well policed and detailed past-performance records are published for all to see, trainers have more trouble fooling the experts, but most of them continue to try. Moreover, the game has developed in such a way as to perpetuate the ancient practice of darkening a horse's form.

The demand for horseflesh with which to fill nine races a day is so urgent that only the most aristocratic and/or affluent stables are allowed to condition their animals carefully. All the others are expected to race the livestock as often as possible. This means entering unready horses. Or, as the saying goes, "racing a horse into shape."

The trainer does not live who has not been called into the racing secretary's office for a favor. "I need to fill the fourth race day after tomorrow," goes the request. "How about helping me and putting your filly in there?"

Stable space is hard to get. The uncooperative barn may find itself without house room at next year's meeting. So the typical response from the trainer is, "Sure! Glad to oblige! Any time!"

A less typical answer: "She isn't ready for a race. Needs a few more workouts. But if you say so, I'll enter her and let her work out in public!"

A veteran trainer comments, "Of course we darken a horse's form. How can we help it? How can a horse fail to look bad when it's not in condition to look good? Two or three bad races and it begins to improve, which is when you have to start worrying. You've paid fifteen grand for the horse and nursed the soreness out of it and you're just beginning to run it into good condition and—bam!—some guy claims it away from you before it's paid for all the time and effort and fees and food you've invested. You've got to try to protect yourself against that, while waiting for it to get in shape to steal a purse.

"If the horse has a pretty fair reputation around the track, you have no choice but to run it over its head—at the wrong distances and at higher claiming prices than anyone in his right mind would pay. And you put stumblebum riders up, who can't handle the horse. And it loses so bad that a lot of people begin to believe you when you cry that something is wrong with it.

"Like as not, the horse is your main meal ticket," he continues. "When it wins, you want it to win at a price. The best way to build the price is to enter it against cheap ones of its own class *before* it is ready to win. Every time you do that, you take an awful chance on having it claimed. But let's say you have the guts to try. You tell the boy not to punish the horse because you've got a better spot picked out for later on. So he lets it pretty much alone and it finishes like sixth. Sure as God made little green mushmelons, half the wise guys in the park notice that the horse picked up five lengths in the backstretch before running into a blind switch on the turn. When next week comes, the horse goes off at 5 to 1 instead of the 20 you've been looking for. Don't let anyone tell you that this is an easy business."

Efforts to inflate the mutuel odds by hiding a horse's improving condition are attributed mainly to smaller stables. But, as I have indicated before, all but the most exclusive barns race their animals into shape. This practice, and the maneuvering whereby trainers seek to protect their cheaper stock from claims, are chiefly responsible for the ostensibly poor form of actually fit and ready horses.

A bad ride by a jockey carrying out the deliberately misleading orders of the trainer sometimes contributes to the build-up, making the horse look worse than it is. But aside from occasional manipulations in trifectas, exactas and the like, no trainer in possession of his sanity knowingly defeats one of his horses when he thinks it ready to win. If it can't win, he may prefer it to lose badly. But if it can win, he strikes while the iron is hot, placing the horse in exactly the right company, at exactly the proper distance, with the best rider available. In other words, stables go all-out to win with any horse that has a chance. They go all-out because they know how briefly most horses retain top form. To enter a ready horse in the wrong kind of race is to risk never winning at all.

All this being so, the crucial task of the player is to penetrate the darkness and locate the signs of improvement tucked away in the past-performance records. At the same time, one seeks out equally significant signs of deteriorating condition among horses thought by others to be in the best of shape.

Schools of Thought

The condition factor is so strategic that many successful players devote most of their attention to it, giving only a lick and a promise to matters such as distance, class, weight, pace and jockey. It is possible to win this way, if the player really understands form and is not downright careless about horses that, good condition or not, are severely outclassed or outdistanced or overweighted, or are likely to suffer from an unfavorable pace or an inadequate ride.

Players who begin their examination of a field of Thoroughbreds by applying the distance and condition factors often find themselves with only two or three qualified contenders when the time comes to proceed to the next phase of their work. This makes life easier.

Other players, especially those who cherish class and consistency, pay no great attention to the condition factor, beyond making sure that the horses they like are not positively out of shape. They often are able to attend to this with a swift glance at the record. If they know what to encompass in the glance, they may be able to survive.

But nobody can ignore the condition factor and come close to winning this game. The more you know about Thoroughbred form and the more attention you give it, the more reliable your selections become.

The Form Cycle

Some horses hold their form for a relatively long time. Others seldom run two really good races in succession. In general, the animals capable of contending for four or five purses in a row are the better ones on the grounds, the ones able to withstand repeated hard efforts. Accordingly, they tend to be males rather than females, and younger rather than older.

Here are typical running lines to demonstrate the form cycle of a cheap seven-year-old claimer. I have omitted the post position, which is irrelevant to the present discussion. The first column represents the horse's running position at the start of each race:

8	9^4	9^5	9^8	9^8
3	4^3	4^2	4^3	6^4
4	3^3	$2^{1/2}$	$1^{1/2}$	1^2
4	4^5	4^4	3^2	$2^{1/2}$
5	4^2	5^2	6^3	7^5
8	9^3	9^4	9^7	9^{10}

The horse won its third race back and the effort knocked it off form. The improvement that foreshadowed that victory came rather suddenly in the fifth race back, when the horse picked up its feet well enough to stay fairly close to the early pace. In its next race it improved again and gained ground in the stretch. An alert player wold have noticed that improvement and would have been careful to consider the animal in its subsequent race, unless it was obviously outclassed or entered at the wrong distance, whereupon the player would have considered it in the race after that. Unless horses of this quality are absolute washouts wihtout a victory in them, they make their winning effort within a race or two of showing improved form. And, unless dropped sharply in class, they seldom run well after winning or finishing close up.

Good horses are always in the money or close to it. If properly managed they hold the winning sharpness for weeks:

4	3^2	4^2	4^3	4^4
3	3^3	2^2	2^2	2^3
2	2^1	$2^{1/2}$	$2^{1/2}$	1no
2	$2^{1/2}$	1^2	1^3	1^4
2	$1^{1/2}$	1^1	1^1	1^2
4	3^2	2^2	2^1	$2^{1/2}$
5	4^5	4^4	4^4	3^3

In its sixth race back, this horse showed that it had approached its best shape. It won three races in succession and now seems to have gone off its feed. It probably will be rested for a month or six weeks and, assuming no injury, will return to the head end of the parade after a preparatory race or two.

Standards of Form

In studying the past-performance records for clues to current condition, the player concerns himself with the following information:

1. The dates and whereabouts of the animal's most recent races and workouts.

2. **The probable effects of this activity on the animal's form.**
3. **Individual variations in the normal form cycle.**

Effective form analysis requires a series of decisions, some negative and others positive. In the negative vein, the player discards animals whose records fail to meet minimum standards. For example, a horse that has been inactive recently might be discarded for that reason alone, regardless of how promising its last race might have seemed at the time. Another horse, recently active, might be discarded because its last race was inexcusably bad, or because the race was too good and unlikely to be repeated!

The records of animals that measure up to the negative standards are then scrutinized for positive indications of winning form. In that phase of the work, the player pits his knowledge against the wiles of the trainer, who may have been trying to conceal or obscure improvement.

Having completed the paper work, you should reserve decision until you have seen the horses in the paddock and walking ring. Here you often find that the animal that looked best on paper is wretched in the flesh. The player's detective work at the paddock will occupy a later chapter. For the present, we deal with studies of past performances.

Recent Action

Every now and then someone breaks into print with the revelation that two thirds of all races are won by horses whose most recent starts occurred within two weeks of the winning effort. Or that a third of all races are won by horses that have had a race within the preceding seven days.

Innumerable systems are based on such statistics. But the facts are that the figures are not nearly so pregnant with meaning as they may seem. For instance, there is no reason why two thirds of all races should not be won by horses that have raced within two weeks: *About two thirds of all horses that go to the post have had a race within two weeks!* And, while horses that return to the races within a week of their latest start win a third of all races, *about a third of all starters have had a race within the previous seven days!*

Because of the large number of two-week and one-week horses that race every day, the probability of cashing a bet on either type of horse (without considering any other factor) is something like one in nine. Mathematically, the natural odds against victory by any random one-week or two-week horse are in the neighborhood of 8 to 1. Which are the exact natural odds against any random horse in any typical field of nine horses! In other words, the player has to know more about a horse than that it has been to the post within a week or two.

I make that assertion not to stage a display of statistical wizardry, but to emphasize a truth that recurs frequently in these pages and is, indeed, the most important truth in handicapping: No handicapping factor stands alone. The date of the last race is often important. But only when related to other vital matters.

At a recent New Jersey meeting, the largest single category of winners was the group of 25 horses that won after layoffs of a month or more. Horses in the next largest group—22—had raced exactly five days before their winning efforts! At a recent California meeting, 11 percent of the races went to horses that had not run in thirty days or more. Another 11 percent were won by horses that had run exactly seven days earlier.

You certainly should concern yourself with the dates of the horse's most recent races. But you must bear in mind that a horse that has not run in a month may often be in good enough trim to defeat something else that ran six days ago.

Recent Action in Claimers

In *The Compleat Horseplayer,* I urged rejection of any horse entered in a claiming race unless its record showed a race or workout within twelve days and, moreover, two races or two workouts, or one of each, within seventeen. Players who continue to follow that rigorous advice report success with it, but I think that the approach is outmoded. Research and personal experience demonstrate that an awful lot of horses win claiming races after being out of competition for a full month. It therefore is wasteful to eliminate an animal solely because it has not raced in four weeks.

To repeat myself, the game has changed. The present era is one of severely overworked Thoroughbreds. The trainer sensible enough to refresh a horse with a few weeks of walking and jogging is often likely to have a much improved runner when the animal resumes competitive activity.

As to published dates and distances and times of workouts, it is always reassuring to see that a claiming racer is fit enough to endure such training between starts. On the other hand, the regulations that govern publication of workout reports vary widely from place to place and time to time. The fact that a horse's record includes no recent workouts does not necessarily mean that it has been spending all its time in the barn. In Kentucky, for one current (but not necessarily permanent) example, the horse may have been training strenuously on a farm, or even on the track itself, without news of the exercise reaching the public.

In analyzing claiming races, the safest approach to the problem of recent action hews fairly close to the following guidelines:

1. A horse entered in a race at seven furlongs or less can be accepted if it has raced within the last calendar month, preferably at the present track, a sister track on the same circuit, or a nearby track of equal or superior quality.

2. A horse entered in a race longer than seven furlongs should show a race within the last calendar month plus at least two workouts in the meantime. If it has raced within the last two weeks and shows a workout since, it is acceptable. And if it has raced within the past week, it need show no workouts.

3. A horse entered in a race at seven furlongs or less can be regarded as a potential contender even if it has been unraced for 45 days, provided that it has been working at intervals of four or five days and has previously won after absences of such length.

4. To accept a horse as a possible contender even though it has not raced in the past couple of weeks is a far piece from assuming that it will win its race. Close consideration of other factors may lead to the animal's elimination. Among those factors are, of course, distance, class, pace, weights, post position, trainer, jockey and how the horse shapes up in the paddock.

The more rigid you become about demanding recent action by claiming horses, the less you need perspire over the remainder of the handicapping, and the less sure you need be of your diagnostic powers at the paddock and walking ring. For an extreme example, it is entirely possible to stay even with the game by playing no claimer that has not had a race within a week—provided one is prepared to apply other simple handicapping rules with equal inflexibility and is willing to pass up a considerable number of races.

With the development of experience and the facile ability to relate form to class, the player becomes more relaxed about recent action (in appropriate cases, that is) and catches some fat mutuel prices that might formerly have been beyond reach.

Recent Action and Better Horses

Allowance, handicap and stakes horses need not race so often to maintain their sharpness. But they seldom are acceptable choices unless they have worked out frequently, recently and with respectable clockings (see pages 160-61). What's more, if the field in an allowance race is composed entirely of authentic allowance horses, the one that has raced well within the last week or two is usually a far better risk than one that has not been to the post for three or four weeks. The most conspicuous exception would be a sparsely raced three-year-old trained by a Laz Barrera, Allen Jerkens or similar top-drawer horseman whose animals invariably have a touch of class and usually go to the well only when ready to fill the bucket.

Another prominent exception is a handicap star returning from vacation for a tune-up in allowance company. If the horse's workouts suggest an effort to win today's race, the player must treat the animal with respect, even if it has not raced in months.

The Workout Secret

Like physicians, art critics and losing horseplayers, professional horsemen manage to disagree on a monstrous variety of subjects. In moments of candor, however, the more experienced and competent among them tend to agree that a horse should be at its very best after a freshening layoff from actual competition, followed by a program of workouts.

Once in a great while, the truth of this theory is demonstrated in a claiming race. An honest old animal benefits so much from a lengthy rest that it wins at first asking and pays a mint. It rarely is possible to tell when one of these miracles is going to happen. The assumption must be that the horse will need two or three or more races before recovering its old form. An equally valid assumption is that it has gone bad and will never recover its old form. Once in a while, however, the player notices unusual signs in the workout line of a claiming sprinter about to return from a rest of six weeks or more:

1. **Frequent workouts, including at least one of real speed.**
2. **Long workouts.**

The claimer returning from a layoff is usually sent to the post after only two or three slow works. If it is a sprinter, two of the workouts are likely to be at four furlongs. The third may be at three. But if it has worked four times in the past two or three weeks and has run one or two of the exercise gallops in close to racing speed, it merits attention. And if one of its works was at the distance of today's race, or longer, the player has a problem: He must decide whether to bet on this impressively fresh animal or pass the race altogether.

Sometimes a horse of this kind runs a grand race but lacks the stamina to carry its speed all the way, because it is still short of top condition. But no less often, the workouts mean what they say. The horse is in remarkable shape for its kind. It wins. The safest procedure for the conservative player is to abstain from betting on the race. A more adventurous type might go for the freshened animal, but only if everything else in the race looked awful.

The reader no doubt noticed that I called frequent, fast, long workouts "unusual signs." In the record of a claiming horse, that is. Cheapsters rarely are asked for speed in their workouts: They do not have the speed to spare. They need it for their races. In fact, whenever a claimer of medium or lower grade ($15,000 or less) shows a swift workout since its last race, the player is entitled to believe that it may be in extraordinarily fine fettle. But, regardless of clockings, the simple presence of a claiming horse on the training track every four or five days between races is ample evidence of physical fitness.

The phrase "workouts every four or five days" recurs throughout this book and so does the synonymous expression "frequent workouts." To avoid misunderstanding, I should emphasize that a lapse of six or seven days between an animal's race and its next race or workout is entirely normal. But when workouts begin, they should almost always recur at regular, short intervals terminated, of course, by the creature's next race. In light of this, the player should wonder about the readiness of a horse that has not raced in three weeks and whose record shows only two workouts during that period. If the latest of the workouts was more than four days ago, doubts should enlarge. Mind you, I say "doubts." Some horses win decisively after going for nine or ten days without a race or workout. Moreover, their victories are predictable on grounds of class, consistency, trainer, jockey, pace and—as far as current condition is concerned—the kind of running the horse did nine or ten days ago.

If I seem to be complicating the reader's existence with these somewhat contradictory interruptions of his train of thought, I apologize. The point, I suppose, is that this is a game in which flexible thinking based on general principles gets more mileage than rigid formulas do. If you absorb the principles of this chapter, and the general guidelines that delineate those principles, you will discover sooner rather than later that you are able to modify the guidelines to suit the unique problems presented by the individual race, the individual horse and, of course, the individual track which may be the kind discussed earlier, where workout information is so scanty that the handicapper simply functions without it. While you will accept recent races and workouts as a good sign in the record of any apparently improving horse entered in a claimer, you will be disinclined to eliminate a relatively classy, consistent horse from consideration in the same race merely because it has been idle for a few days. You will, in sum, relate the factor of condition to that of class, and in due course to those of weights and pace. If you are rigid to that extent—remembering and using the interrelationships among the fundamental factors of handicapping—you will find it necessary to be rigid about little else.

I am sure that all this will become satisfactorily apparent as the reader proceeds through the book.

Workouts by Better Horses

Higher-grade animals that have not raced in recent weeks can be credited with acceptable condition only if they have been working out frequently and show one or two genuinely impressive morning trials. If an allowance or handicap runner produced good speed in a workout seven or eight or nine mornings ago, did not disgrace itself in another gallop four or five days ago, and romped through a final blowout yesterday, it deserves respect. Its last race may have been three or four weeks ago, but the player can be quite sure that the horse is sharp.

Here are standards useful in evaluating the workouts of better-grade horses, including two-year-olds. Obviously, whenever a claiming racer's works approach these standards, it bears watching:

1. At most tracks, a workout is more than satisfactory if the horse breezes (runs entirely without urging) at a rate of approximately 12 seconds for each eighth of a mile. A workout of .36 b (for "breezing") for three furlongs or .48 b for four or 1.00 b for five is a definite sign of life. So is 1.13 b for six furlongs, 1.27 b for seven and 1.42 b for the mile. To determine whether your own track is slower or faster than this, check through a few of the workout columns in your racing paper, and alter your par figures accordingly.

2. If a breezing work at .48 is acceptable, so is .47 h—the symbol for "handily." In such an effort, the exercise boy gives what the trade calls a "hand ride," rolling his knuckles along the horse's neck in the familiar pumping motion, which encourages speed. Thus, if two horses do five furlongs in 1.00, but one of them does it breezing and the other handily, the breezer gets the applause. Persons who enjoy arithmetic usually allow a one-second difference between breezes and hand rides in workouts of five furlongs or less. A second and a couple of fifths is more like it at six or seven furlongs. And three seconds is not too much at a mile or more.

3. Another second of credit is given for a workout that begins in the starting gate (g) rather than from the customary running start. Hence .47 hg is a good as .47 b.

4. If the horses work out on a training track (tr.t.) as well as on the main track (m.t.), the workout lines show it. Training tracks are usually deeper and slower, to help the animals develop stamina. Which is why tr.t .48 h is as good as m.t. .48 b.

5. A longer workout is always more significant than a shorter. It is especially significant if the horse has been away from the races for a while. After a layoff of more than a month, works of three or four furlongs are not too promising for a horse scheduled to race against animals of its own class. But if the race is at six furlongs and the horse spun off six or seven furlongs in good time within the last week or ten days, and has breezed another three or four furlongs in the past 48 hours, one can be reasonably sure that it is ready to try today. Similarly, if today's race is over a distance of ground, the laid-off animal should show a workout or two of at least a mile, and in respectable time.

6. A highly useful way to evaluate workouts is to watch the daily tabulations published by the racing papers. An animal whose exercises are impressive enough to earn comment in the bold-face type at the bottom of those columns is usually worth keeping in mind. So is any cheaper horse whose workout was within a few fifths of a second of the better animal's time on the same morning. An advantage of this method is that it compares horses with each other, rather than with par timings. Daily variations in the speed of the track can alter workout figures considerably—especially on damp mornings.

7. In the record of any horse, especially one that has been racing and working out frequently, a nice breezing effort on the day before the race is a highly reassuring sign of fitness.

8. *Daily Racing Form* has recently begun to include the abbreviation "(d)" in workout reports, signifying that "dogs"—rubber traffic cones—were positioned on the racing strip to keep working horses away from the inside rail and allow that strategic sector of the racing strip to recover from the effects of rain. A workout around the dogs is longer than one along the rail and can be credited as one second faster.

Misleading Workouts

A seldom-mentioned aspect of workouts is that they, too, may help a trainer in his hallowed effort to darken his animal's form. Among the techniques:

1. Using a heavy exercise boy, or boosting the horse's burden with lead weights in the saddle pad. If the animal totes thirty pounds or more above the weight it will carry in the race, slow time is a certainty. But the weights carried on workouts are never reported.

2. Wrapping heavy bandages on the horse's legs. Tinfoil beneath a few layers of flannel and gauze used to be a favorite. The weight slows the horse's stride, worsens its time, builds its mutuel price and develops its physique even more effectively than a heavy exercise boy can.

3. Exercising the horse late in the morning. By that time the track has been chewed up thoroughly by hooves, slowing it considerably.

4. Ordering the boy to keep the animal in the middle of the track until it has completed the turn into the homestretch. This deliberate loss of ground adds seconds to the workout time. It does not fool the official clockers, but the past-performance records have no room to explain why the workout was so slow.

5. Ordering the boy to keep as tight a hold as possible, converting a breezing work into a strangling one, a second or two slower.

6. Exercising the horse at night when the official clockers are not around. This seldom is permitted at major racing centers, but remains a favorite tactic on certain smaller circuits.

7. Working the horse not at the track itself but on a nearby private oval, away from prying eyes. If a trainer begins winning with horses whose records show neither recent races nor workouts, you may discover that, yes, he happens to have a workout strip behind his restaurant.

8. Disguising a horse so that the clockers will not recognize it. This is done by dressing the animal in blinkers and saddlecloth of a color never associated with its stable, or putting a strange exercise boy aboard, or wrapping its legs in bandages (which it has never worn and does not need). Some trainers go so far as to give a wrong name to the clockers when they inquire. Again, practices of this kind are rare in major racing, but far from unknown.

The Form of Two-Year-Olds

Every year, Billy Turner wins maiden-special-weights races with well-schooled juveniles that have never raced before. The same trick is routine—spring, summer and fall—for Jimmy Croll, LeRoy Jolley, Del Carroll, John Veitch and, for sure, someone with horses at the reader's local track. The very presence on the entry list of a two-year-old from one of these barns is enough to give pause to any knowledgeable player.

If the player approaches the distance factor in juvenile races along the lines described in the previous chapter, it can be assumed that any of the logical contenders is in condition, provided it has had a recent race and has been working out briskly at four- or five-day intervals. If it has not raced recently, or has never raced at all, the workouts not only should be frequent but one or more of them should be nice and fast—and the longer the better. A two-year-old in good condition runs as fast as it can at every opportunity. Which is why the speed of recent races or—when real speed is missing in the field—the speed of recent workouts is just about all one needs to make one's selection.

Horses for Courses

I hope you'll agree by now that the winning player prefers a horse that has been running and working out with regularity. And that he and you appreciate it if a horse of that description shows a fast, long workout. And that you hesitate to discard a horse that has been away from the races for a month or so if it is a higher-grade animal and has been working in something close to actual racing speed, preferably at distances longer than the customary three or four furlongs.

In process of noticing how frequently and how recently a horse has been racing and working out, the smart player takes care to see where all this activity has taken place. An allowance animal that ran nicely last week at Hawthorne might be credited with excellent condition if entered today at the same track. It would be a dubious bet if shipped to Laurel.

Many horses withstand long trips remarkably well. But an enormous majority require a race or two before becoming fully acclimated to a new track. Horses that recover quickly from the stress of travel and the tension caused by new surroundings are known as "good shippers." They sometimes manage to win their first race at the new oval without so much as a workout there. But only sometimes. Not often.

A rule honored with unswerving devotion by most experts is this:

1. Unless a horse outclasses its field and has worked out impressively at today's track, its last race must have taken place here or at a sister track on the same circuit.

A Buckpasser can amble into Chicago, work out a couple of times and break the world's record. And every year some European or South American horse wins the Washington, D.C., International at Laurel, outclassing America's best turf runners in spite of its long journey and its lack of local action. Similarly, Jack Van Berg manages to win with his claimers in their first attempts anywhere. And Bill Boniface can train in Maryland, yet win in New York. Again, the reason is an edge in class.

"Horses for courses," say veterans of the backstretch, nodding their heads sagely. Undoubtedly some horses run better at some tracks than at others. A speed horse does better on the pasteboard surfaces of California than on the sandy, holding tracks of the East. A come-from-behind animal does all right at Calder and is lucky to reach third money at Gulfstream. But the real meaning of "horses for courses" is that all horses, regardless of running style, are creatures of habit. Until they have become accustomed to a new track, they run below their best form.

Players who care to pursue this line of reasoning will profit from some additional color.

2. Unless it is entered at a substantially lower claiming price than usual, discard any claiming horse whose last race was at a track of lower class than today's. The only exception would be a local horse returning from a one- or two-race excursion out of town.

3. Throw out any front-running horse in its first start over a track that favors come-from-behinders. The hotshot from Del Mar is a virtual cinch to perish in its first start at Belmont Park.

4. Throw out any come-from-behind horse in its first start over a track that favors front-runners. The only unvarying exception would be a champion like Forego, an exception to everything, anyhow.

5. In choosing between two animals that have run their most recent races at today's track or on today's circuit, give preference to the one that has been working out at today's track. Horses stabled at Hialeah win races there from rivals stabled at Gulfstream. When the action moves to Gulfstream, the horses that regard the Hallandale plant as home begin beating steeds that have to be vanned from Hialeah. At Aqueduct, the most successful stables are invariably ones with stalls on the premises, rather than at nearby Belmont. Horses that work out at Aqueduct sleep there and win there.

Danger Signals

Some of the most popular selection systems are based on the concept of "last-out-in-the-money." The player eliminates any horse that did not finish first, second or third in its last race. If two or more qualify the one with the most recent race gets the bet.

To the extent that such systems take cognizance of class, pace and distance, they are not too bad. Their inescapable weakness is the uncritical assumption that a good race last week foreshadows a good race today. Life is not that simple.

A probable reason that favorites win no more than one race in three is that the crowds tend to make their bets on the basis of "last-out-in-the-money." Failing to appreciate that an animal's good recent effort may have overtaxed its powers, they make it the favorite. But it no longer is in condition to win. The player who recognizes certain signals in the past-performance lines is able to avoid a good many of these false favorites and false second choices. If one finds another bettable horse in the race, one has a good chance to collect a robust mutuel.

1. Throw out any horse that bled, ran sore or finished lame in its last race. The past-performance records in *Daily Racing Form* give that information. Sore-legged animals win every day, but rarely after a race in which the disability was noticeable enough to draw comment. The term "bled" refers to the rupture of blood vessels in the nose or throat under the strain of racing. The flow of blood hampers the animal's breathing. A horse that bled in its last race may not bleed again today, but is unlikely to have recovered from the experience sufficiently to win today.

2. Throw out any horse that lugged in or bore out in its last race. A horse unable to run in a straight line is either badly schooled or ouchy. If it has borne in or lugged out before, it can be discarded without a second thought—unless it seems to enjoy enormous class or speed advantages over the rest of its field, at which point the smart operator resolves to pass the race rather than play roulette.

3. Throw out any horse that is stepping up in class after a race it won while losing ground in a driving stretch run. A horse that has trouble beating its own kind is a poor risk if it tries to tackle superior stock in its next effort. Among cheaper claiming racers, in fact, the exertion of lasting to the finish wire against a gaining rival is usually enough to guarantee that the horse will lose its next start even if it does not go up in class. On the other hand, a horse that merely lopes to the wire, winning easily or handily, can be forgiven if something else gained on it during the stretch.

4. Throw out any cheap four-year-old or older horse that engaged in driving finishes in each of its last two races. Win or lose, a hard drive knocks the average horse off form. Two drives in succession are murder. Notable exceptions to this rule are handicap and stakes racers from leading barns, better-grade two-year-olds, lightly raced three-year-old fillies of high quality and three-year-old colts and geldings of almost any grade. Three-year-old males often come to life in the summer, putting together a series of three or more good races against increasingly tough competition.

If the player likes a six-year-old in a claiming race and wonders whether it can do well today after two successive taxing efforts, its past-performance record may show whether it has ever been able to run well in such circumstances before. In the absence of result charts or helpful *Form* comment lines, the player can assume that the horse was involved in a driving finish if it won by two lengths or less, or finished within a length or less of the winner. If it was similarly situated at the pre-stretch call or stretch call, the drive was that much more prolonged and intense.

It takes a good deal of character to eliminate an animal whose recent record is by far the most impressive in its field, and whose low odds prove that other handicappers think highly of its chances. But the bold step is worth taking—even if nothing else in the race seems worth a play. To fortify determination, and to base the decision on properly comprehensive analysis of the horse, the handicapper should look for other flaws in its credentials. Like as not, its tired body is now being moved up in class to face a caliber of opposition against which it has never been too successful. Or, if not moving up, it probably is being saddled with more weight than before, or an unfavorable post position or, for some strange reason, a non-winning rider.

The very essence of effective handicapping is, after all, the effort to avoid horses on days when their chances are not as good as others may think, and to play horses whose chances are better than the odds indicate. To shun the apparently overworked horse is basic.

5. Throw out any horse aged five or older whose best effort at today's distance occurred in its last race, unless the horse is a male that demonstrated reserve speed in that race. This is an aspect of the overwork discussed above. The cheaper the animal and the more vigorous its latest races, the greater the likelihood that an especially fast performance will exhaust the horse and dull its form for weeks. Failure to produce winning speed in its next start is sometimes facilitated by the tendency of trainers to raise a gallantly competitive runner in class or claiming price after its notably fast race.

Modern trip handicappers and other careful interpreters of equine body language pay close attention to the behavior of horses returning to their handlers in front of the stands after a race. An older horse that has been running fast and frequently and now displays the drooping head and occasional stagger of extreme fatigue can usually be written off as no candidate for a bet in its next outing. This applies whether the latest race was the animal's fastest and best effort or not.

The attempt to evaluate a race as a Thoroughbred's fastest or best is immensely difficult unless the horse has done all of its recent running at a single track. If it has shipped from place to place, the handicapper needs to decide whether a driving finish in 1.11 at one track represented more exertion than a similar finish in 1.12 at another. The ability to make dependable estimates of that kind develops with experience. Published comparisons of track speeds, including those in previous editions of this book, are quickly invalidated by changes in the resilience of racing strips caused by renovative engineering or the irreversible damage of over-use (such as clogged subterranean drainpipes). Accordingly, the printed lore becomes less trustworthy than an individual handicapper's up-to-date awareness of whether Garden State, for example, is faster this month than Philadelphia Park was last month. But given awareness of that kind, a handicapper who attempts comprehensive overviews of a horse's history can tell with some assurance that today's hard race is actually not as demanding as the one last month. Meaning that the animal may be able to perform adequately in its next start, if entered at a suitable distance, in suitable company, after a reasonable absence from competition.

As to the concept of "reserve energy," if the horse won easily or handily, or, as may happen once in a great while, covered the ground without any great exertion in the kind of race known by the chartmakers as an "even effort," it can be accepted as a possibility today. Also, it can be credited with plenty of reserve juice if it won after staying close to the pace, arriving at the stretch call first or second or within a length of the leader, and gained thereafter. Like one of the following, which are the best kind of races. I call them big wins:

$$3 \quad 3 \quad 3^4 \quad 2^1 \quad 1^1 \quad 1^2$$
$$1 \quad 2 \quad 2^1 \quad 2^{1/2} \quad 2^{1/2} \quad 1^{1/2}$$

6. Throw out any claimer whose last race was a big win more than two weeks ago. A horse able to win that powerfully is at the top of its form. The trainer naturally tries to get it another opportunity before it loses its edge. If more than two weeks elapse, the player should suspect that something has gone awry with the horse. Exceptions can be made for animals that have been working steadily while awaiting today's race. But if the horse has had little or no public exercise, the player had better plan to look for signs of distress in the paddock and walking ring.

Before proceeding to our next array of negative signs, it might be a good idea to review the circumstances in which smart players overlook or excuse a poor last race, no matter how bad it may have seemed.

The Airtight Alibi

Because the conditioning process finds horses entered in races they cannot win, it is important not to be misled by their dismal performances in such races. Like the trainer who shoots the works after darkening his horse's form, the expert player dearly loves a situation in which his choice's last race looked so bad that today's odds increase. The handicapper who knows when to disregard a horse's latest race is destined for repeated happiness.

A bad race in the wrong company is, indeed, not a bad race at all. If anything, it suggests to the player that things are working out exactly as he and the maneuvering trainer might wish.

Here is a list of the circumstances in which a poor effort is forgivable. Overlook a horse's last race if:

1. It was on an off-track of a kind that the horse has never negotiated successfully in the past.

2. The horse was entered at the wrong distance.

3. The horse ran against animals of a higher class than it has been able to challenge successfully in its most recent seven or eight efforts.

4. The horse carried substantially more weight than is good for it. (Some Thoroughbreds cannot win under more than 115 pounds and look dreadful with 119 or more. Others, able to win with 117 or 118, die with 121 or 122. If a claimer ran poorly with 119 or more, check its record to see if the high weight constitutes an alibi.)

5. The race was the horse's first in more than a month.

6. The race was the horse's first since arriving on this circuit from another part of the country.

7. The horse showed high early speed before tiring or even stopping or quitting. This often is more than just an alibi for a poor finish. It may be a positive sign of approaching form, and of a trainer's imminent readiness to lower the boom. The past-performance line shows that the animal led or ran within a length or so of the early pace (usually to the pre-stretch call) before conking out. Unless the animal is a chronic quitter that does this sort of thing in almost every outing, the player should be delighted to forgive the eighth-place finish. Dollars to doughnuts, if the horse is well placed today it will show early speed again, and carry it further.

All those solid alibis derive from peculiarities of the modern conditioning process. Other good excuses are more usually attributable to racing misfortune. The expert tosses out the last race if:

8. The jockey had never finished first or second with the horse, is not a national or local leader and, for today's race, has been replaced by a more successful boy.

9. The jockey lost his whip, or a stirrup broke, or a bandage came undone, or some other mishap fouled the tack.

10. The jockey rode weakly or unintelligently enough to attract comment in the result chart.

11. Other horses prevented the animal from running its race. The chart or *Form* trouble line might say "Blocked," "Impeded," "Roughed," "Rough trip," "Forced to check," "Shuffled back," "In close," "Close quarters" or "Forced wide." Or it might say "Wide" or "Ran wide," indicating a bad ride or interference rather than the affliction of bearing out.

12. The horse got off to a poor start, but seldom has that kind of trouble.

Inexcusable Performances

Assuming that the horse ran in its own class range and at its best distance and had no excuse for its last performance, it can be eliminated on grounds of poor condition if:

1. It failed to beat about half its field—finishing fifth or worse in a field of seven, sixth or worse in a field of eight or nine, seventh or worse in a field of ten or more—and earned a speed rating at least 5 points below the ones recorded in its better local races.

2. It failed to gain on the leader at any call in the race and finished out of the money more than six lengths behind. (Some players use this kind of standard in preference to the first. Others use both in sequence.)

3. It lost more than two and a half lengths between the stretch call and the finish.

4. It got off to a poor start, and poor starts have been one of its problems.

5. It earned an uncomplimentary chart comment such as "Dull," "No speed" or "Showed nothing."

Signs of Improvement

"Accentuate the positive, eliminate the negative," wrote Johnny Mercer in a song that was popular during the Stone Age. Numerous horseplayers take the advice literally. They look for horses whose most recent races gave notice of better things to come. They ignore other horses.

In my opinion, a little more work than that pays dividends. Players who follow a sequence similar to the one in this chapter achieve a considerable edge by discarding horses that figure to be out of contention today. They then decide what to do about the remaining horses. If they are really hipped on the condition factor, they can toss out any of the surviving contenders that fail to check out on the positive angles described below. But if they care to consider some advice from an old hand, they may refrain from crossing off such horses until they have evaluated them in terms of class, pace and other fundamentals. My reasons for suggesting this are readily understandable: A horse that has been sufficiently active and has earned no black marks in its recent performances may well be in good enough shape to win today, even if its last race or two were unspectacular. For one thing, the horse might have run an alibi race last time out and this in itself might be a sign that the trainer's gears are meshing. Even without the evidence of an alibi its trainer might be a master at concealing improvement from the public, whereupon the players would live to regret eliminating the animal.

Players not already committed to a different way of doing things really should see if their winning percentage does not increase when they

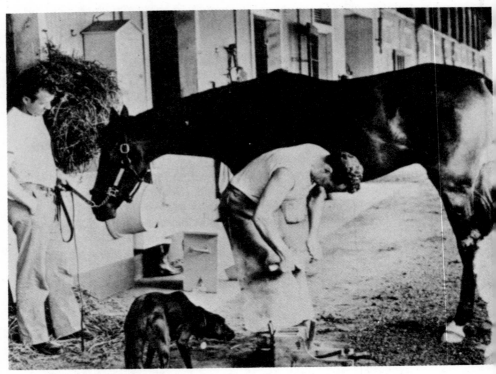

Kelso and the farrier. UPI PHOTO

accept as contenders any animals that qualify on the distance factor and show none of the signs of unreadiness reviewed earlier. A player who does not care to excuse a bad last race on grounds of one of the alibis discussed earlier should then look for negative signs in the horse's next-to-last race. If the race took place in the past three weeks and was a good one, the player had better not eliminate the horse.

In setting forth the following methods of spotting improvement or other signs of current readiness in the past-performance records, I recommend that the player regard them as plus factors. A horse may show none of these angles in his record, but may be the class of the race and win in a walk. Where these factors are especially useful is in separating contenders that (1) qualify on distance, class, pace, etc., (2) have checked out successfully against the negative standards of condition, and (3) need to be differentiated from each other. In such circumstances, a horse that showed one or more of the signs of improvement would ordinarily be the better bet (see Chapter 16). Another use of the signs of improvement is as a homing device for lovers of longshots. As everyone knows, many players hate to handicap, but enjoy a longshot more than anything. If they check out a field of horses against the following series of improvement angles and bet on the longest-priced horse whose record contains one or more of the angles, they can count on an entertaining run for their money.

A horse that has not been eliminated for any of the reasons reviewed earlier can be expected to run a good race today if it:

1. Won its last race easily or handily.

2. Won its last race in big-win style (see page 167).

3. Lost its last race but gained at least two lengths in the stretch, earning favorable comment such as "Rallied," "Gaining," "Game try," "Sharp try" or "Good effort."

4. Lost ground in the middle stages but gained in the stretch. A horse may lose ground to the leader while hunting for racing room, but if it is in a running mood, it often demonstrates that fitness by recovering the lost ground and more:

$$6 \ 6 \ 4^2 \ 4^4 \ 4^3 \ 3^1$$

5. Showed high early speed (see page 168).

6. Ran within the past week.

7. Ran in the money in its first effort after a long layoff or a long journey from another track.

8. Steps down in class today after a race in which it ran well enough to earn a comment like "Evenly" or better.

9. Steps down in class today to a level at which it has never been beaten by more than half a length.

10. Ran the final quarter of its last race in 24 seconds or less. (The famous Colonel E. R. Bradley invented this one. He found that any horse able to cover the last two furlongs that rapidly was an especially good bet next time out. To calculate a horse's final-quarter speed in a six-furlong race, subtract the race's official half-mile clocking from its official final time. For every length the animal gained on the leader from the half to the finish, deduct one fifth of a second. If the horse lost ground, add a fifth for every length it lost. The only other kind of race in which this calculation is possible for most fans is the mile, wherein the three-quarter-mile and final clockings are used.)

11. Ran closer to the early pace than in its previous race or two.

12. Was closer at the stretch call than in its previous race or two.

13. Finished closer to the winner and earned a higher speed rating than in its previous race or two.

14. Gained three or more lengths between the first and second call, or between any other two calls in the race.

15. Is a front-running type that carried its speed farther than in its previous race or two, even though it tired toward the end.

16. Ran an even race, in second or third position all the way, earning a substantially higher speed rating than in its previous race or two.

17. Has earned increasingly high speed ratings in its past three races, even though out of the money in its latest.

As the reader has noticed, many of these positive signs are infinitesimal. Most players overlook all but the more obvious of them. The handicapper sophisticated enough to understand that even slight improvement is often a prelude to major improvement can expect to make extra money by exploiting the above list, along with similar subtleties that will appear in later chapters.

Trip Handicapping

For most full-time professional horseplayers, careful race-watching has always been routine. The sharp eye of an expert may discern a sign of improvement or of decline or may notice that one horse was lucky to win and another unlucky to finish so far behind. Of the hundred other experts watching the same race with vision equally acute, half or more—including the experts from the racing press—may overlook this particular tidbit. To know something unreported to the racing public and unknown by other topnotch handicappers as well is to enjoy a wonderful advantage which professionals never stop trying to achieve.

In recent years, expert race-watching has been facilitated by video replays of each race. In some places, a careful player can see at least one replay shortly after the race ends, another one or two on cable television that evening at home, and at least two more at the track on the following day.

Before the electronic age, old-time race-watchers often worked in teams, one member watching the three or four horses at the rear of the pack, another accepting responsibility for the middle three or four, and a third attending to the three or four in the first and second flight. Pooled observations and interpretations made big money for many a professional combine. But today's trip handicappers (as they call themselves) are more often individual operatives. The repeated televiewings make each expert a one-man gang, able to watch each horse and each cluster of horses in their interactions with each other over and over again on the video screen.

They look for the kinds of signs specified in this chapter, relating apparent improvement or decline to other matters of fundamental importance such as the running style of the horse, the condition of the track at the time of the race, the official clockings of the fractional and final times and, of course, the essential quality of the horse and its rivals. Only full-time players can profit from the effort. And those who have acquired the necessary race-watching disciplines certainly do profit therefrom.

But plenty of other good handicappers do not bother and continue to beat the game on their own terms.

=10=

THE CLASS FACTOR

They claim that the late Saul Silberman, ebullient president of Tropical Park, decided one day to make a splendid and unusual gesture of good-will toward his paying customers. He would go to the grandstand with sheaves of currency and give it all away. For free.

It turned out to be quite an experience. When Silberman offered greenbacks to strangers, many not only refused the gift but behaved as if he were trying in some way to take advantage of them.

I can understand that. Racing is a weird game. A proportion of its clients become so accustomed to calamity that they cannot recognize good fortune when they see it face to face. This self-defeating turn of mind reflects itself in their betting. Let me illustrate.

Class Bonanzas

The nearest thing to a cinch at any track is a sharply conditioned horse of substantial class, when entered at a suitable distance against inferior animals. Did I say racing was weird? Racing is astonishing. One of its most astonishing features is the frequency with which betting oppor-tunities of this kind occur. At the height of the season on major circuits, the discerning player finds at least two such bonanzas every week.

What makes them bonanzas is that the best horse usually wins and almost invariably pays longer odds than it should. Even at Aqueduct, where a relentlessly shrewd crowd sometimes makes odds-on choices of animals that might be 4 to 1 elsewhere, the kind of near-cinch I have in mind (a ready horse of higher class than its rivals) may pay 3 to 2, when it ought to be 4 to 5.

6 GARDEN ST.

1¼ MILES
GARDEN STATE
START FINISH

1 ¼ MILES. (2.00⅘) STARTER HANDICAP. Purse $10,000. 3-year-olds and upward which have started for a claiming price of $8,000 or less since September 1. Closed with 13 nominations Tuesday, June 11. Weights, Wednesday, June 12.

Jo Vins Cannonbomb

Dk. b. or br. rig. 4, by Bombay Duck—Escopeta, by Canonero II
Own.—King joan m
Br.—Jo Vin Farm Inc (NJ)
Tr.—Ferguson Joseph
116
Lifetime 43 8 7 6 $56,538
1985 7 1 3 1 $15,275
1984 26 7 3 4 $37,839
Turf 1 0 0 0 $990

4Jun85- 6GS fm 1⅛ Ⓣ:48 1:12 1:43⅘ 3↑Alw 14000 1 8 65½ 79¾ 49 45½ Pizzo P S b 119 7.90 — — DHGotama 119½ DHDViceless 110½ Sayad 1194 No factor 9
11May85- 9GS fst 1⅛ :47⅕ 1:11⅕ 1:49⅗ Hcp 20000s 3 2 21½ 21 44 58½ Pizzo P S b 110 18.20 72–11 DHSurrender Ground 118¾ DHDisco Dom 117¾ ByAPro1135¾ Tired 7
30Mar85- 6Key fst 2 :50 3:02⅕ 3:28⅕ Hcp 8500s 1 3 41 32 2½ 21 Vigliotti M J b 117 2.80 91–17 FirstTent1181JoVinsCannonbomb117nkComeOnCbin1101¾ Gamely 7
16Mar85- 2Key fst 1¼ :48 1:37⅘ 2:05 Hcp 7500s 5 4 412 47 34½ 32¾ Vigliotti M J b 117 2.80 82–14 First Tent117nkDamascusJet1182½JoVinsCannonbomb1176 Evenly 7
2Mar85- 5Key fst 1⅜ :25⅗ 2:35 3:01⅕ Hcp 6500s 6 1 1½ 1hd 22 21½ Vigliotti M J b 117 *1.30 83–23 CountStefan1191½JoVinsCannonbomb1171FirstTent115hd Gamely 7
16Feb85- 9Key fst 1½ :49⅖ 2:08⅕ 2:34⅖ Hcp 6500s 7 3 1hd 1hd 11 2¾ Vigliotti M J b 117 *1.30 86–20 SinghBoldly116¾JoVinsCnnonbomb117½CountStfn120¾ Weakened 12
19Jan85- 9Key fst 1¼ :47⅗ 1:39⅖ 2:06⅕ Hcp 6500s 1 6 53 1½ 12 14 Vigliotti M J b 113 *1.80 79–19 Jo Vins Cannonbomb 1134EvasiveJohn116nkTopCoat1057 Driving 12
22Dec84- 6Key my 1½ :49⅗ 2:36⅕ 3↑Hcp 6500s 11 4 44 1hd 11 12½ Vigliotti M J b 111 7.60 78–33 JoVinsCannonbomb1112½EvasiveJohn115¾Y.B.Foxy1072 Drew out 11
8Dec84- 5Key fst 1¼ :47 1:37⅕ 2:04 3↑Hcp 6500s 2 2 32 33 2½ 2½ Vigliotti M J b 108 18.00 89–13 LndContrct122½JoVnsCnnonbomb1081½ClssofFftyTw114½ Gamely 9
25Nov84- 5Key fst 170 :46⅗ 1:12⅗ 1:43 Clm 11000 5 4 43½ 3nk 41 67¾ Bolletino N 116 9.10 77–16 NotAWorry118noKatazTrophy1181½ApalacheeWrrior1182 Checked 9
LATEST WORKOUTS May 8 GS 4f fst :51 b

First Tent

Dk. b. or br. c. 4, by Tentam—First Squaw, by First Landing
Own.—American Thoroughbred Ltd.
Br.—Evans T M (Va)
Tr.—Campo Salvatore
120
Lifetime 33 8 4 3 $53,186
1985 13 6 4 1 $39,015
1984 16 2 0 2 $13,151
Turf 4 1 1 0 $6,068

27May85- 8Del fm *1⅛ Ⓣ 1:53 3↑Clm 50000 1 3 31½ 44 33½ 32½ Simpson B H b 115 3.30 91–16 Big Shot 1181¾ DElectrifying 114¾ First Tent 1157 Evenly 5
27May85-Placed second through disqualification
3May85- 9GS fst 1¼ :47⅕ 1:37⅖ 2:03 Alw 16000s 3 3 38½ 511 714 717½ Lloyd J S b 122 4.10 — — Surrender Ground 119nk DHatch 119½ DBy A Pro 1165 Tired 8
20Apr85- 3GS fst 1 1/16 :47⅖ 1:11⅘ 1:44 3↑Alw 15000 6 3 21½ 3½ 22 22 Lloyd J S b 124 4.30 — — Hatch 1182 First Tent 124no Restless Meteor 1186 Held 2nd 6
30Mar85- 6Key fst 2 :50 3:02⅕ 3:28⅕ Hcp 8500s 5 4 3½ 12 1½ 11 Appleby D L Jr b 118 *1.70 92–17 FirstTent1181JoVinsCannonbomb117nkComeOnCbin1101¾ Driving 7
16Mar85- 2Key fst 1¼ :48 1:37⅘ 2:05 Hcp 7500s 1 3 25 23½ 22 1nk Appleby D L Jr b 117 2.60 85–14 FirstTent117nkDamascusJet1182½JoVinsCannonbomb1176 Driving 7
9Mar85- 5Key fst 1¼ :48⅕ 1:38⅘ 2:04⅖ Hcp 6500s 2 3 33 1½ 11 11½ Appleby D L Jr b 115 *1.60 88–19 First Tent 1151½ReasonToMarch1219GotAPrettyFace1143 Driving 6
2Mar85- 5Key fst 1⅜ :25⅗ 2:35 3:01⅕ Hcp 6500s 3 3 42 42½ 44 32½ Appleby D L Jr b 115 4.70 82–23 CountStfn1191½JoVinsCnnonbomb1171FrstTnt115hd Squeezed bk. 7
23Feb85- 5Key fst 1 1/16 :47⅗ 1:12 1:45⅕ Clm 14000 7 3 31½ 31½ 21 22 Appleby D L Jr b 122 7.10 76–18 Hey Man 1162 First Tent 1224 Buck Jump 1161½ Second best 7
17Feb85- 6Lrl fst 1⅛ :48⅕ 1:13⅗ 1:53 3↑Hcp 6500s 3 3 31 21 41½ 43¾ Saumell L b 115 8.90 77–20 Quobow 1152 Dreamers Miracle 1221½ No Blarney 108½ Tired 8
9Feb85- 6Pen gd 1⅛ :49⅘ 1:15⅖ 1:54 3↑Hcp 4000s 2 2 1½ 12 2hd 1nk Appleby D L Jr b 120 *1.80 82–26 First Tent 120nk Royal Anticipation 1223RegalEscort114½ Driving 8
LATEST WORKOUTS Jun 12 GS 5f fst 1:00⅘ h Jun 5 GS 5f fst 1:01 h May 22 GS 5f my 1:01 h May 16 GS 5f fst 1:02 b

Sir Brenda Boy

B. h. 6, by Bold Arian—Brindabella, by Portsmouth
Own.—Linder W J
Br.—Linder W J (Pa)
Tr.—Linder Louis
110
Lifetime 61 5 3 4 $41,562
1985 9 1 1 0 $6,820
1984 15 1 1 1 $9,420
Turf 2 0 0 0 $432

15May85- 4GS fst 1 1/16 :46⅘ 1:11⅘ 1:43⅖ Clm 10000 4 8 811 98 78 612 Alligood M A b 115 29.60 79–12 Shoen 1155¾ Leader Of The Pack 1183 Fresh Deck 108hd Outrun 10
3May85- 9GS fst 1¼ :47⅕ 1:37⅖ 2:03 Alw 16000s 8 4 512 821 820 824¼ Alligood M A b 116 29.70 — — Surrender Ground 119nk DHatch 119½ DBy A Pro 1165 Tired 8
20Apr85-10GS fst 1 1/16 :46⅖ 1:12 1:57 Clm 7000 7 5 58 2½ 1½ 12 Alligood M A b 113 13.90 — — Sir Brenda Boy 1132 Crimson Fleet 1151½ Soudan 1158 Driving 12
31Mar85- 4Key fst 1 1/16 :47⅘ 1:12⅖ 1:45⅘ Clm 6500 2 11 1114 1113 109½ 88¾ Jewell J J b 116 14.40 66–18 Point Man 116½AckEnd1161½TroubleBucks1092 Broke awkwardly 11
24Mar85- 4Key my 170 :47 1:12⅘ 1:44⅕ Clm 6500 4 8 813 57 35 25 Jewell J J b 116 13.80 74–20 Buonofortisimo 1165 Sir Brenda Boy 116½TwoPointer1167 Rallied 8
8Mar85- 5Key fst 1 1/16 :47⅖ 1:11⅗ 1:44 SClm 9000 2 7 719 727 721 725 Lukas M b 114 26.50 59–15 Molasses 1162 Icy Badge 1169 Lotsa Socks 116½ Trailed 7
16Feb85- 9Key fst 1½ :49⅖ 2:08⅕ 2:34⅖ Hcp 6500s 12 10 73¾ 109¾ 1219 1221¾ Cole M A b 110 13.20 66–20 SinghBoldly116¾JoVinsCannonbomb117½CountStefan120¾ Outrun 12
10Feb85- 2Key fst 1⅛ :47⅕ 1:12⅕ 1:52⅕ Clm 6500 4 11 1114 1111 76½ 4½ Gomez M A b 116 48.60 73–19 Recant 112hd Gato De Yarda 116½ Punker 116no Rallied 11
3Feb85- 3Key gd 1 1/16 :47⅘ 1:13⅕ 1:44⅗ Clm 6500 1 7 78¾ 79 711 716 Gomez M A b 116 51.70 65–23 Lucky Key 1206 Super Fashion 1162½ Gato De Yarda1161½ Outrun 9
19Aug84- 4Key gd 170 :47⅖ 1:13⅖ 1:44⅗ 3↑Clm 6500 7 8 810 811 88½ 69¾ Jewell J J b 116 38.10 67–21 Forty More 116¾ Rain Prince 1161 BroadwayBully1184½ No factor 9
LATEST WORKOUTS May 31 GS 4f fst :49⅗ b

Regal Escort

B. g. 5, by Billy Rogell—Scatterbrain, by Dunce
Own.—Indian Mills Stock Farm
Br.—Proctor D L (Ky)
Tr.—Aristone Philip
109
Lifetime 68 10 7 8 $37,969
1985 13 1 0 4 $6,990
1984 25 7 4 2 $22,510
Turf 1 0 0 0

7Jun85- 1GS fst 1 1/16 :47⅗ 1:12⅗ 1:46⅕ 3↑Clm 7000 5 5 53¾ 3½ 31½ 31¾ Cantagallo G J b 114 3.70 75–17 Two Pointer 116¾ Grand Old Herbie 1141 Regal Escort11 Hung 6
18May85-10GS fst 1 1/16 :47⅖ 1:12 1:45⅕ Clm 8000 10 11 1118 915 911 68½ Black A S 115 8.30 73–14 Cajun Lightning 115½ JohnnyBAngry1083½Informal1132 , factor 11

Soudan

Own.—Diamio J

Ch. h, 7, by Soudard—Denova, by Degage
Br.—Cashman E C (Fla)
Tr.—Frey Walter

		Lifetime				
110	1985 9 1 1 1				
	1984 11 0 0 2				
	95 9 9 17	Turf 11 2 2 1			
	$147,888				

Lifetime $147,888

Count Stefan

Own.—Dommell T

Ch. g, 5, by Nizeon—Baby Sally, by Verbatim
Br.—Roach B & T (Ky)
Tr.—Henry Billy J

		Lifetime				
115	1985 10 1 4 1				
	1984 25 5 3 2				
	36 6 7 3				
	$43,367				

3kay65—Placed second through disqualification

Labour Party

Own.—Bull Patricia A

Ch. g, 6, by Hard Work—Esquinapa, by Beau Max
Br.—Pemn W E (Ky)
Tr.—Bull Lee Roy

		Lifetime				
115	1985 10 2 1 2				
	1984 11 1 0 3				
	35 8 3 7	Turf 1 0 0 0 b			
	$74,403				

SIXTH RACE

Garden State

JUNE 15, 1985

1 ¼ MILES. (2.00⅘) STARTER HANDICAP. Purse $10,000. 3-year-olds and upward which have started for a claiming price of $8,000 or less since September 1. Closed with 13 nominations Tuesday, June 11. Weights, Wednesday, June 12.

Value of race $10,000; value to winner $6,000; second $2,000; third $1,100; fourth $600; fifths $150 each. Mutuel pool $73,504. Exacta Pool $72,920.

Last Raced	Horse	Eqt.	A.	Wt	PP	¼	½	¾	1	Str	Fin	Jockey	Odds $1
27May85 ^{8}Del^{2}	First Tent	b	4	120	2	$1\frac{1}{2}$	2^{2}	2^{1}	1^{1}	1^{2}	1^{2}	Thornburg B	1.70
11May85 ^{9}GS^{6}	Count Stefan	b	5	115	6	6^{2}	$6^{2\frac{1}{2}}$	4^{hd}	4^{hd}	2^{4}	2^{5}	McCauley W H	3.20
4Jun85 ^{3}GS^{1}	Labour Party		6	115	7	4	$5\frac{1}{2}$	6^{3}	2^{hd}	3^{2}	3^{1}	Walford J	4.80
27May85 ^{2}GS^{1}	Soudan	b	7	113	5	5^{2}	4^{hd}	$5\frac{1}{2}$	6^{8}	4^{hd}	4^{nk}	Lopez C C	9.60
4Jun85 ^{6}GS^{4}	DH Jo Vins Cannonbomb	b	4	116	1	3^{1}	3^{2}	$3^{2\frac{1}{2}}$	5^{hd}	5^{hd}	5	Vigliotti M J	4.10
7Jun85 ^{1}GS^{3}	DH Regal Escort	b	5	109	4	$2^{1\frac{1}{2}}$	$1\frac{1}{2}$	$1\frac{1}{2}$	$3^{1\frac{1}{2}}$	6^{8}	5^{8}	Cantagallo G J	10.40
15May85 ^{4}GS^{6}	Sir Brenda Boy	b	6	112	3	7	7	7	7	7	7	Murphy D J	14.30

DH—Dead heat.

OFF AT 10:06, Start good, Won driving. Time, :23⅘, :48⅖, 1:13⅘, 1:38⅘, 2:04⅕ Track fast.

$2 Mutuel Prices:				
	2–FIRST TENT	5.40	3.00	2.20
	6–COUNT STEFAN		4.40	2.60
	7–LABOUR PARTY			2.80

$2 EXACTA 2–6 PAID $19.00.

Dk. b. or br. c, by Tentam—First Squaw, by First Landing. Trainer Campo Salvatore. Bred by Evans T M (Va).

FIRST TENT set the pace early, gave way to REGAL ESCORT for a half, moved back outside to regain the lead and proved much the best while kept to pressure. COUNT STEFAN rallied three wide on the final turn to challenge but could nonly prove second best. LABOUR PARTY launched only a mile bid entering the last turn. SOUDAN Saved ground to no avail. REGAL ESCORT pressed or set the pace for a half and steadily weakened.

Owners— 1, American Thoroughbred Ltd.; 2, Dommell T; 3, Bull Patricia A; 4, Diamio J; 5, King joan m; 6, Indian Mills Stock Farm; 7, Linder W J.

Trainers— 1, Campo Salvatore; 2, Henry Billy J; 3, Bull Lee Roy; 4, Frey Walter; 5, Ferguson Joseph; 6, Aristone Philip; 7, Linder Louis.

Overweight: Soudan 3 pounds; Sir Brenda Boy 2.

Opportunities are greater on circuits other than those of New York and Southern California. The crowds are not quite as alert, meaning that the horse usually pays better odds. And the typical field of horses includes fewer genuine contenders, meaning that your choice has fewer horses to beat.

For a typical example, consider the sixth at Garden State on the night of June 15, 1985. Any horse that had raced for a claiming price of $8,000 or less during the preceding ten and a half months was eligible to compete for this $10,000 purse under handicap conditions at a mile and a quarter. Let's consider the records of the four betting favorites.

Jo Vins Cannonbomb has done nothing much on a dirt track since March 30, when a second-place finish behind First Tent was his last outing for six weeks. Returning on May 11, he beat only two horses against a presumably superior field, and did adequately in allowance company on June 4 in his first try on a turf course. He may be ready for a top effort tonight, although that is nothing like a certainty. At his best, he is definitely a threat at today's distance in handicaps open to horses that have started for $6,500 to $7,000.

First Tent, assigned top weight in the field, is a habitual winner who has been in the money in eleven of his thirteen starts this year. In his last start, entered to be claimed for $50,000, he performed creditably in heavy traffic on the grass and was moved up to second on a disqualification. He has since turned in two impressive workouts and can be accepted as fit and ready. His April 20 performance in allowance company with a purse 50 percent higher than tonight's was followed by his only bad performance of the year, as high weight in a starter allowance of quality higher than tonight's race. If he is indeed as ready as he seems, he is better than Jo Vins Cannonbomb.

Count Stefan is from a good barn but seems to back up in the stretch unless facing cheaper company.

Labour Party's upset victory in a $16,000 claimer last out might make him a threat tonight if the distance were shorter. Note that his only two wins of the year were at much shorter distances. His style is generally that of a come-from-behinder, and he might be sharp enough to go all the way tonight, but First Tent surely looks like the class of the field.

For another example of class power, look at the records of the two betting favorites in the eighth at Garden State on June 19. The $15,625 purse was for horses bred in New Jersey. Less than a week ago, Fast Caz almost won the same kind of race at Monmouth Park, a short drive to the north.

Eleven days ago, Crozier Way had his first race over this track and his first since Hialeah two months earlier. He finished a highly creditable third in an allowance race of higher quality than the Fast Caz race. Crozier Way contended with *open company*, not mere Jersey-breds. With

8 GARDEN ST.

START — 6 FURLONGS — GARDEN STATE — FINISH

6 FURLONGS. (1.08⅖) ALLOWANCE. Purse $15,625. 3-year-olds and upward. Registered New Jersey Breds which have not won a race other than maiden, claiming or starter. Weight, 3-year-olds, 115 lbs. Older, 122 lbs. Non-winners of a race other than claiming since May 15 allowed 2 lbs. Such a race since April 15, 4 lbs.

Thirty Seconds

Gr. c. 3, by T V Commercial—Fascination Jude, by Determined
Br.—Bright View Farm (NJ)
Tr.—Bardaro Anthony J
Own.—Bright View Farm
111 Lifetime 2 1 0 0 $5,625 | 1985 2 1 0 0 $5,625 | 1984 0 M 0 0

15May85- 9GS fst 6f :22⅖ :46 1:11⅘ 3↑ S Md 20000 6 7 31 2hd 1½ 11¼ Antley C W 114 9.70 85-12 ThirtySeconds1141¼Satn'sAccomplice114¾HiJimminy1146 Driving 11
2May85- 4GS sly 6f :22⅗ :46 1:11⅘ 3↑ S Md Sp Wt 10 4 22 54½ 815 916½ Antley C W 114 18.90 69-14 Susan'sTeddyBear1141½RighteousPrince114¾SicilinLw1152½ Tired 12
LATEST WORKOUTS Jun 17 GS 4f my :49⅕ b Jun 12 GS 4f fst :48⅕ h ●Jun 7 GS 4f fst :47⅘ h May 31 GS 4f fst :48⅕ h

Fast Caz

B. c. 3, by Hasty Flyer—La Marquise, by Proudest Roman
Br.—Thrush W T II (NJ)
Tr.—Jolin Louis F
Own.—Thrush W T II
111 Lifetime 6 1 1 2 $11,435 | 1985 4 1 1 1 $10,335 | 1984 2 M 0 1 $1,100

13Jun85- 7Mth fst 6f :23⅕ :47 1:12 3↑ S Alw 15000 6 4 31 3½ 2½ 2nk Thomas D B b 113 6.70 80-30 Cinnaminson 113nk Fast Caz 1132 Susan'sTeddyBear1114 Gamely 8
29May85- 7GS fst 6f :22⅕ :45 1:09⅘ 3↑ Clm 32000 7 3 52½ 34 35 36½ Thomas D B b 113 16.70 89-15 Full Venture 1143½ Top Knave 1143 Fast Caz 1131½ Rallied 8
16May85- 2GS fst 6f :22 :45⅕ 1:10⅕ 3↑ Md 32000 9 1 31½ 2hd 12½ 12½ Thomas D B b 114 3.90 91-10 Fast Caz 1142½CommandSpeller1148 DH NorthernSlope114 Driving 10
8Apr85- 3GS fst 6f :21⅘ :45⅕ 1:10⅗ 3↑ S Md Sp Wt 4 2 12 1hd 21½ 56 Vigliotti M J b 112 3.00 — — Sldy'sRuller112noTkeItOnTheLmb1141Perul'sChnt1143 Weakened 10
9Nov84-10Med fst 1 :48⅕ 1:13⅕ 1:40⅖ S Md Sp Wt 12 1 1hd 58 819 828½ Antley C W 118 9.80 51-20 Entrepeau 1185 Ah So Tony 1181½ Chic Weed 113¾ Tired 12
17Oct84- 3Med fst 6f :23 :47⅕ 1:12⅗ Md 50000 7 2 11½ 2½ 33 310 Rocco J 118 18.80 69-24 Four Partners 1099 Sheer Light 1161 Fast Caz 1185 Tired 7
LATEST WORKOUTS Jun 18 GS 3f fst :39⅗ b Jun 12 GS 3f fst :37⅗ b Jun 8 GS 5f fst 1:01 h May 28 GS 3f fst :36⅘ b

V. Formation

Ro. g. 3, by Oxford Flight—Vegitation, by Tatoi
Br.—Brenner Sally G (NJ)
Tr.—Perry Mark
Own.—L & M Stables
115 Lifetime 5 2 1 2 $12,680 | 1984 5 2 1 2 $12,680

25Sep84- 3Med fst 6f :22⅘ :46⅖ 1:13 Clm 20000 2 5 32½ 34 34 36 O'Hara S7 111 *1.50 71-21 Irv's Choice 1155 Inflation's Up 1101 V. Formation 1113 Evenly 6
11Sep84- 3Med fst 6f :22⅘ :46⅘ 1:13⅗ Clm 20000 3 4 34 21½ 1hd 1nk O'Hara S7 110 3.70 75-20 V. Formation 110nk Amorullah 1174 Inflation's Up 1121½ Driving 7
17Aug84- 7Atl fst 5½f :21⅘ :45⅘ 1:05⅗ Clm 20000 2 6 1hd 1hd 1hd 3¾ O'Hara S7 107 12.20 86-22 Patriot'sGold110nkFridayKnight114½V.Formation1072½ Weakened 7
11Jly84- 3Atl fst 5f :23 :47 1:00⅗ S Md Sp Wt 4 4 1hd 12½ 15 15 Ferrucci P Jr7 111 *1.40 85-25 V. Formation 1115 Rockin' Rob 1181½ Trickie Tex 1181½ Driving 6
28Jun84- 3Atl fst 4½f :23⅕ :47 :53⅗ S Md Sp Wt 6 6 48½ 35 25 Ferrucci P Jr7 111 9.80 88-07 T. J's Fool 1185 V.Formation1111½Rockin'Rob1183 Best of others 6
LATEST WORKOUTS Jun 15 Atl 5f fst 1:04 b Jun 8 Atl 3f sly :38 b May 31 Atl 3f fst :37 b May 22 Atl 4f my :50 b

Slady's Ruller

Dk. b. or br. c. 3, by Slady Castle—Blairullah, by Count Amber
Br.—Viggiani F J (NJ)
Tr.—Vincitore Michael
Own.—Viggiani F J
111 Lifetime 10 1 3 1 $19,160 | 1985 6 1 1 1 $14,210 | 1984 4 M 2 0 $4,950

6Jun85- 5Mth fst 6f :23 :46⅘ 1:12⅘ 3↑ S Alw 15000 2 8 89¾ 85¾ 810 816½ Ayarza I b 111 5.60 62-26 Rough Edge116nkHiIdeal1134Susan'sTeddyBear1134 Broke slowly 8
27May85- 6Mth fst 6f :23 :47 1:14 3↑ S Alw 15000 2 6 31 35 23½ 22 Ayarza I b 111 6.70 68-26 A Real Buster 1102 Slady's Ruller 111½ Rough Edge1171½ Gamely 8
7May85- 7GS fst 1 :47⅗ 1:12⅕ 1:37⅘ 3↑ S Alw 18750 4 7 86¼ 98¼ 69¼ 715 Ayarza I b 110 11.10 71-15 SecondEnding110hdTakeItOnTheLmb1146½RngerOne1102¾ Outrun 9
29Apr85- 7GS fst 6f :22⅕ :45⅖ 1:10⅘ 3↑ S Alw 17500 3 5 2½ 1hd 11 32½ Ayarza I b 114 3.10 86-12 Island Fun 1091¾ Tall & Light 114½ Slady'sRuller1142½ Weakened 9
8Apr85- 3GS fst 6f :21⅘ :45⅕ 1:10⅗ 3↑ S Md Sp Wt 10 3 22 2hd 11½ 1no Ayarza I b 112 3.90 — — Slady'sRuller112noTakeItOnTheLamb1141Perul'sChnt1143 All out 10
5Jan85- 3Key sly 6f :22⅘ :47⅘ 1:15 Md Sp Wt 4 8 89½ 69¾ 67¾ 57¾ Simpson B H5 b 114 2.90 58-38 Star Quality 1196½ Sicilian Law119noBroStache119no Rallied wide 10
21Dec84- 1Med sly 6f :22⅘ :46⅗ 1:12⅗ S Md Sp Wt 7 2 12 12 11½ 2nk Ward W A5 b 113 *1.20 79-23 Ernie'sSugarBowl118nkSldy'sRuller11310Ribot'sRun118no Gamely 7
13Dec84- 8Med fst 1 1/16 :47⅕ 1:12⅗ 1:45⅗ S N J Futurity 4 15 1415 1314 1319 1224 Castaneda K 122 80.20 57-20 Another Reef 1224½ D Brother Tom 122¾ Travaux 1227 Outrun 15
23Nov84- 5Med fst 6f :22⅘ :46⅗ 1:14⅕ Md Sp Wt 5 5 43 31½ 22½ 23 Castaneda K 118 42.70 68-26 Centennial Lane 1183 Slady'sRuller118noHasWritten1184½ Gamely 8
17Nov84- 4Med fst 6f :23⅕ :46⅘ 1:14⅕ S Md Sp Wt 1 10 1116 1123 1018 1012½ Castaneda K 118 15.60 58-22 Chic Weed 1133½ Ranger One 118¾ Brother Tom 118nk Outrun 11
LATEST WORKOUTS Apr 24 GS 5f fst 1:01⅗ b

Crozier Way

B. c. 3, by Girl's Castle—Shy Molly, by Idehi
Br.—Florio A (NJ)
Tr.—Helmetag Robert
Own.—Florio Jr & Meloni
111 Lifetime 4 1 1 1 $5,625 | 1985 3 1 0 1 $4,065 | 1984 1 M 1 0 $1,560

8Jun85- 7GS fst 6f :21⅘ :44⅗ 1:10⅗ 3↑ Alw 13000 2 6 32 31½ 32½ 32 Barrera M N 116 24.70 87-12 Grand Horizon's 115hd Chief Louie1132CrozierWay116hd Even try 7
9Mar85- 5Hia fst 6f :22⅕ :45⅕ 1:10⅕ Alw 11500 8 1 52½ 914 1019 918 Klinger O C 121 23.20 72-10 FlyerEscpe118¾Mgloire1151½MedievlScrt115hd Bore out; bumped 10
10Feb85- 4CT fst 4f :23⅕ :48⅗ Md Sp Wt 6 1 1½ 12 18 Melendez J H 118 *1.50 85-19 Crozier Way 1188 Deck'M Captain 118½ Kanrun Sum 118½ Easily 10
31Aug84- 6Atl fst 5½f :22⅗ :46⅘ 1:06⅗ S Md Sp Wt 8 2 1½ 14 13 21½ O'Hara S7 112 7.60 80-24 Sail On Blue 1191½ Crozier Way 1122 Chic Weed 1147½ Gamely 9
LATEST WORKOUTS May 30 GS 6f fst 1:15⅕ h May 21 GS 5f fst 1:01 h May 16 GS 4f fst :50⅗ b

Ranger One

B. c. 3, by Darby Creek Road—Side By Step, by Roberto
Br.—Sterlingbrook Farm (NJ)
Lifetime 12 1 2 3 | 1985 6 0 1 1 $7,760 | 1984 6 1 1 2 $14,750

Master Isais

Own.—Due Process Stable

Ch. g. 3, by Barachois—Raise A Fleet, by Son Ange
Br.—Due Process Stable (NJ)
Tr.—Nobles Reynaldo H

111 $15,247

Lifetime	1984	7 1 2 1
7 1 2 1	Turf	1 0 0 0
$15,247		

3Jun85- 7GS fst 6f	:22 :45 1:10⅗	⑤Alw 18750		Antley C W	b 120	*1.70	66-20 Still Crazy 120no Arthur Teacher 114½ Ranger One 114no	Tired 6
7May85- 7GS fst 1	:47⅖ 1:12⅕ 1:37½	⑤Alw 18750	117	Antley C W	117	18.70	66-16 Endear 117½ Trout Stream 120¹ Sovereign Song 120⁴	Stopped 7
13Apr85- 5GS fst 1	:47 1:11¾ 1:37½	⑤Alw 18750	118	Antley C W	118	*.80e	79-18 Master Isais 118¾ Ah So Tony 118nk Chic Weed 113	Driving 9
9Mar85- 8Key fst 6f	:22¼ :45¾ 1:11¾	Alw 11000	118	Nied J Jr	118	*1.50	77-20 Travaux 118¹¼ Master Isais 118⁹ Still Crazy 118⁷	Weakened 7
26Feb85- 8Key fst 6f	:22 :44⅖ 1:11⅞	Alw 11000	120	Vigliotti M J	b 120	*2.70e	50-17 Varykino 115¹¼ Doubiruby 114¹¼ Manor Parkway 115¹	Tired 10
26Dec84- 8Medfst 6f	:23⅖ :46½ 1:12	⑤Alw 15000	118	Antley C W	118	5.40	89-16 Jacques Rabbit 118no Master Isais 118⁹ Four Flora 110²	Sharp 9
14Dec84- 4Medfst 6f	:23⅖ :46¾ 1:13⅖	⑤Md Sp Wt	118	Antley C W	118	3.70	82-20 Chic Weed 113⅗ Ranger One 118⁸ Brother Tom 118nk	Rallied 11
26Nov84- 7Medfst 6f	:47⅖ 1:13⅖ :45⅔	⑤Md Sp Wt		Antley C W				
17Nov84- 4Medfst 6f	:23⅖ 1:14⅗ :46½	⑤Md Sp Wt						

LATEST WORKOUTS Apr 23 GS 5f fst 1:01 h May 1 GS 5f fst 1:01 h May 25 GS 4f fst :48¾ h Jun 1 GS 5f my 1:01¾ h

Copyright © 1985 by Daily Racing Forms, Inc.
Reprinted with permission of copyright owner.

EIGHTH RACE
Garden State
JUNE 19, 1985

6 FURLONGS. (1.08⅘) ALLOWANCE. Purse $15,625. 3-year-olds and upward. Registered New Jersey Breds which have not won a race other than maiden, claiming or starter. Weight, 3-year-olds, 115 lbs. Older, 122 lbs. Non-winners of a race other than claiming since May 15 allowed 2 lbs. Such a race since April 15, 4 lbs.

Value of race $15,625; value to winner $9,375; second $3,125; third $1,719; fourth $937; fifth $469. Mutuel pool $49,033.
Exacta Pool $48,894.

Last Raced	Horse	Eqt.A.Wt	PP	St	¼	½	Str	Fin	Jockey	Odds $1
8Jun85 7GS3	Crozier Way	3 111	5	2	1½	11½	12½	13	Ferrer J C	2.50
13Jun85 7Mth2	Fast Caz	b 3 113	2	7	4½	31	22	21½	Thomas D B	1.10
10Jun85 5GS2	Ranger One	b 3 113	6	3	63½	44	31	33½	Antley C W	3.70
6Jun85 5Mth8	Slady's Ruller	b 3 111	4	6	5½	54	51½	41	Vigliotti M J	12.40
15May85 9GS1	Thirty Seconds	3 113	1	5	7	7	66	52½	Gomez M A	22.20
6Nov84 3Med6	Master Isais	3 112	7	1	2½	2hd	41	614	Murphy D J	11.00
25Sep84 3Med3	V. Formation	3 116	3	4	3hd	62	7	7	Ferrucci P Jr	28.40

OFF AT 10:59. Start good, Won driving. Time, :22⅕, :45⅖, 1:10⅗ Track fast.

$2 Mutuel Prices:
5-CROZIER WAY ... 7.00 3.40 3.00
2-FAST CAZ ... 2.80 2.60
6-RANGER ONE ... 2.80
$2 EXACTA 5-2 PAID $17.80.

B. c, by Girl's Castle—Shy Molly, by Idehi. Trainer Helmetag Robert. Bred by Florio A (NJ).

CROZIER WAY took the lead soon after the start, set pace just off rail, shook off rivals leaving turn and drew clear. FAST CAZ moved to the rail on the backstretch, eased outside winner when challenging in early stretch but couldn't keep pace. RANGER ONE raced wide and bested the others. SLADY'S RULLER lacked a rally. MASTER ISAIS raced outside and tired. V. FORMATION tired.

Owners— 1, Florio Jr & Meloni; 2, Thrush W T II; 3, T-Bird Stable; 4, Viggiani F J; 5, Bright View Farm; 6, Due Process Stable; 7, L & M Stables.

Trainers— 1, Helmetag Robert; 2, Jolin Louis F; 3, Reid Mark J; 4, Vincitore Michael; 5, Bardaro Anthony J; 6, Nobles Reynaldo H; 7, Perry Mark.

Overweight: Fast Caz 2 pounds; Thirty Seconds 2; Master Isais 1; V. Formation 1.

the leading local rider, Jose Ferrer, and the local race under his belt, he was an easy choice on grounds of class.

At any track, analysis no more elaborate than the kind just demonstrated can be depended on to produce dozens of winners each year. Horses that display even a little foot while being outgunned in stakes races are always threats when entered at the proper distance in allowance fields. Horses lowered in claiming price, or dropping from allowance to claiming company, are always threats if the distance is suitable and recent activity contains signs (however slight) of improving condition. Finally, the handicapper should remain alert to situations in which claiming runners hold class advantages over weak opponents in allowance races. A hard-knocking campaigner with several victories at the track's highest claiming level may romp when entered in an allowance affair for animals that have never won a race or two other than maiden or claiming. Indeed, at Aqueduct's winter meeting each year, former claiming runners invariably win a few stakes without arousing extraordinary surprise. To take advantage of opportunities provided by claiming horses entered in weak allowance or stakes fields, it is helpful to keep track of local purse and claiming-price schedules, noting at which point on the scale certain claiming races command purses roughly equivalent to those offered in certain allowance races. Knowledge of the running times normal for races in these closely related class categories also helps, often revealing that the claiming animal consistently runs faster than the supposedly superior field it faces in its allowance debut.

Leading Money Winners of All Time

As of January 1, 1986, the following horses were the highest earners in the history of the sport.

John Henry	$6,597,947	Life's Magic	2,255,218
Spend A Buck	4,220,689	Wild Again	2,204,829
Slew o' Gold	3,533,134	Chief's Crown	2,191,168
All Along	3,015,764	Majesty's Prince	2,075,200
Spectacular Bid	2,781,607	Kelso	1,977,896
Trinycarol	2,644,516	Proud Truth	1,944,327
Gate Dancer	2,398,945	Forego	1,938,957
Affirmed	2,393,818		

What Class Is

Thoroughbred class, or quality, is easy to recognize and hard to define. From Eclipse to John Henry the horses of highest class—the champions—have been the ones whose physical soundness, speed, stamina and competitive willingness enabled them to beat everything in sight. They won under serious weight disadvantages. They won on off-tracks.

They won by narrow margins after overcoming serious lack of running room in the stretch. And sometimes they won by exhausting their opponents in the first three quarters of a mile and romping home all alone, a city block in front.

Many of the horses they whipped were every bit as sound. Some were speedier. Some had no less stamina and as much courage. But the champions combined those traits in maximum quantity. And, lest we forget, they were trained well enough to remain sound and consistent in race after race. Not many trainers can make a champion of a potential champion. Indeed, nine out of every ten trainers can be relied on to ruin any potential champion they handle. Competence is as rare in this field as in any other.

The Best of the Best

In 1936, *Daily Racing Form* inaugurated an annual poll of its own staff correspondents to determine their choices of the year's champions in each division of Thoroughbred racing. And the divisional champion considered most dominant won the honor of honors—designation as Horse of the Year. The *Form* survey led in time to an annual canvass of leading journalists, the *Form* staff and representatives of the racetrack industry. The prizes, now known as Eclipse Awards, go to a wide range of human beings as well as horses, but the most attention remains where it belongs, on the Horse of the Year.

On the following list of Horses of the Year, the age and sex of each appears in parentheses, with "c" meaning a colt, "h" an entire horse, "f" a filly and "g" a gelding.

1936	Granville (3c)	1956	Swaps (4c)
1937	War Admiral (3c)	1957	Bold Ruler (3c)
1938	Seabiscuit (5h)	1958	Round Table (4c)
1939	Challedon (3c)	1959	Sword Dancer (4c)
1940	Challedon (4c)	1960	Kelso (3g)
1941	Whirlaway (3c)	1961	Kelso (4g)
1942	Whirlaway (4c)	1962	Kelso (5g)
1943	Count Fleet (3c)	1963	Kelso (6g)
1944	Twilight Tear (3f)	1964	Kelso (7g)
1945	Busher (3f)	1965	Roman Brother (4g)
1946	Assault (3c)	1966	Buckpasser (3c)
1947	Armed (6g)	1967	Damascus (3c)
1948	Citation (3c)	1968	Dr. Fager (4c)
1949	Capot (3c)	1969	Arts and Letters (3c)
1950	Hill Prince (3c)	1970	Fort Marcy (6g)
1951	Counterpoint (3c)	1971	Ack Ack (5h)
1952	One Count (3c)	1972	Secretariat (2c)
1953	Tom Fool (4c)	1973	Secretariat (3c)
1954	Native Dancer (4c)	1974	Forego (4g)
1955	Nashua (3c)	1975	Forego (5g)

1976	Forego (6g)	1981	John Henry (6g)
1977	Seattle Slew (3c)	1982	Conquistador Cielo (3c)
1978	Affirmed (3c)	1983	All Along (4f)
1979	Affirmed (4c)	1984	John Henry (9g)
1980	Spectacular Bid (4c)	1985	Spend A Buck (3c)

Class and Speed

At any distance on any dry, fast racing strip, the average running time of higher-class races is faster than the average running time of lower-class races.

The facts are undeniable, having been established in repeated studies at all North American tracks. Horses only a tad better finish only a tick sooner but the averages are there. Class translates into speed.

Undeniable or not, the concept has not penetrated the consciousness of most horsefolk. They all have stopwatches with which they evaluate the workouts of their own livestock, but they adhere to the traditional belief that the running times of races mean nothing. To support the contention, they make an undeniable assertion of their own: A cheap horse can win in 1.10 today and next week go against a classier animal who beats him in 1.11.

In the next chapter we shall clear up all such confusions. For the time being, the reader can rest assured that speed is a dependable indicator of whatever a horse's class may have been when the speed was recorded. The handicapper's problem is to judge whether the horse's class will be at that particular level or higher or lower this afternoon. More later.

Class and Form

We have emphasized that a horse of higher class is physically and temperamentally superior to one of lesser class. If he is a handicap star, he has proved it by starring in handicaps. If he is a $10,000 animal, he can walk way from $7,500 ones. It does not matter how sharp their condition may be, if his own is good. But, no matter how keen his edge, he cannot beat well-conditioned $15,000 stock.

Class and physical condition are closely related. A horse may drop down the scale to $4,000 before it wins a race. If it is still young, it may suddenly iron out its own kinks, get its legs under it and turn hot. Or a new, perceptive trainer may repair the aches and pains or correct the bad habits, as Hirsch Jacobs did in promoting Stymie from a $1,500 claiming race to a national championship.

Rarely does a horse spend an entire career at one class level. Rather, it moves up and down the scale. For most, the peak of class is attained during the three-year-old season. And then injury, overwork and unintelligent handling begin to take effect. Anyone who qualifies as an experienced racing fan has seen more than one former Kentucky Derby contestant struggling to win part of a purse in cheap claimers. At every bull ring in the land, animals of former high class pit their arthritic limbs and stout hearts against beasts that would not have been allowed in the same yard with them a few years earlier.

Quite apart from the pathos of such cases, they demonstrate that the effective class of a horse is related to its current condition. It does no good to ask what kind of fields the horse has beaten. One needs to know what kind it has beaten lately.

The Triple Crown

Only eleven three-year-olds have managed to win the celebrated Triple Crown of American Racing—the Kentucky Derby, the Preakness Stakes and the Belmont Stakes:

1919—Sir Barton	1941—Whirlaway	1973—Secretariat
1930—Gallant Fox	1943—Count Fleet	1977—Seattle Slew
1935—Omaha	1946—Assault	1978—Affirmed
1937—War Admiral	1948—Citation	

The following horses won two of the three great races: Man O' War (1920), Pillory (1922), Zev (1923), Twenty Grand (1931), Burgoo King (1932), Johnstown (1939), Bimelech (1940), Shut Out (1942), Pensive (1944), Capot (1949), Middleground (1950), Native Dancer (1953), Nashua (1955), Needles (1956), Tim Tam (1958), Carry Back (1961), Chateaugay (1963), Northern Dancer (1964), Kauai King (1966), Damascus (1967), Majestic Prince (1969), Canonero II (1971), Riva Ridge (1972), Little Current (1974), Bold Forbes (1976), Spectacular Bid (1979), Pleasant Colony (1981), Swale (1984).

Schools of Thought

Dedicated class handicappers look for the top-quality animal in the race, employing any of several standards and techniques which we shall examine shortly. If they think the horse is in shape, they play it. Otherwise they go to the one that rates second or third or fourth on their scale of class values.

Some class handicappers are as keen on arithmetic as any speed-chart fancier. They assign each contending horse a class rating, usually $\frac{1}{10}$ or $\frac{1}{100}$ of its supposedly true claiming price or class value. They modify the figure by adding or subtracting other homemade numbers in which they try to embody the probable significance of average earnings, consistency, weights, recent form, the winning averages of rider and trainer, and whatever other angles appeal to them.

Players less inclined toward paper work may also concentrate on the class horses in the race, eliminating all but the final choice on the basis of current condition, distance, weight, pace, jockey or whatever.

In my own play, I attend to distance and form eliminations first. I then check the survivors to see if any are clearly outclassed and can be discarded for that reason. By the same token, if one of them is obviously the class of the field, and nothing about jockey or weight assignments or probable pace seems likely to undermine its class superiority, I regard the handicapping process as completed, pending the routine visit to the walking ring. There is, of course, good reason to do a more thorough handicapping job than that on the other contenders, outclassed though they may be. They are, after all, in shape and suited to the distance. If the class horse is scratched, it's nice to know which of the others might become a good bet.

I doubt that anyone who does *not* pay due deference to the class factor can win money at the races. On the other hand, abundant rewards await the player willing to probe beneath the surface of the past-performance records to obtain a really accurate notion of each contender's current class. To adopt any of the procedures that involve such digging is to gain an unbeatable advantage over the rest of the crowd.

Basic Principles

Thousands of racegoers make the costly assumption that a horse has an advantage if it has run against higher-class animals than it meets today. Such reasoning is never valid unless:

1. The horse beat at least half its field or showed high early speed in the higher class.

2. Nothing has happened in the meantime to indicate that the horse has gone bad.

3. The horse is in good enough condition today to demonstrate whatever class advantage it might have.

The first point is basic. Few horses begin their careers in $5,000 claiming races. They descend to that level because they are unable to earn their keep in better company. Until each has found a class in which it can win, or give promise of winning, the experienced horseman assumes, quite properly, that its true class is probably lower.

The horse that never wins but sometimes gets into the money at a given level is usually conceded a good chance of improving when entered against cheaper stock. This is especially true if it has shown pace-setting tendencies or willingness in the stretch. A fairly widespread and entirely valid concept holds that any animal able to finish within three lengths of a winner may be expected to come out on top in the same company at a later date, and should have a class advantage if entered with cheaper animals while still in condition.

In any list of entries at any track, the player finds horses whose records show that they have defeated better fields than challenge them today. A horse is entered at $5,000 today, but has won here at $8,000. Should the player credit it with an edge in class? Not too quickly. In assessing the class of claiming animals that have been racing steadily, without long layoffs, it usually is hazardous to consider any performance that occurred more than three months ago. In fact, the safest procedure is to find the *latest* victory or in-the-money effort and base the class evaluation on it. If the horse won with great authority, or ran close in excellent time, the player should be fairly confident of its ability to hold its own against another field of the same or even slightly higher class. Provided, of course, that it is in shape.

If a claiming horse's record shows an absence from racing of six weeks or more at any time since its good performance in the higher class, the player has stronger reason than ever to suspect that it no longer is able to cut the mustard with better animals. Unless its most recent performances have been powerful enough to indicate that it is as good as it used to be, it should be credited with class no higher than that of the horses it lately has been beating or running close to.

The Purse Is Not Always the Thing

By and large, the better the field of horses, the higher the purse. At your track, allowance races may offer purses as low as $15,000 and as high as $30,000, with numerous gradations between. The best claiming races probably involve purses and horses superior to those of lower-grade allowance races. Lesser handicaps sometimes pay no more than better allowance races and attract the same horses.

Nowadays, *Daily Racing Form* past-performance tables include the purse values of allowance races. Before that innovation, a trainer could steal purses and cash nice bets by letting his horse chase stakes-class animals in classified allowance races, and then drop the animal into the conditioned allowance (for non-winners of two, three or four races) that it could win. Handicappers who did not know the horses by name and did not take the trouble to consult result charts could overlook some decisive differences. Handicappers who paid closer attention won nice bets.

On the other hand, unless you notice a real difference between today's purse and those listed for previous allowance races in the horse's record at the same track, you must not assume that today's race represents a gross rise or fall in class. Purse schedules often are revised upward or downward during a single race meeting, reflecting fluctuations in track revenue. Last month's $15,000 purse has become $14,000 or $16,000. At the same time, if an animal won an allowance for non-winners of two races other than maiden or claiming in its next-to-last race, it was perfectly natural that the purse of the last race be slightly higher, now that the horse was required to compete against non-winners of three.

A related puzzle is the horse who has won a $25,000 allowance pot at Hollypark or Belmont and turns up in apparent readiness to run well for a $15,000 purse at Del Mar or Monmouth Park. It is difficult to keep abreast of the class relationships reflected in purse schedules at one's own track and much more so to be confident about the relationships between purses and the class of the runners at other tracks. When in doubt, the prudent player without direct and dependable knowledge of the horses themselves will regard their races as unplayable, until watching a few clarifies the situation and reduces the number of unplayable races. Sooner or later, one becomes familiar with the situation at the other track. Fewer races are then unplayable.

In recent years, state legislatures have supplied an additional complication. Laws ostensibly designed to foster agriculture and animal husbandry provide enormous bonuses for the breeders and owners of winning Thoroughbreds foaled in the governing states. In some states not previously noted for the quality of their runners, purses awarded to state-bred races (restricted to horses bred in the particular state) are as much as 25 percent higher than those paid to superior fields in open competition. These breeding programs offer large incentives which have already stimulated marked improvement in the quality of horseflesh foaled in New York, New Jersey and the State of Washington, to name a few. But the inflated purses paid in state-bred races confuse and defeat a purse-conscious handicapper who does not take pains to differentiate them from the better races that get lower purses. And a handicapper who still regards an individual horse's gross or average purse earnings as a true index to its class is absolutely doomed wherever state-bred races are programmed.

The Golden Notebook

A player who collects *Daily Racing Form* result charts of all races run on the local circuit has ready access to important information missing from the less spacious past-performance tables. For example, the charts give all details about conditions of eligibility for each race (differences among those conditions may be rewardingly significant). For another, the charts include footnote comments which often reveal excuses for apparently poor performances, or reasons why apparently superb ones were not as good as they seemed. With these kinds of help, deliberations about Thoroughbred class and form become more productive.

Even more efficient than a compilation of result charts is a notebook into which the handicapper transcribes all relevant information about each race. This takes a few minutes per day but saves time later.

The main reason to undertake the work is that it leads to windfalls. The conditions of eligibility for claiming and allowance races are often quite complicated. Just as identical claiming prices may apply to fields of widely diverse quality (ranging from maidens to non-winners this year to non-winners of three in the last two months to no restrictions at all), so may the purses of allowance races. Beyond the state-bred races with which we have already dealt, numerous occasions arise in which a racing secretary finds it expedient to offer identical purses to fields of widely divergent quality.

For example, an allowance race might offer a $7,500 purse to three-year-olds that have not won two races of $2,925 in four months. (Translation: Two races in which the winner's share was $2,925. At some tracks, the winner gets 65 percent of the total purse. In allowance conditions at those tracks, "races of $2,925" are races run for purses of $4,500.)

In offering a purse of $7,500 to animals that have not won twice when competing for far less money in recent races, the racing secretary invites trainers to move some of their three-year-olds ahead in class. He also opens the door to better stock, such as one of last year's juvenile stakes winners in its first or second conditioning start of the season. Or a lightly raced animal whose only victories in a brief career may have occurred in a maiden race and in an allowance of today's value or better!

Another allowance race might offer an identical purse, but confine eligibility to horses that have won a somewhat larger number of recent races, or races of higher purse value. And it might admit older horses along with the three-year-olds.

The player who wants to unearth the opportunities buried in such conditions must know the kinds of races in which the contenders have been competing. He can make the check by referring to a file of result charts, or he can consult the notebook. It might look like this:

9/1. ES Spts, N rtes.
1. 2,4.
2.   NW2 mi 7/1. 5.
3. 10.5–12.5
4. NW2. 1,4.
5. NW3 of 6G 3/31. 3.

Any similar shorthand will do. The objective is ready access to information not included in past-performance records.

The above notations show that on September 1 (9/1), early speed (ES) was advantageous in sprints, and routes were run in whatever style or range of styles is normal (N) at the particular track.

In the first race, the horses that finished second and fourth had excuses. Recent improvements in *Form* past-performance presentations enable the handicapper to omit information about the class of a race which may be adequately described in the past-performance records.

The second race was for animals that had not won twice at a mile or farther since July 1. The race may have been a claimer or allowance race—the p-p's will tell. The fifth-place finisher had a significant excuse (insignificant items do not find their way into the notebook).

The third race was a claimer in which horses could be entered with claiming tags ranging from $10,500 to $12,500. At this writing, the past-performance record of an individual horse who ran in that race shows only the horse's claiming price. It helps to know what the top and bottom prices were.

The fourth race was for non-winners of two races. In some places allowance races are written both for non-winners of two races other than maiden or claiming and for non-winners of two races of any kind. If this was a track of that persuasion and the race had been for non-winners of two other than maiden or claiming, the handicapper would have elaborated the abbreviations. Note that the handicapper credits the winner and the fourth-place finisher with excuses, having made those decisions after seeing the race or after reading the result chart. Perhaps the winner had to overcome interference along the way, meaning that the performance was even better than an unobstructed victory. Or perhaps the winner came from behind on an afternoon when early speed was winning, or won with a run along the rail on a day when that particular path in the homestretch was deep and tiring.

The fifth race was for non-winners since March 31 of three races in which the winner's share was $6,000. The third-place finisher had an excuse.

Absolutely the most de luxe notebooks are the kind maintained by players so enamored of the game that they handicap every race every day. Rather than depend entirely on excuses and eligibility conditions for their evaluation of the quality of a horse's past performances, they jot down the age, sex and class of the horses that finish first, second or third in each race. In the right hands, notes of this kind are like a telescope into the future.

Let us pretend that we are trying to get a line on Horse "A," a five-year-old. The past-performance record shows that its last outing was a strong victory when entered at $6,000. The conditions of the race accommodated four-year-olds and up, at claiming prices of $6,000 to $7,000. So far so good. It was not simply a $6,000 race, as one might conclude from the past-performance record. But it was not simply a $7,000 race, as one might conclude from the conditions.

The player who keeps handicap figures on every race finds in his notebook that "A" beat a four-year-old rated at $5,500, and that the show horse had been a five-year-old rated at $5,000. "A's" own rating prior to that race had been $6,000. If there were any legitimate $7,000 animals in the race they were not in condition to demonstrate that superior class. "A's" rating remains $6,000. If one of its opponents in today's field ran third in a good effort last week, behind horses rated at $8,000 and $8,500, the opponent might be a good bet at splendid odds today.

By the same reasoning, if each of the first three finishers went into the race with $5,000 ratings, the winner would retain that rating. The second and third horses would be reevaluated on the basis of their performances. If it was a close finish, and the two horses ran extremely well, they might remain at $5,000. If they were beaten decisively, or ran in such a way as to suggest a decline in condition, their ratings would be decreased. One man I know operates on the basis of 50 points a length, assuming a truly run race: If "A" and "B" both rated at 5,000 and "A" beats "B" by a length, gaining in the stretch, "A" might emerge from the race with a rating of 5,050, and "B" with 5,000. If "A" won by the length only because "B" tired, "A" might retain 5,000 and "B" get 4,950.

I have had good results by giving full value to a victory or a finish within one length, deducting $500 for a second-place finish or a finish within two lengths, and $1,000 for show. Hence, if the first three finishers went into the race with ratings of 3,700, 3,300 and 3,600, respectively, the winner would retain its original rating (unless it was a young, improving horse that had won most decisively and powerfully). The second finisher might be promoted to 3,700 for running only a jump behind, and the third finisher would end with anything between 2,700 and 3,700, depending on how well it ran, and where the race fit into its own form cycle.

Although this kind of method allows the player to operate at the very nub of the class-condition problem, it requires more attention and is more complicated than the casual hobbyist may like to be bothered with. I include it only because some of the more enthusiastic players in the audience might enjoy a fling at it someday. It works with special efficiency in handicapping allowance races, especially the kinds that find high-priced claimers all mixed up with handicap animals.

Needless to say, if any horse suffers interference serious enough to affect the outcome of a race, the player must make due allowances in assigning post-race ratings. The approach dovetails beautifully with the use of advanced speed figures (which we shall consider later). It also relates closely to the work done by the analytic race-watchers known as trip handicappers.

Track Class

Experienced players usually have sound reason to discount the chances of a horse that has been racing at minor tracks and now makes its first attempt to compete in the big leagues. Until an animal from Charles Town or River Downs or Longacres runs well at Gulfstream or Belmont Park or Santa Anita, it remains a minor-track horse with a great deal to prove.

Class in action. Damascus wins the 1967 Preakness from In Reality and Proud Clarion. UPI PHOTO

The class differences among major and minor tracks are essentially matters of purse money, reflecting individual levels of attendance and pari-mutuel handle. Yet the situation no longer is as simple as it once was. Although Maryland and Massachusetts racing are secondary circuits which hardly achieve the day-in-day-out quality of New York's, shippers from Laurel and Suffolk Downs win more often at Belmont Park, Saratoga and Aqueduct then they used to. And they win in all kinds of competition, including stakes. Handicappers are learning to respect runners that come from secondary tracks in the colors of leading trainers.

If the horse from a top barn at a lesser track is a threat when entered at a better track, what of the one that ships from a major to a minor track? A second question answers the first. Why would anybody stabled at Santa Anita ship a horse to Turf Paradise to compete for much less money than the major track offers in even its lowest-grade claiming race? Answer: The horse has gone bad and the barn hopes it will be claimed.

As a generality subject to few exceptions, no good reason exists to send a horse from high-purse to low-purse territory unless the major circuit is on vacation or the animal is a stakes or allowance type for whom no suitable opportunities appear in the big track's current condition book. Horses of that kind arrive with impressive past-performance records and get the respect they deserve. The others are shipped in desperation and are usually too far gone to win.

Consistency

An honest, relatively sound campaigner is likely to be a factor every time it runs at the right distance against animals of its own quality. Modern conditioning methods are such that a consistent animal's only severe losses occur when it is entered at the wrong distance, or on wet footing, or over its head, or after a long trip or a long layoff. This applies whether the horse be a handicap champion or a $5,000 meal ticket.

In every price bracket, some horses are sounder and more reliable than others. Many are so unreliable that they never win and rarely run in the money. Having failed to establish class of any kind, they warrant betting support by nobody. But what of the creature that has won only once in its last fourteen attempts yet seems properly placed today?

It may be a winner. It may beat off a horse that has won 20 percent of its own races, and has run somewhere in the money half the time. Inconsistent horses beat consistent ones every day.

Some of the worst sucker bets at all tracks are "consistent" horses that run second, third or fourth in race after race, yet almost never win. Another sucker bet is the truly consistent animal that finally runs one race too many and comes out of it incapable of another good race for weeks.

The key to a workable knowledge of consistency is that it means little unless the animal is in good condition and properly placed as to class and distance. And notwithstanding a record of inconsistency, a horse is a threat if entered today at a class and distance that have found it a winner on every similar occasion listed in its record. As far as the record shows, that horse is admirably consistent when in today's company.

Many old-time players refuse to consider an animal that has been unable to win at least one of every five of its starts—the traditional yardstick of Thoroughbred consistency. Some also demand that the horse have finished in the money at least half the time. They count its wins, places and shows, and compare them with its total starts this year, or this year and last.

An even more conservative approach makes additional requirements. Even if its overall record is one of consistency, the horse must show at least one victory in its last two or three races, and two or three victories and/or three to five in-the-money finishes in the published past-performance lines that represent its ten or twelve most recent races. Some players go still further, demanding four in-the-money finishes in the last five races, or not less than four victories in the list of itemized past-performance lines.

Anyone who adheres to such principles of consistency and applies other simple rules involving distance, recent action, basic class and pace can expect to catch a high percentage of winners. Most of the horses turned up by a method of that kind run at short prices, but the player loses very little money betting on them, and may even be a winner in the long run.

Between two horses whose most recent good races were against authentic $7,500 stock, the smart player would naturally tend to favor the one that had been in the money with substantially greater consistency than its rival. And if the more consistent horse had been displaying that enviable quality in its latest races, the proposition would become even more inviting.

But what do you do when confronted by two horses, each entered for $7,500, if one has run at a price that high only once in its career and the other has run at a price that *low* only once in its career? And what if both races at that level were good performances within the last ten days? And what if the horse that stepped up to $7,500 and ran well was a truly consistent animal at lower claiming prices, whereas the other had been quite inconsistent when entered at $8,500 and $10,000, winning only two races of its last fifteen?

Some players automatically go to the "class" horse—the one with victories at a higher claiming price. On any given day, either or both players may be entirely wrong. Assuming both animals are in condition to run their best, the pace of the race may be such as to prevent either form winning. Because pace is so often a determining factor in situations of this kind, I advise the reader to be chary about eliminating relatively inconsistent horses or, at the other extreme, backing them simply because they have won at higher prices in the past.

To my way of thinking, downright inconsistent horses should be eliminated on grounds of class. Horses of middling consistency should be retained—unless obviously outclassed by a truly superior animal.

For anyone who cares to undertake a comprehensive brand of handicapping, moving from distance to form to class to weight to pace to trainer to jockey to special angles and finally the paddock, I recommend the following standards of consistency:

1. Accept as a potential contender any horse with at least one victory in seven to thirteen starts or two victories in fourteen or more starts this year. If it has had fewer than seven races this year, make the computation on the basis of its races this year and last.

2. Accept any horse, regardless of consistency, if it finished in the money or within a length of the winner in its last race, or had an excuse.

3. Accept any horse, regardless of consistency, that steps down in claiming price at least $1,000 to a level at which it has been able to win or run within a length of a winner at today's distance.

These rules are, of course, useless in handicapping maiden races. They also do not apply to two-year-olds. In handicapping older, more experienced claiming horses, they have the great virtue of allowing the player to prepare himself for the upsets that are standard at all tracks—the "surprise" victories by horses that have seldom won but, regardless of prior inconsistency, happen to be well suited to today's race. Handled this way, consistency is not overlooked. On the contrary, the player may find that the only advantages of one horse over its main rival are a more consistent record, plus its superior jockey, plus its superior barn. In a contest of that sort, consistency becomes a plus factor of great significance.

Average Earnings

Most statistical studies of handicapping factors give decent marks to earnings-per-start as an indicator of basic class. I am confident that the statistics were more impressive ten years ago and will be considerably less impressive in the future. As indicated earlier, the proliferation of high-purse races for low-quality horses bred in the individual state has undermined the kind of handicapping that used to depend on a direct correlation between purse and class. I considered omitting this section from the present edition but decided to include it for emphasis. No kind of earnings formula (including the ancient one that calculates the average purse for which the horse has performed effectively in the past) can be trusted in an era of inflated purses for state-bred horses.

Age

A properly handled Thoroughbred achieves the pinnacle of its speed and endurance in the late summer of its four-year-old season and does not necessarily lose these fundamental attributes of racing class until age six or seven. Unfortunately, most Thoroughbreds are not properly handled. Many are so badly abused that they begin to deteriorate at three.

Because of this, one finds three-year-olds winning races of a mile and longer in the spring and summer of the year against older animals that should leave them many lengths behind. If the feat is performed by a Buckpasser or Tom Fool, it should surprise nobody. But when it happens in ordinary races, experts have every right to gnash their teeth.

Four- and five-year-olds are supposed to outclass the threes, especially at distances in excess of seven furlongs. They usually do. Which is one of the chief reasons why the expert player keeps an eye on purse values or on the eligibility conditions of races. The three-year-old that has been losing by narrow margins to older horses does considerably better against animals of its own age. The five-year-old that has been victimizing threes may be unequal to more mature competitors.

On the other hand, many claiming racers are so badly off by the age of four or five that a relatively sound three-year-old handles them with no difficulty—especially toward the end of the year.

Here are some tested rules that help experienced players to cope with the age problem:

1. No horse aged four or older is likely to win a handicap or stakes race unless it usually runs in such company and either has won or finished in the money when so entered.

2. No three-year-old is a good candidate in a handicap or stakes race against older horses unless it has already beaten such a field, or has been running with exceptional power against its own kind, suggesting a clear edge in intrinsic class and condition.

3. No three-year-old is a good bet against older horses in allowance or claiming races during the first eight months of the year unless it has a noticeable advantage in class. In the fall it remains a dubious bet if any older horse is not only in condition but seems superior as to class.

4. In maiden races and races for non-winners of two races, three-year-olds are almost invariably better prospects than the older chronic losers they meet in such fields.

Sex

Except at the lowest claiming prices or in the richest European and American grass races, female Thoroughbreds have less stength and stamina than males. They retain winning condition for briefer periods, and seldom are able to win the second of two successive driving finishes. They need jockeying of intelligence and sensitivity, because they react badly to punishment. Also, their sexual cycle affects their form.

None of this suggests female inferiority. Indeed, except for stakes-quality males, females have greater market value than males for equal racing ability. The reason that a female usually loses when entered to be claimed for $15,000 against colts and geldings is that only about $10,000 of her appraised $15,000 value represents her racing ability. If entered against $10,000 males, she might well win with great authority, but she would be claimed, and no owner wants to lose a $15,000 Thoroughbred for $10,000. Let me explain.

A male worth $15,000 has no value except as a runner. He is no candidate for breeding duty. But a $15,000 filly may have a pedigree attractive enough to earn her subsequent employment as a broodmare. The situation becomes clear when I point out that a stallion impregnates from 30 to 45 mares a year. To earn high stud fees, a stallion needs a good racing record. No such condition attaches to run-of-the-mill broodmares. And so the selling price of an ordinary racing filly or mare is enlarged.

In the upper reaches of long-distance grass racing, fillies and mares have always been able to hold their own against males because their instincts supply them with the ideal running style for that kind of gallop. Impetuous males tend to waste themselves in the early going, while females lope patiently along, waiting until the late stages to make their moves.

In *The Compleat Horseplayer* I disclosed a gimmick that I had found helpful in comparing the class of female and male horses: Deduct 20 percent from the claiming price at which a female beats other females, to determine the kind of geldings, colts (whole males, aged four or less) and entire horses (aged five or more) against which she might have a chance. In short, victory in an f-6,000 is rated at $4,800—not quite good enough to beat a $5,000 colt or gelding.

Among males, geldings usually are regarded as the most reliable claiming racers. Having been castrated, they have nothing in mind but racing. Indeed, they often are easier to train and ride than colts.

Some useful ideas embodying the class distinctions between male and female Thoroughbreds:

1. No female is a likely contender against males unless it has already beaten males of today's value at today's distance or longer, or has run close to males of higher value, or has beaten females when entered at a price substantially (25 percent) higher than today's top claiming price.

2. No female is a likely contender against males if the top claiming price listed in today's conditions is $500 or more above the price for which the female was entered in her last race. If that last race was an f-claimer, reduce its value by 20 percent before making the comparison. An occasional exception to this rule is the filly that scored a powerful win over males in its last race, finishing first by a comfortable margin after gaining in the stretch.

3. No female can be expected to win today against males or females if it is stepping up in class after a race in which it engaged in a driving finish and failed to gain ground during the stretch run.

Rises in Class

Vigorous three-year-olds often improve tremendously. The horse that beat $4,000 claimers at 15 to 1 in June may continue to win, despite boosts in class, and may be a 7 to 5 favorite when it goes to the post against $10,000 animals in August.

Older horses also climb the class ladder, but less often and less spectacularly. Unless a horse ran an exceedingly promising race in its last try, it probably has no business stepping up in claiming price today. The most frequent reason for running it in superior company is that the trainer is trying to work it into condition and wants to protect it from a claim while doing so. If the horse not only is out of its class but is entered at an unsuitable distance, the trainer's motives become that much more apparent.

But the player needs to wrinkle his brow over a rise in class by a horse that won, ran close or showed signs of important improvement in its latest effort. Ability to perceive those signs of improvement (see Chapter 9), when combined with a solid understanding of the class factor, enables a good player to catch winners at nice prices. Racetrack crowds sometimes bet on a horse that moves up in class, but are unlikely to do so unless its most recent race was an obviously strong performance. As the reader now knows, some signs of improvement are by no means obvious.

As in other aspects of handicapping, it is possible to become too mechanical about rises in class, and miss wonderful betting opportunities. The animal that ran well in its last race, entered for $7,500, may not be stepping up in class at all today, even though its price has been raised to $9,000. A notebook-keeper or a collector of result charts would see at a glance that the horse defeated animals every bit as good as those it meets this afternoon. In other circumstances, a horse that remained at $7,500 today might be facing better stock, and might even be tossed out on grounds of inability to handle the assignment.

When dealing with a three-year-old coming off a big win, it makes a good deal of sense to credit it with class no lower than the bottom price in today's eligibility conditions. Horses of that kind should never be underrated, and should be allowed to make huge jumps in class. They can do it. They often are the best bet of the day, week and month.

Here, for persons who depend exclusively on past-performance records, are additional ideas about step-ups in class.

1. To be acceptable as a contender in an allowance race, a horse whose last start was in a claimer (a) should have won an allowance race on this circuit or one of equal class, or (b) should be facing other non-winners of such allowance races, and (c) should not be asked to beat another contender that has run in the money in a handicap race within the last three months.

2. No female may step from a claiming race to an allowance race, or from an allowance to a handicap, unless today's race is for females and no other entrant has ever been able to finish in the money when entered in a race of today's class. An obvious exception is the female stakes winner that tuned up for today's effort by running in an allowance race.

3. A female running against other females may seem to be stepping up in class after a race in which it was entered against males at a lower price. But it may actually be an excellent prospect whose trainer has maneuvered it into a concealed soft spot. For example, if it ran well against males last week, when entered to be claimed for $7,000, it is actually dropping in class if entered against $8,000 fillies and mares today (see page 195).

Drops in Class

A horse rarely drops very much in class unless something is wrong, and the barn has lost hope of winning any money with it at its customary price level. Yet races are won every day by animals entered at lower prices than those listed in their most recent past performances. These are not usually authentic class drops. They merely are proper placements of well-conditioned horses, restoring them to the proper class after running them into shape against better stock.

A player who considers the factors of distance and form before concerning himself with class can save a lot of effort. A horse out of shape is a horse out of shape: it may be dropping in class by $2,500 today, but if it is not in condition to run its current best, nobody should hazard a bet on it.

Assuming that the player restricts attention to animals entered at suitable distances, and in sufficiently good form to qualify as contenders, the following ideas about class drops will prove useful:

1. The horse should improve today if the highest claiming price allowed in the race is lower than the price at which it was entered in its last race.

2. The horse may improve if it stepped down in price for its last race and is entered today at the same price, especially if it ran at the wrong distance in its last race, or will have a better rider today.

3. The horse should improve if it went up in claiming price for its last race and is entered today at a price lower than in its next-to-last. For example, if it is entered at $4,000 today, it might have been entered for $5,000 in its last race, and $4,500 in the race before.

4. A female should improve if it ran against males in its last race and is entered at a lower claiming price today in a race for females. This is a significant reduction in class.

5. A horse should improve today if it is running at a price lower than any listed in its past performances. An allowance horse is invariably a threat when entered in a claiming race for the first time.

6. A horse should be conceded a chance in a claiming race if it has won an allowance race on a major circuit within the last three months.

7. A horse should improve today if it is entered at a price lower than the price at which it was claimed, especially if it was claimed within the past two months and has had not more than three races in that time—all of them losses at a higher claiming price.

The Class of Two-Year-Olds

Until the juveniles are asked to run three quarters of a mile and beyond, nobody has more than a hazy idea of their real class. In the shorter dashes, the two-year-old that has demonstrated its ability to cover the ground in the shortest time is the best bet. He may beat a youngster that goes on to stakes victories at more representative distances. And he may end as a $3,000 claimer himself. Forget it. He remains the best bet today, because speed is all that counts today.

For the same reason, an apparent drop in class from a maiden-special-weights to a maiden claimer, or from one claimer to another of less value is unimportant among two-year-olds entered at distances of less than six furlongs.

Later in the year, when most two-year-olds are running at six and seven furlongs, things change. The player welcomes the presence in a high-priced claimer of a youngster that has run middling well in an allowance race of today's distance. If all other things are equal, the former allowance runner may have a decisive edge in class.

Likewise, the speediest two-year-old in the field is a good bet in any juvenile allowance or stakes race at less than six furlongs, even if its only victory was in a maiden race. But when the distances are stretched out a bit, and the ready stamina of superior class becomes operational, no juvenile should be considered in a stakes unless it has proved its mettle in allowance company.

Class in Handicaps and Stakes

The fields in handicap and stakes events for horses aged three or older are normally so closely matched that victory goes to the animal in best condition—a superiority which may be impossible to foresee in the past-performance lines. On other occasions, especially at secondary tracks, the player may note the presence of a horse that has been doing most of its running in the very best company on the very best circuits. If its rider is one of the nation's best and its barn is also one of the leaders, the horse probably has a class advantage. The player then checks the weights, the condition factor and the probable pace, and often as not finds himself with a nice bet.

11

THE PACE FACTOR

Ask any competent trainer of Thoroughbreds what strategy he would employ with a ready miler on a day when it meets its own kind at its favorite distance. He replies with a shrug: "How do the other horses run? How does my horse run?"

Racing strategy is entirely a matter of pace, which is determined mainly by the running styles of the contestants and partly by class, condition, distance, weights and the texture of the racing strip. After a horse wins a truly run race, the trainer knows that his strategy was correct. Players with negotiable mutuel tickets know that their own handicapping was correct. And they know that—in all particular circumstances of the particular race—the class, condition, distance preferences, weights and running styles of the other horses were advantageous to the winner. In other words, he was a ready Thoroughbred, well placed.

Because pace is the very crux of the trainer's pre-race calculations, it should occupy no lesser position in the mind of the player. Whatever school of handicapping thought may claim one's loyalty, results improve as soon as one budgets a few minutes of intelligent attention for a study of pace.

This applies with special emphasis to speed handicappers, whose arithmetic sometimes overlooks the imperatives of running style and pace. The mutuel machines are invariably kinder to the speed fancier who makes no bet unless reasonably sure that the pace of the race will help his choice to do its best.

Pace wins the race. Sprint races are won or lost in the first half-mile—more often in the first quarter. Longer races are won or lost in the first three-quarters. This remains true whether the ultimate winner be a front-runner which leads all the way, or a stretch-runner which steams out of the pack to win in the last jump. The pace analyst looks for the horse able to set or overcome the fastest probable early pace without tiring too badly in the homestretch. It is as starkly simple as that.

How Pace Works

Most thoroughbreds are able to produce top speed for about three furlongs. The rider's problem is to consume this energy efficiently. His ability to do so is limited by the physique and temperament of his mount, which govern its racing style.

The cheap front-runner has only one way of going—lickety-split from the gate and decelerating from exhaustion in the last quarter-mile.

Better front-runners can be rated on the lead, restrained just enough to avoid premature fatigue while staying in front.

The familiar "one-run" horse allows itself to be rated behind the pace and then expends its strength in a single burst—losing if the jockey lets it run too soon, or if he waits too long, or cannot find racing room, or if the leader simply ran too fast and too far.

A really useful horse of rare versatility may be able to lead from wire to wire in some races, or run slightly behind the early pace in others, allowing the rider to adapt to the demands of the situation.

The rider is limited not only by his mount's style but by the effect of the racing surface on that style and, of course, the effect on the horse of its opponents' styles. A front-runner is fortunate if (1) it races on a day when the track is kindly to early speed and (2) its opponents include no other front-runner of equal class and condition. In such circumstances, the jockey wins by rating the animal, allowing it to run just quickly enough to stay in front, but slowly enough to have plenty left in the stretch. Even a rank quitter can win once in a while when the situation is so favorable that it develops an early lead too large for the plodders to overcome.

Any front-runner encounters trouble when opposed by another early speedster or two of equal or superior class. In such competition, the outclassed horse gives way a few seconds after it is challenged. On days favorable to early speed, one of the other two may go on to win the race, if its class and condition permit. When the track is deeper and more tiring, the two surviving front-runners are more likely to defeat each other, giving way in the stretch to a horse that has run slightly behind the early pace, awaiting its turn. Or, if the track is exceptionally deep and holding, the winner may be a horse that was many lengths behind the early pace but comes along in the final yards.

In any truly run race a decided class advantage tells the tale. A genuinely superior horse wins if in shape to do so, regardless of running style. If a front-runner, it pickles others of that persuasion and proceeds to win. If it prefers to run behind the early pace, it turns on the engine in the stretch and leaves the others behind, like a Forego or John Henry.

Without a pronounced edge in class, a stretch-gainer wins its race pretty much by default. It wins by staying sufficiently close to the early leaders and waiting for them to beat each other. Quite often, they have no choice. Should one of them slow down in the early running, in an attempt to conserve strength, its front-running rival almost invariably does the same. When both slow down too noticeably, the shrewd rider of an off-pace horse smells the rat, speeds up, takes the lead ahead of schedule and holds it to the wire. Eddie Arcaro used to do that sort of thing at every opportunity.

The Right Track

Since most Thoroughbreds are prisoners of their own inherited or acquired running styles, owners and trainers select their stock with that in mind. Horses with early speed are found in greatest profusion at tracks most favorable to that style. Horses more laggard out of the starting gate are in demand at places where the finishing kick has a better chance to win.

One of the most important handicapping discoveries of the century was made separately by Frederick S. Davis in Pennsylvania and Dr. William L. Quirin in New York. Each found that North American tracks are considerably more hospitable to early speed than to the late gain in the homestretch. Slightly more than 55 percent of all races are won by horses with enough early speed to run first, second or third at the half-mile pole. Davis reported that horses of that kind won 62 percent of all races on dry footing at the main track at Aqueduct. When the strip was wet, the percentage rose to 75. At Belmont Park, long thought to favor come-from-behinders, dry tracks enabled quick-starting animals to win 52 percent of the time, a record that improved to 70 percent in slop and mud. At Monmouth Park, the figures were 62 percent when dry, 60 when wet. And at Fair Grounds, although early speedsters won but 45 percent of the races on a dry strip, they took 65 percent when the New Orleans track was in its familiarly soggy state.

Modern techniques of track construction, drainage and maintenance have moderated some of the pronounced biases for which some racing strips were formerly notorious. In bygone days, Gulfstream, Del Mar, Monmouth Park and Golden Gate were justly regarded as unusually favorable to horses with early speed. Churchill Downs, Ellis Park, Fort Erie and Sportsman's Park were at the opposite extreme. Things have changed.

At any North American one-mile track in the final years of this century, the player will encounter days on which the racing strip is so glibly resilient that the first horse to reach the half-mile pole is a virtual cinch to arrive at the finish line no worse than second. On other days, the horses with early speed will fade in the homestretch. And there will be days when the best horse wins, regardless of running style.

On most days in most places it therefore has become absolutely crucial to appraise the existing condition of the racing surface in terms of its effect on the racing. Nothing can be taken for granted.

Many years ago, in *The Compleat Horseplayer,* I presented a pace-rating formula which handled track variations by avoiding them. Play was confined to fast tracks and such sloppy ones as benefited early speed. The fact was overlooked that fast tracks also vary from day to day and even from race to race. The procedure remained in the black only because it permitted play on few races and only on horses that were conspicuous standouts. Because of that book and the success many players had with its advice, I became identified as an all-out pace handi-capper, dependent on arithmetical calculations. I am not. In these pages I hope to persuade uncommitted readers that pace *analysis* is far prefera-ble to numerical pace ratings, and that the essence of pace analysis is knowledge of how early speed is doing on the particular track that particular afternoon or evening.

Pace on Grass

Most grass racing places a premium on the ability of better horses to save ground on the turns, cut the corner into the homestretch and come on strong at the end. The texture of the footing usually favors race tactics of that kind. But the popular growth of turf racing seems to have produced new generations of grass horses able on occasion to overcome traditional track biases. Just as the best horse on the dirt can win a big stakes by coming from off the pace on a day when the main track favors early speed, so can the best horse win from wire to wire on grass.

The Illusion of Stretch Speed

Because of the dominance of early speed on most days at most tracks, and because the rider who falls too far behind the early pace invites other horses to run away and leave him hopelessly behind, the fast start has become a fundamental of the sport. Precious speed is spent in the rush from the gate and the duel for favorable position at the head of the line, and/or on the rail, and/or on the dry center of the strip, or wherever the riders want to be.

The finish being a product of what took place earlier, practically all races are run more rapidly in the beginning than at the end. Most players are unaware of this. But it is crucial to an understanding of pace and of jockeying.

The front-runners in a typical six-furlong sprint at Aqueduct cover the first quarter-mile in less than 23 seconds. They require at least 25 seconds to run the final quarter. Whenever a horse runs the last quarter in .24 it rates headlines.

The sensational sight of a Thoroughbred coming on strong to pass four or five others in the stretch is mostly optical illusion. It obviously is running faster than the others. But it may actually be slowing down: It passes its rivals because they are "backing up"—decelerating more rapidly. Whether slowing down or not, the stretch-gainer in no circumstances runs as rapidly as it did in earlier stages of the race. If it manages to win, its victory is attributable not only to its class, condition and rider, but to the inability of earlier leaders to keep going.

The optical illusion deserves further comment. A come-from-behind type that wins a six-furlong race in 1.11⅗ very possibly ran the first quarter in .23⅗, the second in .23⅗ and the last in .24⅖. This is what the racing brotherhood knows as an "even race." The horse holds its stride comfortably all the way to the stretch and loses relatively little motor power when it gets there. To the crowd in the stand the horse may seem to be flying, but it is not. Good riders run such races on good horses. Riders like Bill Shoemaker, Angel Cordero, Steve Cauthen, Jorge Velasquez, Chris McCarron, Laffit Pincay, Sandy Hawley and other masters of pace do it frequently. A speed-minded, whip-conscious public chews its fingernails and unburdens itself of oaths when such a horse loses by a nose, wondering why the boy did not let it run sooner. But pace is tyrannical. Energy expended earlier is unavailable later. When Shoemaker wins or loses by a nose, it is an odds-on bet that a whoop-de-doo rider would have lost by lengths, having wasted the horse prematurely.

Varieties of Pace Handicapping

The public confuses pace with speed. Some persons who call themselves pace handicappers are no such thing. They are speed handicappers. Rather than study the records for a clue as to the possible pace of the race, they use ordinary speed-rating charts and deal entirely with final time. Some of the charts are known as "average pace" charts, on the assumption that the horse with the best final time has covered each yard of ground at the swiftest average pace. This is beyond refute: As final time improves the horse can be said to run the distance at a faster rate, or pace. But this is word-mongering. "Average pace" is merely a different way of expressing final time. It has nothing to do with the running style of any Thoroughbred, and is no help whatever to a player who cares to figure out how today's race may be run.

Confusion about the meanings of speed (or final time) and pace may explain why Damon Runyon pinned the label "Speed Boys" on the brilliant pace handicapper Jule Fink and his colleagues. Fink specialized, and still does, in cashing large bets on speed horses. But he bets them only after analyzing track conditions and pace and satisfying himself that the speed horse has a better chance of remaining in one piece all the way.

Many practitioners of pace handicapping concentrate their attention on the two, three or four horses in the race that seem to deserve the highest pace ratings. By whatever methods they assign such ratings, they single out the best of the lot and ignore everything else. For some reason, they usually rate the horses indiscriminately, on the basis of races run anywhere, in any year, at any distance. Their choice, more often than not, is the highest-rated animal whose recent record suggests that the trainer may be trying. They hit enormous mutuel prices. But their indifference to distance, current class and the fine points of form produces a lamentably high percentage of losers.

A somewhat more rational group tosses out entrants that have not raced in the last week or two, accepts the rest as contenders, and pace rates them. Again, little attention is given to class or distance. Speed or pace charts (which are one and the same thing) are used to compare a race at Fair Grounds with one at Suffolk Downs, or a race at Hawthorne with one at Calder. These players also get high prices, but enough losers to condemn them to the scrambler category. The high prices they get are by no means accidental, of course. Any horse that has ever run well enough to deserve a superior pace rating is a threat to jump up and win whenever it gets into shape.

In my view, the most profitable pace handicapping consists of analyzing the running styles of all sharply conditioned horses that are suited to the distance and are neither outclassed nor (much rarer) overweighted. If the day appears to be one on which a particular running style is at a serious disadvantage, we eliminate horses encumbered by that running style. The only exception would be an animal of sufficient class to overcome the disadvantage—as a top-grade stakes winner might when entered against an inferior bunch. A key to handicapping, after all, is to waste no time on animals whose records (in this case their running styles) disqualify them as logical contenders.

Analyzing Pace

Let us examine the fractional times and running lines of the best recent races of two horses. For present purposes, we shall make the totally unrealistic assumption that track conditions were identical for those races, justifying arithmetical comparison of raw times.

"A":	22⅖	45⅗	1.10⅖	4	2	1^{2}	$1^{1/2}$	$1^{1/2}$	1no
"B":	22⅖	45⅕	1.10⅗	5	4	4^{3}	3^{1}	$2^{1/2}$	1^{2}

Given no important difference in the weights, a conventional speed handicapper or "average pace" handicapper would regard Horse "A" as better by a fifth of a second, or one full length. It broke swiftly, was well in front after a quarter-mile, led at the half in .45⅗ and held its lead to the finish, although closely pressed. Horse "B" was not too far off the pace in the early stages (a fact that most speed handicappers and other arithmeticians might overlook), but took a full fifth longer to get home. The believers in charts would go to "A" by a large majority, and would be wrong.

A pace analyst would prefer "B" and would be right. His object, as described earlier, would be to find the animal able to set or overcome the fastest early pace and hold its lick to the end. "B" overcame a half-mile pace of .45⅕ and had so much left at the end that it won going away. Its own time to the half-mile was faster than "A's," about .45⅖ (figuring six or seven lengths per second). The power of its subsequent performance suggests that it would have enough juice for a stout stretch run even after chasing a pace-setter that did the half in .45 or .44⅘. An early pace of that kind would wreck "A." Indeed, it is possible that "B" might pickle "A" shortly after they leave the half-mile pole, and might beat the poor thing by ten lengths. The only kind of front-runner with a reasonable chance against a well-conditioned "B" would be one able to finish comfortably in 1.10⅖ or better after reaching the half in .45 or better.

For an example of another kind, try this:

"C":	23	45	1.23⅘	5	2	2^{1}	2^{1}	1^{1}	1^{2}
"D":	23	45⅗	1.23⅖	3	5	5^{5}	4^{4}	3^{2}	2^{1}

This time the speed handicapper picks the off-pace horse because its final time is better. But the on-pace horse happens to be the superior risk, unless today's track is unfriendly to its style. "C" was able to run the half in less than .45⅕, yet retained enough energy to pull ahead and draw out in the stretch. If his only problem today is "D," he can throttle all the way back to .46 or more, which will make him unbeatable in the stretch. Worse, if "D" tries to stay close to "C" in the early stages, so as to be in striking range later, he will have less left at the end that he did in his best race. The record shows that "D's" ability to win in 1.23⅖ depends on the presence of one or two tiring front-runners. But "C" was able to outclass the leader in his own race, and could probably have done 1.23⅖ if pressed through the last eighth of a mile.

Ruffian carries Jacinto Vasquez to an easy victory over an Aqueduct allowance field on April 14, 1975. During that brief season, which ended with her tragic death in July, the three-year-old filly established herself as one of the greatest runners of all time. NEW YORK RACING ASSOCIATION (BOB COGLIANESE)

Numerical Pace Ratings

Previous editions of this book went to some length in explaining the simple arithmetic of pace handicapping. This time I shall be more concise. I see no necessity for ratings of that kind, much preferring the analysis of track conditions and running styles already described.

I would have eliminated this section altogether if pace ratings of various types were not still in vogue, accompanied by a good deal of confusion.

The purpose of the rating process is to obtain a numerical expression of the fastest pace that a contending horse can set or overcome when in keen form. Without precise knowledge of how fast or slow the track may have been on previous days, it is unwise to base a horse's pace rating on a single past performance. A more sensible approach is to use two or three good local performances per animal, if that much material is available in the record. By permitting the handicapper to strike an average, the extra past performance or two may possibly smooth out distorted figures produced on days when the track was excessively fast or slow.

At distances up to seven furlongs, it is conventional to base the rating on the official half-mile time of the race plus the final time of the horse itself. With races of a mile or longer, the official three-quarter-mile time and the individual's final time are used.

For rating purposes, the handicapper looks for the recent past performances at today's exact distance over today's track on occasions when the strip was dry and fast. The past races should feature relatively rapid fractional and final times and a victory or otherwise impressive finish by the animal. It is vital to choose past performances reasonably representative of the horse's present condition—recent enough to typify the horse as it now is, rather than as it may have been in better days.

Let us now consider Horse "E," whose recently relevant performances follow:

```
.44⅘   1.09⅘
.45    1.10⅕
.45⅕   1.10
```

Remember, these conventional pace ratings are based on the official half-mile running times (the times of the horses leading the way) and the individual horse's own final times. The picture is seldom as symmetrical as in the model case of Horse "E," but the example will serve us better than a more complex one would.

Clearly, the pivotal times of this horse's better races cluster around .45 and 1.10. The fact that the horse's one race with that fractional time ended in 1.10⅕ rather than 1.10 might persuade the handicapper to use the slower time.

Unfortunately, the entire procedure involves so much compromise to begin with that little is gained by fretting over a vagrant fifth of a second. As often as not, the decision to add or subtract a fifth will cancel some other error. Without accurate track-speed variants with which to translate final running times into numbers more truly reflective of a horse's actual speed, the handicapper does well to assign the horse whatever final time it seems most likely to achieve in a race with the average fractional time. In the case of Horse "E" the obvious choice of fractional time is .45 and it seems sensible to use 1.10 for the final time.

In our example we shall rate "E" against rivals "F" and "G" whose own fractional and final time figures have been chosen by the approach just demonstrated. The race we are pretending to handicap is a six-furlong affair with a top claiming price of $15,000. Nine entrants have been eliminated for failure to measure up in terms of distance, form or class. Each of the surviving contenders has run good recent races in

$15,000 company and less impressive ones when entered for $20,000. Here are the figures:

"E":	.45	1.10
"F":	.44⅘	1.10⅗
"G":	.45⅘	1.11⅕

The simplest method of comparing these performances awards 10 points to the fastest time in each column, and deducts a point for each fifth of a second by which other times are slower. Here is how it works in the present example:

"E":	9 + 10 =	19
"F":	10 + 7 =	17
"G":	5 + 4 =	9

A player who cares to undertake a bit more work can make finer distinctions by using one of the speed formulas discussed on page 205. Regardless of methodology—and there are many, including some that use miles per hour or feet per second—the exercise is effective only to the degree that the handicapper eliminates horses that lack decisive class advantages yet have running styles unsuited to the existing characteristics of the track. But, as I keep saying, the handicapper who can make such eliminations seldom needs numerical pace ratings.

A Better Way

Here is the best recent race of Horse "H," with the fractional and final times omitted but with the *Daily Racing Form* speed rating and track variant added:

$$3^5 \quad 3^2 \quad 2^1 \quad 2^{no} \quad 84\text{-}17$$

In the next chapter we shall consider the subject of speed ratings and track variants, including those published in the *Form*. To understand the present example, with which we wind up this discussion of pace ratings, the reader should understand that a *Form* speed rating of 100 means that the horse equalled the track record for the distance of the race. The 84 rating of Horse "H" means that its final running time was 16 fifths of a second slower than the track record (100 − 84 = 16). The adjoining number 17 on the past-performance line of Horse "H" is the *Form*'s daily track variant. It states that the animal ran an 84 on a day when the average winning time of the races was 3⅖ seconds, or 17 fifths, slower than the track records for the distances of those races.

The total of Horse "H's" rating plus the daily variant of 17 was 101. Since "H" was beaten only by a nose, the winner of the race and the race itself also get a total rating of 101. If "E" had finished two lengths behind while earning the identical 84–17, the winner's and race's rating would have been 103.

To give "H" a pace rating as useful as the kind considered earlier but much easier to calculate, we need recognize that he reached the quarter pole (the second number, or call, in the running line) only two lengths behind in a 101 race. That gives him a pace rating of 99.

If we were using more precise speed figures than those of the *Form,* the identical pace-rating procedure—subtracting from the final speed figure of the race one point for each length that the individual horse trailed the leader at the second call—would give us an even more accurate pace rating.

Although an advocate of non-arithmetical pace analysis, I found it useful to run pace figures on Spend A Buck and Eternal Prince before the 1985 Kentucky Derby, to test my belief that Spend A Buck would run away from the other colt in a duel of early speed. Using the speed figures of my associate Henry Kuck, I found that Spend A Buck rated at least a point higher on pace than did Eternal Prince, and considerably higher than that on final time. As the reader may recollect, Eternal Prince was slow out of the gate at Churchill Downs on that day and the speed duel never happened. But the pace figures supported my belief that the outcome would have been no different even if Eternal Prince had emerged from the gate in a hurry. Spend A Buck would have won, and big.

Pace and Post Position

The inside post positions—the closer to the rail the better—are a great advantage to a fast-breaking front-runner when the first turn is only a few hops from the starting gate. The situation occurs most often in middle-distance races involving two turns. Logically enough, an outside post is a serious disadvantage to such a horse in a race of that kind, unless it is very much the class of its field.

Having to get to the rail so that it can run with maximum ease at the slowest possible pace over the shortest possible route, the front-runner needs extra quality and stamina to overcome the handicap of the outside post. Lacking those attributes, but imprisoned by its running style, it may defeat itself in the effort to get to the rail, in front, before reaching the first turn. Or, if the rider does not try to reach the rail that soon, the mount must cover extra ground on the turn.

In circumstances of that sort, a stretch-running type with a more favorable post position is often a better bet. When ridden by a good postboy able to get it out in a hurry and find a good position in the pack, it is able to lay slightly off the pace and, with ordinary luck, find the room it needs to pass the fatigued front-runner in the stretch.

Races with a long, straight run to the first turn are quite different for the jockey and the player. The front-runner is at no serious disadvantage in any post position. Even if it breaks from the extreme outside, its rider has plenty of time. He may ease over to the rail at any point before the first turn occurs, losing little ground and expending practically no extra energy in the process.

The slow-breaking horse with an inside post position is in grave trouble, however. Unable to get out of the gate as fast as many of the others, it often is pinched back as they fight their way toward the rail. To its difficulty in gathering stride and momentum is added the exertion of staying out of trouble and, finally, the problem of trailing everyone around the turn and, as the stretch arrives, finding—as often as not—that the only way home is on the outside of the pack, covering extra ground.

An added complication, for front-runner and off-pace horse alike, is the condition of the running surface. On muddy days, the deepest, most difficult running is often along the rail. The speed horse, which usually needs to save as much ground as possible, can now do so only at the risk of tiring itself in the deep gumbo. The competition now becomes a struggle for room in mid-track. The stretch-runner with a touch of stamina and class sometimes manages to come on along the rail at the end, deep footing or not.

Handicappers can make extra money by keeping tallies of the winning post positions at each distance and in each kind of track condition. To note that the inside post is a detriment at six furlongs on days when the track is labeled "fast" is to become aware of a situation not at all uncommon in many places, yet often overlooked by the crowd. And to discover that one or more of the middle posts is a great advantage when the track is drying out after rain is to place oneself in the way of jackpots.

12

THE SPEED FACTOR

We turn now to a fascinating subject which causes enormous confusion among horsefolk and intense rancor among handicapping authorities. Let us begin with the following interrelated yet apparently contradictory facts:

1. Over the course of any track's season, in races at any distance, the slowest winning times are recorded by horses of the lowest quality.

2. In the same season, faster winning times are usually those of better horses.

3. Nevertheless, relatively cheap horses often win in faster times than better horses do.

4. Yet better horses often defeat relatively cheap ones in times noticeably slower than each produces in other circumstances.

5. For persons who know how to deal with these paradoxes, speed becomes an accurate indicator of Thoroughbred class.

6. Losses penalize handicappers who depend too heavily on numerical speed ratings or speed figures, neglecting other factors.

Some Background

Confronted as they have always been by the first four of the odd realities listed above, many excellent horsemen conclude that running times mean absolutely nothing in the appraisal of a horse or a race. But they continue to depend on stopwatches to help them evaluate their horses' morning workouts.

Generations of handicappers and would-be handicappers have embraced the wisdom contained in Item 5 above. Seeking to save time and energy, they have stampeded to the error described in Item 6.

For many years, until about thirty years ago, each annual edition of the conservative and authoritative *American Racing Manual* included a speed-handicapping procedure essentially indistinguishable from literally hundreds of others that I have seen (some of which are still being sold). It consisted of a so-called parallel time chart which tabulated all race distances and their supposedly normal running times, assigning a numerical value to each, with the faster times getting higher ratings.

A supplementary chart prescribed numerical adjustments for inherent deviations from normal speed at the track and/or distance at which the rated race was run. Finally, the author supplied a scale of point deductions for the number of lengths or partial lengths by which the horse in question had finished behind the winner. Additional points were added or subtracted to reflect the number of pounds more or less to be carried by the animal in its upcoming race. The instructions suggested basing all this on the official final time of whatever past race had found the individual horse performing most successfully. Nothing was said about the horse's present form, or its suitability to the distance or footing or likely pace of today's race. The numbers were supposed to take care of everything. Which they unquestionably did, now and then, but not nearly often enough. It was sheer Item 6.

Putting the Problem in Focus

The primary influence on Thoroughbred running time is the ability of the animals. All studies of average or median running times logged on normally dry and fast racing strips show that the slowest are in races involving the cheapest maidens on the grounds, whereas the fastest are in the best of the season's stakes races. The seasonal averages recorded between these extremes can be plotted as a straight-line graph, with the normal time intervals between adjoining classes or claiming prices turning up at just about a fifth of a second. The only irregularities are more apparent than real, involving distances or classes so unusual at the given track that the sampling of official times is too small to be representative.

Secondary influences on running times are often powerful enough to produce strange effects. Chief of these factors is the weather, including precipitation, wind and air temperature. Yesterday, when everything was normal, the better races involved the better running times. Last night and this morning it rained. This afternoon it was sunny and breezy. The track

**Buckpasser sets a new world record for the mile—1.32⅗—in winning the
1966 Arlington Classic. Creme de la Creme was second.** UPI PHOTO

was drying out. Times were faster in early races than in later, as the track
became gummier. Thus, $15,000 fillies ran more rapidly in the first race
than $20,000 colts did in the ninth.

In the cruel cold of northern winter, relatively good horses log slower
running times than their inferiors do in the balm of summer. But when
the temperature exceeds 90 and humidity is low, some horses dehydrate
so badly that they run seconds slower than in more tolerable circumstances.

Another notable factor is track maintenance. Modern tracks become
dead slow when at their driest. A few trips by the watering trucks restore
some of the resilience. Deep harrowing of the cushion atop the racing
strip may then slow things down. Rolling and scraping have the contrary
effect.

But the phenomenon of the cheaper horse turning in a time faster than
that of the better horse is not always attributable to weather or track
maintenance. It often has a lot to do with the nature of the Thoroughbred
itself.

Horses are herd animals, most content in company. Centuries of
selective breeding have not abolished the heredity of the Thoroughbred
racer. For every extraordinary Secretariat who runs at world-record
speed even when unchallenged and a hundred yards in front, thousands
slow down and wait for other horses to join them as soon as they get the
lead in a race. Those who retain the lead in those circumstances are
simply tractable animals that have learned what is expected of them, or
are responsive to reminders provided by their jockeys.

American Speed Records

Distance	Time	Horse, Age, Weight	Track	Date
5f	.55⅕	Chinook Pass (3) 113	Lga*	9/17/82
5½f	1.01⅗	Zip Pocket (3) 129	TuP	11/19/67
6f	1.07⅕	Grey Papa (6) 116	Lga	9/4/72
		Petro D. Jay (6) 120	TuP	5/9/82
6½f	1.13⅘	Best Hitter (4) 114	Lga	8/24/73
		Trooper Seven (4) 122	Lga	8/10/80
7f	1.19⅖	Rich Cream (5) 118	Hol	5/28/80
		Time to Explode (3) 117	Hol	6/26/82
1m	1.32⅕	Dr. Fager (4) 134	AP	8/24/68
1m70y	1.38⅖	Win Stat (7) 112	OP	3/7/84
1¹⁄₁₆	1.38⅖	Hoedown's Day (5) 119	BM	10/23/83
1⅛	1.45⅖	Secretariat (3) 124	Bel	9/15/73
1³⁄₁₆	1.52⅖	Riva Ridge (4) 127	Aqu	7/4/73
1¼	1.57⅘	Spectacular Bid (4) 126	SA	2/3/80
1⅜	2.14⅕	Man O' War (3) 126	Bel	6/12/20
1½	2.24	Secretariat (3) 126	Bel	6/9/73
1⅝	2.38⅕	Swaps (4) 130	Hol	7/25/56
1¾	2.52⅘	Noor (5) 117	SA	3/4/50
2	3.19⅕	Kelso (7) 124	Aqu	10/31/64

American Turf-Course Records

Distance	Time	Horse, Age, Weight	Track	Date
5f	.55⅘	Beautiful Glass (3) 113	Hol*	12/12/82
5½f	1.02⅕	Faneuil Hall (5) 108	Hia	2/25/71
6f	1.08	Out of Hock (4) 117	Bel	7/4/83
6½f	1.15⅖	Avowal (3) 125	WO	7/10/82
7f	1.20⅘	Beau Bugle (4) 112	Bel	6/6/74
1m	1.32⅗	Royal Heroine (5) 123	Hol	11/10/84
1m70y	1.37⅕	Aborigine (6) 119	Pen	8/20/78
1¹⁄₁₆	1.38	Told (4) 123	Pen	9/14/80
1⅛	1.45⅖	Tentam (4) 118	Sar	8/10/73
		Crystal Water (4) 116	SA	2/20/77
		Waya (4) 115	Sar	8/21/78
1³⁄₁₆	1.51⅖	Toonerville (5) 120	Hia	2/7/76
1¼	1.57⅖	Double Discount (4) 116	SA	10/9/77
1⅜	2.11	Cougar II (6) 125	Hol	4/29/72
1½	2.23	Fiddle Isle (5) 124	SA	3/21/70
		John Henry (5) 126	SA	3/16/80
1⅝	2.37	Tom Swift (5) 110	Sar	8/23/78
2	3.18	Petrone (5) 124	Hol	7/23/69

*Abbreviations of track names explained beginning on page 313.

Thus, comparatively good horses often run no faster than required to. In a race against a lesser Thoroughbred, a good horse may well put the other away and then loaf all the rest of the trip to the finish line, with a final time slower than the defeated animal may have earned in beating its own class on a previous occasion (when weather may have contributed to the particularly fast time). Furthermore, when one speaks of the better horse "putting the other away," the truth may be that the other cooperated.

Like all animals, horses have their own pecking order in which the physically superior dominate the rest. It begins in the broodmare pasture. There the foal of the boss mare gets the most desirable space and begins to expect submission from its companions. It enjoys a particularly good chance of retaining dominance in later life, considering who its momma was. When a dominant horse flattens its ears and swings its muzzle toward another, the other retreats.

And when neither is especially dominant over the other but both are in good trim and ridden by competent jockeys, the final time of their thrilling rush down the homestretch can be the fastest that either has ever traveled the particular distance.

The horse that loses when challenged is reviled as a quitter by the human beings who handle it or bet on it. Yet, every now and then an animal of that kind finds itself unopposed on the lead in the first stages of a race and, as the saying goes in the barn area, it "gets brave when loose on the head end" and simply breezes to victory in the fastest time of its career. Which is why animals with early speed are often real threats when dropped in class sufficiently to gain an unopposed lead.

The sharply contrasting patterns of behavior just reviewed are neither exceptional nor contradictory. They merely illustrate the range and variety of equine personality plus a sample of the challenges encountered by handicappers in the study of Thoroughbred speed.

Basic Objectives

It is entirely possible to play the races successfully without attempting to compare final times recorded on different days and/or at different distances and/or at different tracks. Moreover, proper handling of the speed factor is a realistic objective only for professionals or for such hobbyists as combine intense motivation with a luxury of extra time and talent. Still, enormous advantage compensates persons who take the trouble of compiling their own accurate speed figures and using them in the context of an adequately comprehensive handicapping program.

Good speed figures come as close as humanly possible to factoring out all influences on running time except the ability of the horses. Thus, the handicapper who has such figures knows with justifiable confidence how good each horse was on the days of its best races. This is invaluable information for someone facing the most crucial problem in handicapping—the attempt to decide which of the horses will turn out best in the particular realities of the upcoming race.

Now let us survey the different levels of approach to all this.

Speed Ratings

As we observed in the last chapter, these are standing features of every running line on the past-performance pages of *Daily Racing Form*. A speed rating of 100 means that the horse's running time equalled the track record for the distance. Each fifth of a second slower earns a point less. Thus an 85 is three full seconds (15 fifths) slower than the local track's record.

Among the main drawbacks here is the handicapper's need (or wish) to compare performances at different distances and tracks. Obviously, if the local track record at one distance was set by a superhorse like Chinook Pass, ordinary Thoroughbreds will forever after get lower-than-normal local speed ratings at that distance, being unable to approach the time achieved by the great one. Ordinary Thoroughbreds from other tracks will have higher speed ratings at the distance than the locals do. The higher numbers will not necessarily indicate actual superiority.

But now comes a comforting fact. The great analyst of Thoroughbred performance patterns Frederick S. Davis found that raw *Form* speed ratings of the kind just discussed were statistically valid indicators of future performance. For instance, when he compared the higher of each starter's latest two *Form* speed ratings with those of every other starter in a series of six-furlong sprints, he discovered that 62 percent of the races were won by one of the horses with the top three ratings. But those horses represented only 31 percent of all the starters in the races. Thus, they won twice their fair share.

Track Variants

When reviewing pace, we noted that *Daily Racing Form* accompanies each speed rating with another number known as the daily track variant. A combination of 85-16 means that the horse earned a speed rating of 85 on a day when the winners ran an average of 3 ⅕ seconds (16 fifths) slower than the local track records for the distances of their races. As experienced handicappers know and others will quickly understand, the purpose of a track variant is to express the track's relative slowness or glibness and thus its effect on running times. But with the yardsticks being track records, it can be seen that the variant will be lower on days when comparatively good horses compete, and higher on days when cheaper horses compete—quite regardless of the true condition of the track.

Yet the true condition of the track is a component influential enough to make the published variant a useful supplement to its companion speed rating. Many years ago I published a handicapping procedure in which horses that qualified as contenders in playable races got figures that added the most recent and/or relevant speed rating to its variant. Subsequent wrinkles added or subtracted points in a quite satisfactory program from which lots of people extracted fun and profit. More recently, William L. Quirin's computer studies demonstrated that the sum of speed rating and variant was more effective than the speed rating alone. He also showed handicappers how to achieve even better results by using formulas based on each track's average *Form* variant, which he spelled out in his books.

Better Figures

Although the kind of prepackaged parallel time chart described at the beginning of this chapter has been available in hundreds of versions for many decades, and still is, it holds no appeal for sophisticated handicappers. Making arbitrary adjustments for races run on different tracks without compensating for the effect on running times of actual track conditions is undoubtedly better than no adjustment at all, but is naive. For one thing, by the time the canned track-adjustment figures appear in print, some of them are totally out of whack because the nature of the individual racing strip has been modified by resurfacing.

Good handicappers who decide to avail themselves of the advantages of speed figures usually start by attending to an indispensable requirement: They compile a dependable list of the normal (average or median) running times on dry, fast tracks for each class of horses at each distance on each of the tracks for which they will need figures.

This sounds like a large assignment and is even more arduous than may be evident. The class categories need to be broken down according to age—separating races for two-year-olds, races in which only three-year-olds participate and races involving horses aged four or more. Races for fillies and mares must be recorded separately from others.

The works of Quirin include formulas that facilitate the research by enabling the worker to concentrate on key distances and classes. But a good deal of careful checking is essential. As already mentioned, track-speed formulas have a tendency to become outdated.

Having compiled the recently or currently normal (known usually as "par") times for the relevant track or tracks, the handicapper then calculates daily variants on the basis of each race's deviation in fifths of seconds from its own par. The general custom is to add up all the deviant pluses and minuses and divide by the number of races, striking a crude average. More knowing operatives separate sprint times from those of longer races, and do two variants per day.

The results of this can be very satisfactory. But there is a still better way.

Best Figures

One of the shortcomings of the conventional variant based on par times is the underlying assumption that a *daily average* deviation from par reflects the actualities of horse racing. Calculating an average per day is convenient, but Mother Nature does not change all of her patterns and cycles at 12:01 A.M. and wait twenty-four hours to change them again. In fact, the resilience of a track may change for better or worse, faster or slower, several times during a single program.

Matters of this kind fall neatly into place when the emphasis in variant calculation shifts from the racing strip to the horses themselves. A handicapper who begins with properly calculated par times can progress in a few weeks or months to accepting as the par of each upcoming race whatever figure seems plausible for the particular group of horses. Into that projection goes every handicapping skill, especially the ability to recognize horses improving or declining, plus the effects of immediate track conditions on horses of various running styles.

Having compared the final time of a race with the pre-race projection, and having seen how the deviations turned out in the races that preceded and followed, the handicapper has an excellent idea what the final time would have been if weather and other track conditions had been absolutely neutral. And there, in fifths of seconds, stands the variant for the race.

While developing their projective abilities, some handicappers prefer not to overburden themselves with estimates of how much a given horse may improve or decline. They use the horse's last speed figure in a comparable situation, or (among more mechanical and less realistic handicappers) its last speed figure in any situation. Or they may strike an average between its last two speed figures, or latest two relevant ones.

Sixths and Other Fine Points

It galls the meticulous among us that Thoroughbreds more often travel at the rate of six or seven lengths a second than the traditional five. Even slowing down, as all do in the homestretch, five lengths per second is dismally slow.

This particular error may be the kind that works out well enough for practical purposes, cancelling as many mistakes as it causes, but I doubt it. Horses do not run five lengths per second, and a fifth of a second of running time is not equivalent to a length ahead or behind.

It seems to me that someone starting afresh might edge closer to reality and do beaten-length computations in terms of sixths of seconds. For example, let the final time of 1.08 earn a rating of 500 for the winner of a six-furlong race, and let a win in 1.09 fetch a rating of 440—60 points less. This means that a final time of 1.08 ⅕ is worth 488 at the rate of 12 points for each fifth of a second of official running time. But just see what happens with beaten lengths, which are charged at the rate of 10 points each.

Returning to the example of a race run in 1.08, the winner gets 500. The horse that finishes second, two lengths back, loses 10 per length, netting 480. Half a length is charged 5, and quarter-lengths or necks 3. The few persons I know who have adopted 12 points per fifth of time and 10 points per beaten length of horse have reported happiness with the results.

An even more interesting method may be to abandon the fifths or sixths for beaten lengths, as have some followers of the extraordinarily prolific researcher John H. Meyer of the Turf Investment Society of San Clemente, California. Refining suggestions made many years ago by the late Robert S. Dowst, who proposed that handicappers compute speed in miles per hour, Meyer developed tabulations that give rates of speed in feet per second for fractional and final times. Ingeniously, he suggests that the race be considered over for all the horses as soon as the winner's nose reaches the finish line. If a horse was beaten by one length in a race run in 1.12, its rate of speed is calculated on the supposition that it ran 11 feet (Meyer's preferred horse length) fewer than the 3,960 feet of a full six-furlong sprint. The animal's rate of speed was 54.85 feet per second, as one sees after dividing the 3,949 feet traveled by the 72 seconds of traveling time. One probably would do as well to call a horse 10 feet long and simplify the arithmetic a bit.

Meyer observes that it is as easy to calculate par times, variants and speed figures in this way as in the conventional fifths of seconds. It may well be more satisfactory.

Back to Basics

Let me now deal with an issue that was implicit but not spelled out in earlier sections of this chapter. Although it is an extremely basic consideration, it is often overlooked by enthusiasts of speed arithmetic, many of whom tend to ignore fundamentals in the best of circumstances. Here goes:

Although accurate speed figures are splendid indicators of class (as it existed at the time a speed figure was earned), they need to be analyzed in the context of the distance of the race and the class of the competition in which the horse performed on the given occasion.

That is, good speed figures are interchangeable from distance to distance, but most horses are not. Before extrapolating in that way, develop a concrete idea of the horse's adaptability to today's distance. The same applies with equal force to rises in class. The horse that earns a high figure against its own kind is by no means sure to approach that figure when outclassed.

Now to the turf course. A handicapper who produces good speed figures for dirt racing is exempt from the usual difficulties that conventional speed handicappers encounter in grass racing. Even the "about" distances and uncertain clockings that characterize turf races at some tracks are no great problem for someone whose figuring emphasizes the horses rather than the racing surface.

Of course, this does not mean that a horse's grass figures can be used in evaluating its chances in a race on dirt, unless the animal has already shown equal talent for both surfaces. The same applies to handicapping for races on sloppy, muddy or other off-tracks. A horse's dry-track figures are not usually replicated in off-footing. Lacking a line on the off-track ability of the horses, your best course often is to favor the ones whose running styles seem best suited to the existing situation. When you find a horse with a record of good performance in today's kind of off-going, plus the particular running style that appears to have the advantage, you face a nice opportunity.

13

THE WEIGHT FACTOR

To differentiate themselves from mere horseplayers, racing fans who analyze the past performances of Thoroughbreds like to call themselves handicappers. It is an impressive term, well deserved. Technically and traditionally, however, a handicapper is a racing official, not a customer. His job is to heighten the sporting aspects of the game—and make life more difficult for its players—by attempting to equalize the winning chances of horses. He does this by saddling better horses with relatively heavy weights, allowing inferior horses to carry relatively light weights.

The procedure is at least four centuries old. It originated in common sense: A horse with less weight on its back retains more energy for the stretch run. Whenever a longshot carrying 110 pounds noses out a favorite carrying 123, there is little room for doubt that the favorite could have reversed the order of finish under a lighter burden.

In contests among well-conditioned Thoroughbreds of approximately equal quality, with first-rate riders aboard, the only measurable, tangible, fully predictable advantage is lighter weight. During the actual race, this advantage may be insufficient, of course. Horses carrying heavier loads may prove to be in sharper condition, or better suited to the pace, or unapproachably superior in class, or better ridden. Professional horsemen know all this very well. It is their duty to avoid or minimize whatever disadvantages they can. So they look for spots in which their horses will be required to carry the lightest possible weights. In some circumstances, they try to augment that advantage by employing apprentice jockeys, reducing weight by the additional three, five, seven or ten pounds allowed as bonuses to trainers who risk the services of inexperienced riders.

When the late Ben Jones trained for the mighty Calumet Farms, he kept his horses out of countless rich races in which they would have been freighted with a few more pounds than he liked. His son and successor, H. A. "Jimmy" Jones, allowed the great Citation to carry as much as 130 pounds only four times. The horse lost all four of the races and never won with more than 128 throughout its career. As far as the Joneses were concerned, track handicappers had but one goal in life—to beat Calumet with high weights.

At the bottom of racing's totem pole, Trainer Joe Blow maneuvers for months with an arthritic nag until he finds a cheap race in which the poor thing must carry only 109 pounds. He fires the gun. The horse wins in a walk. Joe Blow feels like a genius. His horse might have whipped the identical field under 119 pounds, but don't try to argue that with Blow. He wants the largest possible bulge in the weights. In a game of perilous uncertainty, weight is something of which he can be sure. Only a fool, says Blow, would think that 109 pounds ain't ten pounds less weight than 119.

The commonsensical belief that a horse is best off with least weight on its back has become a kind of springboard. From it, horsemen, track officials and vast numbers of paying customers dive headlong into error and confusion. "Weight," they say, "brings 'em all together." By this they mean that a competent racing secretary–handicapper can assign weights of such exquisite accuracy that all entrants in a given race will have almost exactly equal chances to win. Nonsense.

Condition, class, distance, pace and jockey are factors of such fundamental importance that weight differentials seldom obscure them. Of the 54 races run every week at a major track, the outcome of one or two may be attributable to the effects of weight. In the other 52, weight is one factor among many, and not decisive.

The Scale of Weights

The tabulation on page 224–225 is the most honored of all the weight formulas. It derives from rulings propounded in the middle of the last century by Admiral John Francis Rous, who was unchallenged czar of British racing. The old salt knew something about Thoroughbreds and a great deal about human beings. His scale put the damper on certain larcenies by using weights to neutralize the natural advantages of older horses over younger, and males over females, at various distances and at various times of year.

It is quite a good scale. It is so good that it virtually eliminates weight as a prime factor in weight-for-age stakes races. When both horses are weighted according to the scale, victory in a contest between a three-year-old and a four-year-old invariably goes to the animal that rates best on the distance, condition, class, pace and jockey factors. To observe that this probably would remain true if the scale's weight differentials were lowered or increased by a pound or two does not belittle the admiral's accomplishment.

When assigning weights for handicaps, or in writing conditions for allowance and claiming races, track officials employ the scale's guidelines, but seldom its exact poundages. For example, the conditions of a typical allowance race at six furlongs in April stipulate basic weights of 113 pounds for three-year-olds and 126 for older horses. Non-winners of a certain number of races, or of races of a specified value, get lighter imposts than these. But the deductions are made from the basic weights, according to the age of each horse. The purpose of using 113 and 126 instead of the official scale's 117 and 130 is to make the proposition more attractive to trainers. It allows mediocre older horses to run under weights they are able to carry.

There can be no doubt that the differentials suggested by the official scale of weights are highly useful in the management of the sport. They bestow rules and standards on an area where chaos and chicanery might otherwise prevail. But there is no magic in them. They are far from precise in their effects on Thoroughbred performance. They do not begin to nullify class and condition—nor are they intended to.

Some horsemen complain that the scale is considerably off base in its treatment of four-year-olds during the early months of the year. They argue, with considerable justice, that it is unfair to require these young horses to run at equal weights with older, stronger animals in March, April, May and June.

The complaint would be worth acting on if significant numbers of races found horses running under weights at all close to the basic age differentials prescribed by the official scale. But factors like class, consistency and form are *also* embodied in the eligibility conditions of races. By the time weight concessions have been granted for failures to win, or for entry at slightly lower claiming prices, or for lower earnings, the extra poundage which a trainer might regard as unfair to his four-year-old has been compensated.

Handicapper's Weight Formulas

Because weights are precisely measurable, are an integral part of the eligibility conditions of every race, and are much on the mind of every horseman, efforts have been made to develop formulas expressing the

Jockey Club Scale of Weights

(a) The following weights are carried when the weights are not stated in the conditions of the race.

Distance	Age	Jan.	Feb.	Mar.	April	May	June	July	Aug.	Sept.	Oct.	Nov.	Dec.
Half Mile	Two years	x	x	x	x	x	x	x	105	108	111	114	114
	Three years	117	117	119	119	121	123	125	126	127	128	129	129
	Four years	130	130	130	130	130	130	130	130	130	130	130	130
	Five years & up	130	130	130	130	130	130	130	130	130	130	130	130
Six Furlongs	Two years	x	x	x	x	x	x	x	102	105	108	111	111
	Three years	114	114	117	117	119	121	123	125	126	127	128	128
	Four years	129	129	130	130	130	130	130	130	130	130	130	130
	Five years & up	130	130	130	130	130	130	130	130	130	130	130	130
One Mile	Two years	x	x	x	x	x	x	x	x	96	99	102	102
	Three years	107	107	111	111	113	115	117	119	121	122	123	123
	Four years	127	127	128	128	127	126	126	126	126	126	126	126
	Five years & up	128	128	128	128	127	126	126	126	126	126	126	126
One and a Quarter Miles	Two years	x	x	x	x	x	x	x	x	x	x	x	x
	Three years	101	101	107	107	111	113	116	118	120	121	122	122
	Four years	125	125	127	127	127	126	126	126	126	126	126	126
	Five years & up	127	127	127	127	127	126	126	126	126	126	126	126

One and a Half Miles	Two years	x	x	x	x	x	x	x	x	x	x	x	x
	Three years	98	98	104	104	108	111	114	117	119	121	122	122
	Four years	124	124	126	126	126	126	126	126	126	126	126	126
	Five years & up	126	126	126	126	126	126	126	126	126	126	126	126
Two Miles	Three years	96	96	102	102	106	109	112	114	117	119	120	120
	Four years	124	124	126	126	126	126	126	125	125	124	124	124
	Five years & up	126	126	126	126	126	126	126	125	125	124	124	124

(b) In races of intermediate lengths, the weights for the shorter distance are carried.

(c) In races exclusively for three-year-olds or four-year-olds, the weight is 126 lbs., and in races exclusively for two-year-olds, it is 122 lbs.

(d) In all races except handicaps and races where the conditions expressly state to the contrary, the scale of weights is less, by the following: for fillies two years old, 3 lbs.; for mares three years old and upward, 5 lbs. before September 1, and 3 lbs. thereafter.

(e) Welterweights are 28 lbs. added to the weight for age.

(f) In all overnight races except handicaps, not more than six pounds may be deducted from the scale of weights for age, except for allowances, but in no case shall the total allowances of any type reduce the lowest weight below 101 lbs., except that this minimum weight need not apply to two-year-olds or three-year-olds when racing with older horses.

(g) In all handicaps which close more than 72 hours prior to the race the top weight shall not be less than 126 lbs., except that in handicaps for fillies and mares, the top weight shall not be less than 126 lbs. less the sex allowance at the time the race is run; and scale weight for fillies and mares or three-year-olds may be used for open handicaps as minimum top weight in place of 126 lbs.

(h) In all overnight handicaps and in all claiming handicaps, the top weight shall not be less than 122 lbs.

(i) In all overnight races for two-year-olds, for three-year-olds, or for four-year-olds and upward the minimum weight shall be 112 pounds, subject to sex and apprentice allowances. This rule shall not apply to handicaps, nor to races for three-year-olds and upward.

The mighty Citation, shown winning the 1948 Kentucky Derby, never won a race when carrying more than 128 pounds. UPI PHOTO

effects of poundage on running time. One set of formulas is widely accepted among racing secretaries, newspaper selectors, trainers and players, many of whom concede it the authority of Holy Writ:

1. Four extra pounds of weight slows a horse by one fifth of a second, or one full length, in a sprint.
2. Three extra pounds have the same effect at a mile.
3. Two extra pounds have the same effect at a mile and an eighth.
4. One extra pound has the same effect at a mile and a quarter.

It may be so. But nobody can prove it. Horses are living beings whose fitness and mood improve or deteriorate from day to day according to the fluctuations of the individual form cycle. Condition, class, pace and jockey invariably are so decisive in the running of a race that the effects of small differences in weight become less exact than the formulas pretend.

Horse "A" loses by a neck under 115 pounds this week. Next week, under 110, the creature runs the same distance in the same time, losing by five lengths. Or runs slower and wins. Horse "B" does three quarters in

1.11⅖ under 112 pounds this week, losing to a classier animal. Next week, with 119, he beats his own kind in 1.11 flat. Someone who pays close attention to the weight formula at the expense of other factors condemns himself to grief.

Where the weight formula is more useful is in the work of racing secretaries. Like the official scale of weights, the formula has the virtue of being orderly. It is as good an aid as any in the process of deciding how many pounds to assign to each horse entered in a handicap race. Traditionally, and justly, the horse that has been winning the biggest races is burdened with higher and higher weight in each succeeding effort. The horses that have been chasing him get less and less. When one of them finally beats him, weight may be to blame—especially if he has been required to carry genuinely high weight. More often, however, his handlers refuse to run him under really heavy imposts. He loses simply because he has reached the downcurve of his form cycle, and another horse not only has rounded into shape but is able to demonstrate it under a low impost.

Weight in Handicap Races

The handicap race is the supreme test of the theory that "weight brings 'em all together." Here the racing secretary has comparatively free rein. The only limitation on his experiments is the reluctance of certain barns to accept high weights. He sometimes solves the problem by assigning their champion horses the minimum top weight allowable under the rules of racing, and lightens the weights on all other entrants as much as necessary to provide a reasonable handicap.

If his calculations result in a close finish, he not only is good at his work, but lucky. Weight does not bring 'em all together. Not even in handicaps.

I have just reviewed the charts of the 66 richest handicap races run in the United States during 1984. They dispel for all time the theory that weight differentials come close to equalizing the chances of horses whose class, condition, jockeys and pace and distance preferences are unequal. If the theory were valid, horses carrying the highest weights in each handicap field would win no more races than horses carrying the lowest weight. But here is what actually happened in 66 races:

1. Horses carrying the lowest weight in their fields won only three of the races and finished second or third in only 14.

2. Horses carrying the highest weight in their fields won 24 of the races and finished second or third in 24 others.

3. Horses carrying the highest weight finished last in only six of the races.

4. Horses carrying the lowest weight finished last in 16 of the races.

These statistics indicate most strongly that the weight concessions given to inferior horses and the weight penalties imposed on better horses do not cancel the more fundamental factors of class, condition, pace and jockey.

The number of high-weighted winners was strikingly below normal. High weights usually win about 33 of every hundred handicaps. That an indeterminate number of the high-weighted losers might have done better with lower weights is undeniable.

A perhaps more convincing indicator of the failure of weight to "bring 'em together" is the margin of victory that separates the typical handicap winner from the horses that pursue him. Of the 100 leading handicaps during another representative year, only 36 were won by a margin of half a length or less. And in only 26 of the races was the last horse to cross the finish line as close as 15 lengths to the winner! The usual gap was about 30 lengths, weights notwithstanding!

When Weight Counts

As the results of handicap races demonstrate, large weight concessions rarely make winners of outclassed or unfit horses. The principle stands up in all kinds of races, including the cheapest claimers.

For this reason, the expert turns his attention to weight only after deciding which horses are in decent form, are not outclassed, are suited to the distance and, therefore, qualify as contenders. At this point, the following ideas become helpful:

1. Weight usually is no factor in two-year-old races at less than six furlongs. If the fastest animal gets in with as many as five pounds less than its leading rivals and is being handled by a good rider, the bet becomes more inviting. But weight spreads large enough to neutralize superior speed are unheard of in these short dashes.

2. Three-year-old and older horses, and two-year-olds entered at distances of six furlongs and beyond, vary in their weight-carrying ability. If well-placed as to class, distance, condition and pace, and if assigned a weight no higher than it has carried in previous strong performances, a horse can be backed confidently, regardless of any weight concessions to other entrants. But if the horse has never run well at today's distance when carrying as much weight as it is assigned today, it probably is a bad bet. This is especially true of front-running horses with a tendency to tire in the stretch. It is almost equally true of one-run horses that win only by coming from far off the pace.

Handsome Boy, with 116 pounds, defeats the mighty Buckpasser, who carried 136, in the 1967 Brooklyn Handicap at Aqueduct.

3. If today's weight is higher than the horse has ever carried in the past, but if the assigned weight is below 120 pounds, the player checks to see how the horse has fared with three or four pounds less. Is it the kind of cheapie that seems comfortable only with 114 and below? Does it die in the final stages whenever it has 116 or more? If it seems a fairly courageous runner, and qualifies on other counts, it usually can be conceded ability to carry four or five pounds more than it has ever won with in the past—provided today's race is a sprint. At longer distances, three pounds is an equally safe assumption.

4. For most horses, 120 pounds is the beginning of difficulty at any distance. Except for young, sharp animals of allowance quality or better, no horse should be granted ability to carry 120 or more unless (a) it has already done so with aplomb in a race of today's distance or longer, or (b) it has run a powerful, reasonably recent race at the distance or longer, under 118 or more.

5. In races at a mile or longer, weights in excess of 120 pounds become most burdensome. A horse entered in a race of that kind under such an

Quick Pitch shows that weight is not everything by carrying 172 pounds to victory over the jumps at Aqueduct in 1967. UPI PHOTO

impost can be backed with confidence only if (a) it has demonstrated its ability to tote the load, (b) it is in superb form and does not come to the race off a recent tough effort under similar high poundage, and (c) no other fit animal of equal class has a weight advantage of five pounds or more.

6. In races at a mile or more, it pays to keep an eye peeled for weight shifts. Assuming that Horse "A" had a five-pound advantage when it beat "B" by a nose last week, "B" deserves consideration if the advantage is canceled or reversed today.

7. At any distance, weight in excess of 120 pounds becomes additionally unfortunate if the track is muddy or slow or heavy, and other contenders have lighter burdens.

8. A horse running with less weight than it carried in its last race should be viewed with extra respect when it qualifies on the distance, form and class factors. Trainers being poundage-conscious, today's weight shift, however slight, may represent opportunity to the barn.

9. If the track announcer reports that a horse will carry four pounds or more in excess of the weight prescribed in the conditions of the race, the horse is probably out for exercise. Being weight-watchers, horsemen want every pound of advantage they can scrounge, and do not ordinarily accept the services of an overweight jockey on a day when the horse has a good chance to win.

10. If the track announcer says that the horse will carry one pound of overweight in an important race, the player has reason to suspect the physical fitness of the rider. Presumably the horse has a good chance—or the player would be paying no attention to it. Presumably the rider has tried to make the low weight to which the horse is entitled. If he has failed by a pound, he may be woozy-headed from dehydration. Has he been winning many races lately? If he has been in a slump, his weight problem may be the answer. The horse should be viewed with extreme caution.

11. If a trainer waives an apprentice weight allowance in order to put a leading rider on his horse, the bettor should perk up and take notice. On the other hand, if the trainer has switched from a hot apprentice to a run-of-the-mill boy who never has won with the horse, the player should beware.

12. Except in dealing with races over a distance of ground among extremely well-matched horses of superior class, it is a waste of time to worry about weight shifts or weight advantages of less than three pounds. A pound or two does not make that much difference, but other factors do.

13. When in doubt as to the weight-bearing ability of your leading contender, pass the race.

14

THE STABLE FACTOR

In Chapter 3 we saw that about 98 percent of North American racing stables lose money. That is why stable owners are called "sportsmen and sportswomen" by the racing press. The sport is founded on their willingness to spend more than they take in.

Most can afford it. If they could not, they would quit. To be sure, many remain owners for only a few years, moving to other pursuits after Internal Revenue no longer permits them to deduct stable losses from their taxes. To be tax-deductible, a racing stable must show occasional profits, like a business rather than a hobby. Some manage to qualify as profit-making enterprises by buying and selling horses in claiming races, or by merchandising attractive livestock at the auction sales that punctuate race meetings.

Socialites and Pros

Owners come in all shapes, sizes, sexes and ages, from all walks of life. Those who form the political backbone of the big-time sport and supply it with most of its famous glamour are persons of inherited wealth. The breeding and racing of Thoroughbreds is a traditional avocation of their families. They share dominance of the pastime with a few millionaires of more recent vintage and a scattering of professional horsemen who rose to the top the hard way and now own important stables.

Diverse though owners may be, they fall into two categories. The smaller (by far) is composed of those with sufficient sense and taste to leave horsemanship to horsemen. A more numerous group includes owners whose desire for prominence exceeds their interest in horseflesh. If certain trainers behave like con artists and seem to know as much about soft soap as they do about the care and schooling of Thoroughbreds, it is from years of coping with bubble-headed employers.

Many owners want the trainer to pretend that they know something about horses. They crave to make strategy. They sulk if the trainer fails to adorn each horse with a popular rider. They want to know why the trainer spends so much money on straw. They get sore if the trainer doesn't tip them off to a longshot once in a while. They fume if they don't win stakes races and get on television. They make general nuisances of themselves. But they pay bills.

One of the most celebrated owners of modern times was Elizabeth (Arden) Graham, the cosmetics queen who owned Maine Chance Farms. During her thirty-five years in the sport, she employed at least sixty-five trainers. Some of the most competent horsemen of the era were unable to achieve lasting rapport with the lady. For examples, Eddie Neloy, Clarence Buxton, Eddie Holton, H. Guy Bedwell, George Odom, Frank Christmas, Tom Barry, Mose Shapoff, Ivan and Monte Parke, Ben Stutts, W. O. Hicks, Frank Merrill, Jr., Casey Hayes, Willie Molter, Randy Sechrest, Al Scotti and George Poole.

The player needs to know something about owners. He especially needs to know the names of the most successful ones. Generally, he will pay much more attention to the doings of trainers, who are the most decisive influences in the life of a Thoroughbred. But trainers move from owner to owner, their fortunes rising or falling according to the kind of livestock the owner provides. And year after year the same owners appear on the list of leading money winners. It pays to know who is who.

Leading Owners

To qualify for the player's alert respect, a racing stable not only should win a great deal of money but should finish first in at least 15 percent of its attempts. Those listed below have established their ability to meet those standards. For the reader's convenience, I list them alphabetically and omit the words "stable" or "farm" that occur so often.

R. J. AMENDOLA
ARTHUR I. APPLETON
ARENEL
AUGUSTIN
W. M. BACKER
DALE BAIRD
OSCAR S. BARRERA

BEL ROB
BKY
PETER M. BRANT
ROBERT BRENNAN
BRIGHT VIEW
BROOKFIELD
BUDANN

CALUMET

CANADA WEST

CARDIFF STUD

CHRISTIANA

CLAIBORNE

BROWNELL COMBS II

LESLIE COMBS II

ALVIN DAVIS

HENRIK DE KWIATKOWSKI

J. J. DEVANEY

JOSEPH P. DORIGNAC, JR.

ELMENDORF

EQUUSEQUITY

MARTIN L. FALLON

BERTRAM R. FIRESTONE

A. J. FOYT, JR.

JOHN FRANKS

FRANCES A. GENTER

GOLDEN EAGLE

DOLLY GREEN

GREENTREE

HARBOR VIEW

W. R. HAWN

RICHARD HAZELTON

AARON U. JONES

STANLEY I. JOSELSON

KINGHAVEN

KINGSBROOK

EUGENE V. KLEIN

GLENN LANE

BLANCHE P. LEVY

LIVE OAK

LOBLOLLY

W. A. LOFTON

BILL MARKO

JOHN D. MARSH

O. C. MAXWELL

JEROME S. MOSS

D. C. MUCKLER

NORTH AMERICAN
   THOROUGHBREDS

OAK MANOR

T. P. PAPAGALLO

CHARLENE R. PARKS

W. C. PARTEE

PEN-Y-BRYN

WILLIAM HAGGIN PERRY

OGDEN PHIPPS

RUSSELL L. REINEMAN

RENA-KIM

ROKEBY

THEODORE M. SABARESE

SAM-SON

SANDERA

ROBERT E. SANGSTER

JOHN M. SCHIFF

SCORPIO

FARID SEFA

EDWARD A. SELTZER

FRANK STRONACH

SUMMA

TARTAN

TRESVANT

TRIPLE AAA

JACK VAN BERG

R. H. VERMILLION

WINDFIELDS

WOODSIDE

Owners of Champions

The first family of modern American racing is named Phipps. Ogden Mills (Dinny) Phipps succeeded his father, Ogden Phipps, as Chairman of the New York Racing Association, which operates Aqueduct, Belmont Park and Saratoga. His grandmother, Mrs. Henry Carnegie Phipps, headed the celebrated Wheatley Stable. Dinny Phipps, his parents and his sister, Cynthia, have all owned and raced good horses. Among them, the members of this dynasty have owned twenty American champions, and at least that many near-champions. They head the list of currently or recently active stables that have won six or more championships.

PHIPPS-WHEATLEY: Ancestor, Bold Lad, Bold Ruler, Buckpasser, Castle Forbes, Christmas Past, High Voltage, Impressive, Mako, Misty Morn, Neji, Numbered Account, Oedipus, Queen Empress, Queen of the Stage, Relaxing, Straight and True, Successor, Top Bid, Vitriolic.

CALUMET: A Glitter, Armed, Barbizon, Before Dawn, Bewitch, Citation, Coaltown, Davona Dale, Forward Pass, Mar-Kell, Our Mims, Real Delight, Tim Tam, Twilight Tear, Two Lea, Whirlaway, Wistful.

GREENTREE: Bowl Game, Capot, Devil Diver, Jungle King, Late Bloomer, Malicious, Stage Door Johnny, Tom Fool.

ALFRED G. VANDERBILT: Bed o' Roses, Discovery, Native Dancer, Next Move, Now What, Petrify, Social Outcast.

ROKEBY: American Way, Amerigo Lady, Arts and Letters, Fort Marcy, Key to the Mint, Run the Gantlet.

C. V. WHITNEY: Bug Brush, Career Boy, Counterpoint, First Flight, Phalanx, Silver Spoon.

Man vs. Horse

Horsemen sometimes convey the impression that the sport would be more to their liking if a way could be found to eliminate the horses.

Eddie Arcaro once complained that three out of four horses don't want to win their races. Other riders say that unwillingness is even more prevalent than that. Throughout the industry, a standard conversational theme is the perverse, mulish, erratic contrariness of these animals.

After centuries of selective breeding, racing apparently remains alien to the essential nature of the Thoroughbred. Despite training routines intended to bring any fairly sound horse into some kind of racing trim, the breed continues to balk.

Exactly what is wrong?

Human stupidity and greed, intensified by the economics of a highly precarious business.

Responsible racing journals are replete with articles on the techniques of breaking and schooling yearlings, maintaining equine health, and preparing a horse for its race. Regardless of disagreements on technical matters, virtually all the articles play variations on a single theme: A Thoroughbred treated with rough impatience is unlikely to amount to much.

If kindness, patience and intelligence were dominant characteristics of the racing industry, such articles would be unnecessary. But they are necessary. Anyone can prove it by wandering around the barns of a morning, or keeping eyes and ears open at the paddock in the afternoon.

Many trainers, stablehands, exercise boys and jockeys truly love and understand horses. Many more do not. The heart of the misunderstanding seems to be the unwarranted assumption that modern racing is a natural activity for horses and that the animals, though mentally dim, should adopt a more human attitude toward their work and be grateful for the opportunity to participate. When the bland manageableness that passes for equine gratitude is withheld, and sulkiness or rebelliousness sets in, the tendency of the human being is to react with resentment of his own. In due course, there arises the peculiarly negative, self-defeating, quite widespread feeling that the meal-ticket, the horse, is an infernal nuisance, a necessary evil.

The truth is that racing is no more natural for horses than the hundred-yard dash is for men. To engage successfully in activities of that kind, a horse (or man) must be carefully schooled and tended. To survive any great number of races or training workouts without breaking down, the muscles, joints, heart and lungs of horse or man must be trained for undue stress. The difference, of course, is that a human footracer can discuss his pain. And he can make choices.

But horses cannot. They are entirely dependent on man. Like other domesticated animals such as the dog, they thrive or wilt according to the treatment they get from humans. A well-nurtured Thoroughbred tolerates the hullabaloo of the track, the repeated exhaustion of training and racing, the sometimes frightening ministrations of handlers, blacksmiths and veterinarians. He is willing to race. He sometimes even seems to like it. When he is retired he may act, like an Exterminator or Kelso, as if he missed the excitement, and may perk up considerably when brought back to a track to parade in front of the stands.

But the unwilling Thoroughbred is a different specimen. He fears noise or people, or some particular handler, or his knee hurts after repeated concussion of hoof on racing strip, or his lungs are congested, or he was soured on the whole game by unpleasant early experiences. Sometimes he can be whipped into cooperating and running a good race. More often, the punishment frightens him into losing his stride. Or he retaliates in the only ways he knows, which are to sulk or swerve or duck or stop.

As the Hirsch Jacobs experience with Stymie illustrates, and as has been shown in many other cases of the same kind, a trainer with time, skill and motivation may sometimes undo the previous experiences or present afflictions that cause unwillingness in a Thoroughbred. Unfortunately, the tempo and pressures of the business make most such speculative experiments uneconomical. The horse is a commodity on which a quick return is craved. Either it delivers or it goes elsewhere. The need for the quick dollar, earned from minimum investment, affects what happens to most Thoroughbreds from the moment of birth. Financial pressures influence the behavior of trainers, grooms, exercise boys and stablehands—all but a lucky few trainers and their backstretch employees.

While most owners fully expect to lose money, each wants to win every purse he can—and some specialize in nagging about it. The goal of the average trainer and his staff is to keep the owner quiet—if not happy—by providing maximum action. Moreover, backstretch incomes are tied to purse revenues. The trainer gets 10 percent. Bonuses go to everyone else, including the humblest swipe.

Under those pressures for quick returns, and with the track's racing secretary screaming for horses with which to fill out his programs, it is perhaps no wonder that comparatively sound animals are grievously overworked. And that they continue to race even after overwork begins to take its toll. And that they finally break down forever. And that the year never passes without half a dozen good three-year-olds going permanently bad before they ever get to Churchill Downs. And that many three-year-old champions poop out at four. And that a topnotch six-year-old is a rarity.

You can argue until you turn blue that a horse might last longer and earn a great deal more money if raced more sparingly, prepared more carefully for each race. The trainer answers with a grimace, "Horses make no money standing in their stalls or browsing in pastures. I'm not John Nerud or Woody Stephens. I'm not working for Mr. Whitney or Mr. Guest. I've got payrolls to meet and my owners are breathing down my back. Horse either gets up and does it or I go rustle me another horse."

Scores of trainers—possibly hundreds—do the very best that can be done for their animals, on the sound theory that proper care will be repaid at the finish wire some afternoon. Their ability to function this wisely depends not only on their own competence but on the dispositions of their employers—the owners—and on the quality of their stable help. Good stablehands are hard to find nowadays. The others tend to give as little time and care as possible to a horse, thereby helping to worsen whatever quirk or ailment may be preventing it from winning. I have seen the trainers of world-famous stables seethe in helpless rage at the barbarically stupid impatience with which exercise boys and grooms handle frightened animals. "I'll fire that bum as soon as I can find another" is a familiar refrain in the front offices of racing barns.

How Horses Learn

All scientific studies of horses reveal them to be less intelligent, in the human sense, than apes, dolphins, elephants, pigs or dogs. But they are keenly sensitive to their surroundings and to the experiences they undergo at human hands. And they have memories that would do credit to any elephant. It is easier for them to learn than to forget what they have learned. A bad habit implanted by a misused whip, an ill-advised shout or cuff, or an accidental collision, may persist for years.

It is unlikely that any horse actually understands the difference between winning and losing. Yet horses obviously do what they can to avoid or resist discomfort. There seems no doubt that they do best when taught their trade with a minimum of fear and pain, and when convinced by repeated experience that the rewards of good performance are worth the considerable effort.

It all begins with the yearlings. Patient, gentle treatment being costly, because it consumes the time of expensive personnel, an appalling number of Thoroughbreds are ruined at this, the earliest stage of their careers.

The process known as "breaking" is meant to accustom the young horse to the feel of the rider and his tack. It is a hideously frightening experience for the yearling, unless the handlers take their time. All writings on the subject (and trade journals are at it constantly) emphasize that human violence during the breaking period often spoils the disposition of a horse, leaving it dispirited or fractious.

Damage at that stge is compounded for many horses by impatience and carelessness during their first months of drill on the training track. They must learn to run straight, and to respond to the rider's voice, hands and reins, and to change leads on the turns, and to break from a standing start at the gate. It is a tricky business in which, once again, the future abilities of the animal may be impaired by unintelligent handling.

Yet the pressures are to school 'em as fast as possible (to save money) and get 'em to the races as early in the two-year-old season as possible (to get the money back). Thousands never make it to actual competition, having broken down from running too fast too early in their lives.

Horses do not grow a complete set of adult teeth until they are five! One of the chief reasons why young horses break down is that their immaturely soft bones give way under the concussion of running full tilt over hard surfaces. Incredibly, some veterinarians assert that the problem is worsened and disaster assured by ill-fitting shoes, which throw the animals off balance when they run.

Among horses that finally get to the races, few are without quirks of temperament or running style. Horsemen ascribe many of the idiosyncrasies to equine family traits. But candid ones agree that proper handling from the very start of schooling could minimize the effects of these inherited characteristics and, above all, could prevent development of other bad habits.

When the jockey grumbles that he always has to whip a particular horse to get some run from it in the early stages of a race, he refers in most cases to an animal whose earliest handlers taught it, altogether unintentionally, to behave that way. Horses that panic in the paddock or do not like to run on the rail, or between horses, or behind horses, or in front of horses, or on the turns, or that quit when whipped, or refuse to run unless whipped, are victims of their early conditioning. Horses whose tongues must be tied down with straps are, most often, horses whose first handlers did not know how to break them to the bit.

One of the best-known facts about Thoroughbreds is that their first experiences in competition often have a decisive effect on their later performances. A horse whose trainer is careful to give it an easy first race or two has a much better chance of going on to better things than a horse that almost expires of exhaustion in its first outings. Even better at the beginning is an easy *winning* race. The horse that loses its first races in all-out efforts may take months to recover from the experience. It usually behaves as if it is *supposed* to chase the others, not beat them.

In 1961, *The Thoroughbred Record* provoked considerable debate with a series of articles by the veteran horseman Colonel Phil T. Chinn. Among other statements uncomplimentary to modern racing, Chinn declared that the bucked shins, osselets and other arthritic ailments that afflict today's overworked two- and three-year-old horses were virtually unknown in his era. Horses were not subjected to premature strain when he was a lad. When they turned sore, he said, they were rested. And rest was more beneficial to bones and joints worn and torn by overstrain than the modern practice of cauterizing damaged tissue with a red-hot iron.

During the ensuing uproar, *The Thoroughbred Record* polled horsemen for their opinions. Three out of five agreed that the modern Thoroughbred is less sound than its ancestor of thirty years before. Those who agreed tended to blame today's harder tracks, the demand for more speed, the failure to rest modern horses during the winter and the strain of breaking from the stationary starting gate.

Some of the comments were enlightening.

Sam Sechrest said, "It's not a question of soundness. If horses were given more time as two-year-olds and at the time of breaking, and not started so soon, I don't believe there would be so many bucked shins and osselets.

Max Hirsch: "Horses not raised with common sense."

Robert L. Dotter: "Asking for too much speed from horses that have not finished growing."

Stephen Di Mauro: "Bad exercise boys—snatching, twisting and turning horses too sharply. Same for hot walkers. All in all, careless help."

John H. C. Forbes: "Thirty years ago there was time to rest a horse."

R. H. McLellan: "Starting juveniles at the start of the year and racing the majority of them too often thereafter."

W. C. Freeman: "Too many sprint races which force a trainer to rush his young horses before they have achieved their growth."

Dale Landers: "Racing and breaking colts too young."

Other articles in authoritative trade periodicals have deplored abuses visited on horses that survive the rigors of premature racing. Writer after writer pleads with horsemen to give ailing or jaded Thoroughbreds the rest they need. But rest takes time. And time is money. From stakes winners to $1,000 derelicts, lack of rest is a prime factor in the development of disability.

Veterinarians agree, and many have written, that a horse with cold symptoms should be rested. In recent years, outbreaks of what horsemen call "cough"—actually influenza—have caused alarm throughout racing. The proper treatment includes rest—an absolute termination of training and racing. But the lung capacities of innumerable Thoroughbreds have been impaired permanently by the strain of racing while infected with flu.

"I know, I know," says a top trainer. "I'm as sad as you are that the sport is not as gracious as it was when lords and their ladies sat under parasols and watched Arabian chargers run around their pastures for side bets. But this thing is bigger than all of us. It's just a reflection of changes that have taken place in every area of life. If you want to get indignant about the industrialization of the Thoroughbred, be my guest. But while you're at it, you might consider the industrialization of everything else. When was the last time you saw a piece of homemade bread, or milk fresh from a cow, or a new-laid egg, or an automobile that looked like the guy who made it cared about his work? You go get indignant about horses. Me, my main worry is whether I can get my horses onto the track for their exercise tomorrow morning before the strip is shut down for rolling. And whether I can talk some snot of an exercise boy into taking my filly around the track twice before he runs off to pick up another few bucks working some other guy's horse. And whether tomorrow's shipment of feed will have mold in it like the last one. And whether the damned accountant will get the stable's books in order for the next damned tax examination."

All of this has a good deal to do with the handicapping of horse races. The player is better off when he realizes that most trainers are not more competent than most haberdashers or auto mechanics and are under no greater compulsion to be. That realization surely clears the air for the player and inspires greater respect for the feats of those very few trainers who manage somehow to surmount all obstacles, winning far more than their share of races every season. These are the trainers the smart player favors. They have better horses and/or induce more racing readiness and willingness in their stock than other trainers do. Between two evenly matched contenders—one trained by a national or local leader and the other by a scrambler—the expert player grants an advantage to the horse from the more successful barn.

Trainers to Watch

Charles Whittingham handles nothing but good horses, or potentially good horses and—except for the occasional maiden—races them only when he believes they are ready for a genuine effort. Such horsemen operate that way because they prefer to, and because they are fortunate enough to be employed by owners willing to be patient. Other trainers may be every bit as knowing but have less to work with. Handling the discards of better barns, or struggling with stock spoiled by others, they hang on by their fingernails and wait for luck to smile.

Who are the best trainers in the business? Insiders award the palm to those who manage to make the most of whatever horseflesh they may have. All lists include the aforementioned Whittingham and the remarkable H. Allen Jerkens, who for years has specialized in transforming apparently ordinary animals into authentically good ones—and beating champions with them.

Held in much lower regard are horsemen lucky enough to train the expensively bred stock of wealthy stables yet seldom able to keep the animals in condition long enough to win the big victories to which their bloodlines may have entitled them. And almost nobody has a kind word for trainers who (1) win races but ruin their horses in the process or (2) seldom enter horses at the right distance or in the right company yet consider themselves victims of ill fortune when smarter operatives claim the horses and begin winning with them.

It is fun to nominate trainers as best or nearly best. And it is essential to know, as implied above, that a horse claimed by Barn "A" from Barn "B" is likely to improve dramatically. One's ability to know such things has less to do with the difficult job of comparing horsemen's talents than with the relatively easy one of comparing their performance statistics. Whether Trainer "A" actually is more gifted than "B" is beside the point. What counts is "A's" superior record as revealed in statistical compilations during the present race meeting and those of the recent past.

Here is how to do it:

1. Never bet on the trainer alone. In the long run, the best seldom win more than one race in every four or five attempts.

2. If the horse seems to be a leading contender in its race and is being handled by a reliable trainer, it deserves extra favor. Indeed, it is rarely a mistake to differentiate closely matched horses on such grounds. Successful trainers get that way by beating the unsuccessful ones.

3. A contending horse deserves special consideration if its trainer meets one of the following standards:

a. Mention on the published daily list of leading trainers at the current meeting, with a winning average of at least 17 percent.

b. Mention on the list of consistent trainers that appears below. The list should be revised and updated by consulting *The American Racing Manual* each year. From the player's point of view, a high percentage of victories is more important than high total earnings.

The suggestion that a winning average of 17 percent be the timberline between reliably consistent trainers and their rivals is based on the knowledge that the most reliable trainers manage in the long run to win a race in every four or five attempts. A trainer capable of such a winning average can be regarded as off his feed or in bad luck if he falls much below 17. But, unless he loses his good horses, he will improve his average before long. This is why the list on the following pages should be used in conjunction with the current list of local leaders, and should be updated annually.

Superconscientious handicappers carry the statistics beyond the trainer's winning percentage. They record his performances with horses returning from layoffs, and with previously unraced horses, and with newly claimed horses, and with routers as distinguished from sprinters. Not content with discovering whatever strengths, weaknesses and areas of specialization may seem evident in these records, the handicappers also try to ascertain training patterns that might be associated with the individual's all-out attempts to win. What about drops in class? Rises in class? Switches in distance? Frequency of workouts? Preferences for one or another rider?

Factual compilations of that kind are a great deal of work but reward any handicapper sufficiently attuned to the realities of the sport to understand that a good trainer's methods are dictated not only by personal preferences but by the variable nature of the horses in his barn and, of course, by pressures from owners.

The Consistent Ones

Among the thousands of licensed Thoroughbred trainers in the U.S. and Canada, most of the best and some of the best-connected are listed here. Whenever they have the livestock, they can be expected to win consistently.

FRANK ALEXANDER	DALE BAIRD
RON ALFANO	TONY BARDARO
NED ALLARD	LAZARO S. BARRERA
SUE ALPERS	OSCAR S. BARRERA
ROGER ATTFIELD	MARIO BENEITO

VINNIE BLENGS
BILL BONIFACE
ALLEN BOROSH
NEIL BOYCE
JIM BRACKEN
LOU BRANDT
FRANK BROTHERS
BOB CAMAC
GORDON CAMPBELL
SAL CAMPO
JOE CANTEY
DEL CARROLL II
HENRY CARROLL
GEORGE CARTER
MARK CASSE
TOM CAVINESS
NELSON CHAMPAGNE
HENRY CLARK
WARREN (JIMMY) CROLL
BILL CURTIS
DUKE DAVIS
JIM DAY
GROVER (BUD) DELP
RICHARD DELP
DICK DE STASIO
JOEY DORIGNAC
MIKE DOYLE
NEIL DRYSDALE
STURGES DUCOING
DICK DUTROW
LARRY EDWARDS
MARTY FALLON
JERRY FANNING
MIKE FERRARO
PETER FERRIOLA
JOHN R. S. FISHER
BERNARD FLINT
JOHN H. FORBES
BOBBY FRANKEL
JUAN GARCIA
GEORGE GETZ
GREG GILCHRIST
ALLEN GOLDBERG
LOU GOLDFINE

FRANK GOMEZ
JOHN GOSDEN
NEWCOMB GREEN
ED GREGSON
MEL GROSS
TOMMY GULLO
CHARLES HADRY
JERRY HAMMOND
DAN HASBANY
RICHARD HAZELTON
BRUCE HEADLEY
DENNIS HEIMER
BILLY HENRY
ROYSTON HENRY
JOHN HICKS
ROBERT HILTON
STANLEY HOUGH
PETER HOWE
LARRY JENNINGS
KAY JENSEN
ALLEN JERKENS
PHIL G. JOHNSON
BRUCE JOHNSTONE
LEROY JOLLEY
GARY JONES
FORREST KAELIN
DAVE KASSEN
EDDIE KELLY
EDDIE KELLY, JR.
LARRY KELLY
PAT KELLY
THOMAS J. KELLY
BOB KLESARIS
CLIFF LAMBERT
ROGER LAURIN
RAY LAWRENCE
KING LEATHERBURY
JOHN (BUTCH) LENZINI, JR.
BUDD LEPMAN
BRUCE LEVINE
JACK LUDWIG
WAYNE LUKAS
DICK LUNDY
RICHARD MANDELLA

Woody Stephens

Charlie Whittingham

H. Allen Jerkens

D. Wayne Lukas

Jack Van Berg

Frank Martin

Laz Barrera

Bobby Frankel

Jonathan Sheppard

Lynn Whiting

Oscar Barrera

Gary Jones

Dick Dutrow

Shug McGaughey

King Leatherbury

Frank Gomez

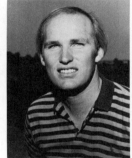

John Gosden

Jim Day

Cracker Walker

Jerry Fanning

Walter Greenman

Walter Reese

Billy Turner

Eddie Kelly

JOE MANZI
BILL MARKO
FRANK (PANCHO) MARTIN
JOSE MARTINEZ
RON McANALLY
CLAUDE (SHUG) McGAUGHEY
FRANK MERRILL
MACK MILLER
MIKE MITCHELL
MARVIN MONCRIEF
HENRY MORENO
JIM MORGAN
STEVE MORGUELAN
GASPER MOSCHERA
BILL MOTT
JIM MURPHY
JAN NERUD
REYNALDO NOBLES
LUIS OLIVARES
HECTOR PALMA
JOHN PARISELLA
JIMMY PASCUMA
WARREN PASCUMA
ANGEL PENNA
ANGEL PENNA, JR.
STEVE PENROD
AL PEPINO
RON PEREZ
BEN PERKINS, JR.
DANNY PERLSWEIG
BILL PERRY
JOE PIERCE, JR.
MITCHELL PREGER
WILLARD PROCTOR
HY RAVICH
WALTER REESE
SCOTT REGAN
MARK REID
ROBERT REINACHER
ROBERT RIBAUDO

TOM ROBERTS
LYMAN ROLLINS
GIL ROWNTREE
MIKE SEDLACEK
SUE SEDLACEK
JONATHAN SHEPPARD
PHIL SIMMS
ROBERT SIRAVO
TOM SKIFFINGTON
BRUCE SMITH
JERE SMITH
BERT SONNIER
WOODY STEPHENS
MEL STUTE
JOHN SULLIVAN
JOHN TAMMARO
HOWARD TESHER
WILLARD THOMPSON
NOBLE THREEWITT
EDDIE TRUMAN
BILLY TURNER
JACK VAN BERG
DAVE VANCE
DARRELL VIENNA
DAVID VIVIAN
DON VON HEMEL
CHARLES (CRACKER)
   WALKER
ART WARNER
SID WATTERS
TED WEST
GENE WEYMOUTH
DAVID WHITELEY
LYNN WHITING
CHARLIE WHITTINGHAM
DON WINFREE
RANDY WINICK
GARY YAGER
JUDY ZOUCK

When They're Hot

In Chapter 4 we saw that a handicapper might be drawn to close consideration and ultimate selection of a winner partly because of its pedigree and partly because of the circumstances and price of its sale at a yearling auction two years before. And now we turn thumbs down on a fetchingly bred animal with a smashing victory and some excellent workouts.

In the seventh at Belmont Park on June 5, 1985, the betting favorite was Spectacular Spy, by no less than Spectacular Bid out of a Buckpasser mare. The three-year-old colt had broken its maiden by five lengths, drawing away under a hand ride. Now, twenty-six days later, after some brilliant morning works, he was seeking his first allowance victory. One could understand the enthusiasm of the crowd, including some of its heaviest bettors. It was not unreasonable to make this colt a 9 to 5 favorite.

But the kind of handicapping advocated around here requires the player to take a carefully considered look at the credentials of every horse in the race. We start at the top.

Rambling Rector took a long time breaking his maiden at three but returned running on May 25, beating half of a good field and promising to improve today if he could overcome his habit of starting too slowly to beat good horses in short races.

Atom Smasher would probably need some racing before recovering the ability he had displayed as a three-year-old maiden in 1983.

Spectacular Spy has already earned our admiration.

Takka Takka and Stomper have been away and have plenty to prove.

Moon Prospector's promising two-year-old season ended in its second start when he finished second as odds-on favorite in the Juvenile. In his return on May 16 he gained a ton of ground in the stretch, losing by only four lengths. Improvement was expected next time, but he ran into trouble ("lacked room"). He is from a good barn and today the rider is Angel Cordero.

Passing Thunder has shown little, Benediction has been absent and Wednesday Golf wants more distance.

Boutinierre makes his first start of the year. He is the subject of a hot tip and goes as second favorite. The workouts are nice but not nicer than those of Spectacular Spy, who has raced recently.

Blushing Guest demands an extremely close look. The trainer, D. Wayne Lukas, leads everybody at the Belmont meeting with nine wins in twenty-four starts for an elegant 38 percent. The rider is Jorge Velasquez, second only to Cordero in the jockey standings. After a four-month recess, the colt came back running, leading to the head of the stretch under 121 pounds in tough company at seven furlongs. That kind of performance bespeaks improvement today.

7 BELMONT 6 FURLONGS — BELMONT PARK

6 FURLONGS. (1.08⅗) ALLOWANCE. Purse $24,000. 3-year-olds and upward which have never won a race other than Maiden, Claiming or Starter. Weights, 3-year-olds 114 lbs. Older 122 lbs. Non-winners of a race other than Claiming since May 15 allowed 3 lbs. Of such a race since May 1, 5 lbs.

Rambling Rector — B. c. 4, by Blushing Groom—Admiring, by Hail to Reason
Own.—Rokeby Stables Br.—Mellon P (Va) Tr.—Miller Mack
117   Lifetime 16 1 4 1 $33,460   1985 1 0 0 0 $1,440   1984 12 1 3 1 $27,180

Atom Smasher — Ch. h. 5, by Explodent—Something Gall, by Hilll Gall
Own.—Sigel M E Br.—Sigel & Wolfson (Fla) Tr.—Hough Stanley M
117   Lifetime 11 1 1 3 $25,836   1985 8 1 1 3   1984 0 M 0 0

Spectacular Spy — Gr. c. 3, by Spectacular Bid—Lassie Dear, by Buckpasser
Own.—Kilroy W S Br.—Farish & Kilroy (Ky) Tr.—Carroll Del W II
111   Lifetime 1 1 0 0 $13,200   1985 1 1 0 0   1984 0 M 0 0 $13,200

Takka Takka — B. c. 4, by Ack Ack—Horn Quarter, by First Landing
Own.—Martin Charlene Br.—Brant P M (Ky) Tr.—Martin Frank
117   Lifetime 10 1 1 1 $21,830   1985 4 0 0 1   1983 6 1 M 0

Stomper — B. c. 4, by Run Dusty Run—Hunters Song, by Amber Morn
Own.—L'Adila Farm Br.—Moorfield Corp (Ky) Tr.—Combs Don
117   Lifetime 11 1 1 1 $24,665   1984 8 1 3 1   1983 3 1 M 0 $24,655
Turf 1 0 0 0

18Apr84- 2Kee my 6f :23⅕ :47⅘ 1:13⅘ Md Sp Wt 2 5 41½ 1½ 11 11¾ Allen K K 120 *.70 81-19 Stomper 1201¾ Soy Espada 120²⁰ Paul's Preference 120⁴ Driving 7
10Apr84- 4Kee gd 7f :22⅘ :46 1:24⅕ Md Sp Wt 1 8 64¼ 56 36½ 38½ Maple S 119 5.30 76-22 Pemcor 119⁶ Brigadoon 1192½ Stomper 119⁶ 9
29Sep83- 4Bel fst 6f :22⅘ :46⅕ 1:11⅘ Md Sp Wt 10 13 12¹⁴ 914 711 710¾ Bailey J D b 118 15.40 74-17 CountryManor1182½LoudAndClear118⁵MealTicket118¾ Slow start 13
LATEST WORKOUTS Jun 4 Bel tr.t 3f sly :38⅘ b

Moon Prospector

B. c. 3, by Northern Prospect—Ask For The Moon, by Sky High II
Br.—Peskoff P (Fla)
Tr.—Schulhofer Flint S
Own.—Peskoff S D
109
Lifetime 4 1 1 0 $27,168 | 1985 2 0 0 0 | 1984 2 1 1 0 $27,168

25May85- 9Bel fst 6f :22⅕ :45⅗ 1:10⅗ Alw 24000 9 5 64¼ 85 68 57¼ Graell A 117 3.30 81-11 Taylor Road 117² Lucky Belief 1222½ Bolinger 110½ Lacked room 11
16May85- 9Bel fst 6f :23⅕ :45⅗ 1:11⅘ 3↑Alw 24000 6 2 9⁹ 11¹⁴ 88 8⁴ Graell A 110 7.20 81-18 Magicus 121nk Lord Montague 121nk Taylor Road 110nk Outrun 12
20Jun84- 8Bel fst 5½f :22⅗ :46⅗ 1:05⅗ Juvenile 1 1 2½ 32½ 32½ 22½ Bailey J D 115 *.90 84-18 SkyCommnd1152½MoonProspctor1151DoItAginDn1131¾ Game try 10
24May84- 4Bel fst 5f :22⅗ :45⅗ :57⅗ Md Sp Wt 4 3 22½ 21½ 1hd 13 Bailey J D 118 3.80 99-15 MoonProspector118³NickelBack118⁶BetMeDdy1183½ Drew clear 8
LATEST WORKOUTS Jun 2 Bel 4f fst :46⅘ h May 24 Bel 3f fst :36⅕ b May 11 Bel 5f fst 1:00 h May 6 Bel 6f fst 1:18 b

Passing Thunder

Ch. c. 3, by Valdez—Happy Summer, by Summer Tan
Br.—Galbreath J W (Ky)
Tr.—Ferraiola Frank
Own.—Dougie G Farm
109
Lifetime 4 1 1 0 $17,060 | 1985 3 0 1 0 $5,060 | 1984 1 1 0 0 $12,000

14Apr85- 5Aqu fst 7f :23⅗ :47 1:24 3↑Alw 22000 2 8 42½ 42½ 55½ 76½ Maple E 114 1.70 75-22 Cutlass Reality 113no Hillside View 1162¾ Chief Louie 109½ Tired 8
4Apr85- 7Aqu fst 7f :23⅕ :46⅕ 1:23⅘ Alw 22000 7 4 62¾ 52½ 43½ 55½ Velasquez J 117 1.40 80-19 Summitry 117¾ Truth Be Told 1191¾ See The Way 117³ Wide 7
6Jan85- 1Aqu fst 170 ⊡:48⅕ 1:12⅗ 1:42⅘ Alw 23000 2 2 2½ 1hd 1hd 2hd Maple E 117 1.90 89-17 First Blast 122hd Passing Thunder1173¾Kilts'Nashua1121¾ Gamely 6
19Dec84- 6Aqu fst 6f ⊡:22⅘ :47 1:13⅘ Md Sp Wt 9 11 10¹⁴ 711 73½ 1½ Maple E 118 19.40 78-25 PssingThunder118½ⒹRewrded1181½FirstBlst118nk Greenly, drvng 12
LATEST WORKOUTS Jun 3 Aqu ⊡ 3f fst :36⅘ h May 29 Aqu ⊡ 5f sly 1:02 b (d) May 23 Aqu ⊡ 4f fst :47⅘ h May 1 Aqu 4f fst :50 b

Benediction

Ch. c. 4, by Princely Native—Parody, by Prince John
Br.—Jacobs J W (Ky)
Tr.—Jacobs Eugene
Own.—Jacobs J W
117
Lifetime 6 1 0 1 $9,880 | 1984 6 1 0 1 $9,880 | 1983 0 M 0 0

25Sep84- 5Med fst 6f :22⅘ :46⅗ 1:12 3↑Md Sp Wt 7 5 44½ 31½ 3½ 11 Cruguet J 117 *1.30 82-21 Benediction 117¹ Sacred Motion 117⁴ PrinceO'Rullah117⁴ Driving 7
14Sep84- 3Bel fst 6f :22⅗ :46⅗ 1:11⅗ 3↑Md Sp Wt 11 3 3nk 32½ 68 69½ Cruguet J 118 *1.80 75-18 AnotherKing117³RmblingRector1181½Mgnetize1182¾ Fin. after 1/2 12
27Aug84- 9Sar fst 6f :22⅘ :46 1:11⅗ 3↑Md Sp Wt 5 2 1hd 21 2hd 31 Cruguet J 117 4.50 82-16 Incite 117¹ Take A Talc 117no Benediction 117½ Tired 11
5Mar84- 8Hia fst 6f :22⅘ :45⅕ 1:10⅗ Md Sp Wt 9 9 43 46 511 512½ Perret C b 120 6.60 76-23 GreenCedars120³VideoReplay120⁴MedievlScholr1203½ Weakened 12
20Feb84- 5Hia fst 6f :22⅘ :45⅗ 1:10⅗ Md Sp Wt 6 6 54½ 69½ 58½ 47¾ Vasquez J 120 6.70 81-16 Ends Well 1202½ Anderson Spring 1201½ Pinckney 120⁴ No threat 12
14Jan84- 3Hia fst 6f :21⅘ :45⅗ 1:10⅗ Md Sp Wt 2 7 811 1016 64½ 47½ Vasquez J 120 — 82-11 Night To Remember 120⁵FrazierBay120¹MellonBalls1201½ Rallied 12
14Jan84-No wagering, tote malfunction
LATEST WORKOUTS Jun 2 Bel tr.t 4f fst :49 b May 28 Bel tr.t 1 fst 1:45⅘ b ●May 23 Bel tr.t 7f fst 1:28 b May 17 Bel 6f fst 1:13⅗ hg

Wednesday Golf

B. c. 3, by Honest Pleasure—Dr Mary Lou, by Dr Fager
Br.—Tartan Farms (Fla)
Tr.—Nerud Jan H
Own.—Tartan Stable
109
Lifetime 9 1 0 1 $13,140 | 1985 5 1 0 1 $13,140 | 1984 4 M 0 0

18May85- 5Bel gd 1 :46⅗ 1:11⅕ 1:36⅖ 3↑Alw 25000 6 6 44½ 78½ 78½ 712½ Guerra W A b 110 6.30 71-15 Anecdote 1214¾ Geologist 121¹ Naked Emperor 103hd Tired 8
4May85- 3Aqu fst 7f :22⅗ :45⅕ 1:22⅕ 3↑Alw 22000 7 1 31½ 41½ 45 310 Guerra W A b 110 9.30 80-15 Lightning Leap 112⁴ Attribute 110⁶ Wednesday Golf 110nk Wide 7
11Apr85- 7Aqu fst 7f :22⅘ :46 1:23⅘ Clm 100000 5 6 65½ 66½ 712 610 Cordero A Jr b 122 6.90 72-24 FadedImage112nkCoyoteDncer1181½TylorRod1124¾ Steadied start 7
27Mar85- 6Aqu fst 1 :46 1:11⅕ 1:38⅗ Md 75000 1 5 42½ 31½ 2½ 12½ Cordero A Jr b 122 11.30 74-20 Wednesday Golf 1222½ Bruciefruit 1131¾ Bucktracer1221½ Driving 9
4Mar85- 6Aqu fst 6f ⊡:23 :46⅗ 1:11⅗ Md Sp Wt 2 10 1010 1021 1025 1021¾ Santagata N 122 17.60e 65-22 Eternal Prince122⁶ChangeTheLock122nkAlex'sGame122no Trailed 10
2Dec84- 6Aqu fst 6f :22⅘ :47 1:12⅗ Md Sp Wt 9 9 104½ 913 917 919½ Ward W A⁵ 113 49.40 60-24 Proud Truth 1182¾ Take Control 1181½ Buckner 118³ Outrun 10
13Sep84- 4Bel fst 6f :22⅗ :46⅕ 1:12 Md Sp Wt 14 9 1013 1418 1418 1315½ Espinosa R E⁷ 111 62.60 67-21 Script Ohio 118¾ Cullendale 1181½ Mighty Courageous1181½ Wide 14
25Aug84- 6Sar fst 6f :22⅕ :45⅗ 1:10⅗ Md Sp Wt 11 7 915 1024 924 926½ Miranda J 118 49.00 61-18 Herat 1187¼ Another Reef 118¼ Testimonial 118¾ Outrun 11
30Jly84- 4Bel fst 5½f :22⅘ :46 1:04⅗ Md Sp Wt 9 9 1029 1030 1033 1034½ Venezia M 118 22.50 57-19 Tiffany Ice 1187¾ Varick 1182½ Coyote Dancer 118nk Bore out st. 10
LATEST WORKOUTS May 26 Bel tr.t 4f fst :48⅘ b May 12 Bel 4f fst :50⅕ b Apr 29 Bel 5f fst 1:01⅘ h Apr 20 Bel 4f gd :50⅘ b

Boutinierre

B. c. 3, by Bold Forbes—Rosespray, by Bagdad
Br.—Peters L J (Ky)
Tr.—Kelly Larry
Own.—Peters L J
109
Lifetime 2 1 0 1 $12,120 | 1984 2 1 0 1 $12,120

8Sep84- 3Med fst 6f :22⅗ :45⅘ 1:10⅗ Alw 12000 5 5 22½ 33 34 39 Migliore R 118 *1.10 79-18 DoItAginDn1151½FuturRlty1187½Boutnrr1184½ bobbled-bumped st 5
24Aug84- 4Sar my 5f :22⅕ :45⅗ :57⅗ Md Sp Wt 10 7 21 21 2hd 11½ Migliore R 118 3.40e 101-09 Boutinierre1181½StrikeUp1185½MedivlLov118² Bumped st,driving 11
LATEST WORKOUTS May 28 Bel 5f fst 1:00 b May 21 Bel 5f fst 1:03 b May 15 Bel 4f fst :48⅘ b May 8 Bel 3f fst :36 b

Blushing Guest

Ch. c. 4, by Blushing Groom—Justaguest, by Groton
Br.—Hamilton & Hymphrey & Watt (Ky)
Tr.—Lukas D Wayne
Own.—Klein Mr-Mrs E V
117
Lifetime 7 1 3 1 $26,785 | 1985 3 1 0 1 $14,760 | 1984 4 M 3 0 $12,025 | Turf 2 0 2 0 $8,000

25May85- 4Bel fst 7f :22⅗ :45⅗ 1:23⅘ 3↑Alw 24000 4 3 1hd 1hd 3½ 53½ Velasquez J 121 7.40 82-11 Lord Montague 1211½ Mr. Jimmy G. 103nk Aswan High 112½ Tired 8
30Jan85- 7Aqu fst 170 ⊡:48⅘ 1:14 1:45⅘ Alw 23000 10 3 42 32 2⁴ 35½ Lovato F Jr 117 *1.10 69-25 MorningThunder1174½FlmeBerr112¹BlushingGust117nk No excuse 10
14Jan85- 4Aqu fst 6f ⊡:22 :45⅘ 1:12⅕ Md Sp Wt 9 7 55½ 31½ 11½ 14½ Lovato F Jr 122 *.40e 83-20 Blushing Guest 1224½ Barrilla 122³ Relation 122² Ridden out 9
6Jly84- 6Hol fm 1⅛ ①:47⅗ 1:12⅗ 1:50⅗ 3↑Md Sp Wt 7 6 88¾ 84¾ 75½ 2hd Pincay L Jr 117 *.60 78-22 Solid Print 122hd Blushing Guest 117½ Dorilord 1151¾ Rallied 11
16Jun84- 7Hol fm 1⅛ ①:48 1:12⅗ 1:49⅘ Alw 22000 11 1 1½ 2hd 1½ 21¾ Day P 114 21.50 82-16 StarMaterial1141¾BlushingGuest114hdPromontory117² Weakened 11
27May84- 6Hol fst 1 :46⅗ 1:11⅕ 1:37⅗ 3↑Md Sp Wt 2 4 52 32 34½ 24 McCarron C J 115 *1.20 75-18 Idol 115⁴ Blushing Guest 1151¾ Fabuleux Prince 1152¾ Evenly 8
20May84- 1Hol fst 6f :22⅘ :45⅗ 1:10⅗ 3↑Md 2 8 73½ 710 76½ 54½ McCarron C J 115 *1.60 80-17 Melodisk 117² QuackQuackQuack123nkBillikin115² Shuffled back 8
LATEST WORKOUTS May 16 Bel 4f fst :49⅘ b May 6 Bel 6f fst 1:14⅗ h Apr 27 Bel 5f fst 1:03⅘ b Apr 21 Bel 4f fst :50⅘ b

SEVENTH RACE
Belmont
JUNE 5, 1985

6 FURLONGS. (1.08⅘) ALLOWANCE. Purse $24,000. 3–year–olds and upward which have never won a race other than Maiden, Claiming or Starter. Weights, 3–year–olds 114 lbs. Older 122 lbs. Non–winners of a race other than Claiming since May 15 allowed 3 lbs. Of such a race since May 1, 5 lbs.

Value of race $24,000; value to winner $14,400; second $5,280; third $2,880; fourth $1,440. Mutuel pool $114,966, OTB pool $135,748. Exacta Pool $212,175. OTB Exacta Pool $211,315.

Last Raced	Horse	Eqt.	A.	Wt	PP	St	¼	½	Str	Fin	Jockey	Odds $1
25May85 ^{4}Bel^{5}	Blushing Guest		4	117	11	8	$2^{1\frac{1}{2}}$	2^{3}	1^{2}	1^{8}	Velasquez J	4.90
25May85 ^{9}Bel^{5}	Moon Prospector		3	111	6	1	$1^{\frac{1}{2}}$	$1^{\frac{1}{2}}$	2^{4}	$2^{1\frac{1}{4}}$	Cordero A Jr	6.80
25May85 ^{4}Bel^{4}	Rambling Rector	b	4	117	1	9	9^{hd}	6^{3}	$4^{\frac{1}{2}}$	3no	Bailey J D	7.10
10May85 ^{3}Bel^{1}	Spectacular Spy		3	111	3	7	7^{1}	$5^{1\frac{1}{2}}$	3^{2}	$4^{6\frac{1}{2}}$	Davis R G	1.90
26Jly84 ^{5}Bel^{8}	Stomper		4	117	5	6	6^{2}	$3^{\frac{1}{2}}$	5^{6}	5^{3}	Vasquez J	28.70
17May84 ^{6}Bel^{8}	Takka Takka		4	117	4	2	4^{1}	9^{5}	8^{2}	$6^{\frac{3}{4}}$	Hernandez R	28.80
18May85 ^{5}Bel^{7}	Wednesday Golf	b	3	109	9	10	11	$10^{1\frac{1}{2}}$	10^{6}	$7^{\frac{3}{4}}$	Thibeau R J	19.10
8Sep84 ^{3}Med^{3}	Boutinierre		3	111	10	4	5^{1}	$7^{\frac{1}{2}}$	6^{hd}	$8^{\frac{3}{4}}$	Migliore R	4.00
14Apr85 ^{5}Aqu^{7}	Passing Thunder		3	109	7	11	10^{5}	$8^{\frac{1}{2}}$	7^{hd}	9^{4}	Ward W A	21.60
14Apr84 ^{5}Aqu^{7}	Atom Smasher	b	5	117	2	3	$3^{1\frac{1}{2}}$	$4^{\frac{1}{2}}$	$9^{\frac{1}{2}}$	$10^{7\frac{1}{2}}$	MacBeth D	13.60
25Sep84 ^{5}Med^{1}	Benediction		4	117	8	5	$8^{\frac{1}{2}}$	11	11	11	Cruguet J	58.40

OFF AT 4:01. Start good, Won ridden out. Time, :22⅖, :45⅖, 1:08⅘ Track sloppy.

$2 Mutuel Prices:

12–(N)–BLUSHING GUEST	11.80	7.20	4.00
7–(I)–MOON PROSPECTOR		7.60	3.40
1–(B)–RAMBLING RECTOR			3.80

$2 EXACTA 12–7 PAID $85.20.

Ch. c, by Blushing Groom—Justaguest, by Groton. Trainer Lukas D Wayne. Bred by Hamilton & Hymphrey & Watt (Ky).

BLUSHING GUEST prompted the pace, took over after entering the stretch and drew away quickly. MOON PROSPECTOR showed speed to the stretch while saving ground and weakened. RAMBLING RECTOR came out while moving leaving the turn but failed to seriously menace. SPECTACULAR SPY saved ground into the stretch but lacked a late response. STOMPER moved up approaching the stretch but had nothing left for the drive. TAKKA TAKKA was finished early. BOUTINIERRE showed some early foot. ATOM SMASHER gave way leaving the turn.

Owners— 1, Klein Mr-Mrs E V; 2, Peskoff S D; 3, Rokeby Stables; 4, Kilroy W S; 5, L'Adila Farm; 6, Martin Charlene; 7, Tartan Stable; 8, Peters L J; 9, Dougle G Farm; 10, Sigel M E; 11, Jacobs J W.

Trainers— 1, Lukas D Wayne; 2, Schulhofer Flint S; 3, Miller Mack; 4, Carroll Del W II; 5, Combs Don; 6, Martin Frank; 7, Nerud Jan H; 8, Kelly Larry; 9, Ferraiola Frank; 10, Hough Stanley M; 11, Jacobs Eugene.

Overweight: Moon Prospector 2 pounds; Boutinierre 2.

Can this four-year-old improve enough to beat Spectacular Spy? Chances are he could beat Spectacular Spy without improving very much at all. Notice how much faster he ran the early fractions on 25 May than Spectacular Spy had. But his record is not that of an impetuous speedball who needs the early lead. Check his winning race of January 14, when he came from behind and won in relatively faster time than Spectacular Spy would. Check the respective *Form* speed ratings for a crude comparison. Use the sums of *Form* speed ratings plus variants for a somewhat finer comparison.

Those who generate good speed figures make even more accurate comparisons. The figures of my colleague Henry Kuck awarded Spectacular Spy a 76 for his victory on May 10. The January win by Blushing Guest was also worth 76, but the pace of the race was two points superior to that of the Spectacular Spy race.

Furthermore, Blushing Guest is a more mature animal. Three-year-olds often beat older runners in these allowance races for non-winners of one or two or three, but only on the basis of superior class. If there is nothing to choose on that score, the older horse has the advantage. And as local statistics indicate, so does a horse from the barn of Wayne Lukas and ridden by Jorge Velasquez.

The track has come up sloppy on June 5, favoring horses with adequate early foot. Blushing Guest should accommodate to the going.

Any remaining doubt should be obliterated by the odds. At almost 5 to 1, Blushing Guest offers much better value than does the other colt at less than 2 to 1.

15

THE JOCKEY FACTOR

Even in an era of millionaire quarterbacks and other players of ball, some American jockeys are among the richest athletes on earth. A really successful one takes home from $500,000 to more than $1 million per year for a decade or two, if he keeps his weight down, his nose clean and his mind on his work.

By tradition, the victorious rider gets 10 percent of the purse. Many owners sweeten this bonus with other gifts, such as the proceeds of a large bet on the horse. As pin money, the big-league jock also gets as much as 5 percent of the horse's earnings for finishing second or third, plus tokens of $35 to $100 for finishing out of the money. These rates vary from track to track.

This sounds like a splendid career for any little person who likes horses. It certainly is, in the same sense that a top executive position with General Motors is a splendid career for anyone who likes cars. The trouble is that a man can be wild about cars and spend his career in the grease pit of a filling station. And a little fellow who likes horses may become a jockey without ever making big pay at it.

Success as a race rider requires more than small size and large desire. Talent is essential. Luck helps. An ingratiating personality does no harm. The top riders have those qualities in abundance. Most do not, which is why there are so few top riders.

Many jockeys are untalented to begin with. Others, fearful of injury, fail to exercise what little talent they may have. It is not at all unusual to see races in which one or more of the riders do nothing but cling to the reins and wave the whip.

An amazingly small group of riders dominates the profession. They own the winner's circle, lock, stock and bonus. They are so much more successful than their colleagues that there simply is no comparison.

About 5,000 men and women have riding licenses. In the course of a year, barely 3,000 of them ride in actual races. Of those who do, almost half get 100 or fewer mounts, compared with the 1,000 to 1,800 assignments obtained by successful jockeys.

Of those who ever ride during a year, about a third win not a single race. More than half the races are won by perhaps 200 riders—the middle and upper classes of the profession.

And now we reach the heart of the matter. An elite group of less than four dozen riders—not even 1 percent of the profession—wins more than 9,000 races a year. Members of this tiny elite win one race in every seven! Moreover, they win about $140 million in purses for their employers— fully a quarter of the purse money paid at all tracks!

Betting on Jockeys

Awareness of the enormous statistical edge enjoyed by a handful of leading riders leads some players to center their handicapping on the jockey rather than the horse. If the handicapping is fairly competent, taking due account of the horse, the player who refuses to bet on any but a top rider has an excellent chance to get by. Unfortunately, such players usually ignore the horse. They "follow" individual jockeys, often betting according to the formulas supplied by progressive betting systems. As points out on page 55, this leads straight to ruination. Any jockey inevitably encounters streaks of from twenty to fifty consecutive losers.

Neither do players do themselves a favor by going to the opposite extreme. "The horse is the thing," some say. "All I do is look for the live horse in the past performances. I let the trainer pick the jockey." Bad logic. The actual "liveness" of a horse often is revealed in the identity of its rider.

Players are right in supposing that most trainers know which riders to put on their horses. But most jockeys and their agents know something, too. They know which horses are the likeliest contenders. Successful riders have their pick of the best mounts. The presence on a horse of an obscure or relatively ungifted rider is frequently a sign that the trainer is marking time, or that the horse is less ready than its record implies.

In any case, the probability of victory by a leading rider is so disproportionately high that it should not be overlooked. The past performance of the jockey should always be evaluated, as part of the evaluation of the horse.

The Importance of the Ride

In 1966, Avelino Gomez led all North American riders with 318 victories in 996 attempts. His winning average of .321 was a record among champions in the races-won department, surpassing the .301 achieved by Bill Shoemaker in 1954. Gomez had long been one of the finest reinsmen in the world, an extraordinarily consistent winner wherever he rode. He preferred to ride in Canada and Mexico. He had his choice of mounts in those places. When he rode in New York, pickings were less easy. Other outstanding jockeys competed with him for the best mounts. He got fewer winners.

The point of this is that no rider can make a winner of a non-contender, except by accident. To be a consistent winner, the jockey must get the mounts. And even the consistent winner loses about eight of every ten races in which he rides. Most of the losses are simply part of the form cycle. It's a nice horse, but it won't win for another two or three weeks, and the leading rider is content to stay with it in the meantime, so that he may cash in later.

Other losses find the topnotcher on some downright rotten animals. Contractual commitments, the politics of the business or the wish to do a friend a favor often result in Pat Day or Bill Shoemaker going postward on a hopeless hulk. Because the Shoe has the mount, the odds drop. But the chances of victory remain as slim as they would be if Joe Nobody were aboard.

Where good jockeys come into their own is on fit, well-placed horses. As their riding records illustrate, they bring something extra to the assignment. They win the big ones and the close ones. The trainer able to induce one of them to ride his animal knows in his heart that he has done everything possible for victory. The owner loves him for it. And if the horse loses, the owner blames the horse and consoles the trainer. Trainers would rather be consoled than blamed.

Does the second- or third-best horse in the race win because its rider is the best in the race? It happens somewhere every day. And it happens everywhere several times a week. The frequency with which it happens depends, of course, on the class of the track. In a field of nine horses at the height of the Southern California or New York season, one usually finds that each of the three or four logical contenders is being ridden by a first-rate jockey. Yet there are occasions when this is not so, and the player is able to make his choice on grounds that one or two of the contenders are carrying outgunned boys.

Some horsemen maintain that New York riders are so evenly matched that none can move a horse more than a neck farther than any of a couple of dozen others. Races are won, however, by necks and heads and noses. Cordero, Velasquez, Migliore, Bailey, MacBeth, Maple and Vasquez do it often enough in New York to warrant the eagerness with which trainers seek their services. Yet, if the best horse in the race is ridden by Robbie Davis, Antonio Graell, Jean-Luc Samyn or Mike Venezia, no knowledgeable player would refrain from betting on that account. These four jockeys seldom win more than 10 percent of their starts in the extraordinarily difficult competition of New York race-riding, but would be unchallenged leaders almost anywhere else. Among them, they account for more than $12 million in purse money each year.

What is the New York player to do? If so many of the riders there are better than their records indicate, how is he to tell one from another?

He should do exactly what he would do at any other track, where the distinctions among riders are often easier to recognize. He should bear in mind that the most successful riders are those most sought after by trainers. They get the best mounts. They get more good mounts—and the statistics prove it—than are assigned to riders who may be equally good but are less successful. Therefore, the player bears the percentages in mind. He scrutinizes the field in terms of distance, condition, class, weights, pace, barns. At some point—whether sooner or later depends entirely on his preference—he eliminates horses to which non-winning riders are assigned. A leading rider should never be dismissed, of course. But a good rider with unimpressive winning statistics can often be ruled out. A bit later I shall present some ways of making these decisions.

Riding Ability Defined

The ideal rider has an instinctive sense of the needs, capacities and peculiarities of his mount. Developed through years of experience in the barns, on the training tracks and in money competition, this sensitivity enables him to get extra effort from any kind of horse, with or without helpful instructions from the trainer.

The ideal rider is an expert judge of pace. He can tell whether the early going is too slow or too fast for his horse, and he adjusts the animal's stride accordingly. Unless the horse is unmanageably rank, he runs it as slowly as possible before the final turn for home, giving it the breather it needs for that last burst of effort.

The ideal rider is a master strategist. He takes the trouble to learn all about changes in the footing, so that he can navigate his horse over the fastest part of the track. If the rail is the place to be, he will be there, even if behind horses. His knowledge of his own mount, and of its rivals, and of the other riders, usually enables him to find daylight and come through at the end, still on the rail.

The ideal rider has extraordinarily quick reflexes and remarkable powers of anticipation. In the split second that he recognizes the development of a potential traffic jam, he steers his horse away from the trouble. In the split second that a hole begins to open in front of him, he takes advantage of it.

The ideal rider is unswervingly courageous. His confidence is unshaken by the dreadful spills that he and all other jockeys suffer from time to time. He takes calculated risks. He goes through holes from which battle-weary jockeys back off. Yet he is not reckless. He knows when to take up or go wide rather than risk harm to himself, his horse and the others in the race.

Leading Riders of All Time

As of January 1, 1986, the records of *Daily Racing Form* showed that the following jockeys had won more often than any others in the history of American racing. The names of those no longer active are followed in parentheses by the years in which they retired.

	Victories	Total Purses
Bill Shoemaker	8,507	$103,593,768
Laffitt Pincay, Jr.	6,267	106,054,127
Johnny Longden, (1966)	6,032	24,665,800
Angel Cordero, Jr.	5,734	104,535,898
Jorge Velasquez	5,587	90,018,389
Larry Snyder	5,285	33,053,842
Sandy Hawley	4,902	52,117,159
Dave Gall	4,833	12,502,774
Eddie Arcaro (1961)	4,779	30,039,543
Steve Brooks (1975)	4,451	18,239,817
Walter Blum (1975)	4,382	26,497,189
Bill Hartack (1974)	4,272	26,466,758
Chris McCarron	4,238	73,815,359
Donald Brumfield	4,227	32,959,081
Jacinto Vasquez	4,205	53,906,795
Avelino Gomez (1980)	4,081	11,777,297

The ideal rider is alert at the gate. He keeps his horse on its toes in readiness for the start. He gets out of there as quickly as the horse can manage it, to achieve the all-important racing position that enables him to save ground later.

The ideal rider has unlimited competitive spirit. As long as his mount has a chance, he refuses to give up. He continues trying until the race is over. This, combined with his knowledge of pace and strategy, makes him what the trade calls a "strong" rider—a strong finisher. If he wasted his mounts in the early going, they would have nothing left at the end, and his finishes would be less strong.

The ideal rider uses the whip no more than necessary. He gets all he can by exploiting the pace of the race, and by distributing his weight evenly on the withers (which is comfortable for the animal), and by using voice, reins, legs and, above all, hands. He rolls his hands on the horse's neck, in rhythm with its stride, urging it forward. When he whips, the emphasis means something to the horse, and it usually reacts by lengthening stride.

The ideal rider spares his horse in other ways. He is able to win by a neck when less capable jockeys might need the security of a three-length lead. Similarly, if the horse is clearly beaten, he does not bother to whip it in a spurious display of determination. He eases it, saving it for next time.

The ideal rider has no weight problems. Without having to resort to the self-denial, the steam baths and the deliberate heaving after meals which make ashen, wasted, weakened, prematurely old men of other jockeys, he rides at full strength. A well-nourished, clear-headed rider is an asset to a horse. A starved rider is likely to conk out at any time.

The ideal rider brings absolute concentration to the job. Like any other athlete, he does whatever is necessary to remain in decent physical and mental condition. His private life is an orderly one that helps, rather than disrupts, his frame of mind. If he boozes or wenches, the recreation is never excessive enough to harm his performance and generate disfavor among trainers. If he gambles, he does it according to the rules, betting only on his own mounts, through their owners. He does not become so immersed in the gambling aspects of the game that his "investments" distract him from his riding.

Among riders now active, many come close to these ideal standards. With all due respect to the good old days (whenever they were), I doubt that any era has seen as many authentically great race riders as now compete in the major races of the East and West coasts. Chris McCarron, Laffit Pincay, Angel Cordero, Jorge Velasquez, Eddie Delahoussaye, the immortal Bill Shoemaker and the carpet-bagging Midwesterner Pat Day are so good that handicappers safely credit them with adding lengths to the ability of any fit horse entered at the proper distance. On their best days, which means most of the time, they display no weaknesses, riding every race with supreme skill.

Riders for Courses

During 1966, Bill Shoemaker accepted 246 mounts in New York. He won on 37 of them, for a batting average of .150. Outside New York—mainly in California—he won 194 times in 791 attempts, for an average of .245. This made his overall statistic a nifty .213.

It is no disgrace to score with only 15 percent of one's mounts on the New York circuit. But Shoemaker always does better than that elsewhere. He is one of the rare riders able to win at least once in every five races—the brand of consistency most significant to players. But he

Laffit Pincay, Jr.

Pat Day

Chris McCarron

Angel Cordero, Jr.

Bill Shoemaker

Jorge Velasquez

Don Miller, Jr.

Craig Perret

Randy Romero

Larry Snyder

Eddie Delahoussaye

Chris Antley

Robin Platts

Gary Stevens

Sandy Hawley

Alexis Solis

Don Brumfield

Earlie Fires

Eddie Maple

Robbie Davis

Herb McCauley

Jerry Bailey

Richard Migliore

Russell Baze

cannot win that often if he does not get the horses. The reason he has fewer good horses to ride in New York is simple enough: Trainers tend to stay with topnotch boys who they know will remain available for the entire season. If rider Doe is good enough to be among the six or seven leaders at Aqueduct, he is good enough for any horse—even though he may lack the virtuoso qualities of a Shoemaker. Rather than antagonize Doe and Doe's noisy agent by using Shoemaker during the champ's irregular trips East, the trainer says with the local rider, and Shoemaker has to take the leavings.

Earlie Fires, leading apprentice rider of 1965, when he scored in 19 percent of his starts, invaded New York in 1966 and made a splendid impression. But he won only 8 percent of the time, as contrasted with the 15 percent he was able to log during the same year in less rugged company elsewhere.

Sammy Boulmetis and Jimmy Stout, heroes of New Jersey racing and thorough pros in their own right, could never get much in New York. Nor could Johnny Longden, the wizened godling of the West Coast. On the other hand, Laffit Pincay, Jr., a 1966 sensation in Illinois, was no less sensational in New York, and proceeded to maintain the level when he shifted headquarters to California.

Generally speaking, a rider who has distinguished himself sufficiently to earn national ranking is a fair bet to win on any track—provided his horse qualifies for support. However, he *usually is a much better bet on his home circuit or on some lesser circuit.* To take an extreme, hypo-

The Very Best

The following riders win high percentages of their starts in the fastest company and are threats to win the biggest races on any circuit. When the spirit and the potential revenues move them, Pincay, Day and Cordero commute by air from one end of the country to another, winning enormous purses. Others are less inclined toward frequent travel. All must be regarded as serious contenders at home or away. Their birth years appear in parentheses.

CHRIS ANTLEY (1966)
ANGEL CORDERO, JR. (1942)
PAT DAY (1953)
EDDIE DELAHOUSSAYE
 (1951)
SANDY HAWLEY (1949)
CHRIS McCARRON (1955)
RICHARD MIGLIORE (1964)

CRAIG PERRETT (1951)
LAFFIT PINCAY, JR. (1946)
ROBIN PLATTS (1949)
RANDY ROMERO (1956)
BILL SHOEMAKER (1931)
GARY STEVENS (1963)
JORGE VELASQUEZ (1946)

thetical case, if he breaks records in Arizona, he must prove himself all over again before meriting support in New Jersey. But if he is Day, he rates as tops anywhere.

Among the first things the expert does in handicapping a field of horses is check the current jockey standings at the track. He carefully notes the names of the two or three top riders, and any others whose listings show that they have been winning at least 16 or 17 percent of their starts. These are the boys who are getting the live horses. And who are justifying the trainers' confidence.

In conjunction with this, the player refers to national listings. Good ones appear on pages 260, 262 and 263.

Apprentice Jockeys

The chronic shortage of first-rate riders impels horsemen to beat the bushes for promising new talent. To encourage the search and expedite the development of newcomers to the trade, trainers are allowed weight concessions for any horse on which they seat an apprentice jock.

If the apprentice wins a race or two in fairly authoritative style, he usually gets more work than his skills warrant. He rides and wins, while full-fledged journeymen sit in idleness and grumble about the politics of the game.

Politics has something to do with it. The notorious eagerness of many owners to see fashionable riders aboard their horses combines with the weight allowance to make the "hot" apprentice an attractive proposition to certain trainers.

Of course, apprentices often lose on horses that might win with better jockeying. But this is not always a negative factor from the trainer's point of view. A player who takes ten minutes to study any random issue of *Daily Racing Form* will notice that some horses seem to lose when the apprentice is up, and win only with a leading rider. The function of the apprentice in such cases is to give an unready horse a brisk workout in actual competition under light weight. If the horse accidentally wins, so much the better. Certain stables specialize in manipulations of that kind, and attentive players have no trouble recognizing the signs in the records.

A more wholesome, widespread and significant reason for the popularity of apprentices is their eagerness. They ride the cheapest race as if it were the Kentucky Derby. When the eagerness occurs in combination with genuine ability—as sometimes happens—the trainer of a cheap horse often prefers the apprentice to an older hand. The boy may be green, but his spirit is beyond doubt. It frequently enables him to finish ahead of more experienced riders whose own competitiveness has been dulled by prosperity. Apprentices rarely get mounts in important races, and seldom win when they do. But they have an extra something going for them in lesser races.

Dependable Pros

In the riding profession, last year's hero is this year's bum. The jockeys on this list have had their seasons as heroes and remain able to become national leaders at any time. Some prefer life on lesser racing circuits. Others continue to ride with distinction in the major leagues. None harms the chances of a well placed horse.

MARY ANN ALLIGOOD (1956)
JERRY BAILEY (1957)
GARY BAZE (1955)
DAN BECKON (1951)
DAVE BORDEN (1956)
VINCE BRACCIALE, JR.
  (1953)
DON BRUMFIELD (1938)
MARCO CASTANEDA (1950)
ROBBIE DAVIS (1961)
JUVENAL DIAZ (1954)
LARRY DUPUY (1955)
BRYAN FANN (1949)
EARLIE FIRES (1947)
DAVE GALL (1941)

CARL GAMBARDELLA (1939)
JULIE KRONE (1963)
JEFF LLOYD (1956)
DON MacBETH (1949)
HERB McCAULEY (1957)
EDDIE MAPLE (1948)
JEAN-LUC SAMYN (1956)
RAY SIBILLE (1952)
VIOLET SMITH (1949)
LARRY SNYDER (1942)
GARY STAHLBAUM (1952)
PAT VALENZUELA (1962)
JACINTO VASQUEZ (1944)
RICK WILSON (1953)

In recent years Don Miller, Chris Antley, and Wesley Ward have each been an authentically hot apprentice. After losing the weight allowance, each has continued to get good mounts and win numerous races. The transition from bug-boy to journeyman is usually more difficult than that. Most leading apprentices disappear from prominence as soon as the rules require them to ride at equal weights against polished jockeys. Trainers no longer assign them the live horses. The boy who could do nothing wrong suddenly becomes an also-ran.

As might be expected, apprentices do their best work on horses that require the least jockeying. To win a six-furlong sprint on a sharply conditioned pace-setter, the boy need only get out of the gate in a hurry and remain in the saddle for an additional minute and eleven seconds or so. A more experienced rider might use the animal's energies more efficiently, but horsemen often prefer the five- or seven-pound weight concession for a sprinter of that type.

The Comers

Any of the promising riders listed below is capable of national leadership.

RUSSELL BAZE (1958)   JACK PENNEY (1962)
VERNON BUSH (1961)   JOSE SANTOS (1961)
WALTER GUERRA (1962) DON SEYMOUR (1960)
RON HANSEN (1960)   ALEX SOLIS (1964)
JACK KAENEL (1964)   WESLEY WARD (1968)
DONALD A. MILLER, JR.
  (1963)

As apprentices, Sandy Hawley, Chris McCarron and Steve Cauthen were remarkable for their precocious ability to win at all distances on horses that required rating off the pace. Ordinarily, off-pace horses are poor risks when ridden by apprentices. At sprint distances, the kid has too little time to recover from his mistakes or solve the problems presented by traffic jams. At longer distances, he is worse off: His sense of pace is not yet trustworthy. Also, the extra turn of the track presents additional headaches for which the best cure is experience.

Accordingly, expert players bet on an apprentice jockey only if his mount is a front-running sprinter or, in rare cases, if the boy has shown that he can win at the distance with the particular come-from-behinder.

Match the Rider to the Horse

An approach to the jockey factor becomes sensible as soon as it embraces a key reality: the high percentage of races won by the leading riders. The player who favors leading riders directs himself toward live horses.

Yet the player must reckon with the fact that other riders also win races. And that some of those less prominent riders are uniquely suited to certain horses which refuse to run for more successful jockeys.

Here is a good way to handle the jockey problem:

1. Accept as a contender any ready, well-placed horse ridden by a journeyman jockey who (a) is a national leader or (b) is a leader in the current standings at the track or (c) has won at least 16 percent of his races at the meeting or (d) has won with the horse in the past.

2. Eliminate any horse ridden by an apprentice jockey unless (a) it is a front-running type entered in a race around not more than one turn or (b) the boy has won with the horse in the past or (c) the boy rates among the most successful riders at the current meeting and has been winning at least 16 percent of his starts.

3. Play no apprentice in route races unless he has demonstrated in the past that he can handle assignments of that kind.

4. When appraising the chances of a horse about to benefit from a switch from some ordinary rider to a genuinely hot one, one reasonably can assume that the successful jockey is not riding the horse for mere entertainment. To get the most accurate line on the horse's ability, the handicapper should find its best race in the past-performance lines and assume that the horse can approach that level of performance today. This wrinkle works much more often than it fails, but works only when the rider in question is on a real roll, at or near the top of the standings, and winning in clusters.

Needless to say, these suggestions are valid only as part of a comprehensive approach to handicapping.

The most convenient and productive time to analyze the rider's qualifications is at the end of the handicapping process, after the more fundamental questions of distance, condition, class, weight and pace have been attended to. It makes no sense to eliminate a horse on the jockey factor until then. The penalty for doing so is exacted on the afternoon of the race, when the trainer switches from the unsuccessful jockey to Velasquez or Gary Stevens. If the player has not checked the horse for distance, class, etc., it is impossible to guess whether the rider change is as immediately significant as it might seem.

16

58 PLUS FACTORS

You have eliminated seven of the eight horses, including the favorite in the race. The remaining animal seems admirably situated as to distance, class, weight and pace. It is in good form. The jockey's name is Velasquez. The crowd is letting it go to the post at 4 to 1. You buy a ticket.

The horse finishes second, a few jumps ahead of the favorite. The winner is a 20 to 1 shot. You turn back to the past-performance records to see if you missed anything. No. The horse had fallen on its face every time it had tried to go farther than a mile. And it had never been in the money against animals of today's caliber.

On the other hand, the horse was ridden by the only jockey who had ever won with it before. And was carrying seven fewer pounds than in its last race. And had worked out only yesterday. As they say in the trade, it had a few angles going for it.

Because racing is a game in which victory rewards the shrewd as often as it does the swift, innumerable players do their handicapping entirely in terms of angles—patterns in the past-performance record which reveal significant maneuvers by a trainer or possible improvement by the horse itself. Distance, form, class, pace and jockey are all surveyed in such figuring, but seldom in any fundamental way. The angle player hits longshots, as does anyone else who takes a cavalier attitude toward the basics of the sport. Naturally, he also suffers long droughts and generally ends by losing more money than he wins.

But angles have their place in handicapping. They are especially useful as a means of separating well-placed, legitimate contenders whose fundamental ratings are too close for easy decision.

Readers of *The Compleat Horseplayer* and *Ainslie on Jockeys* will recall that each contained a compilation of selection angles helpful in singling out live horses. I called them "plus factors" and urged the reader to use them only *after* more fundamental analyses. I renew the advice in this chapter, with the admission that almost any of the plus factors might constitute the basis of an interesting selection system. Players drawn to the idea of mechanical systems, which require no effort beyond the application of rules, will find that Chapter 18 of the present volume offers the most fetching array of possibilities ever published in one place. Before attempting to adapt any of the upcoming plus factors to system play, it might be a good idea to look through the assortment in the later chapter.

In the meantime, anyone who prefers to do his own handicapping will find the following wrinkles a useful adjunct to whatever method he favors. If unable to separate two or three horses by ordinary means, see whether any of the following factors applies to one or more of the horses. Generally, a contender is a good bet if it earns four more of these credits than any other contender does.

1. Winning Favorite: A horse that goes to the post as betting favorite in its race deserves extra credit if its barn customarily wins more than a third of the races in which its horses run as favorites.

2. Consistent Stable: Whether the horse is favorite or not, it deserves credit if its trainer is among the leaders at the current meeting or is shown by *The American Racing Manual* or the daily racing program or the tabulations in this book to be exceptionally consistent.

3. Consistent Jockey: If the rider is an unusually consistent winner or a national or local leader, the horse gets credit. If the horse happens to be the betting favorite and the jockey is good on favorites, the horse gets an additional check or star or whatever symbol you prefer.

4. Favorable Jockey Shift: Credit any contender that lost its last race but is to be ridden today by a different jockey, provided the boy is a national or local leader, or has a winning percentage of at least 16 at the meeting, or has won with the horse in the past. Likewise, a shift to the hot apprentice of the meeting also deserves credit. A switch to a winning rider is almost invariably a sign of readiness, especially in a horse that qualifies as a legitimate contender on more fundamental grounds.

5. Won Last Race Easily: Such horses are among the best bets to repeat unless the last race was against cheap stock or the horse led all the way, without being challenged for the early lead.

6. Won Last Race Handily: The difference between "handily" and "easily" is not great. An animal that wins handily usually retains enough of its form to win at the next asking, provided it is properly placed (a question that should be settled at earlier stages of the handicapping).

7. Last Race a Big Win: The most powerful kind of victory is that in which the horse leads at the stretch call, or is close to the pace, and wins going away.

8. Lost Last Race but Gained in Stretch: If the result chart or past-performance line says "rallied," "just missed," or "finished fast" and the horse picked up at least two lengths in the stretch, it may do better today. Unless, of course, the effort dulled its form (which the player should have noticed in analyzing the form factor).

9. Lost Ground in Middle Stages but Gained in Stretch: A horse may be shuffled back by heavy traffic after a good start. If it at least regains the lost ground, it demonstrates the willingness and condition that wins races. The past-performance line might look like this:

$$3 \quad 3 \quad 2^3 \quad 5^5 \quad 4^4 \quad 2^2$$

In seeking this angle—known to old-time punters as the "Up and Down System"—little attention need be paid to running position. Lengths behind the leader are more important, although it is nice to note that the horse managed to pass others while closing in on the leader.

10. Gained Three Lengths or More at Any Call: A burst of speed at any stage of a race is often a sign of improvement:

$$3 \quad 4 \quad 5^5 \quad 3^2 \quad 4^3 \quad 5^4$$

The horse turned it on sufficiently to gain three lengths between the quarter-mile and pre-stretch calls. Or, if it was a route race, between the half-mile and three quarters.

11. Passed More than Half the Field: If an animal that usually breaks alertly got off to a poor start and, though losing, passed more than half the other horses in the race, it probably will improve today.

12. Ran Closer to the Early Pace than in Its Previous Two Races: An almost invariably reliable sign.

13. Was Closer at the Stretch Call than in Its Previous Two Races: Ditto.

14. Finished Closer to the Winner than in Its Previous Two Races: Ditto.

15. Is a Front-Running Type that Carried Its Speed Farther than in Either of Its Two Previous Races: More of the same.

16. Ran an Even Race, No Worse than Fifth All the Way, Earning a Higher Speed Rating than in Either of Its Previous Two: A particularly telling sign, often overlooked.

17. Has Earned Increasingly High Speed Ratings in Each of Its Last Two Races: Not necessarily as obvious a sign as it might seem, especially if horse has not been finishing in the money.

18. Has Earned Increasingly High Speed Ratings in Each of Its Last Three Races: Dynamite.

19. Has Early Speed: A fast start is often a better sign than a fast finish. Unless the horse is an habitual quitter (which should have been eliminated early in the handicapping), it deserves credit for leading or running close to the leader of its last race.

20. Led or Ran Within Two Lengths of the Winner to the Stretch Call before Losing Ground in the Stretch Run of a Longer Race than Today's: The reference, as usual, is to the animal's last race. The horse might have won if the race had been at today's comfortable distance. The distance switch, combined as it often is with a class drop and jockey shift, is a dead giveaway that the stable is shooting.

21. Has Led from Wire to Wire in a Race at Today's Distance: The type of horse able to get out on top and stay there is an extra-good bet when in shape and properly situated. He encounters none of the problems that befall off-pace animals.

22. Last Race Easy, Previous Race Good: The last race was easy if the horse never challenged for the lead, finished fourth or worse, and earned chart comment like "No excuse," "No mishap," "Ran evenly," "Wide," or "No rally." If everything else in the record suggests a good performance today, and if the animal's next-to-last race was a good one, the chances are that its last outing was a conditioning effort—a tightener.

23. Alibi: A horse that lost because it was misplaced or because it ran into trouble is often a nice bet when properly placed in its next effort. The public often overlooks the reason for its last defeat, seeing only that it lost badly.

24. Last Race within Seven Days of Today: A horse good enough to survive close scrutiny in terms of distance, condition, class, weight, jockey and pace deserves extra consideration if its trainer is running it within seven days of its last race. There can be little doubt that the animal is ready and that the barn is trying.

25. Last Race within Five Days of Today: Five days is so much more impressive than seven that the player can give the animal an extra star on that account.

26. Second or Third Start after Long Layoff or Long Trip: Horses usually do far better in the second or third effort at a new track or after a layoff.

27. Ran in Money after Long Layoff or Long Trip: If the horse ran second or third in its first attempt at the new track (or after a vacation), and did so without the all-out effort of a hard stretch drive, it almost certainly will improve today. An especially good sign is early speed that petered out in the later stages of the race. The horse was undoubtedly short of wind, and should improve today.

28. Stabled at Today's Track: Horses stabled at Belmont Park win a lower proportion of races at Aqueduct than horses that sleep at Aqueduct. The workout line in the past-performance record tells where the horse lives—a good plus factor at any track.

29. Worked Yesterday: Many trainers believe in giving the horse a breezing workout on the day before a winning effort.

30. Recent Long Workout: If the horse has been tiring in the stretch, or has been away from the races for a while, a six-furlong workout for today's sprint or a workout of a mile or more for today's route is an indication that the trainer has been building the animal's stamina. The workout should have occurred at least three days ago, to enable the horse to recover from it.

31. Four Workouts in Last 20 Days: A racer that works every five days is in good physical condition and is being prepared for a good effort. Nowadays, many trainers race their horses so often that it is not possible to have any workouts. The reader should be happy to find that the horse has had four activities—a total of four races and/or works—in the last 20 days (or less).

32. Six Pounds Less Weight than in Best Race: If the trainer has found the spot in which the horse can run with considerably less weight than it carried in its best effort at the distance, he is likely to want to cash in on the opportunity. The fact that the horse qualifies as a contender suggests that the trainer knows what he's up to.

33. Five Pounds Less than in Last Race: Trainers like to get weight off. Even though the last race may have been a much different kind of affair than today's, the lighter burden remains significant.

34. Distance Switch: Today the horse is running at a suitable distance or the player would (I hope) have eliminated it. If it ran at the wrong distance last time, the effort probably was for conditioning purposes, which may pay off today.

35. Down in Class: If the top claiming price at which horses may be entered in today's race is lower than the price at which the horse was entered in its last start, today's company is probably easier pickings.

36. Steps Down after "Even" or Better Race: A horse bears watching when it drops in class after a race in which it neither exerted itself nor earned unfavorable comment. If the comment was "Even," the player can assume that the trainer had today's race in mind and was merely preparing the horse. If the comment was "Good try" or "Rallied" or something equally complimentary, the horse probably will be an odds-on favorite today.

37. Steps Down Today and Stepped Down Last Time: If the horse's recent record qualifies it as a contender, repeated drops in class may not be the woeful signs that they are in the case of a worn-out animal. They may only mean that the barn is desperate for a purse and a bet.

38. Stepped Down Last Time, Runs in Same Class Again:
The trainer evidently thinks that the horse has found its best level. Since the horse is plainly one of the leading contenders in the race, the trainer may be right. If the check mark is added to others earned on the bases of distance switches, weight shifts, jockey switches and the like, the player may be in on a betting coup.

39. Up One Notch Last Time, Down Two Today: Good manipulators get nice prices with this one. For example, the horse might be entered for $5,500 today and its last two races might look like this:

Clm 6500
Clm 6000

If the $6,000 race was fairly good and the $6,500 one pretty bad, the trainer may be wound up for a killing. Racetrack crowds seldom penetrate the past-performance records deeply enough to notice maneuvers of this kind. They see that the horse is dropping $1,000 in price after a bad race. They do not notice that it also is dropping $500 in price after a previous, but recent, good race. Naturally, the good race should have taken place within two or three weeks.

40. Drops from Claimer to f-Claimer without Face-Value Drop: A filly or mare entered in a race for $5,000 females is dropping in class and will have a better chance than she did if her last race was for $5,000 animals of both sexes.

41. Drops from Claimer to f-Claimer with Apparent Value Rise: A filly that ran in a Clm 5000 last week is not stepping up in class if today's is an f-6000. At most tracks, she will pay extraordinarily good odds, because the crowd will think she is being pushed up the class ladder. Review the 20 percent formula.

42. Properly Placed Three-Year-Old: A three-year-old that has been running fair races against older horses is a cinch to move ahead by several lengths when the trainer finally drops it in with its own kind. If the maneuver is combined with an apparent increase in class—a rise in claiming price of not more than $1,000—it is an especially powerful gimmick and should get a second check mark.

43. New Low Class Today: A contender deserves credit if it is meeting the cheapest field of its career.

44. Has Never Lost by More than Half a Length at This Distance against This Class or Lower: A strong indication that the trainer has found the right spot for the horse.

45. Highest Class Rating: A horse should be credited if its class rating is the highest among the leading contenders.

46. Highest Class Rating by 15 Points: A $1,500 edge in class merits an extra check mark.

47. Has Won Allowance Race at Major Track: This is significant in handicapping claiming races.

48. Has Won Handicap or Placed in Stakes at Major Track: This occurs in claiming races sometimes, and should get an extra check. It also is well worth noticing in allowance races.

49. Recently Claimed: The rules of racing require a recently claimed animal to be run in a higher bracket during the first month it is in the new hands. Exceptions occur when one meeting ends and a new one starts, whereupon the animal is let out of jail and can run at any price the trainer chooses. Horses claimed within the last month that have not yet won for the new proprietors are among the best bets a handicapper finds—provided he has already assessed distance, condition, class, weights, jockeys and pace.

50. Drops Below Price at Which It Was Claimed: A busy claiming trainer does this all the time—winning his first attempt with a newly

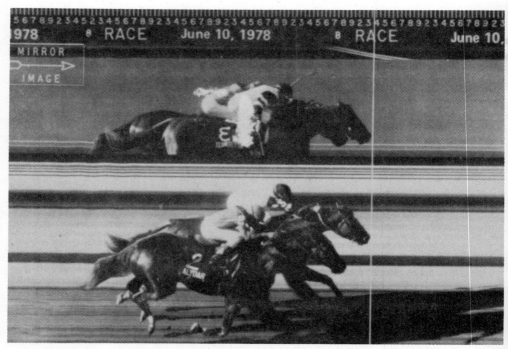

Official finish-line photo shows Affirmed beating Alydar in the 1978 Belmont Stakes. Steve Cauthen rode Affirmed, Jorge Velasquez was on Alydar.
NEW YORK RACING ASSOCIATION

claimed horse, and insuring the win by entering it for less than he paid. In general, if a horse qualifies as a live contender, was claimed within two or three months, and is running for the first time at a price lower than the owner paid, an all-out effort should be expected.

51. Consistency: This is one of the most powerful of plus factors, provided, of course, that the horse has adequate pace and class ratings, is in shape and likes the distance. A horse qualifies for the credit if it has won 20 percent of six or more races this year or, if less active this year, has won 20 percent of all its races this year and last.

52. Only Consistent Horse: If no other contender meets the consistency standards, the consistent one should get a second check mark.

53. Gelding: A gelding in shape to run its best is the most trustworthy of Thoroughbreds.

54. Entry: A contender coupled in the betting with another horse has something extra on its side. Because the contender is ready to go, the trainer undoubtedly will use the other half of the entry to make the pace easier for the contender. Therefore, if the contender is a stretch-running type, and its stablemate is a front-runner, and the contender's chief rival in the race is another front-runner, it pays to give the contender not one but two checks. The player is safe in assuming that the stablemate will run the rival pace-setter into the ground, clearing the way for the winning half of the entry.

55. Fast Final Quarter: Colonel E. R. Bradley, the professional gambler who had the Kentucky Derby in his hip pocket, used to make money betting on horses that had run the final quarter-mile of their latest races in 24 seconds or better. The angle is especially useful if the horse qualifies on other counts. To tell how fast a horse traveled the final quarter of a six-furlong race, subtract the half-mile time of the race from the final time. If the horse gained ground from the pre-stretch call to the finish, allow one fifth or one sixth of a second for each length it gained and subtract from the previous figure. Or, if the horse lost ground, add. If the horse's last race was at a mile, subtract the three-quarter-mile clocking from the final time, and then adjust the result according to the number of lengths gained or lost by the horse. It is impractical to attempt this calculation except if the race was at six furlongs or a mile. The angle is so good that it deserves not one but two check marks.

56. Lone Speed. Very occasionally, a horse shapes up as the only animal in its field with good early speed—good, at least, by comparison with that of other starters. If the horse likes today's footing and not only promises to capture the early lead without serious challenge but has showed in the past that it is sufficiently stout of heart and lung to run the required distance, it is an extraordinarily good bet.

57. First Time on Furosemide: This chemical, known in racing as Lasix, is used in most places to prevent bleeding in the respiratory tract, which occurs in some horses during the stress of a race. This is not the only effect of the drug. For one thing, when administered the first time or two, it makes many horses perform at their best. In states that require the tracks to identify horses running on the stuff, alert players pounce on animals getting it for the first or second time.

58. Blinkers On or Off: Many good horsemen disapprove of blinkers, contending that a properly schooled Thoroughbred is best off with vision unobstructed. But not that many runners are that well schooled. The application or removal of blinkers—especially after a race in which the animal showed some signs of improvement—may make a decisive difference next time out. Watch for this in conjunction with switches in distance and/or rider.

17

PADDOCK AND POST PARADE

Uncountable thousands of horseplayers go to racetracks without ever looking at a horse except in electronic miniature when the video screen stops showing the odds and displays the race. That's no great way to look at a horse.

The reason that so many racegoers sit in front of video monitors instead of going outdoors at the track is that they do not know any better. In a typical racing crowd of 15,000, hardly 1,000—many of them tourists—go to the paddock and walking ring to inspect the animals. A much larger faction mills around beneath the stands, hoping to stumble onto a hot tip. One would like to think that most fans who understood the advantage of looking at the horses before the race might be motivated to seize the advantage. So here goes.

The paddock and walking ring are where experts make their final decisions about the winning chances of horses. One animal may have seemed clearly superior on paper. Others generate serious interest when the logical choice turns out to present a paddock portrait of unwillingness or other unreadiness. In closer situations, the study of horses in the flesh continues through the parade in front of the stands, and the pre-race gallops.

Recognizing Readiness

When a good barn sends a fit horse to the races, the animal looks the part. Whether a two-year-old maiden or a five-year-old handicap champion, its class and condition are usually recognizable without the aid of a scoreboard. Its healthy coat glows like well-oiled, hand-rubbed wood. Its mane and tail are carefully groomed. Its eyes are bright, head up, ears erect and forward, muscles firm, ribs barely visible. Its stride is long, easy and free. Its nervousness, if any, resembles the wound-up tension of a human athlete eager for action.

The handsomest, soundest-looking, best-behaved, most devotedly groomed horse in the field is an extraordinarily good bet—but only if it seemed a likely winner during the paper-and-pencil phases of the handicapping. Relatively unimposing Thoroughbreds often win championships, and some of the finest-looking horses you ever saw never got beyond the allowance stage.

Kelso was unimpressive in the walking ring. There have been $4,000 horses with snazzier-looking coats. Yet the player who noted from the past-performance records that Kelso was the best horse in the race could not possibly have been put off by the great gelding's looks. Kelso did not look bad. He just looked unremarkable.

And there you have the main point of the jaunt to the saddling enclosure. You go there to see if there is any reason to refrain from betting on your choice. You hunt for negative signs.

The professional horseman and professional bettor enjoy a considerable advantage in this setting. Because they are on the scene every day, they know which few horses are able to run well even after displays of pre-race fretfulness. They know which horses are running in bandages for the first time. They know which horses customarily race with special shoes or special bits, and which are heavier or skinnier or more languid than usual.

The hobbyist or infrequent player is unable to keep abreast of such things. But if he knows what to look for and what, in general, it all means, he guarantees himself more winners, fewer losers and a higher rate of profit than can possibly be achieved by omitting the paddock visits.

Nervousness and Reluctance

Loyd (Boo) Gentry was roundly criticized because Graustark, the best-looking colt in years, broke down before getting to the Kentucky Derby. I sang in that critical chorus myself and shall never believe that the horse's ruination was unavoidable.

If Gentry offered any excuses, I did not read about them. A man with an ironic, rather cynical view of things, he kept his own counsel. He also kept his job as trainer of the high-class animals which his father, the celebrated Olin Gentry, bred and raised for John W. Galbreath's Darby Dan Farm.

The next year, word got around that Boo might have a fresh chance at the Derby with a nice colt called Cup Race, a half brother of Graustark. But Cup Race went the way of so many others. Injuries knocked it out of the entry box. Gentry then decided to see what might be done with a second colt, Proud Clarion.

This particular animal had suffered so severely from the sore shins that plague today's hard-worked two-year-olds that it had raced only three times at age two, and had failed to win. A slow learner, and set back still further by the shin ailments, it also suffered from extreme nervousness. However, it showed enough promise early in the year to deserve a shot at Louisville.

On two afternoons during the week before the Derby, Gentry took the trouble to come to grips with Proud Clarion's nervousness. He paddocked the horse. That is, he brought it to the paddock amid the uproar of actual racing and saddled it, as if for actual competition.

"He shook so, his teeth rattled," said Gentry.

On each occasion, the horse did not recover its composure until safely back in the barn.

Derby Day came. Gentry again brought Proud Clarion to the paddock—this time not merely to be saddled but to run in the big race. This time the horse was quite calm. It finally had become accustomed to the noise of the track. Proud Clarion won the Kentucky Derby at 30 to 1.

The betting favorite on that day was Damascus, trained by Frank Y. Whiteley, Jr. Like other Whiteley horses, this handsome son of Sword Dancer had been the beneficiary of patient, careful handling. It had long since overcome its natural fear of human crowds and of the special tension associated with pre-race ritual. It might get keyed up, but was not the skittish type that exhausts itself before the race starts.

Yet Damascus was nervous before the Derby. Unaccountably nervous. So nervous that certain New Yorkers who had seen the horse win the Wood Memorial at Aqueduct now changed their minds about betting on it in the big one. They suspected that something was wrong. So did Frank Whiteley.

Bill Shoemaker brought Damascus from the gate in a rush, found the horse unusually rank, but managed to snug it back slightly off the pace until the turn for home. Coming into the stretch, he located daylight, pointed Damascus at it and asked for speed. The colt started after the leader, Barbs Delight, as if able to eat it up and win by yards. And then the predictable happened. Damascus ran out of gas and was lucky to finish a well-beaten third. It had left its race in the paddock.

I do not know why Damascus was nervous on Derby Day. But I do know that 99 out of 100 noticeably nervous horses use up so much energy before the start of their races that they stop in the stretch.

Among two-year-olds and certain lightly raced threes such as Proud Clarion, the chief cause of serious nervousness is fear of a strange environment. A frequently complicating factor is dread of the discomfort which the animal has learned to associate with the sights, sounds and tugs and hauls to which it is subjected on the day of a race. Many horses seem literally to dread the prospect of the stressful dash from the starting gate or the punishing drive to the wire.

Later, after becoming adjusted—or resigned—to the demands of racing, Thoroughbreds manifest reluctance—or the nervousness it often begets—only when returning to the track from a long vacation, or when running for the first time at a strange place, or when ill or in pain or when jaded from too much work.

Here are signs of reluctance severe enough to warn the player that the horse may be out of kilter:

Fractiousness. Instead of walking cooperatively from the receiving barn to its paddock stall, the animal fights its handler. It tosses its head, swishes its tail restlessly, kicks, tries to wheel. The behavior may become more intense in the stall, or may not erupt until that point (as if the animal suddenly realized that it had not merely been out for a stroll but was actually going to be asked to race). It may try to kick down the walls of the stall. It may resist the saddle. It may try to savage its handlers with its teeth.

Later, in the parade around the ring, the horse may calm down—a good sign, if accompanied by other good signs to be described below. But if the fractiousness or unhappiness persists, the player knows that precious, unrecoverable energies are being squandered.

Note well that a horse that jogs, toe-dances and whinnies before its race should not be charged with undue nervousness unless it presents other signs of the condition. It may simply be keyed up, which is better than being uninterested.

Note also that inexperienced horses display more nervousness than seasoned animals do. Allowances must be made for this, although the really frantic juvenile seldom has anything left for its race. It is most comforting to discover that the two-year-old with the best previous clockings is also a cool cat in the walking ring.

Human Failure. The reaction of the horse's handlers to its fractiousness is frequently a dead giveaway to their estimate of the animal's prospects. When the groom or trainer displays viciousness or impatience of his own, he reveals that he has no more liking for the race than the horse does. If the horse had a substantial chance, the handler would do everything possible to protect his bet and his share of the purse. This, incidentally, is why stakes horses of notoriously erratic temperament, such as certain members of the Nearco-Nasrullah-Nantallah line, win even after giving their handlers fits. The thing is that they *are* stakes horses and the handlers are under orders to accept the trouble or find employment elsewhere. A fractious claiming racer seldom is treated with such deference. Once the battle starts in the paddock, little is done to improve the animal's disposition, or relieve the fears that account for the misbehavior. Not, that is, unless the horse has an excellent chance in the race and the handlers are willing to suffer injury and indignity in an attempt to salvage the situation.

Washiness. A lather of nervous sweat appears early in the paddock proceedings and the dampness spreads along the horse's neck and flanks like a stain.

In very hot weather, all healthy horses are expected to sweat. Indeed, horsemen worry about the condition of an animal that remains dry when most others are wet. But a nervous, washy horse has a particularly distressed air, no matter what the weather may be. His handlers sponge off the foam, yet he generates more. The sweatiness usually occurs in combination with other signs of nervous strain, such as rapidly flicking ears, or ears that lie flat, or a tossing head, or outright fractiousness.

Kidney Sweat. Nervousness betrays itself with an accumulation of white foam between the animal's rear legs. Occasionally, this is the only visible sign of unease. If the nervousness is not severe, the kidney sweat should diminish or disappear before the horses leave the walking ring for the track. If it becomes more profuse, the horse is probably out of sorts. On closer or more expert inspection, other signs of unreadiness may become apparent.

It is useless to speculate about the causes of any individual case of paddock distress. Whether produced by inexperience, physical discomfort or a sudden, perverse reluctance to play the game, it prevents horses from winning. The player need know no more than that. Even if the horse's record proclaims it the best runner in the race, the player who sees signs of serious reluctance or apprehensiveness had better not risk real money, unless the horse snaps out of its difficulties in short order. Or unless it is the kind of freak that always acts like a loser before it wins.

Bandages

Short bandages around fetlock and pastern are beneficial to a horse that tends to scrape its ankles on the surface of the track, a difficulty known in the trade as "running down." If the horse seems otherwise fit, these short bandages can be ignored.

Long bandages on the hind legs often are applied for much the same reason that a handball player wears a wrist strap—to give extra support. In this case, muscles and ligaments held firmly together enable the animal to propel its weight forward with greater comfort. A really sound horse requires no such artificial assistance, but hind bandages are acceptable unless the horse seems reluctant to race. In those circumstances, the bandages can be accepted as an additional sign of trouble and the horse should be tossed out.

Long bandages on the forelegs are strong signs of tendon trouble where the horse can least tolerate it. If an animal wearing these things seems ready to run, and figures to be the best in its field, the wise player passes the race. The horse might indeed win, but nobody should bet on it. Sooner or later, horses with foreleg ailments break down. Naturally, if the leading contender bobs up in front bandages and shows no liking for the day's activity, the player goes to his second choice with considerable confidence.

Soreness and Lameness

Some gallant old campaigners have legs so gnarled and knotted with wear-and-tear that it hurts to look at them. It surely hurts worse to run on them. But the horses get out there and win. Accordingly, the player should hesitate to rule out a contender whose knee is swollen or who has an alarmingly prominent tendon. Far better to assume, as racing officials do, that any horse able to get to the post is probably "racing sound" and may occasionally overcome its ouchiness and finish on top.

The trick is to recognize "racing sound" animals that are hurting too badly to stand the gaff. Most give fair warning by the unwillingness with which they surrender to saddle, rider and post parade. Others, more stoical about it, seem quite content to run, but reveal in their short, choppy strides that they are too stiff and sore to do it well. The goings-on in the paddock stall also help the player to spot such trouble.

In Arkansas, New York and New Jersey, which forbid pain-killing drugs for racing purposes, the law-abiding trainer of a lame or sore horse is forced to rely on bandaging, liniments and the analgesic properties of cold water. It is by no means unusual to walk into a receiving barn and find half the entrants in a claiming race standing in tubs of ice. The ice relieves discomfort by dulling the nerves that transmit pain. It also counteracts inflammation, at least briefly. To prolong its effects, trainers often wrap the sore member in a bandage soaked in the ice water. On arrival at the paddock stall, the bandage is removed. So are less significant bandages known as shipping, standing or stall bandages, which protect the legs from accidental kicks and scrapes.

It is not a particularly good idea to cross out the name of a contending horse that comes to the paddock in cold-water bandages. The soothing comfort may be all the animal needs to run in its best possible form.

Before making up his mind, the player should watch what goes on in the stall after the bandage is unwrapped. If trainer and groom fuss over the suspect joint, feeling it for signs of inflammation, one can assume that they are worried. Or if the horse shies away from the attention, the player knows that it hurts at a touch and is unlikely to run well.

After a few weeks of experience, the player can recognize horses that are stiff and sore. Their walking gait is less fluid than it might be. They favor the ouchy limb or foot, getting off it as quickly as possible in what amounts to a limp.

In the absence of an outright limp, the horse's head or hips may tell the tale. The head rises when a sore foreleg touches the ground, and then it nods to the opposite side. In the case of a painful rear leg, the opposite hip drops noticeably while walking. If the forelegs spread and seem about to straddle, as if the animal were on a skating rink, it has a sore knee or two, and will confirm the diagnosis with a mincing, choppy stride when it tries to run.

Every now and then, a horse's gait is so stilted in the walking ring that the player has no trouble deciding to bet on something else, or pass the race entirely. Perhaps more often, the player waits to see whether the animal eases out of its stiffness en route to the starting gate.

The Final Minutes

The horse that arouses expert suspicion in the walking ring generally confirms it during the post parade or the pre-race gallops. Like a child being dragged to the woodshed for punishment, it sweats, strains, has difficulty keeping its feet under it, and needs to be escorted under a tight hold by an outrider on a lead pony. Head high, eyes wild, chewing on the bit, the horse looks like the embodiment of defeat. Its occasional victory does not make a sucker of the player who refuses to bet on it. This kind of animal is not a good bet to begin with, and it proves this over the long haul by losing far more often than not.

Other unready horses do not have to be carried to the post, or held in check to prevent them from bolting to the stable. They simply run sore. The jockey sets them down for a gallop in front of the stands and they do not step out with the characteristically long stride of the Thoroughbred. Short, choppy steps, often with head unusually high or unusually low, reveal soreness. When the rider gets to the backstretch and busts the horse a couple of times with his whip, it may seem to lengthen stride and run more easily, a sign that it is working out of the trouble and may be able to run. No magic formula can be offered to help the player decide whether to bet or not. The only safe prescription is familiar enough: When in doubt, pass.

For my taste, the best bet is the horse that navigates to the starting gate under its own power, without a lead pony and without any special exercises beyond a brief gallop or two. Lead ponies have become so common in modern racing, however, that the bettor would cut his play

Affirmed and Steve Cauthen are unable to overtake Seattle Slew and Angel Cordero in the 1978 Marlboro Cup at Belmont Park. NYRA (BOB COGLIANESE)

below the reasonable minimum if he made the lack of a pre-race escort a large factor in his handicapping.

Shoes

Horseshoes come in a multitude of varieties, most of which are of absolutely no interest to the player.

In the old days, when horsemen solved their economic problems by conniving with each other to cash large bets on fixed races, deliberately poor shoeing was a favorite means of stiffing a horse. Nowadays, purses are more numerous, and big-time horsemen have little incentive to hobble a potential winner. The ancient custom of stiffing it today so that it may win at long odds next time is hard to practice in an era of overworked horses which seldom retain winning form from one race to the next. And an era of relatively vigilant policing. And of claiming races which help a trainer to darken improving form until ready to crack down at a price.

It also is an era in which some veterinarians swear that horses would last longer if greater attention were paid to their shoes. I mention this only for background. The player may deplore the incompetent handling of horses, but is powerless to act against it. As far as shoes are con-

Bobby Ussery enjoys the scent of roses and the taste of triumph on Proud Clarion after the 1967 Kentucky Derby. UPI PHOTO

cerned, his role begins and ends with a glance at the official shoe-board and a close look at the feet of his horse.

He should bet money on no horse that wears steel shoes, now that aluminum ones are the mode. The aluminum weighs several ounces less than steel and, as the saying goes along shed row, "an ounce on the foot is like a pound on the back."

The player also should bet no money on a horse that wears bar shoes. These differ from the usual open-ended footwear. A bar is built across the opening. The purpose is to prevent a weak hoof from spreading and cracking under the animal's weight. Winners rarely wear these.

On tracks that tend to get gooey when wet, or any kind of track labeled muddy or heavy, the player should favor a sharp, well-placed horse whose handlers have spent the few dollars necessary to equip it with mud calks. These cleats provide extra traction.

Blinkers and Bits

The track's printed program advises the player whether a horse that has been running in blinkers will run today without them ("blinkers off") or vice versa ("blinkers on"). The purpose of the hoods is to keep the horse running in a straight line, with his mind on his work. They prevent him from seeing what he might ordinarily shy away from or veer toward— such as other horses, or the inside rail or the grandstand. The heavy reliance of horsemen on trial-and-error is demonstrated by their experimentation with blinkers. A two-year-old that runs a couple of unaccountably erratic races when blinkered is quite likely to be sent postward without them in its next attempt. Sometimes the change works wonders, but don't bet on it. By and large, the change to favor is "blinkers on," when the two-year-old is from a smart barn, has never run hooded, and needs only to improve its previous clockings by a fifth or two to win a maiden race.

Bits come in as many varieties as shoes. The only interesting one is the extension, run-out bit. If the horse has been lugging in, it may go to the post with a bit that is longer on the off (right) side, enabling the rider to develop greater leverage with the reins. Similarly, a bearing-out horse benefits from an extension on the near (left) side. If the player gets to the races frequently enough to notice this change in equipment, and if the horse shapes up well with respect to class, condition, distance and the like, the mutuel ticket may be a better investment than usual.

Drugging and Stiffing

Heroin is known as "horse" because trainers used to dose racehorses with it. The dreaded opium derivative is a powerful stimulant of horses. Its effect is exactly the opposite of the lethargy associated with human addiction. Indeed, a heroin-stimulated horse may become uncontrollably wild, thereby frustrating its handlers, who had hoped only to dull its pain and shock its nervous system into condition for a winning effort.

I mention heroin because it is interesting. What is perhaps most interesting about it is that it has gone out of fashion at the tracks. More reliable, less dangerous, and far less easily detected stimulants and pain-killers are now in use.

The rules of racing forbid the administration of such chemicals. Concern for the betting public, to say nothing of concern for the well-being of the Thoroughbred, explains why official laboratories test blood or urine samples taken from all winners and (in more sensible jurisdictions) all favorites and all animals that ran surprisingly well or surprisingly badly. Pre-race blood sampling is also coming into vogue, and for good reason.

Unfortunately, the intent of all this policing is more impressive than the results it achieves. For one thing, at least three of every four horses need medication of some kind to withstand training and racing. Secondly, in an age of wonder drugs, horsemen constantly stumble upon marvelous new preparations which not only help relieve pain but stimulate a horse's nervous system and, when administered in proper dosage, are exceedingly difficult to detect in saliva or urine samples.

In racetrack chemistry, as in war, the offense is always a jump or two ahead of the defense. By the time the track chemists have discovered how to detect a new drug, unscrupulous horsemen have found an even newer one.

Thus, one of racing's strongest weapons against stimulation of horses is its network of undercover intelligence agents. In plain language, spies. If these shoeflies were not padding around the barns pretending to be other than what they actually are, and if trainers and stablehands were not thoroughly conscious that Big Brother is watching, the game would be much less orderly and predictable than it is.

Every year, about one tenth of 1 percent (.001) of the lab tests turn out positive. Which is to say that racetrack chemists find traces of one or another banned drug. Heads roll. The crime often is blamed on a stable boy, who then vanishes. Once more, calm descends on shed row. Or the trainer, after serving a brief term of suspension, becomes more vigilant than ever. In some cases this means vigilance against hanky-panky. In other cases it means vigilance against getting caught at hanky-panky.

Nobody really knows how many horses go postward under the influence of drugs which relieve discomfort and augment the animals' natural energies. But the high degree of predictability in racing strongly suggests that the problem need alarm no player. Most races are won by horses whose records of increasing readiness are confirmed by good appearance and pleasant deportment in the paddock. If, as seems highly improbable, the victory is often a triumph of medication, the situation is potentially dangerous and deserves even more attention than it already gets behind the scenes of the sport. But, as nearly as I or anyone else can tell at present, drugs have not yet become a factor as important as distance, class, condition, pace or jockey. Nor are they likely to.

Another use of drugs is for purposes of preventing victory by the best horse in the race. It would be naive to pretend that horses never are stiffed, either by their handlers or some other bettor. Barbiturates, which turn up in twenty or thirty horses a year, are a favorite means of inducing languor and defeat. No doubt other chemicals, less easily detected, are also in use. But cases of chemically induced slowness are rare in major racing and by no means standard elsewhere.

One of my authorities for that assertion is the most successful race-fixer in history, Anthony Ciulla, a gigantic thief who became a multimillionaire during the 1970s by prearranging hundreds of races in New England, Michigan, Pennsylvania, New Jersey and New York. While perfecting his craft in Rhode Island and Massachusetts, he discovered that drugging was an undependable way to detain a Thoroughbred. A dosage that induced torpor in one animal might merely relax another just enough to suppress its nervousness and make a competitive tiger of it.

Accordingly, Ciulla abandoned equine medicine and began to bribe jockeys. When finally caught, convicted and imprisoned, he accepted government protection as a member of the Federal witness program. Some of the regional underworld syndicates which had franchised his operation were planning to have him killed, to silence him. He beat them to it. His testimony at a succession of Federal trials resulted in the imprisonment of a large number of underworld honchos and some fall-guy trainers and riders. Racing meanwhile spruced up its security apparatus. An occasional race may be rigged, but that appears to be the extent of such corruption.

Tote-Board Tips

Privileged insiders, who supposedly have a better-than-fair idea about what's what before the race starts, are known enviously as the smart money. When the odds on a horse drop sharply before post-time, the crowd convulses. Hundreds stampede to the windows to join the smarties in the good thing, thereby weighing down the odds still more.

It is true that stable owners, trainers, grooms and clockers—and their relatives, friends and clients—bet thousands of dollars on a horse deemed ready to win. If the horse is unready, or is considered so, they don't bet on it. And if they *do* bet, the odds decline.

Is it possible to tell whether smart money is on a horse? Sometimes. Is smart money smart enough to bother about? Sometimes.

In my opinion, the tote board is an interesting object but should be allowed to play no role whatever in the player's handicapping. His first problem is to find himself a horse. If he finds it, the tote board tells him whether the odds are reasonable. The better his handicapping, the less attention he need pay to the odds, of course. But if he is a neophyte, and not sure whether his horse merits a bet, low odds may well be sufficient reason to abstain.

This, of course, flies in the face of the belief that the player's handicapping is confirmed whenever his horse goes to the post at lower odds than expected. Confirmed by what? By smart money? But what about the two or three other platoons of smart money that have sunk the family jewels on two or three other horses in the same race?

The smart money is not a formally organized league of superlatively knowledgeable bettors. It does not move in a single phalanx to the mutuel windows. Any individual insider or group of insiders is as likely to be wrong about a horse as anyone else. Assuming, of course, that "anyone else" is a good handicapper.

The test of whether smart money is on a horse is whether relatively more is bet on it to win than to place or show. The insiders bet to win, because that's where profit lies. Accordingly, if bets on the horse account for a fifth or sixth of the win pool but only a seventh or eighth of the place or show pool, the player knows that certain presumably smart plungers expect big things and have backed their opinion with cash. Exception: an odds-on horse. The public often bets as heavily on such a horse to place or show as to win.

A last-minute drop in the odds on a horse may or may not reflect inside action by the stable. Occasionally, it means nothing but the infectiousness of a wild rumor. Not so many years ago, I was buttonholed by two hustlers in five minutes, each trying to tout me onto the same two-year-old. I thought it had no chance in its race, and was fascinated to see the odds drop. The horse ran out of the money at 7 to 5. A 4 to 1 shot won. That night I heard from a quite reliable source that several thousand dollars had been wagered on the winner by some smart guys who had employed a few hot-walkers to circulate through the crowd touting the other nag. This kind of thing happens quite often at smaller tracks.

At all racetracks in this country, a sharp drop in the tote-board quotation during the final minutes before post-time usually is a result of a rumor that somebody has loaded up on the horse in the win pool. The news spreads and the rush begins. For the record, let it be noted that the smart money, if it be involved at all, usually feeds its bets into the machines gradually, in an effort to elude discovery. Or, in some cases, it bets at the very start of wagering.

Now that I have done my level best to discourage the reader from allowing himself to be swayed by what he sees on the tote board, I should admit that it seldom pays to buck such betting trends in maiden races at major tracks. This is particularly true when a first-time starter goes postward at odds considerably lower than its morning-line quotation. The reason is simple enough. The only reliable dope about first-starters and lightly raced maidens is the opinion of clockers and other horsemen who have seen it in the mornings. Including, of course, its own handlers. When the slightest amount of extra cash shows up for such a horse in the win pool, the word spreads through the crowd with great rapidity and the odds plummet. I have never kept records of the results attainable through bets on such maidens, but I should not be surprised if profits await anyone who bets on them—provided that he does so only when he thinks that nothing else in the race has an obviously superior chance.

Another kind of tote action worth watching is the *lack* of change in the quotation on a medium-odds horse when the odds drop on another. Plainly, when odds drop sharply on one horse, carrying it into the even money range or thereabouts, odds should rise on everything else in the race. If one horse holds steadily in the 3 to 1 to 6 to 1 range, somebody is hurrying the money in on it. If your handicapping has already singled out that animal, it might pay you to increase your bet.

=18=

HOW TO BUILD YOUR OWN SYSTEM— 60 PRINCIPLES THAT WORK

The purpose of this chapter is to provide the reader with working material for weeks, months and years of constructive fun. Because the word "system" has disreputable overtones for serious handicappers, let me begin by defining terms.

As presented to generations of gullible horseplayers by hundreds of mail-order charlatans, selection systems almost invariably are gross oversimplifications which bear only the most accidental relationship to handicapping. The system seller promises riches to any customer able to follow two or three simple rules. One of the main supporting assurances of all such flim-flammery is the unqualified pledge that the system demands no exercise of judgment by its user. In short, you remain as ignorant as ever, and as uninformed, but you now can beat the races with a few rules.

When the miracle system arrives in the mail (and I have several hundred in my files) it inevitably turns out to be a formula that points out one or another type of horse in one or another type of race—*with little or no attention to the qualities of the other horses entered in that race.*

And there stands the essential difference between mail-order magic, which does not work, and handicapping, which does. In the analysis we call handicapping, the player attempts to appraise horses in relation to each other and to the challenges presented by the distance, footing and other realities in which the race will be contested. Handicapping requires enormous judgment and endless comparison of things. The typical selection system exempts the user from all such effort.

Nevertheless—and here we approach the basis of this chapter—good handicapping is always *systematic*. The player who uses pen, work sheets, pocket calculator and private notebooks is most certainly systematic. But so is the veteran who depends entirely on the printed matter in the *Form* as supplemented by personal memory. No good handicapper can do a race haphazardly.

What follows are procedures designed to help the reader develop—through trial, error and other experimentation—an appropriately systematic method of handicapping. In the end, the process will yield a workable method. It will bear the stamp of the handicapper's individual tastes and skills. It will be no more elaborate than the handicapper finds pleasing. Yet it will be recognizably comprehensive enough to qualify as real handicapping.

The Basic Components

The development of any handicapper involves phase after phase of increasingly sophisticated experimentation with back issues of *Daily Racing Form*. The reader can choose among literally thousands of concepts and profit from the effort—provided that the fundamental launching pads of handicapping are included. Let each series of trials begin as follows:

1. Elimination of horses that seem unsuited to the distance of the race (see Chapter 8).

2. Elimination of horses that do not seem in sufficiently sharp condition to qualify as contenders (see Chapter 9).

3. Elimination of horses that seem outclassed. In time the reader will find this merging with the one above. (see Chapter 10).

4. Elimination of such horses as have survived the previous eliminations but are at a serious disadvantage on today's footing or in light of prevailing track biases, if any (see Chapter 11).

From this point forward, the developing handicapper can flesh things out with speed figures and/or attractive plus factors located in Chapter 16 and/or with any of the dozens of wrinkles contained in other chapters. Before committing yourself to one course or another, I suggest that you browse through the remainder of the present chapter and see whether any of the formulas assembled here strike your fancy. If so, try to work one or more of them into a personalized handicapping method, and see how it does in dry runs with old *Form*s.

Most of the principles that follow could be peddled through the mail as selection systems in their own right. In fact, many have been. What removes the curse and makes the ideas worthy candidates for the reader's consideration is that they have been rescued from the usual oversimplification.

That is, before putting any of the principles to the test of a dry run, the reader will have applied the fundamental elimination procedures set forth above. The reader will have identified the contenders in the race. This transforms a simple-minded system into a legitimate component of authentic handicapping.

Class-Consistency

Principle 1: Play a contender entered for a claiming price at least $2,000 below any price tag it has carried in the past, provided it is the only such horse in the race and is regarded highly enough to go postward at odds of 15 to 1 or less.

Reasoning: Class will tell.

Comment: All minor tracks and some major ones are replete with gimpy, cut-rate horses that used to win allowance races or $50,000 claimers. However, the published past-performance records are brief. They seldom cover more than the most recent six or eight months of an active animal's career. For that reason, this system tends to point out horses that have only recently declined in market value. Such a Thoroughbred unquestionably has gone sour, but it may still have enough class to beat the cheapies it faces this afternoon.

Fantastic results have been recorded in tests of this idea. E. R. DaSilva and Dr. Roy M. Dorcus, faculty members at the University of California at Los Angeles, reported in their interesting book *Science in Betting* (Harper, New York, 1961) that the method turned up 27 plays at a 55-day meeting at Hollywood Park. Thirteen of the bets won, at a profit of $1.50 on every wagered dollar! Somewhat more action—37 plays in 55 days— occurred at Santa Anita, with only a slight reduction in profits. At Aqueduct, a 50-day workout produced 11 plays and an 82 percent profit.

I ran through three weeks of a Delaware Park meeting and found that plays arose at the rate of three or four a week. The sample was too small for significance, but I was interested to note that four of ten selections won and that the prices were long enough to return almost exactly 100 percent on every dollar invested. To achieve this, however, certain elaborations were necessary. Like other apparently simple notions about racing, the one embodied in this system produces endless confusion unless shored up with additional rules.

Suggestions: The player should avoid maiden races, because drops in claiming price mean little in such company. Similarly, if an entrant in a straight $5,000 claimer once ran in a race for $10,000 maidens, it does not qualify on such grounds, but should qualify on the basis of a race for previous winners.

Another problem is that of the horse whose only qualification is that it ran in an allowance race or a higher-bracket claimer at a minor track. Such stock should be ignored. Finally, high-priced claiming races at major tracks frequently involve animals that have run in allowance company. Unless the player is satisfied that the allowance race was substantially classier than today's claimer, he should toss out the horse.

Principle 2: Play any contender running in a claiming race for the first time, provided it has been racing and working out regularly, was beaten by not more than five lengths in its last start, and either led or was within two lengths of the leader at some stage of the race.

Reasoning: An allowance or maiden-special competitor in good enough physical condition to race and work frequently must be conceded an excellent chance when it drops into claiming company after a race in which it showed signs of life.

Suggestions: If in doubt as to what constitutes sufficient recent action, consult Chapter 9. Or require at least one race in the past eighteen days, with workouts at the rate of one per five days for any horse that has not raced in eight days or longer. A distance rule is probably less necessary with this system than in other methods of selection: The trainer who drops a formerly promising horse into a race from which it may be claimed is likely to put it where it can do its best.

Principle 3: Play a contender that led or ran within a length of the leader at one or more of the early calls of its last race and drops down today to a class at which it has won in the past.

Reasoning: Trainers do this sort of thing all the time.

Comment: A pace-setting type that tires in the late stages after showing some run is usually brought back to the races in a hurry, to exploit its apparently improving form. When dropped in with cheaper company than it has been facing, it usually holds its speed longer. The trainer probably places it at the right distance in a situation of this kind.

Principle 4: Bet any contender that was claimed in one of its last three races and is entered today at a price lower than the new owner paid for it.

Reasoning: Horsemen sometimes make dreadful claims, but not very often. If the horse has been running and working regularly and the owner now risks losing it for less than he paid, the player knows that the barn wants today's purse. Badly.

Comment: An occasional horse goes to pot during the very race from which it is claimed. Others conk out during their first days in the new barn. But a majority of the remainder give the new owners some run for the money, having been chosen on grounds of impending good form. Certain shrewd haltermen often win with the horse on the first try, even though it runs against better company than it has been meeting in the recent past. Others take a couple of races to prepare the animal for the crackdown, and do not hesitate to enter it for $500 or $1,000 less than the purchase price, to insure the best possible results. This idea probably will not make money if played indiscriminately, but should be a powerful instrument for anyone who knows the habits and gimmicks of his local track's leading trainers.

Suggestions: The system is unworkable with maidens. It gains strength if the player checks the horse in the paddock, to make sure it is ready.

Principle 5: Play a contender stepping down in class after a race in which it ran out of the money, provided that (1) it had stepped up in class for that race and (2) it was never worse than third at any call in its next-to-last race.

Reasoning: This combines Plus Factors 22 and 23 (see Chapter 16). They often are accompanied by as many as six or seven others, signifying an authentic "go."

Comment: Formal handicapping procedures often single out this system's horse as a contender, yet it may pay a handsome mutuel because of its apparently bad last race.

Principle 6: Play a contender stepping down in class after a race in which the chartmaker's comment indicated that it ran an "even" or better race.

Reasoning: This is Plus Factor 36. A horse that did not disgrace itself in competition with better horses might move ahead a few lengths today.

Comment: Years ago, I used to finish no worse than even, and sometimes with a nice seasonal profit, using this system in races where I could find (1) no truly consistent horse with a clear edge in class and (2) none that ran powerfully enough in its last race to look like a serious threat on grounds of current form. I believe the system is most effective in races for animals aged four and older and, of course, only when more fundamental factors fail to suggest a likely play.

Principle 7: Play a contender that finished second in its last race if (1) it runs in the same company or cheaper today and (2) the winner of its last race has subsequently stepped up in class and won.

Reasoning: The horse lost to something that was much too good for the field. But it beat everything else and should be a good bet today.

Comment: This is what is called a "follow-up" system. A player who already keeps a notebook record of results, the true class of races, and the like, can turn a pretty penny with this angle. It produces not more than one or two plays a week, but the winning percentage ranges between 33 and 50, depending on how careful the player is about avoiding three-year-olds against older horses and horses that have not had sufficient recent work.

Suggestions: If you do not maintain a notebook, the infrequent plays produced by this system may not seem worth the trouble. On the other hand, the results are most gratifying for anyone with the necessary patience. The system is particular dynamite with fillies and mares that finish second to males and seem to be stepping up in class when entered at a slightly higher price against females. As readers of Chapter 10 are aware, such a step up is really a step down. The system gets equally good results with three-year-olds that race against their own kind after running second to older horses. In any case, careful observance of the form cycle is necessary. A horse that runs second may get so tuckered out that it can't beat anything in its next effort. Check Chapter 9 and devise rules to assure bets on ready horses.

Principle 8: Play a contender that has gone to the post as betting favorite in at least 40 percent of the races described in its past-

performance record, provided that it (1) has finished in the money in at least half the races for which detailed past-performance lines are published and (2) has won no less than 25 percent of its total races this year and last.

Reasoning: A horse of established consistency and recognized class (note the frequency with which it runs as favorite) is seldom a hopeless risk.

Comment: Strangely enough, this system puts the player on cheapies as well as stakes runners. It gets surprisingly good prices at times. The crowd often discounts the chances of a vigorous young three-year-old against better stock than it has faced in the past. Odds also rise when a well-backed horse loses two or three times in succession.

Suggestions: The system is at its best when the player takes pains to avoid jaded horses. Sufficient late action and, among older horses, not too many hard recent races should be minimum requirements. Two-year-olds are not covered by this system, which calls for consistency over a period of two years.

Principle 9: Play a contender that has won at least 25 percent of no fewer than six races this year, or this year and last combined, provided that it (1) has run within the past ten days at this track and (2) has won at today's distance against animals of today's class.

Reasoning: An authentically consistent horse, properly placed and physically fit, is usually a real contender.

Principle 10: Play a contender that has won and/or finished second at least ten times during this year and last, provided that it (1) has finished first or second in at least half its races during that period and (2) has won at least 25 percent of its total starts during that period and (3) has raced within the past eight days and (4) has won or finished second within the past two months.

Reasoning: A genuinely consistent horse that ran eight days ago should be fit enough to live up to its record today.

Comment: This one seldom gets more than two or three plays a week. Prices range from odds-on to $30 and better, with the majority at 2 to 1 and 5 to 2. *Turf and Sport Digest* published a full-season New York workout of a closely similar system many years ago. It hit 40 percent winners and the profit exceeded 100 percent.

Principle 11: Of contenders that ran within the past ten days and finished out of the money, play the one whose record shows a victory at today's exact distance in a field of today's class.

Reasoning: The recent losing race and the proper placement suggest an effort to win at a price.

Comment: Like so many angles of its kind, this one leads to the poorhouse unless the player fortifies it with sensible condition rules. Otherwise, its losing streaks will be more compelling than the longshots it finds.

Suggestions: With condition rules, this kind of play becomes an especially promising bet, particularly when the maneuvering trainer assigns the mount to a leading jockey.

Principle 12: Play a contender that lost its last race but earned a "Form" speed rating of 95 or better.

Reasoning: It takes an exceptionally good horse to earn such a rating, win or lose. An animal of such class should win next time out if given any part of a break.

Comment: Like most systems, this one improves in the hands of a player willing to supplement mechanical rules with knowledge of the game. An analysis of fitness is most important, and so is analysis of the assigned weights. The player who uses the idea in that fashion should find it helpful in big races.

Principle 13: Play the contender that has won or finished closest to the front end most often in its last seven races. Add the finishing positions in those races, counting a victory as 1, a second-place finish as 2, and so on, but giving nothing worse than a 5, even if the horse finished tenth in one of its races. The horse with the lowest total is the play. If any horse has fewer than seven races, but has won any, pass the race.

Reasoning: Recent consistency is the best kind.

Comment: Surprisingly good prices await anyone who plays this mechanically after due attention to distance, class and recent action.

Form

Principle 14: Bet a contender that won its last race easily, provided that the race took place not more than a week ago.

Reasoning: An easy winner is at top form. The trainer seeks a repeat victory as soon as possible.

Comment: A sound idea, except when the animal steps up to meet one or two classier animals whose own condition is sharp.

Suggestions: Worth trying if the horse is the only one of its kind in the race. In allowances, handicaps and stakes, and in top-grade claimers at major tracks, the one-week rule might be eased to ten days.

Principle 15: Play a contender that won its last race by gaining in the stretch after leading or running within two lengths of the leader at the stretch call, provided the race occurred within two weeks.

Reasoning: The big win is the most reliable sign of powerful, winning form. But if the horse is kept out of action for more than two weeks, one must assume that illness or injury has prevented the trainer from cashing in again.

Comment: The player who is careful about age, sex and jockey can beat the game with this.

Suggestions: Play no race in which more than one horse qualifies. Avoid three-year-olds against older, except in allowance sprints, or if you know that the three-year-old beat older in its big win. Also avoid females against males. Otherwise, do not worry about animals moving up in class. This kind does it and wins. Flexibility about the two-week rule also helps: If the horse has been working briskly at four- or five-day intervals, it can be allowed up to three weeks since its last race. Obviously, however, the situation is rosier if not more than a week elapses.

Principle 16: Bet a contender that gained in the stretch in its last race provided that it beat at least three horses and does not step up in class.

Reasoning: Class and form.

Comment: An excellent spot-play method for claiming races, but only when not more than three animals qualify and no other apparently sharp entrant has superior consistency. Gets excellent prices.

Suggestions: Try combining this with 13 and 14, using it when they fail to produce a play in a medium-grade claimer. A severe late-action rule is needed for the best results. I would not bother with a horse unraced for more than two weeks unless it had worked out at least twice in the last eight or ten days. To break ties, favor the horse stepping down in price. If still a tie, go to the one that raced most recently and/or got the most favorable chart comment.

Principle 17: Play a contender that ran close to the early pace of its last race, slowing down in the later stages, provided that (1) it had not showed as much early speed in its previous two races and (2) it earned a higher speed rating in the last race than in either of the previous two.

Reasoning: Early speed is a reliable sign of improvement.

Comment: Innumerable systems derive from this idea. Their virtue is in steering the player away from obvious choices, many of which turn out to be past the peak of form.

Suggestions: Try this with horses that have raced in the past seven days or have worked out at short intervals since racing not more than two weeks ago. Concentrate on claiming races, and notice whether results improve if the jockey factor is introduced.

Principle 18: Play a contender that lost its last race provided that it was first, second or third at the pre-stretch call and that (1) it had been at least two positions farther back at that call in each of its previous two races and (2) it earned a higher speed rating than in either of the two previous races.

Reasoning: Another sign of improvement, representing a sign of life in the semifinal stages of the race.

Comment: Everything said about 17 applies here.

Principle 19: Play a contender that was first, second or third at the stretch call and, while losing, earned a higher speed rating than in its previous two races.

Reasoning: Another hint of imminent victory.

Principle 20: Play a contender that finished two positions closer to the winner and earned a higher speed rating than in its previous two races.

Reasoning: Still another sign of improvement.

Principle 21: Play a contender that ran an even race, in second, third or fourth position (it does not matter which), at each of the four calls. The horse should have earned a higher speed rating than in either of its previous two races.

Reasoning: Such a horse is on the verge.

Principle 22: Play a horse that has earned increasingly high speed ratings in each of its last three races without winning, and has been increasingly close to the winner at each of the four calls in each race. Judge closeness to the winner in terms of either running position or number of lengths behind. If the horse led at any call in its third race back or its next-to-last race, it should have led at the same call in the following race.

Reasoning: The occasional animal whose record shows an overall improvement of this kind is on its way to the winner's circle.

Suggestions: Consider combining all these improvement-angle systems into one. A careful study of results at your own track will disclose the blend that yields the most satisfactory profits.

Principle 23: Play a contender that raced twice in the past fourteen days but did not win, provided that it has won at today's distance and class at some time in the past three months.

Reasoning: A properly placed animal fit enough to race three times in two weeks is fit enough to win, perhaps at a price.

Suggestions: Things improve considerably if the player requires that the horse's record show a bit of improvement in either of its last two efforts. It also pays to avoid any four-year-old or older animal that lost in close, driving finishes in both of its most recent starts.

Principle 24: Play a contender that has raced within two weeks, has worked out every five days since, worked out yesterday, and is dropping in claiming price.

Reasoning: Such a recent record portrays a trainer getting ready to shoot the wad with a physically able animal.

Principle 25: Among contenders that have raced in the past seven days, finishing out of the money, play the one that has run in the highest-grade race in the last two months.

Reasoning: A race within seven days is always a good sign. Many successful players refuse to bet on any other kind of animal.

Principle 26: Play the contender that finished in the money most recently.

Reasoning: What better clue to top form than a recent good performance?

Comment: The last-out-in-the-money system may be the most popular of them all. It protects the player against serious losing streaks by choosing animals whose trainers are trying to cash in on good form. It can be used in any kind of race.

Suggestions: The player who understands the form cycle increases the winning percentage by ruling out horses whose in-the-money finishes are forecasts of deterioration rather than improvement.

Principle 27: Play a contender that finished in the money in its last two starts, provided that it (1) won not more than one of them, (2) was out of the money in its third race back, (3) steps up not more than 25 percent in claiming price today and (4) is the only qualifier in the race.

Reasoning: The horse demonstrated improvement in its next-to-last and either improved still more in its last or ran well enough to get some of the money. It may still have enough on the ball to win today.

Comment: Frank Bouche served this one to readers of *American Turf Monthly*. It gets good prices, encounters few long losing streaks and locates a play or two on most racing days. Its ingenious rules cover the kind of animal that lost last time because it was stepped up in class after a victory. Also covered are the animals that won last time but which may be able to win again because they step up only slightly today. The rule against races with more than one qualifier prevents confusion. It also tends to turn up races in which the one horse, regardless of odds, is a form standout.

Principle 28: By reading the official charts, including the chartmaker's comments, note the name of any horse that finished fast in the stretch and reached the wire not more than two lengths behind the winner. Note also horses that encountered interference of some kind but showed late speed. And horses that go off at 2 to 1 or less but finish out of the money after a poor start or interference of some kind. Play each horse each time it races again until it wins, but do not play it more than four times. Compile the list from charts of all races except jumps, two-year-old and maiden races.

Reasoning: The stout stretch finish is a splendid clue to impending victory. The alibi is a strong plus factor in cases of this kind.

Comment: The man who introduced me to Thoroughbred racing half a century ago used to make a pretty penny with a follow-up system quite similar to this. In 1949, R. H. Matthews explained the present version to readers of *Turf and Sport Digest*. He published a workout covering 1,752 bets at seven tracks in a period of almost a year. The winning percentage was 23 (418 winners) and the profit was a robust 57 cents for every wagered dollar. Some of the mutuel payoffs were extraordinary—one horse paid $94.90, another $87.20, another $86.70. And so on, including dozens at 4 to 1 or better. The system beat every one of the seven meetings.

Principle 29: Play a contender that runs within four days after being scratched from a race, provided that (1) the track was fast on the day the horse was scratched and (2) the horse was assigned a post position for the race from which it was scratched and (3) the horse has been racing and working out regularly.

Reasoning: The trainer scratches the horse because a better opportunity is in prospect a few days later. If he were not hoping to win with the animal, he would let it get its tightener in the earlier race and would not bother to scratch it.

Comment: A sound enough idea, limited by the inescapable fact that the wish to win and the ability to win are two different things. The post-position rule is important. Often, more entries are received than can be accommodated in a race. The extra horses are placed on an "also-eligible" list and are assigned no post positions. If one of the others is scratched, a horse is moved into the race from the also-eligible list. Therefore, a horse whose name appears on the also-eligible list may be scratched for no reason other than that the race was filled.

Principle 30: Consider only contenders that ran within ten days and finished out of the money. Determine the number of lengths by which each was beaten in each of its three most recent races (counting a victory as zero). Add the number of beaten lengths. Play the horse with the smallest total.

Reasoning: A horse that has been getting close to the winner, or winning itself, benefits from an easy out-of-the-money race. If it then returns to the wars within ten days, it is in adequate physical condition. Its poor last race will inflate the mutuel price.

Comment: This is a nice angle for players sensible enough to steer away from animals that are on the downgrade.

Principle 31: Play a contender that finished fourth in its last race provided that it (1) gained at least two lengths in the stretch or (2) led or ran within a length of the leader at any calls or (3) steps down in claiming price.

Reasoning: The fourth-place finish, being out of the money, discourages a certain amount of public play, augmenting the odds. A horse that ran fourth after giving notice of improvement, or that steps into easier company, should never be overlooked.

Principle 32: Play a contender that returned to racing after a layoff of six weeks or more and, in its first or second outing, led or ran within a half length of the leader at the first three calls, but tired in the stretch and lost.

Reasoning: The "short" horse needed that race to build its stamina and demonstrate the benefits of its freshening layoff.

Comment: A player who exercises the slightest discrimination about the pace factor should be able to make profits with this, especially at tracks that favor horses with front-running styles.

Principle 33: Play a contender that finished out of the money but within five lengths of the winner.

Reasoning: The apparently poor finish conceals the fact that the horse was actually quite close to the winner. Good mutuels are likely.

Comment: This is a cousin of 31. It gets enormous prices. The difficulty is that as many as four or five horses in a single field may qualify.

Suggestions: When playing this there seldom is any sense in betting at less than 4 to 1.

Principle 34: Play a contender that ran out of the money in its last race, if (1) it finished not more than a length behind the second-place horse and (2) the winner of the race crossed the wire at least five lengths in front.

Reasoning: A horse that wins by five lengths or more has demonstrated unusual superiority over its field. In those circumstances, an out-of-the-money finish, a length or less behind the second-place horse, is evidence of form.

Comment: This gets prices because of the failure of racing crowds to differentiate between a badly outclassed or badly conditioned horse and one that ran quite close to the leaders, even though it failed to get into the money.

Principle 35: Play any contender that ran as betting favorite within the past six days and finished in the money.

Reasoning: The trainer strikes while the iron is hot.

Comment: This gets a high percentage of winners, which can be increased by closer attention to the form factor.

Principle 36: Play a contender that has been in the money in each of its last four races.

Reasoning: The horse is due.

Comment: No horse is ever "due" on these grounds alone. Furthermore, some horses, especially two- and three-year-olds, become habitual runners-up, unwilling to pass the leader. Within these limitations, the system can be used to catch a fair percentage of winners. Moreover, the prices are often not bad, possibly because the crowd tends to lose faith in horses of this type.

Suggestions: Confine play to secondary tracks, or to horses stepping down in class, or horses switched from ordinary jockeys to local or national leaders.

Principle 37: Play a contender that was the favorite in its last race but lost, provided it gained in the stretch.

Reasoning: The animal wanted to run. Perhaps it was victimized by lack of racing room or a badly judged ride.

Comment: Some racegoers play every beaten favorite they can find. The advantage of this approach is its usual avoidance of false favorites, the sucker horses that get the public's money after they have begun to los their racing sharpness.

Suggestions: If the selection was entered at the wrong distance last time, expect big things today. If the last race was at the right distance, it is safest to require that the horse stay in the same class or step down a bit. Make sure that the last race was recent, or that the animal has been working out regularly. Welcome a change of riding assignments, especially if today's jockey is a leader.

Repeaters

Among the rules most familiar to system fanciers is "Eliminate any horse that won its last race." The reason is statistical: Many horses are incapable of winning twice in succession. Yet many others win two or three or four in a row.

Principle 38: Play a contender that goes to the post within six days after a race in which it led at every call and won by two lengths or more.

Reasoning: The horse is hot.

Comment: Indeed it is.

Suggestions: Unless the horse gained in the stretch it is unlikely to repeat the victory in a substantially higher claiming bracket. If the top claiming price in the last race was $6,000 or less, today's should be not more than 20 percent higher. If the last race was in a higher range, the animal can step up 25 percent. An exception would be the horse that previously has won in today's class or better.

Principle 39: Play a contender that won its last race "handily," "easily" or "going away" provided that (1) the race took place within ten days and (2) the horse has won at least 25 percent of its starts, finishing out of the money in fewer than half.

Reasoning: This catches good horses at the peak of their form.

Comment: Incredibly, not all the horses unearthed by this system are short-priced favorites.

Suggestions: If the horse has had ten or more races this year, it is safe to calculate its consistency on this year's record alone. Otherwise, combine this year's total with last year's. Do not attempt to use this method with two-year-olds. Somewhat bigger class rises can be permitted than in 38. But if the animal moves from a claimer to an allowance race, do not bet on it unless it has already won in such company.

Favorites

Endless profits await the player able to identify 45 percent of winning favorites *before* their races. System fanciers tinker by the hour with gimmicks designed to eliminate false favorites. Here are a few wrinkles well worth studying.

Principle 40: In races with a purse value of $10,000 or less for four-year-olds and up, play the favorite if (1) it has won at least 20

percent of its races this year and (2) it has won at least 20 percent of its races this year and last and (3) its list of recent performances includes at least three wins and two places, or four wins and one place, or five wins and (4) it finished in the money in its last start, which occurred at today's track not more than eighteen days ago and (5) it has won at today's exact distance.

Reasoning: A four-, five- or six-year-old of proved consistency and fitness is the steadiest of all Thoroughbreds. This is especially true in races of less than top quality, where the competition is less severe. The system bars races open to three-year-olds only because animals of that age frequently have not yet found their proper class level: An apparently inconsistent one might actually be the class and speed of its field. A handicapper could discern this, but the means of doing so are too complicated for inclusion in a system of this kind.

Comment: When Lawrence Lalik published this method in *American Turf Monthly,* the magazine reported that tests at Bowie, Fair Grounds and New York had produced winners in 55 to 63 percent of its selections, with profits ranging between 40 and 60 percent. Plays arise two or three times a week.

Principle 41: Play an odds-on favorite to place in any non-claiming race with a purse of $5,000 or more.

Reasoning: Year in and year out, bets of this kind show a small profit.

Comment: As far as I know, this is the only kind of place or show betting on which profit is assured without resort to handicapping. The explanation is that the animals are especially good ones, less susceptible than others to sudden lapses of form. They win or finish second about two thirds of the time. The place prices are customarily wretched, but perk up a bit when the place pool is shared with backers of a longshot.

Suggestions: Unless yours is a track of authentically major caliber, you had better test this on the few races of $15,000 value that were run there last season. In my experience, odds-on favorites are most reliable at New York, California, Illinois, Florida, Arkansas, Maryland and New Jersey.

Principle 42: When the track is sloppy, play a front-running horse that goes to the post as favorite.

Reasoning: Front-runners have a special advantage in the slop.

Suggestions: If the horse happens to qualify under one of the other systems concerned with favorites, it can be supported with considerable confidence. Otherwise, the player should see whether the animal is the only apparently fit front-runner in the field. In case another seems capable of running with it, and there is doubt about the favorite's staying power in such circumstances, the next factor to examine is class. If the favorite is moving up in class and does not seem completely capable of surviving early competition for the lead, pass the race.

Principle 43: Play a favorite if (1) it is male, (2) it raced not more than five days ago and (3) it won the race.

Reasoning: It may still be at peak form.

Comment: In 1956, *Turf and Sport Digest* reported a fifteen-month test, covering about 2,800 races at all major tracks. This simple system yielded a profit of 13 cents on every wagered dollar.

Principle 44: If the favorite did not win its last race, or goes to the post at odds higher than even money, play the second choice in the betting, provided that (1) it is male and (2) it won its last race within the last five days (ten days if today's purse is $15,000 or higher).

Reasoning: The crowd's second choice wins about one race in five. This means that, in almost two races on an "average" afternoon, the crowd overestimates the favorite's winning chances by comparison with those of its second choice. This system directs the player to a kind of race in which the crowd errs rather frequently.

Comment: Jud Onatsirt, who also devised 43, reported a six-month test of this one. It cranked out a 55 percent profit. Plays occurred at the rate of about two a week at major tracks. In combination with 43, this is as simple and rewarding as any purely mechanical angle I have ever seen.

Speed and Pace

Principle 45: In sprints no longer than six furlongs, find the highest total of "Form" speed rating plus track variant earned by each contender when running at today's exact distance in the past

month. Allow 1 point for each three pounds of difference between today's assigned weight and the weight carried in the rated race. If today's weight is lower add the points to the previously calculated speed figure. If today's weight is higher, subtract the weight points. Play the horse with the highest net figure.

Reasoning: Many conventional users of speed ratings do little more than this.

Comment: Dorcus and DaSilva, who gave us Principle 1, recorded profits of almost 50 cents on the dollar in lengthy workouts with this one. About 40 percent of the selections won. When dealing with two-year-olds racing at distances shorter than six furlongs, the weight factor can be omitted.

Principle 46: From each contender's last two races, take the higher total of speed rating plus track variant. Play the horse with the highest figure.

Reasoning: Frederick S. Davis showed that the horse chosen this way won 62 percent of sprints. His study was restricted to dry, fast tracks—a good idea.

Principle 47: Add the running positions of each contender at the pre-stretch and stretch calls of its last two races. Play the horse with the lowest total.

Reasoning: The horse closest to the front during the middle stages of its last two races is certain to be in contention today.

Comment: Best suited to tracks that favor front-runners. Gets good mutuels sometimes.

Principle 48: Among contenders that finished in the money within the past week, play the one that has earned the highest speed rating in a race of today's exact distance on the present circuit during the past three months. If a tie, play the one that carried the highest weight when earning the top rating.

Reasoning: A horse that races twice in a week is physically fit and might show its previously superior speed.

Principle 49: To the highest speed rating earned by each contender during the past thirty days, add 1/100 of the claiming price for which it was entered, and add the weight it carried. Play the horse with the highest total.

Reasoning: Speed, weight and class are the bases of many successful handicapping procedures.

Comment: This one gets winners. It would be fun to see what combination of consistency and jockey rules might improve results.

Jockeys

Followers of jockeys learn in time that it is a good idea to pay some attention to the horses which the youngsters ride. Almost any of the more solid systems in this chapter will suffice. And here are a few others designed expressly for the purpose.

Principle 50: Play one of the five leading jockeys at the current meeting when he rides a contender that (1) lost its last race, (2) finished in the money in at least one of its latest three attempts, (3) has won 20 percent of its starts this year and last combined and (4) raced not more than ten days ago.

Reasoning: A fit, consistent horse that lost its last race should go off at better-than-usual odds today.

Suggestions: Break ties by going to the higher-class animal.

Principle 51: Play a contender that lost its last race provided that (1) the jockey has won with it at today's exact distance but in better company than today's and (2) the jockey is either a national leader or ranks among the top riders at the current meeting.

Reasoning: This is another fairly reasonable effort to get occasionally higher mutuels than one might expect when a leading jockey is aboard a class horse.

Suggestions: Note how often horses of this type come to life when switched from an apprentice or a rank-and-file journeyman to a leading reinsman or one who has won with the animal in the past.

Principle 52: Play the contender listed at lowest odds in the track program's morning line, provided that it is ridden by one of the two leading jockeys of the meeting.

Reasoning: Hot jockey, hot horse.

Comment: The morning-line favorite does not always turn out to be the public's choice, but seldom pays better than 5 to 2. The stinginess of the odds are compensated by a good winning percentage.

Suggestions: The player may not believe that the jockeys listed at the head of the official "leading riders" tabulation are the best on the grounds and is probably correct. You can use the two jocks with the highest winning averages.

Tote Board

The handicapper usually gains confidence from significant tote-board activity on the horse. Certain system players omit the handicapping and look for omens on the tote board. Here are some of the more sensible approaches.

Principle 53: Play a contender when the tote board shows that disproportionately high sums are being bet on it to win, by comparison with what is being bet on it to place or show.

Reasoning: Horsemen do not fool around with place and show betting. When they bet, they bet to win.

Comment: If the bets on a horse account for 20 percent of the win pool and only 15 percent of the place pool, it is obvious that someone is loading up on the front end. Indeed, if the place bets account for 17 percent of that pool a similar supposition is warranted. The only time place or show bets should be high in proportion to win bets is when the horse is odds-on. In such circumstances, lots of money, smart and otherwise, goes on place and show tickets.

Principle 54: Bet on a contender that lost its last race and steps up in class today but goes to the post at lower odds than in the cheaper, losing race.

Reasoning: The insiders must have a coup cooking.

Comment: Ordinarily such a horse should be running at higher odds today. If the player's handicapping suggests that the animal is in shape, the lower odds may indeed be a sign of inside action.

Principle 55: If one horse is heavily bet and its odds fall below 8 to 5, any contender whose odds do not rise is worth backing.

Reasoning: When the odds on the favorite drop, the odds on the other horses should rise. If the 4 to 1 or 5 to 1 shot holds steady when the favorite drops from 5 to 2 to 7 to 5, you know that many people have been buying tickets on the longer-priced animal.

Comment: Again, good handicapping is the key. If the favorite looks to you like a sucker horse, and you like the other, the steadiness of its odds is an indication that other smart players feel the same way.

Principle 56: In the second race of the day, play a contender on which proportionately more money was bet in the daily double than is being bet in the win pool of the race.

Reasoning: Rather than drive down the odds on his entrant in the second race, many a trainer or owner buys daily-double tickets on it. After the first race, the track posts the mutuel price that the double will pay on each horse in the second race. If the daily-double price on a horse is lower than it should be, considering the odds at which the horse is held in the win pool of the race itself, somebody must have plunged on the double.

Comment: Such things happen. If the stable holds a sufficient number of daily-double tickets which couple its horse with the winner of the first race, and if the daily-double price is right, the boys can sweeten the profit with only modest bets on the win end. Modest bets at high odds. This is preferable to betting a wad on the horse, driving the odds down, and collecting peanuts later.

Suggestions: Two minutes before post-time for the second race, divide the posted daily-double price on each horse by the latest tote-board quotation. Thus, if the daily-double price is $200 and the present odds against the horse are 20 to 1, the answer would be 10. If the daily-double price on another entrant is $24 and the odds against it to win the second race are 2 to 1, the answer in its case is 12. Clearly, the longshot was heavily backed in the daily double. Horses of this kind win once in a while. The time to bet one is when its record identifies it as a contender.

Public Selectors

Thousands of systems handicap the newspaper handicappers. Starting with the assumption that a good public selector, or a consensus of several, names horses with legitimate chances to win, the systems deploy simple handicapping procedures in an attempt to avoid the losers. Some of these systems produce lengthy strings of winners at low prices. Like other systems, they perform best when the track is fast.

Principle 57: Play the contender that is the "Form" consensus choice in an allowance, handicap or stakes race, provided that the horse (1) has won a third of its races since the beginning of last year and (2) either was in the money in its last race or lost by not more than two lengths and (3) has been in the money in at least five of its last seven races and (4) carries not more than 124 pounds, unless the race is a weight-for-age stakes.

Reasoning: Not only do the experts like it, but it clearly is an outstanding Thoroughbred.

Comment: A system like this hits few losers, and few payoffs above $4. Profits are possible.

Suggestions: Beware of cheaper allowance races at secondary tracks.

Principle 58: Play the consensus ("Form") choice, provided that it has had a race and one workout within seven days.

Reasoning: A high proportion of winners have had a race and a workout in seven days. When the racing paper's consensus favors a horse with those qualifications, it ought to have a splendid chance.

Comment: This system has been around for years. It finds about one play a day at a typical major track, and is quite reliable.

Principle 59: Bet the contender that is the consensus choice when no other horse in the field has raced more recently or is more consistent or has earned a higher speed rating in its last three races.

Reasoning: Consistency, fitness, overall speed and the high regard of experts should produce winners.

Comment: Do not be surprised if this one produces seven or eight short-priced winners in succession—at the rate of one play every ten days or so.

Principle 60: Clip the "Horses to Watch" column which appears in the "Form" on Mondays. Play each horse three times or until it wins—whichever occurs sooner.

Reasoning: These are tips from chart-callers, clockers and other experts.

Comment: Profits are conceivable for a player who makes sure the animals are legitimate contenders.

Suggestions: Do a dry run in which no paper bet is made unless the horse has had a race or a workout within a week, is entered at a suitable distance, and is assigned a leading jockey.

19

HOW TO READ PAST PERFORMANCES

Not one racegoer in a thousand is fully conversant with the symbols and abbreviations employed by *Daily Racing Form* in past-performance records. Spending a few minutes with this chapter is highly recommended. The first section of the chapter reproduces the *Form*'s own instructions for users of the tabloid editions published in the middle and far West and Canada. The second section contains instructions for users of the full-size Eastern editions, followed by instructions for use of the tabloid editions.

Abbreviations for North American Tracks

Abbreviations below designate tracks in *Daily Racing Form* charts and past-performance tables.

AC	Caliente, Mex.	**Atl**	Atlantic City, N.J.
Aks	Ak-Sar-Ben, Neb.	**Ato**	Atokad Park, Neb.
Alb	Albuquerque, N.M.	**Bel**	Belmont Park, N.Y.
AP	Arlington Park, Ill.	**Bil**	Billings, Mont.
Aqu	Aqueduct, N.Y.	**BM**	Bay Meadows, Cal.
ArP	Arapahoe Park, Col.	**Bmf**	Bay Meadows Fair, Cal.
AsD	Assiniboia Downs, Can.	**Bml**	Balmoral Park, Ill.

Boi	Boise, Ida.	Pay	Payson Park, Fla.
BRD	Blue Ribbon Downs, Okla.	Pen	Penn National, Pa.
Cby	Canterbury Downs, Minn.	Pha	Philadelphia Park, Pa.
CD	Churchill Downs, Ky.	Pim	Pimlico, Md.
Cda	Coeur d'Alene, Ida.	PJ	Park Jefferson, S.D.
Cls	Columbus, Neb.	Pla	Playfair, Wash.
Crc	Calder Race Course, Fla.	Pln	Pleasonton, Cal.
CT	Charles Town, W. Va.	PM	Portland Meadows, Ore.
Dar	Darby Downs, Oh.	Pmf	Portland Meadows Fair
DeD	Delta Downs, La.	Pom	Pomona, Cal.
Del	Delaware Park, Del.	PP	Pikes Peak Meadows, Col.
Det	Detroit Race Course, Mich.	PR	El Comandante, P.R.
Dmf	Del Mar Fair, Cal.	Pre	Prescott Downs, Ariz.
Dmr	Del Mar, Cal.	Rap	Rapid City, S.D.
EIP	Ellis Park, Ky.	RD	River Downs, Oh.
EnP	Enoch Park, Can.	Reg	Regina, Can.
EP	Exhibition Park, Can.	Ril	Rillito, Ariz.
EvD	Evangeline Downs, La.	Rkm	Rockingham Park, N.H.
Fai	Fair Hills, Md.	Rui	Ruidoso Downs, N.M.
FE	Fort Erie, Can.	SA	Santa Anita Park, Cal.
Fer	Ferndale, Cal.	Sac	Sacramento, Cal.
FG	Fair Grounds, La.	Sal	Salem, Ore.
FL	Finger Lakes, N.Y.	San	Sandown Park, Can.
Fno	Fresno, Cal.	Sar	Saratoga, N.Y.
Fon	Fonner Park, Neb.	SFe	Santa Fe, N.M.
FP	Fairmount Park, Ill.	SJD	San Juan Downs, N.M.
GBF	Great Barrington, Mass.	SLR	San Luis Rey Downs, Cal.
GD	Galway Downs, Cal.	Sol	Solano, Cal.
GF	Great Falls, Mont.	Spt	Sportsman's Park, Ill.
GG	Golden Gate Fields, Cal.	SR	Santa Rosa, Cal.
GP	Gulfstream Park, Fla.	STC	Spendthrift, Ky.
Grd	Greenwood, Can.	Stk	Stockton, Cal.
GrP	Grants Pass, Ore.	StP	Stampede Park, Can.
GS	Garden State Park, N.J.	SuD	Sun Downs, Wash.
HaP	Harbor Park, Wash.	Suf	Suffolk Downs, Mass.
Haw	Hawthorne, Ill.	Sun	Sunland Park, N.M.
Hia	Hialeah Park, Fla.	Tam	Tampa Bay Downs, Fla.
Hol	Hollywood Park, Cal.	Tdn	Thistledown, Oh.
HP	Hazel Park, Mich.	Tim	Timonium, Md.
JnD	Jefferson Downs, La.	TuP	Turf Paradise, Ariz.
Jua	Juarez, Mex.	Wat	Waterford Park, W.Va.
Kee	Keeneland, Ky.	WO	Woodbine, Can.
LA	Los Alamitos, Cal.	Wyo	Wyoming Downs, Wyo.
LaD	Louisiana Downs, La.	YM	Yakima Meadows, Wash.
LaM	La Mesa Park, N.M.		
Lar	Nuevo Laredo, Mex.		**HUNT MEETINGS**
Lat	Latonia, Ky.		
Lga	Longacres, Wash.	Aik	Aiken, S.C.
LnN	Lincoln State Fair, Neb.	AtH	Atlanta, Ga.
Lrl	Laurel Race Course, Md.	Cam	Camden, S.C.
MD	Marquis Downs, Can.	Clm	Clemens, N.C.
Med	Meadowlands, N.J.	Fai	Fair Hills, Md.
Mex	Mexico City	Fax	Fairfax, Va.
MF	Marshfield Fair, Mass.	FH	Far Hills, N.J.
Mth	Monmouth Park, N.J.	Fx	Foxfield, Va.
NP	Northlands Park, Can.	Gln	Glyndon, Md.
OP	Oaklawn Park, Ark.	GN	Grand National, Md.
OTC	Ocala Training Center, Fla.	GrM	Great Meadows, Va.

GV	Genesee Valley, N.Y.		**Pro**	Prospect, Ky.
Lex	Lexington, Ky.		**PW**	Percy Warner, Tenn.
Lig	Ligonier, Pa.		**RB**	Red Bank, N.J.
Mal	Malvern, Pa.		**SH**	Strawberry Hill, Va.
Mid	Middleburg, Va.		**SoP**	Southern Pines, N.C.
Mon	Monkton, Md.		**StL**	St. Louis, Mo.
Mor	Morven Park, Va.		**Try**	Tryon, N.C.
Mtp	Montpelier, Va.		**Uni**	Unionville, Pa.
Oxm	Oxmoor, Ky.		**War**	Warrenton, Va.
PmB	Palm Beach, Fla.			

Abbreviations for Foreign Tracks

AbA	Aberdeen, Aus.		**CeA**	Cessnock, Aus.
Af	Africa		**Cha**	Chantilly, Fra.
Ain	Aintree, Eng.		**Che**	Cheltenham, Eng.
AEP	Aix-en-Provence, Fra.		**ChA**	Cheltenham, Aus.
Aix	Alexandra Park, Eng.		**Chep**	Chepstow, Eng.
Amie	Amiens, Fra.		**Chs**	Chester, Eng.
And	Andelys, Fra.		**CiJ**	Cidare Jardim, Brazil
Ang	Angers, Fra.		**Cla**	Clairfontaine, Fra.
Ast	Ascot, Eng.		**Cln**	Clarendon, Aus.
Auc	Auckland, N.Z.		**HdS**	Club Hipico de Santiago, Chile
Aus	Australia		**Clge**	Cologne, Ger.
Aut	Auteuil, Fra.		**CSA**	Colombia, S.A.
Ayr	Ayr, Scot.		**Com**	Compiegne, Fra.
BaB	Baden Baden, Ger.		**Cor**	Cordoba, Arg.
Bal	Baldoyle, Ire.		**Cd'A**	Cote d'Azur, Fra.
Bo-D	Bangor-on-Dee, Eng.		**Cra**	Craon, Fra.
Bat	Bath, Eng.		**C-L**	Croise-Laroche, Fra.
BtA	Beaudesert, Aus.		**Cur**	Curragh, Ire.
Belg	Belgium		**Dea**	Deauville, Fra.
Bell	Bellestown, Ire.		**Dev**	Devon-Exeter, Eng.
BlnE	Berlin, East Ger.		**Diep**	Dieppe, Fra.
Bern	Bernay, Fra.		**Don**	Doncaster, Eng.
Bev	Beverley, Eng.		**Dor**	Dortmund, Ger.
Brtz	Biarritz-Bayonne, Fra.		**DRoy**	Down Royal, Ire.
Bir	Birmingham, Eng.		**Ddt**	Duindigt, Holland
Bgta	Bogota, Col.		**Dun**	Dundalk, Ire.
Bog	Bogside, Scot.		**Dus**	Dusseldorf, Ger.
Boik	Boiktort, Belgium		**Edn**	Edinburgh, Scot.
Bor	Bordeaux, Fra.		**Elb**	Elbeut, Fra.
Braz	Brazil		**Eng**	Enghien, Fra.
Bri	Brighton, Eng.		**Epm**	Epsom, Eng.
Bris	Brisbane, Aus.		**Esk**	Esk, Aus.
Bru	Brussels, Belgium		**Fy**	Fairyhouse, Ire.
Bgh	Buckfastleigh, Eng.		**FlA**	Flemington, Aus.
Bda	Budapest, Hungary		**Fol**	Folkestone, Eng.
Cgs	Cagnes, Fra.		**Font**	Fontainebleau, Fra.
Can	Canterbury, Aus.		**Fwl**	Fontwell, Eng.
Cara	Caracas, Venez.		**Fra**	Frankfort, Ger.
Car	Carlisle, Eng.		**Gal**	Galway, Ire.
Ctk	Catterick, Eng.		**Gwd**	Goodwood, Eng.
Cau	Caulfield, Aus.		**GoA**	Gosford, Aus.
Cav	Cavaillon, Fra.		**GoP**	Gowran Park, Ire.

Ham	Hamburg, Ger.
Hml	Hamilton, Scot.
Han	Hanshin, Japan
H.B.	Hawkes Bay, N.Z.
Hay	Haydock Park, Eng.
HnA	Hazeldean, Aus.
Hfd	Hereford, Eng.
HAr	Hipodromo Argentino, S.A.
HCh	Hipodromo Chile, Chile
Hor	Horst-Emscher, Ger.
HuP	Hurst Park, Eng.
If-Ba	Iffezheim-Baden, Ger.
I.S	Isle Sorgue, Fra.
BWI	Jamaica, B.W.I.
Kel	Kelso, Scot.
KG	Kembia Grange, Aus.
Kem	Kempton Park, Eng.
Kilb	Kilbeggan, Ire.
Kill	Killarney, Ire.
Kfd	Knutsford Park, B.W.I.
Koi	Koi, Ger.
Kre	Krefeld, Ger.
Kret	Kretein, Ger.
Kyo	Kyoto, Japan
LaC	La Capelle, Fra.
Lan	Lanark, Scot.
LaP	LaPlata, S.A.
Layt	Layton, Ire.
Lgn	Leghorn, Italy
Lei	Leicester, Eng.
Leo	Leopardstown, Ire.
Tre	Le Tremblay, Fra.
Lew	Lewes, Eng.
Peru	Lima, Peru
LimJ	Limerick Junction, Ire.
Lin	Lincoln, Eng.
Lfd	Lingfield, Eng.
List	Listowell, Ire.
Liv	Liverpool, Eng.
Lon	Longchamp, Fra.
Lou	Loudeac, Fra.
Lud	Ludlow, Eng.
Lvov	Lvov, Ukrania
Lyon	Lyons, Fra.
Mai	Maissons-Laffitte, Fra.
Mall	Mallow, Ire.
Man	Manchester, Eng.
Msl	Marseille, Fra.
Mas	Masterton, N.Z.
Mtu	Manawatu, N.Z.
Mda	Mendoza, Arg.
Mer	Merano, Italy
Mil	Milan, Italy
Mto	Monterrico, Peru
MVA	Moonee Vly, Aus.
Mor	Mornington, Aus.
Mrpt	Morphetville, Aus.
Mos	Moscow, Russia
Muh	Mulheim, Ger.
Mul	Mullinger, Ire.
Naas	Naas, Ire.
Nak	Nakayama, Japan
Nan	Nantes, Fra.
Nap	Naples, Italy
Nav	Navan, Ire.
Nus	Neuss, Ger.
Nby	Newbury, Eng.
NeA	Newcastle, Aus.
Nec	Newcastle, Eng.
New	Newmarket, Eng.
Ntn	Newton Abbott, Eng.
N.Z.	New Zealand
NoE	Nort Erdre, Fra.
Not	Nottingham, Eng.
Orl	Orleans, Fra.
Oslo	Oslo, Norway
Ost	Ostend, Belgium
OtM	Otaki Maori, N.Z.
Pal	Palermo, Arg.
Pan	Panama
Per	Perth, Scot.
PhP	Phoenix Park, Ire.
Plu	Plumpton, Eng.
Pomp	Pompadour, Fra.
Pon	Pontefract, Eng.
Pow	Powerstown Park, Ire.
Pun	Punchestown, Ire.
QdA	Queensland, Aus.
Raf	Rafaela, Arg.
Rand	Randwick, Aus.
Red	Redcar, Eng.
Rei	Reims, Fra.
Ren	Rennes, Fra.
Rin	Rinconada, Venez.
R.J.	Rio de Janeiro, Brazil
Rip	Ripon, Eng.
Rom	Rome, Italy
Rio	Rosario, Arg.
Rmn	Roscommon, Ire.
Ros	Rosehill, Aus.
Rou	Rouen, Fra.
StC	Saint-Cloud, Fra.
Sby	Salisbury, Eng.
Sdn	Sandown, Eng.
SF	San Felipe, Peru
SI	San Isidro, Arg.
Sant	Santiago, Chile
Sed	Sedgefield, Eng.
Sli	Sligo, Ire.
SthA	South Africa
Sll	Southwell, Eng.
StM	St. Malo, Fra.
Stkl	Stockel, Belgium
Stock	Stockholm, Sweden
Stn	Stockton, Eng.
SoA	Stratford-on-Avon, Eng.

Syd	Sydney, Aus.	**Vna**	Vienna, Austria
Tau	Taunton, Eng.	**Wto**	Waikato, N.Z.
Tsk	Thirsk, Eng.	**Wan**	Wanganui, N.Z.
Thur	Thurles, Ire.	**Wsw**	Warsaw, Poland
Tok	Tokyo, Japan	**Wak**	Warwick, Eng.
ToA	Toowoomba, Aus.	**WarF**	Warwick Farm, Aus.
Toul	Toulouse, Fra.	**Wa-T**	Waterford-Tramore, Ire.
Tou	Touquest, Fra.	**Wel**	Wellington, N.Z.
Tow	Towcester, Eng.	**Wer**	Werribee, Aus.
Tra	Tralee, Ire.	**Wet**	Wetherby, Eng.
Trm	Tramore, Ire.	**Win**	Windsor, Eng.
Tur	Turin, Italy	**Wolv**	Wolverhampton, Eng.
Uru	Uruguay	**Wdn**	Woodend, Aus.
Utx	Uttoxetter, Eng.	**Wor**	Worcester, Eng.
Val	Valparaiso, Chile	**Wye**	Wye, Eng.
Van	Vannes, Fra.	**Wyo**	Wyong, Aus.
Var	Varese, Italy	**Yar**	Yarmouth, Eng.
Ver	Vernon, Fra.	**Yor**	York, Eng.
Vich	Vichy, Fra.	**Yugo**	Yugoslavia
Vic	Victoria, Aus.		

DETAILED EXPLANATION OF DATA IN PAST PERFORMANCES

Past Performances include up-to-date lifetime records of every starter, lifetime turf statistics for every horse who has raced on the grass in the U.S. and foreign countries; purse values for allowance races; an indication of races for 3-year-olds and upward 3↑; a symbol Ⓕ denoting races for fillies or fillies and mares; a symbol [S] pointing out races for state-bred horses; an [R] symbol denoting races with other eligibility restrictions; and a "bullet" ● denoting superior workouts (the best workout of the day at the track and distance).

FOREIGN-BRED: An asterisk (*GOOD HOPES) preceding the horse's name indicates he was not bred in the United States or Canada. The country of origin (abbreviated) appears after the breeder's name, as does the state or province of all horses foaled in the United States, Puerto Rico or Canada.

MUD MARKS: One of the following symbols after a horse's name reflects an expert's opinion of his ability on an off track:

*** Fair Mud Runner** **× Good Mud Runner** **⊗ Superior Mud Runner**

RECORD OF STARTS AND EARNINGS: Each horse's complete lifetime racing record (on dirt, grass and over jumps) is given in addition to the current and prior year, or the last two years in which he competed. The letter M in the current year's record indicates the horse is a maiden. M in the previous year's record indicates the horse was a maiden at the end of that year. The Turf Record shows his lifetime number of starts, wins, seconds, thirds and purses in races run on the grass.

Horse	Mud Mark	Claiming Price / Color Sex Age	Pedigree	Today's Weight (With Apprentice Allowance Claimed)	Lifetime Record	Complete Record For Two Years
Good Hopes Own.—Good Hopes Farm	*	Ch. f, 4, → $12,000	by Ridan—Miss Hopes, by Jet Ribot Br.—Jones H G (NY) Tr.—Jones H G	117⁵	Lifetime 32 3 5 0 $11,575	1983 14 3 2 0 $9,825 1982 18 M 3 0 $1,750 Turf 3 0 0 0 $200
LATEST WORKOUTS		May 31 Bel 3f fst :37 bg	●May 27 Bel 4f fst :46 h	May 23 Bel 3f fst :36⅘ b	May 14 Bel 4f gd :49 b	

NOTE: Latest workouts are printed under each horse's past performances when they are available. The "bullet" ● indicates it was the best workout of the day at the track and distance. Abbreviations used in workouts: b—breezing; d—driving; e—easily; h—handily; bo—bore out; g—worked from gate; Ⓣ—turf course; trt—training track; [•]—inner dirt track; (d)—worked around dogs.

EVERYTHING YOU WANT TO KNOW IS IN THE PAST PERFORMANCES!

30Jun85—6Bel fst 6f :22⅘ :46 1:11⅗ 3↑ⒻS Clm c-12000 3 5 2³ 3hd 3¹ 1no Smith T5 b 117 *.70e 88-14 Good Hopes 117no Bad Baya 112² Lacily 1071½ Blocked, just up 12

DATE RACE WAS RUN — The day, month and year. This race was run on June 30, 1985.

30Jun85—6Bel fst 6f :22⅘ :46 1:11⅗ 3↑ⒻS Clm c-12000 3 5 2³ 3hd 3¹ 1no Smith T5 b 117 *.70e 88-14 Good Hopes 117no Bad Baya 112² Lacily 1071½ Blocked, just up 12

NUMBER OF RACE AND TRACK RACED ON — This was the sixth race at Belmont Park. A complete list of track abbreviations is published in the past performance section of each issue of Daily Racing Form. A ◆ symbol preceding race number denotes track located in foreign country.

30Jun85—6Bel fst 6f :22⅘ :46 1:11⅗ 3↑ⒻS Clm c-12000 3 5 2³ 3hd 3¹ 1no Smith T5 b 117 *.70e 88-14 Good Hopes 117no Bad Baya 112² Lacily 1071½ Blocked, just up 12

TRACK CONDITION — The track was fast. Track condition abbreviations are, for dirt tracks: fst-fast; fr-frozen; gd-good; sl-slow; sly-sloppy;

DISTANCE OF RACE — The race was at 6 furlongs (or 3/4 of a mile — there are 8 furlongs to a mile). An asterisk * before distance means it was not exact (*6f—"about" 6 furlongs). Turf course symbols (following distance): Ⓣ—main turf course; [T]—inner turf course; [•]—inner dirt track (at racecourses that have two dirt strips).At tracks where there are different starting points for races of the same distance on the same surface (on the main surface or out of a chute), races that are started from the chute are indicated by the symbol + after the time of the race. Separate tracks records and speed ratings are compiled for these races.

30Jun85—6Bel fst 6f :22⅘ :46 1:11⅗ 3↑ⒻⓈ Clm c-12000 3 5 2^3 3^{hd} 3^1 1no Smith T^5 b 117 *.70e 88-14 Good Hopes 117no Bad Baya 112^2 Lacily $107^{1\frac{1}{2}}$ Blocked, just up 12

FRACTIONAL TIMES — The first fraction (:22 4/5) is the time of the horse in front at the quarter; the second fraction (:46) is the time of the horse in the lead after a half-mile. Fractional times used vary according to the distance of the race. For a listing of the fractions at various distances, see table below.

30Jun85—6Bel fst 6f :22⅘ :46 1:11⅗ 3↑ⒻⓈ Clm c-12000 3 5 2^3 3^{hd} 3^1 1no Smith T^5 b 117 *.70e 88-14 Good Hopes 117no Bad Baya 112^2 Lacily $107^{1\frac{1}{2}}$ Blocked, just up 12

FINAL TIME — This is the time of the first horse to finish (when the winner is disqualified, this is HIS time, not the time of the horse awarded first money).

30Jun85—6Bel fst 6f :22⅘ :46 1:11⅗ 3↑ⒻⓈ Clm c-12000 3 5 2^3 3^{hd} 3^1 1no Smith T^5 b 117 *.70e 88-14 Good Hopes 117no Bad Baya 112^2 Lacily $107^{1\frac{1}{2}}$ Blocked, just up 12

RACE FOR 3-YEAR-OLDS AND UPWARD — This is used ONLY when 3-year-olds and upward started in the race.

30Jun85—6Bel fst 6f :22⅘ :46 1:11⅗ 3↑ⒻⓈ Clm c-12000 3 5 2^3 3^{hd} 3^1 1no Smith T^5 b 117 *.70e 88-14 Good Hopes 117no Bad Baya 112^2 Lacily $107^{1\frac{1}{2}}$ Blocked, just up 12

RACE FOR FILLIES AND MARES — The symbol Ⓕ means the race was restricted to fillies or fillies and mares.

30Jun85—6Bel fst 6f :22⅘ :46 1:11⅗ 3↑ⒻⓈ Clm c-12000 3 5 2^3 3^{hd} 3^1 1no Smith T^5 b 117 *.70e 88-14 Good Hopes 117no Bad Baya 112^2 Lacily $107^{1\frac{1}{2}}$ Blocked, just up 12

STATE-BRED RACE — The symbol [S] means the race was open only to horses foaled in a specific state (a closed race). The state where the horse was foaled follows the name of his breeder, directly below the horse's pedigree. The symbol [R] is used to indicate other types of restricted races, such as events limited to horses owned by residents of a certain state, to horses sired by stallions standing in a certain state, to horses sold at a certain auction, etc.

30Jun85—6Bel fst 6f :22⅘ :46 1:11⅗ 3↑ⒻⓈ Clm c-12000 3 5 2^3 3^{hd} 3^1 1no Smith T^5 b 117 *.70e 88-14 Good Hopes 117no Bad Baya 112^2 Lacily $107^{1\frac{1}{2}}$ Blocked, just up 12

CLAIMING PRICE OR TYPE OF RACE — The horse was entered to be claimed for $12,000. The letter c preceding the claiming price indicates the horse was claimed. Stakes races are identified by name; purse values are given for allowance races (Alw 12000). North American Graded Stakes, plus Canadian Graded Stakes, are indicated in a supplementary line. For a complete list of the various race classifications, see table below.

30Jun85—6Bel fst 6f :22⅘ :46 1:11⅗ 3↑ⒻⓈ Clm c-12000 3 5 2^3 3^{hd} 3^1 1no Smith T^5 b 117 *.70e 88-14 Good Hopes 117no Bad Baya 112^2 Lacily $107^{1\frac{1}{2}}$ Blocked, just up 12

POST POSITION — The horse left the starting gate from post position number 3. This figure can differ from the official program number because of late scratches, horses coupled in the wagering (an "entry") or horses grouped in the mutuel field.

30Jun85—6Bel fst 6f :22⅘ :46 1:11⅗ 3↑ⒻⓈ Clm c-12000 3 5 2^3 3^{hd} 3^1 1no Smith T^5 b 117 *.70e 88-14 Good Hopes 117no Bad Baya 112^2 Lacily $107^{1\frac{1}{2}}$ Blocked, just up 12

FIRST CALL — The horse's position immediately after leaving the starting gate. He was fifth at this point. Points of call vary according to the distance of the race. In races of 1 mile and longer, the start call is omitted and the horse's position at the 1/4-mile or 1/2-mile is given instead. A table listing the points of call for races at the most frequently run distances is printed below.

30Jun85—6Bel fst 6f :22⅘ :46 1:11⅗ 3↑ⒻⓈ Clm c-12000 3 5 2^3 3^{hd} 3^1 1no Smith T^5 b 117 *.70e 88-14 Good Hopes 117no Bad Baya 112^2 Lacily $107^{1\frac{1}{2}}$ Blocked, just up 12

SECOND CALL — The horse was second, three lengths behind the leader (2^3) at the 1/4-mile point. The large figure indicates the horse's running position; the small one his margin behind the leader. If the horse had been in front at this point (1^3), the small figure would indicate the margin by which he was leading the second horse.

Copyright © 1985 by *Daily Racing Forms, Inc.* Reprinted with permission of copyright owner.

30Jun85—6Bel fst 6f :22⅘ :46 1:11⅗ 3↑ⒻⓈ Clm c-12000 3 5 2^3 3^{hd} 3^1 1no Smith T^5 b 117 *.70e 88-14 Good Hopes 117no Bad Baya 112^2 Lacily $107^{1\frac{1}{2}}$ Blocked, just up 12

THIRD CALL — The horse was third at this call, at the 1/2-mile point, a head behind the leader (3^{hd}).

30Jun85—6Bel fst 6f :22⅘ :46 1:11⅗ 3↑ⒻⓈ Clm c-12000 3 5 2^3 3^{hd} 3^1 1no Smith T^5 b 117 *.70e 88-14 Good Hopes 117no Bad Baya 112^2 Lacily $107^{1\frac{1}{2}}$ Blocked, just up 12

STRETCH CALL — The horse was third, one length behind the leader (3^1), at this point. The stretch call is made 1/8 mile from the finish.

30Jun85—6Bel fst 6f :22⅘ :46 1:11⅗ 3↑ⒻⓈ Clm c-12000 3 5 2^3 3^{hd} 3^1 1no Smith T^5 b 117 *.70e 88-14 Good Hopes 117no Bad Baya 112^2 Lacily $107^{1\frac{1}{2}}$ Blocked, just up 12

FINISH — The horse finished first, a nose before the second horse (1no). If the horse is second, third or unplaced, the small figure indicates the total distance he finished behind the winner.

30Jun85—6Bel fst 6f :22⅘ :46 1:11⅗ 3↑ⒻⓈ Clm c-12000 3 5 2^3 3^{hd} 3^1 1no Smith T^5 b 117 *.70e 88-14 Good Hopes 117no Bad Baya 112^2 Lacily $107^{1\frac{1}{2}}$ Blocked, just up 12

JOCKEY — The horse was ridden by T. Smith. The small figure following the jockey's name (Smith T^5) indicates the amount of the apprentice allowance claimed. When an apprentice allowance is claimed the exact number of pounds of the claim is listed.

30Jun85—6Bel fst 6f :22⅘ :46 1:11⅗ 3↑ⒻⓈ Clm c-12000 3 5 2^3 3^{hd} 3^1 1no Smith T^5 b 117 *.70e 88-14 Good Hopes 117no Bad Baya 112^2 Lacily $107^{1\frac{1}{2}}$ Blocked, just up 12

EQUIPMENT CARRIED — The letter b indicates the horse was equipped with blinkers. Other abbreviations which may appear here: s-spurs; sb-spurs and blinkers.

30Jun85—6Bel fst 6f :22⅘ :46 1:11⅗ 3↑ⒻⓈ Clm c-12000 3 5 2^3 3^{hd} 3^1 1no Smith T^5 b 117 *.70e 88-14 Good Hopes 117no Bad Baya 112^2 Lacily $107^{1\frac{1}{2}}$ Blocked, just up 12

WEIGHT CARRIED IN THIS RACE — The horse carried 117 pounds. This is the weight of the rider and equipment (saddle, lead pads, etc.) and includes the apprentice allowance when an allowance is claimed.

30Jun85—6Bel fst 6f :22⅘ :46 1:11⅗ 3↑ⒻⓈ Clm c-12000 3 5 2^3 3^{hd} 3^1 1no Smith T^5 b 117 *.70e 88-14 Good Hopes 117no Bad Baya 112^2 Lacily $107^{1\frac{1}{2}}$ Blocked, just up 12

CLOSING ODDS — The horse was 70 cents to the dollar (he was 7-10 in the wagering). The star * preceding the odds indicates he was the favorite. The symbol ♦ between the weight and the odds would mean he finished in a dead-heat with one or more horses. The letter e following the odds means the horse was coupled in the betting (an entry) with one or more horses. The letter f in this position would indicate he was in the mutuel field; the symbol [D] means that the horse was disqualified.

30Jun85—6Bel fst 6f :22⅘ :46 1:11⅗ 3↑ⒻⓈ Clm c-12000 3 5 2^3 3^{hd} 3^1 1no Smith T^5 b 117 *.70e 88-14 Good Hopes 117no Bad Baya 112^2 Lacily $107^{1\frac{1}{2}}$ Blocked, just up 12

SPEED RATING AND TRACK VARIANT — The first figure is the speed rating, a comparison of this horse's time with the 100-par track record; the second figure is the track variant, showing how much below par the times for all races were that day.

30Jun85—6Bel fst 6f :22⅘ :46 1:11⅗ 3↑ⒻⓈ Clm c-12000 3 5 2^3 3^{hd} 3^1 1no Smith T^5 b 117 *.70e 88-14 Good Hopes 117no Bad Baya 112^2 Lacily $107^{1\frac{1}{2}}$ Blocked, just up 12

FIRST, SECOND AND THIRD HORSES AT THE FINISH — The horses who finished 1-2-3 in the race, the weight each carried and the margins separating each one from the next horse. If any of these horses was disqualified or finished in a dead-heat, the symbol [D] for disqualified or [DH] for dead-heat precedes the horse's name.

30Jun85—6Bel fst 6f :22⅘ :46 1:11⅗ 3↑ⒻⓈ Clm c-12000 3 5 2^3 3^{hd} 3^1 1no Smith T^5 b 117 *.70e 88-14 Good Hopes 117no Bad Baya 112^2 Lacily $107^{1\frac{1}{2}}$ Blocked, just up 12

COMMENT LINE — A capsule description of the horse's performance, with special emphasis on pointing out any trouble he may have encountered.

30Jun85—6Bel fst 6f :22⅘ :46 1:11⅗ 3↑ⒻⓈ Clm c-12000 3 5 2^3 3^{hd} 3^1 1no Smith T^5 b 117 *.70e 88-14 Good Hopes 117no Bad Baya 112^2 Lacily $107^{1\frac{1}{2}}$ Blocked, just up 12

ABBREVIATIONS USED FOR RACE CLASSIFICATIONS

"Alw 12000"—Allowance race, with race's purse value.

"Clm 10000"—Claiming race. (Entered for $10,000.)

"Stk 50000"—Claiming stakes. (Entered for $50,000.)

"ⒸM 10000"—Fillies or fillies & mares, maidens, claiming. (Entered for $10,000.)

"Handicap"—Handicap.

"Hcp 10000"—Handicap, claiming. (Entered for $10,000.)

"Inv H'Cap"—Invitational handicap.

"Md Allow"—Maidens, allowances.

"Md 10000"—Maidens, claiming. (Entered for $10,000.)

"Md Sp Wt"—Maidens, special weight.

(Note: In all "starter" races, the figure given is the claiming price eligibility required.)

"Match R."—Match race.

"Clm °10000"—Optional claiming race—NOT entered to be claimed.

"Clm 10000°"—Optional claiming race—WAS entered to be claimed.

"Hcp °10000"—Optional claiming handicap—NOT entered to be claimed.

"Hcp 10000°"—Optional claiming handicap—WAS entered to be claimed.

"Spec'l Wt"—Special Weight.

"Alw 10000s"—Starter allowance race.

"Hcp 10000s"—Starter handicap.

"Md 10000s"—Starter maiden race.

"Spw 10000s"—Starter special weight race.

In stakes races, with the exception of claiming stakes, the name or abbreviation of name is shown in the class of race column. The letter "H" after name, indicates the race was a handicap stakes. The same procedure is used for the rich invitational races for which there are no nomination or starting fees. The letters "Inv" following the abbreviation indicate the race was by invitation only.

POINTS OF CALL AND FRACTIONAL TIMES IN PAST PERFORMANCES

The points of call and the fractional times in the past performances vary according to the distance of the race. The points for which the fractional times are given correspond to the points of call of the running positions (except in some races at odd distances). In all races, the stretch call is made 1/8 mile from the finish. The points of call and fractional times for the most frequently raced distances are:

Distance of Race	1st Call	2nd Call	Points of Call 3rd Call	4th Call	5th Call	Fractional Times Given At These Points of Call
2 Furlongs	Start	—	—	Stretch	Finish	—
2 1/2 Furlongs	Start	—	—	Stretch	Finish	—
3 Furlongs	Start	—	—	Stretch	Finish	1/4
3 1/2 Furlongs	Start	1/4	—	Stretch	Finish	1/4
4 Furlongs	Start	1/4	—	Stretch	Finish	1/4
4 1/2 Furlongs	Start	1/4	—	Stretch	Finish	1/4
5 Furlongs	Start	3/16	3/8	Stretch	Finish	1/4
5 1/2 Furlongs	Start	1/4	3/8	Stretch	Finish	1/4
6 Furlongs	Start	1/4	1/2	Stretch	Finish	1/4
6 1/2 Furlongs	Start	1/4	1/2	Stretch	Finish	1/4
7 Furlongs	Start	1/4	1/2	Stretch	Finish	1/4
1 Mile	1/4	1/2	3/4	Stretch	Finish	1/2
1 Mile 70 Yards	1/4	1/2	3/4	Stretch	Finish	1/2
1 1/16 Miles	1/4	1/2	3/4	Stretch	Finish	1/2
1 1/8 Miles	1/4	1/2	3/4	Stretch	Finish	1/2
3/16 Miles	1/4	1/2	3/4	Stretch	Finish	1/2
1 1/4 Miles	1/4	1/2	1 mile	Stretch	Finish	1 mile
1 5/16 Miles	1/4	1/2	1 mile	Stretch	Finish	1/2
1 3/8 Miles	1/4	1/2	1 mile	Stretch	Finish	1 mile
1 1/2 Miles	1/4	1/2	1 1/4	Stretch	Finish	1/4
1 5/8 Miles	1/4	1/2	1 3/8	Stretch	Finish	1/4
1 3/4 Miles	1/2	1 mile	1 1/2	Stretch	Finish	1 1/2
1 7/8 Miles	1/2	1 mile	1 5/8	Stretch	Finish	3/4
2 Miles	1/2	1 mile	1 3/4	Stretch	Finish	3/4
2 1/16 Miles	1/2	1 mile	1 3/4	Stretch	Finish	1 3/4
2 1/8 Miles	1/2	1 mile	1 3/4	Stretch	Finish	3/4
2 1/4 Miles & Longer	1/2	1 mile	2 miles	Stretch	Finish	2 miles

NOTE: When the 1/4 mile or 1/2 mile call is substituted for the start call, only the horse's position at that point is indicated. The margin separating the horse from the leader is not given.

FOREIGN-BRED HORSES

An asterisk (*) preceding the name of the horse indicates foreign-bred. (No notation is made for horses bred in Canada and Cuba.)

MUD MARKS

*—Fair mud runner   X—Good mud runner
⊗—Superior mud runner

COLOR

B—Bay   Blk—Black   Br—Brown   Ch—Chestnut   Gr—Gray
Ro—Roan   Wh—White   Dk b or br—Dark bay or brown

SEX

c—colt   h—horse   g—gelding   rig—ridgling   f—filly   m—mare

PEDIGREE

Each horse's pedigree lists, in the order named, color, sex, age, sire, dam and grandsire (sire of dam).

BREEDER

Abbreviation following breeder's name indicates the state, Canadian province, place of origin or foreign country in which the horse was foaled.

TODAY'S WEIGHT

With the exception of assigned-weight handicap races, weights are computed according to the conditions of the race. Weight includes the rider and his equipment; saddle, lead pads, etc., and takes into account the apprentice allowance of pounds claimed. It does not include a jockey's overweight, which is announced by track officials prior to the race. The number of pounds claimed as an apprentice allowance is shown by a superior (small) figure to the right of the weight.

TODAY'S CLAIMING PRICE

If a horse is entered to be claimed, the price for which he may be claimed appears in bold face type to the right of the trainer's name.

RECORD OF STARTS AND EARNINGS

The horse's racing record for his most recent two years of competition appears to the extreme right of the name of the breeder and is referred to as his "money lines". This lists the year, number of starts, wins, seconds, thirds, and earnings. The letter "M" in the win column of the upper line indicates the horse is a maiden. If the letter "M" is in the lower line only, it indicates the horse was a maiden at the end of that year.

TURF COURSE RECORD

The horse's turf course record shows his lifetime starts, wins, seconds, thirds and earnings on the grass and appears directly below his money lines.

LIFETIME RECORD

The horse's lifetime record shows his career races, wins, seconds, thirds and total earnings. The statistics, updated with each start, include all his races—on dirt, grass and over jumps—and are located under the trainer's name.

DISTANCE

a—preceding distance (a6f) denotes "about" distance (about 6 furlongs in this instance.)

FOREIGN TRACKS

◆—before track abbreviation indicates it is located in a foreign country.

POST POSITION

Horse's post position appears after jockey's name—Smith T[3]

FILLY OR FILLY-MARE RACES

Ⓕ—preceding the race classification indicates races exclusively for fillies or fillies and mares.

RESTRICTED RACES

Ⓢ—preceding the race classification denotes state-bred races restricted to horses bred in a certain state (or a given geographic area) which qualify under state breeding programs.

Ⓡ—preceding the race classification indicates races that have certain eligibility restrictions other than state where bred, sex or age.

RACE CLASSIFICATIONS

10000—Claiming race (eligible to be claimed for $10,000). Note: The letter c preceding claiming price (c10000) indicates horse was claimed.

M10000—Maiden claiming race (non-winners—eligible to be claimed).

10000H—Claiming handicap (eligible to be claimed).
010000—Optional claiming race (entered NOT to be claimed).
100000—Optional claiming race (eligible to be claimed).
Mdn—Maiden race (non-winners).
AlwM—Maiden allowance race (for non-winners with special weight allowances).
Aw10000—Allowance race with purse value.
HcpO—Overnight handicap race.
SplW—Special weight race.
Wfa—Weight-for-age race.
Mtch—Match race.
A10000—Starter allowance race (horses who have started for claiming price shown, or less, as stipulated in the conditions).
H10000—Starter handicap (same restriction as above).
S10000—Starter special weight (restricted as above). Note: Where no amount is specified in the conditions of the "starters" race dashes are substituted, as shown below:

A———   H———   S———

500000S—Claiming stakes (eligible to be claimed).

STAKES RACES

In stakes races, with the exception of claiming stakes, the name or abbreviation of name is shown in the class of race column. The letter "H" after name indicates the race was a handicap stakes. The same procedure is used for the rich invitational races for which there are no nomination or starting fees. The letters "Inv" following the abbreviation indicate the race was by invitation only.

SPEED RATINGS

This is a comparison of the horse's final time with the track record established prior to the opening of the racing season at that track. The track record is given a rating of 100. One point is deducted for each fifth of a second by which a horse fails to equal the track record (one length is approximately equal to one-fifth of a second). Thus, in a race in which the winner equals the track record (a Speed Rating of 100), another horse who is beaten 12 lengths (or an estimated two and two-fifths seconds) receives a Speed Rating of 88 (100 minus 12). If a horse breaks the track record he receives an additional point for each one-fifth second by which he lowers the record (if the track record is 1:10 and he is timed in 1:09⅗ his Speed Rating is 102). In computing beaten-off distances for Speed Ratings, fractions of one-half length or more are figured as one

RACES OTHER THAN ON MAIN DIRT TRACK

⊡—following distance denotes inner dirt course.
⊕⊙—following distance indicates turf (grass) course race.
⊙—following distance indicates inner turf course.
[S]—following distance indicates steeplechase race.
[H]—following distance indicates hurdle race.

TRACK CONDITIONS

ft—fast   fr—frozen   gd—good   sl—slow   sy—sloppy
m—muddy   hy—heavy
Turf courses, including steeplechase and hurdles:
hd—hard   fm—firm   gd—good   yl—yielding   sf—soft

SYMBOLS ACCOMPANYING CLOSING ODDS

*(preceding)—favorite   e (following)—entry
f (following)—mutuel field

APPRENTICE OR RIDER WEIGHT ALLOWANCES

Allowance indicated by superior figure following weight—117^5

ABBREVIATIONS USED IN POINTS OF CALL

no—nose   hd—head   nk—neck

DEAD-HEATS, DISQUALIFICATIONS

▲—following the finish call indicates this horse was part of a dead-heat (an explanatory line appears under that past performance line).

†—following the finish call indicates this horse was disqualified. The official placing appears under the past performance line. An explanatory line also appears under the past performance of each horse whose official finish position was changed due to the disqualification.

‡—before the name of any of the first three finishers indicates the horse was disqualified from that position.

hurdle events, for races of less than three furlongs, or for races for which the horse's speed rating is less than 25.

When Daily Racing Form prints its own time, in addition to the official track time, the Speed Rating is based on the official track time.

Note: Speed Ratings for new distances are computed and assigned when adequate time standards are established.

TRACK VARIANTS

This takes into consideration all of the races run on a particular day and could reflect either the quality of the competition, how many points below par the track happened to be, or both. The Speed Rating of each winner is added together, then an average is taken based on the number of races run. This average is deducted from the track par of 100 and the difference is the Track Variant (example: average Speed Rating of winners involved is 86, par is 100, the Track Variant is 14). When there is a change in the track condition during the course of a program the following procedure is employed in compiling the Variant: races run on dirt tracks classified as fast, frozen or good, and those listed as hard, firm or good on the turf, are used in striking one average. Strips classified as slow, sloppy, muddy or heavy on the dirt, or yielding and soft on the turf, are grouped for another average. If all the races on a program are run in either one or the other of these general classifications only one average is used. The lower the Variant the faster the track or the better the overall quality of the competition.

Note: A separate Track Variant is computed for races run on the turf (grass), straight course races, and for races run around turns at distances of less than 5 furlongs.

TROUBLE LINES

When a horse experiences trouble in a race, this information is reported, with the date of the incident, in a capsule description directly below the past performance line for that race.

WORKOUTS

Each horse's most recent workouts appear directly under the past performances. For example, Jly 20 Hol 3f ft :38b indicates the horse worked on July 20 at Hollywood Park. The distance of the work was 3 furlongs over a fast track and the horse was timed in 38 seconds, breezing. A "bullet" ● appearing before the date of a workout indicates that the workout was the best of the day for that distance at that track.

Abbreviations used in workouts:

b—breezing   d—driving   e—easily   g—worked from gate   h—handily   bo—bore out   ①—turf course   Tr—trial race
(d)—worked around "dogs"   tr.t following track abbreviation indicates horse worked on training track.

Distance	1st Call	2nd Call	3rd Call	4th Call
1 Mile	1/2 Mile	3/4 Mile	Stretch	Finish
1 Mi., 70 Yds.	1/2 Mile	3/4 Mile	Stretch	Finish
1 1/16 Miles	1/2 Mile	3/4 Mile	Stretch	Finish
1 1/8 Miles	1/2 Mile	3/4 Mile	Stretch	Finish
1 3/16 Miles	1/2 Mile	3/4 Mile	Stretch	Finish
1 1/4 Miles	1/2 Mile	1 Mile	Stretch	Finish
1 5/16 Miles	1/2 Mile	1 Mile	Stretch	Finish
1 3/8 Miles	1/2 Mile	1 Mile	Stretch	Finish
1 1/2 Miles	1/2 Mile	1 1/4 Miles	Stretch	Finish
1 5/8 Miles	1/2 Mile	1 3/8 Miles	Stretch	Finish
1 3/4 Miles	1/2 Mile	1 1/2 Miles	Stretch	Finish

POINTS OF CALL—PAST PERFORMANCES

The points of call in the past performances vary according to the distance of the race. The points of call of the running positions for the most frequently raced distances are:

Distance	1st Call	2nd Call	3rd Call	4th Call
2 Furlongs	Start	—	Stretch	Finish
5/16 Mile	Start	—	Stretch	Finish
3 Furlongs	Start	—	Stretch	Finish
3 1/2 Furlongs	Start	—	Stretch	Finish
4 Furlongs	Start	1/4 Mile	Stretch	Finish
4 1/2 Furlongs	Start	1/4 Mile	Stretch	Finish
5 Furlongs	3/16 Mile	3/8 Mile	Stretch	Finish
5 1/2 Furlongs	1/4 Mile	3/8 Mile	Stretch	Finish
6 Furlongs	1/4 Mile	1/2 Mile	Stretch	Finish
6 1/2 Furlongs	1/4 Mile	1/2 Mile	Stretch	Finish
7 Furlongs	1/4 Mile	1/2 Mile	Stretch	Finish

NOTE: The second call in most races is made 1/4 mile from the finish; the stretch call 1/8 mile from the finish.

HOW TO READ DAILY RACING FORM PAST PERFORMANCES

Past Performances include cumulative statistics for every horse who has raced on the grass in the U.S. and foreign countries; a symbol Ⓢ designating races restricted to horses bred in a certain state; a symbol Ⓡ indicating races that have certain eligibility restrictions other than sex or age, and a "bullet" ● denoting superior workouts (the best workout of the day at that track for that distance).

FOREIGN-BRED: An asterisk preceding the horse's name indicates he was bred in a foreign country. The country of origin (abbreviated) appears after the breeder's name, as does the state or place and Canadian province of all horses foaled in the United States, Puerto Rico or Canada.

MUD MARKS: One of the following symbols after a horse's name reflects an expert's opinion of his ability on an off track:

✱ **Fair Mud Runner**   ✕ **Good Mud Runner**   ⊗ **Superior Mud Runner**

RECORD OF STARTS AND EARNINGS: Each horse's lifetime statistics are given as well as his complete racing record for the current and prior year, or the last two years in which he competed. The letter M in the current year's record indicates the horse is a maiden. M in the previous year's record indicates the horse was a maiden at the end of that year. TURF RECORD shows his lifetime starts, wins, seconds, thirds and earnings on the grass.

Horse	Mud Mark	Today's Weight	Color Sex Age Pedigree	Today's Claiming Price		Earnings Record				
Good Hopes	✱	**1175**	Ch. f. 4 by Ridan—Miss Hopes, by Jet Pilot	$12,000	1984	12	3	2	1	$20,280
Own.—Good Hope Farm			Br. Jones H G (Cal)		1983	4	M	0	2	$1,100
			Tr. Jones H G		Turf	4	1	0	1	$6,500
			Lifetime 20 3 3 4 $23,600							

30Jun84-6Hol 6f :224 :46 1:113 ft *6-5e 1175 33 32 21 1no SmithT3 Ⓔ Ⓢ c12000 81-12 GoodHpes,LionTmr,HppyDys 12
Jly 28 Dmr 3f ft :37b   ●Jun 25 Hol 4f ft :46h   ●Jun 20 Hol 3f ft :362h   May 25 Hol 4f ft :49b

NOTE: Latest workouts are printed under each horse's past performances when they are available. The "bullet" ● indicates it was the best workout of the day at the track and distance.

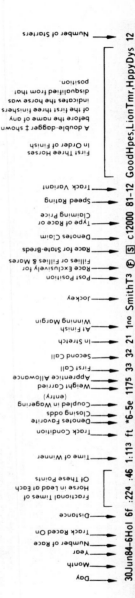

Number of Starters
First Three Horses in Order of Finish
A double-dagger ‡ shown before the name of any of the first three finishers indicates the horse was disqualified from that position.
Track Variant
Speed Rating
Type of Race or Claiming Price
Denotes Claim
Race for State-Breds
Race Exclusively for Fillies & Mares
Post Position
Jockey
At Finish Winning Margin
In Stretch
Second Call
First Call
Apprentice Allowance Weight Carried
Coupled in Wagering (entry)
Closing odds
Denotes Favorite
Track Condition
Time of Winner
Fractional Times of Horse in Lead at Each Of These Points
Distance
Track Raced On
Number of Race
Year
Month
Day

30Jun84-6Hol 6f :224 :46 1:113 ft *6-5e 1175 33 32 21 1no SmithT3 Ⓔ Ⓢ c12000 81-12 GoodHpes,LionTmr,HppyDys 12

30Jun84-6Hol 6f :224 :46 1:113 ft *6-5e 1175 33 32 21 1no SmithT3 (F) [S] c12000 81-12 GoodHpes,LionTmr,HppyDys 12
DATE RACE WAS RUN The day, month and year. This race was on June 30, 1984.

30Jun84-6Hol 6f :224 :46 1:113 ft *6-5e 1175 33 32 21 1no SmithT3 (F) [S] c12000 81-12 GoodHpes,LionTmr,HppyDys 12
NUMBER OF RACE AND TRACK RACED ON This was the sixth race at Hollywood Park (Hol.) See the Past Performance section of Daily Racing Form for a complete list of track abbreviations. The ◆ symbol before track indicates it is located in foreign country.

30Jun84-6Hol 6f :224 :46 1:113 ft *6-5e 1175 33 32 21 1no SmithT3 (F) [S] c12000 81-12 GoodHpes,LionTmr,HppyDys 12
DISTANCE OF RACE The race was at 6 furlongs or ¾ of a mile (there are 8 furlongs in a mile). An "a" before the distance (a6f) denotes an "about" or inexact distance (about 6 furlongs). A circled Ⓣ following the distance denotes the race was run on the main turf course; a squared Ⓣ a race run on track's inner turf course; Ⓘ indicates race run on the inner dirt strip.

30Jun84-6Hol 6f :224 :46 1:113 ft *6-5e 1175 33 32 21 1no SmithT3 (F) [S] c12000 81-12 GoodHpes,LionTmr,HppyDys 12
FRACTIONAL TIMES The first fraction (:22⅘) is the time of the horse in front after a quarter-mile; the second fraction (:46) is the time of the horse in front at the half-mile point.

30Jun84-6Hol 6f :224 :46 1:113 ft *6-5e 1175 33 32 21 1no SmithT3 (F) [S] c12000 81-12 GoodHpes,LionTmr,HppyDys 12
FINAL TIME OF FIRST HORSE TO FINISH This is the winner's final time (6 furlongs run in 1:11⅗). In all cases, this is the time of the first horse to finish (when the winner is disqualified, this is HIS time, not the time of the horse awarded first money.)

30Jun84-6Hol 6f :224 :46 1:113 ft *6-5e 1175 33 32 21 1no SmithT3 (F) [S] c12000 81-12 GoodHpes,LionTmr,HppyDys 12
TRACK CONDITION The track was fast (ft).

30Jun84-6Hol 6f :224 :46 1:113 ft *6-5e 1175 33 32 21 1no SmithT3 (F) [S] c12000 81-12 GoodHpes,LionTmr,HppyDys 12
APPROXIMATE CLOSING ODDS The horse was approximately 6-5 in the wagering. An asterisk (*) preceding the odds indicates the horse was the favorite; an "e" following the odds indicates the odds that it was part of an entry (two or more horses coupled in the wagering); an "f" that horse was in the mutuel field.

30Jun84-6Hol 6f :224 :46 1:113 ft *6-5e 1175 33 32 21 1no SmithT3 (F) [S] c12000 81-12 GoodHpes,LionTmr,HppyDys 12
WEIGHT CARRIED IN THIS RACE The horse carried 117 pounds. The superior (small) figure following the weight indicates that, in this instance, a 5-pound apprentice allowance was claimed. When an apprentice allowance is claimed, the exact amount of the claim is listed.

30Jun84-6Hol 6f :224 :46 1:113 ft *6-5e 1175 33 32 21 1no SmithT3 (F) [S] c12000 81-12 GoodHpes,LionTmr,HppyDys 12
FIRST CALL The horse was running third, three lengths behind the leader at this stage of the race (at the ¼ mile in this instance). The larger figure indicates the horse's running position, the superior figure his total margin behind the leader. If he had been in front at this point (1²), the superior figure would indicate the margin by which he had been leading the second horse.

30Jun84-6Hol 6f :224 :46 1:113 ft *6-5e 1175 33 32 21 1no SmithT3 (F) [S] c12000 81-12 GoodHpes,LionTmr,HppyDys 12
SECOND CALL The horse was third at this stage of the race (at the ½ mile in this instance), two lengths behind the leader.

30Jun84-6Hol 6f :224 :46 1:113 ft *6-5e 1175 33 32 21 1no SmithT3 (F) [S] c12000 81-12 GoodHpes,LionTmr,HppyDys 12
STRETCH CALL The horse was second at this stage of the rac a length behind the leader. The stretch call is made about ⅛ mile from the finish.

30Jun84-6Hol 6f :224 :46 1:113 ft *6-5e 1175 33 32 21 1no SmithT3 (f) [S] c12000 81-12 GoodHpes,LionTmr,HppyDys 12
FINISH The horse finished first, a nose in front of the second horse. If second, third or unplaced, the superior figure indicates his margin behind the winner.

30Jun84-6Hol 6f :224 :46 1:113 ft *6-5e 1175 33 32 21 1no SmithT3 (f) [S] c12000 81-12 GoodHpes,LionTmr,HppyDys 12
JOCKEY AND POST POSITION T. Smith rode the horse, who started from post position number 3.

30Jun84-6Hol 6f :224 :46 1:113 ft *6-5e 1175 33 32 21 1no SmithT3 (f) [S] c12000 81-12 GoodHpes,LionTmr,HppyDys 12
CLAIMING PRICE OR TYPE OF RACE The horse was entered to be claimed for $12,000 and the "c" indicates she was claimed; the (f) that the race was exclusively for fillies and mares; the [S] a race restricted to horses bred in a certain state. (An [R] in this space would indicate a race that had certain eligibility restrictions other than state where bred, sex or age). If it is an allowance race other than maiden or starter, the purse is given. If it is a stakes race, the name of the race is given.

30Jun84-6Hol 6f :224 :46 1:113 ft *6-5e 1175 33 32 21 1no SmithT3 (f) [S] c12000 81-12 GoodHpes,LionTmr,HppyDys 12
SPEED RATING The horse's speed rating was 81.

30Jun84-6Hol 6f :224 :46 1:113 ft *6-5e 1175 33 32 21 1no SmithT3 (f) [S] c12000 81-12 GoodHpes,LionTmr,HppyDys 12
TRACK VARIANT The track variant that day was 12.

30Jun84-6Hol 6f :224 :46 1:113 ft *6-5e 1175 33 32 21 1no SmithT3 (f) [S] c12000 81-12 GoodHpes,LionTmr,HppyDys 12
FIRST THREE FINISHERS These are the first three finishers in the race.

30Jun84-6Hol 6f :224 :46 1:113 ft *6-5e 1175 33 32 21 1no SmithT3 (f) [S] c12000 81-12 GoodHpes,LionTmr,HppyDys 12
NUMBER OF STARTERS Twelve horses started in the race.

20

THE RACEGOER'S DICTIONARY

Acey deucy—Riding style in which right stirrup is shorter than left, enabling jockey to balance more easily on turns.

Across the board—Three bets—win, place and show—on one horse.

Added money—Purse money with which track management supplements stakes posted by owners and breeders.

Aged—Of a horse, aged seven or older.

Airing—A workout; a racing performance in which horse runs as if it were only out for exercise.

All-out—Maximum exertion.

Allowance race—A non-claiming affair in which published conditions stipulate weight allowances according to previous purse earnings and/or number or type of victories.

Also eligible—Official entrants that will not run unless other horses are scratched and vacancies occur in field.

Also-ran—Horse that finished out of the money.

Alter—To castrate, geld.

Ankle boot—Protective covering for fetlock, usually leather or rubber.

Ankle cutter—Horse that cuts a fetlock with opposite foot while running.

Apprentice—Student jockey.

Apprentice allowance—Weight concession granted animal ridden by apprentice.

Arm—Foreleg, between elbow and knee; forearm.

Armchair ride—Easy victory without urging by rider.

Baby—Two-year-olds, especially during first months of year.

Baby race—Two-, three- or four-furlong race for two-year-olds, early in year.

Back at the knee—Defective conformation in which foreleg bends slightly backward at knee.

Backstretch—Straight part of track on far side; stable area.

Back up—Slow down noticeably.

Bad actor—Fractious horse.

Bad doer—Horse that lacks appetite, usually because of illness, pain, fatigue, nervousness or loneliness.

Badger—Cheap horse that qualifies owner for track privileges; "badge horse."

Bald—Of a horse, with a white face.

Ball—Pill; physic.

Bandage—Leg wrapping.

Bangtail—Tail bobbed or tied short; journalese for horse.

Bar plates—Horseshoes with bars across rear.

Barrel—Horse's torso.

Barrier—Starting gate.

Baseball—Daily-double play in which bettor couples a horse in one race with all horses in the other; "wheeling."

Bat—Whip (a term used by writers, not jockeys).

Bay—Brown or tan horse with black mane and tail.

Bear in—Running toward inside rail instead of straight.

Bear out—Running toward outside, especially on turns.

Beat—An unfortunate defeat, as when a horse is caught in the last stride and a losing bettor moans, "What a tough beat!"

Beef—Protest, usually by jockey about another's riding tactics.

Bell—Signals start of race and termination of betting.

Bend—A turn of the track.

Big Apple—A major racing circuit.

Bill Daly—Rider who takes lead as soon as possible is "on the Bill Daly." Famous trainer, "Father Bill" Daly, used to tell jockeys, "Get on top right away and improve your position."

Bit—Metal mouth bar to which reins are attached.

Blanket finish—Extremely close finish.

Blaze—Large white marking on horse's face.

Bleeder—Horse that bleeds during heavy exertion, usually from ruptured blood vessels of nose.

Blind switch—In which rider finds his mount pocketed behind horses and must decide whether to hope for an opening or take back and go around.

Blinkers—Eye pieces that limit a horse's vision and sometimes help him to concentrate on running.

Blister—Treatment of damaged tissue with chemical irritant or heat, causes blistering and encourages development of scar tissue.

Block heel—Horseshoe with raised heel, to prevent running down.

Bloodline—Pedigree.

Blow out—Short exercise to limber a horse before its race.

Blue roan—Horse with coat of black, white and yellow hairs, producing blue-gray effect.

Boat race—A fixed race.

Bobble—Stumble; break stride clumsily.

Bog spavin—Puffy swelling on inside of hock. Caused by strain.

Bold eye—Prominent eye, supposedly sign of courage.

Bold front—Long, well-muscled neck, another sign of courage.

Bolt—To run off in wrong direction, as when horse tries to return to barn instead of going to starting gate.

Bone spavin—Bony swelling, usually below the hock joint.

Book—Jockey's schedule of riding assignments; bookmaker; bookmaker's tally of amounts bet on each horse and odds necessary to assure him of profit.

Boot—To kick horse, as when booting it home in race; rubber or leather anklet.

Boots and Saddles—Bugle call sounded when riders mount and when horses enter track for post parade.

Bottom—Equine stamina; horse assigned outside post position and listed last in program of race; sub-surface of racing strip.

Bottom line—Bottom, or female side of pedigree.

Bow—When strained sheath of flexor tendon ruptures, allowing tendon to stand out behind cannon bone like string of a bow.

Boy—Jockey.

Brace—Horse liniment.

Brackets—Victory, because index numbers with which official result charts identify previous race of each horse are enclosed in brackets if horse won that race.

Break—Start of race; accustoming young horse to saddle, bridle and rider.

Breakage—Difference between true mutuel odds and lesser, rounded amounts given to winning players. The resultant millions usually are divided between track and state.

Break down—Become unable to race because of lameness or injury.

Break in the air—Leap upward at the start, instead of hustling forward.

Break maiden—When horse or rider wins first race of career.

Breastplate—Leather passed across chest of horse and fastened to each side of saddle, keeping it in place. Used on thin horses.

Breather—Restraining horse to rest and relax it before stretch drive.

Breed—To mate horses.

Breeder—Owner of mare at time she drops foal.

Breeze—Running under a stout hold, easily, without encouragement.

Bridge-jumper—Bettor who specializes in large show bets on odds-on favorites.

Brisket—Area of horse's body between forelegs.

Brittle feet—Hooves that chip easily and are difficult to shoe.

Broken knees—Skin lesions at knee.

Broken wind—When overstrained lung tissue breaks down, causing breathing problems; "heaves."

Broodmare—Female Thoroughbred used for breeding.

Broodmare dam—Mare whose female offspring become good broodmares.

Boodmare sire—Male horse whose female offspring become good broodmares.

Bruce Lowe system—A method of identifying Thoroughbred families by number, according to the female ancestor from which each family descends.

Brush—Light collision during race.

Brushing—Horse scrapes fetlock with opposite shoe. Caused by improper balance, poor shoes or fatigue.

Bucked shins—Shins painfully inflamed by overstrain.

Bug boy—Apprentice jockey, because of asterisk with which newspapers identify apprentice in entry lists.

Bull ring—Small track, because of sharp turns.

Bushes—Small-time, bush-league racing.

Buy the rack—Purchase every possible daily-double or other combination ticket.

Buzzer—Battery-powered oscillator or vibrator used illegally to frighten horse into running; machine.

Calculator—Clerk who computes parimutuel odds.

Calk—Horseshoe cleat for greater purchase in mud or on grass.

Call—To announce progress of race for purposes of offical result charts (chart-caller); to describe race to audience; stage of race at which running positions are recorded, like "half-mile call."

Canker—Foot infection that softens the hoof.

Cannon—Foreleg between knee and ankle. Rear leg between hock and ankle.

Canter—Slow gallop; lope.

Capped—Swollen, as of elbow or hock rubbed or bumped in stall.

Card—Program of racing.

Car fit—Severe fright while being shipped in van, train or plane.

Carry the target—Run last all the way.

Cast—Fallen and unable to rise, as of a horse; lost or "thrown," as of a horse-shoe.

Chalk Horse—Betting favorite.

Chalk player—Bettor on favorites.

Challenge—To vie for lead.

Chart—Result chart.

Chase—Steeplechase.

Chestnut—Brown or tan horse with brown tail and mane; horny growth (called "night eyes") on inside of horse's legs.

Choppy—Of stride, shortness, often reveals soreness.

Chute—Extension of stretch to permit long, straight run from starting gate to first turn.

Circuit—Geographical grouping of tracks whose meetings are coordinated to run in sequence.

Claim—To buy horse in claiming race.

Claimer—Claiming race; horse that runs in such races.

Claiming box—Where claims are deposited before race.

Clerk of the scales—Weighs riders and tack before and after race.

Clever—Of a horse, kindly, easily managed, able.

Client—Purchaser of betting information from horseman or other tipster.

Climb—To run with unusually high motion of forelegs, usually when flustered or tired.

Clocker—Person who times workouts, usually for betting information.

Close—Of final odds on horse ("closed at 2 to 1"); to gain ground on leader.

Close-coupled—Of a horse, short-backed.

Close fast—Finish fast, gaining on leader.

Clothes—Horse blanket.

Clubhouse turn—Turn of track nearest clubhouse; first turn of races that begin on homestretch.

Coffin bone—Main bone in equine foot.

Cold—Of a horse, unreadiness to win because of physical condition or stable's intentions.

Cold-blooded—Of a non-Thoroughbred horse.

Colors—Distinctively patterned rider's costumes identifying owner.

Colt—Unaltered male horse aged four or less.

Combination—Across-the-board bet for which a single mutuel ticket is issued.

Come back to—Of a horse, to tire and slow down, allowing other horse to close gap.

Condition—Equine form or fitness; to train a horse.

Condition book—Publication in which track announces purses, terms of eligibility and weight formulas of races.

Conditions—Terms of race, including purse size, eligibility for entry, and weight concessions.

Connections—Owner, trainer and other custodians of horse.

Consolation double—When horse is scratched from second race after daily-double betting begins, money is set aside to pay those who have bought tickets pairing horse with winner of first race.

Contract rider—Jockey on whose services an owner, by contract, has first call.

Cooler—Covering draped on horse while it cools out after race or workout; horse that is restrained to prevent it from running well.

Corn—Horny callus caused by irritation from horseshoes.

Coronet—Area just above hoof; "crown of hoof."

Cover—Of a stallion, act of coupling with a mare.

Cow hocks—Hocks that turn toward each other, like cow's.

Cresty—Of horse, thick-necked and probably not nimble.

Cribber—Horse that bites parts of its stall, sucking air into lungs; "wind-sucker"; "crib-biter."

Cropper—Spill, usually in jump race.

Croup—Top hindquarters of horse.

Crowd—To race too close to another horse, forcing its rider to take up or change course.

Cryptorchid—Male horse with undescended testicle.

Cuff—Horse anklet; credit ("on the cuff").

Cull—Unwanted horse disposed of by owner.

Cup—Type of blinker.

Cup horse—Good router.

Cuppy—Of a track, when surface breaks into clods and shows hoofprints.

Curb—Sprain at back of hock; a powerful bit equipped with extra strap or chain beneath horse's chin.

Cushion—Subsurface of track.

Cut down—Of a horse, injured during race by shoe of another horse or by striking itself with own shoe.

Daily double—Form of mutuel betting in which player attempts to pick winners of two races, buying a single ticket on the double choice.

Dam—Horse's mother.

Dark—Of a track at which or a day on which there is no racing.

Dark horse—Underrated animal that wins or has good prospects of winning.

Dash—Sprint race.

Dead heat—When two or more horses reach finish wire simultaneously.

Dead weight—Lead slabs carried in saddle to increase weight of jockey and tack.

Declaration to win—Public announcement by owner of more than one entrant in a race that he will try to win with one but not with the others.

Declare—To withdraw horse from race.

Deep—Of racing surface recently harrowed or to which extra top soil has been added, increasing holding qualities.

Derby—Stakes race for three-year-olds.

Destroy—To kill a horse.

Disqualify—To lower horse's actual finishing position by official act after deciding it interfered with others during race, or carried improper weight or was drugged.

Distaff side—Female ancestry, shown in lower half of pedigree.

Distance of ground—A route race.

Division—When too many entries are made in an important race, track may divide it into two races.

Doer—Of a horse, eater.

Dog—Obstructions placed near rail when track is muddy, to prevent horses from running there and kicking up the surface during workouts; cheap horse; quitter.

Dope—Information about races or horses; drugs.

Draw Away—To win going away; "draw clear"; "draw out."

Drench—To give horse liquid medicine.

Drive—All-out exertion, under heavy punishment, especially in home-stretch.

Drop—Give birth to foal.

Dun—Mousy, grayish color in brown to gold range, usually with black mane and tail.

Dutch—To take advantage of booking percentages by eliminating heavily bet non-contenders, betting on others in exact proportions necessary to yield profit no matter which wins.

Dwell—Of a horse that breaks slowly from the gate

Early foot—Good speed at beginning of race.

Ease up—To slow horse's stride, sparing it exertion.

Easy ride—Performance in which jockey fails to try.

Eggs (walking on)—Of a sore horse.

Eighth—Furlong; 220 yards; 660 feet.

Eighth pole—Colored post at the inside rail exactly one furlong from finish wire.

Empty—Of a horse that lacks energy for finishing drive.

English Stud Book—Official repository of English Thoroughbred records.

Entire—Of an unaltered male horse.

Entry—Two or more horses owned by same interests, or trained by same person, entered in same race and coupled in the betting.

Ewe-necked—Of a horse with concave neck, a sign of clumsiness.

Exacta—Form of betting in which player attempts to pick winner and second horse, buying one mutuel ticket on the double choice. Also exactor or perfecta.

Excused—Permitted to withdraw horse after official scratch time.

Exercise boy—Rider in training workouts.

Extend—To force horse to go all out.

Fade—To tire and drop out of contention.

False quarter—Horizontal crack in hoof, caused by coronet injury.

Falter—To tire badly.

Farrier—Horseshoer.

Fast track—Dry, hard strip on which horses run fastest; a track at which typical running times are relatively fast by comparison with most other tracks.

Feather—Extremely light weight.

Fetlock—Horse's ankle.

Field—All entrants in race; in pari-mutuel betting, two or more lightly regarded horses grouped as a single betting entry.

Figure—To have a winning chance; the handicapper's rating number that identifies the winning chance; also "fig."

Filly—Female horse, aged four or less.

Film patrol—Crew that records running of each race on movie film or television tape, for possible review by stewards when questions arise about behavior of horse or rider.

Fire—Cauterization of ailing tissue with red-hot needle or firing iron.

Fit—Of a horse, physical readiness.

Five-eighths pole—Post at inside rail, exactly five furlongs from finish wire.

Flag—Signal held by official flag man a few yards in front of the gate, where race actually starts. Timing begins when horses reach that point and he drops flag.

Flag down—To wave at an exercise rider to indicate horse is working too hard.

Flash—Change of odds information on tote board.

Flat—Conventional racing surface, contrasted with grass or jump course.

Flatten out—Of an exhausted horse that stops, often dropping its head flat-level with body.

Foal—Newborn horse; of a mare, to give birth.

Foot—Speed; soft tissue beneath hoof.

Footing—Condition of track surface.

Forearm—Horse's foreleg between elbow and knee.

Forked—Of horse's conformation where forelegs join body.

Form—Of a horse, current condition; *Daily Racing Form*.

Form player—Bettor who makes selections from past-performance records.

Fractions—Clockings at quarter-mile intervals in races and workouts.

Free lance—Jockey not under contract to one stable.

Freemartin—Filly twin of a colt.

Freshener—Layoff designed to restore energies of overworked horse.

Frog—Triangular fleshy cushion on sole of horse's foot.

Front runner—Horse that prefers to run in front.

Furlong—One eighth of a mile.

Futurity—Race in which horses are entered before birth.

Gad—Jockey's whip.

Gait—Equine walk, trot or gallop; horse's action or "way of going."

Gallop—Fastest gait; workout; an easy race or workout, compared with one in which horse is urged.

Garrison finish—Victory by a come-from-behind horse, such as those ridden by the famous Snapper Garrison.

Gaskin—Hind leg between thigh and hock.

Gate—Starting gate; entrance to track.

Gelding—Castrated male horse.

Gentleman jockey—Amateur rider.

Get—Offspring of stallion.

Getaway day—Last day of race meeting.

Get into—Of a rider, to whip horse.

Gimpy—Of a lame, sore, "ouchy" horse.

Girth—Saddle band.

Go—Of a stable or horse, to start in a race; an effort to win.

Going—Condition of racing surface; of a horse, its stride ("way of going").

Going away—Winning while increasing the lead.

Good bone—Impressive bone structure indicative of weight-bearing ability and ruggedness.

Good doer—Of a horse, a hearty eater.

Go on—Of a horse, to win at a new, longer distance. "I think he'll go on."

Goose-rumped—Of a horse, high hindquarters with a sharp slope at base of tail.

Grab—To catch foreleg with a hind foot, because of faulty conformation. Causes stumbling, loss of stride.

Graded race—One in which eligibility is limited to horses in one or another classification, as determined by racing secretary. Graded allowances and graded handicaps are common.

Graduate—To break maiden.

Grandam—Equine grandma.

Grandsire—Equine grandpa.

Gray—Equine color composed of black and white hairs.

Groom—Stable employee who tends horse, brings it to a paddock for race.

Grounded—Of a jockey, suspended from competition for infractions of rules.

Grunter—Horse whose noisy breathing indicates unreadiness for hard exertion.

Guinea—Stablehand, because winning British owners used to tip the groom a guinea.

Gumbo—Heavy mud.

Gun—All-out effort by jockey.

Gypsy—Itinerant owner-trainer; "gyp."

Half—Half-mile; time "to the half" is fractional time after half a mile of running.

Half brother—Male horse out of same dam as, but by different sire than another horse.

Half-mile pole—Vertical pole at infield rail exactly four furlongs from finish line.

Half-miler—A track of that distance; horse that prefers such a track.

Half sister—Female horse out of same dam as, but by different sire than another horse.

Halter—Hand-held rope or strap by which horses are led; to claim a horse.

Halter man—Owner or trainer who specializes in buying horses from claiming races.

Hand—Four inches of equine height.

Handicap—Race in which racing secretary or track handicapper assigns weights designed to equalize winning chances of entrants; to study horses' records in effort to determine winner of race.

Handicap Triple Crown—Mythical award to horse that wins the three classic handicaps—the Brooklyn, Suburban and Metropolitan—in one season.

Handily—Of a comparatively easy victory achieved without hard urging; of a fairly strenuous workout under a hand ride without whipping.

Handle—Total sum bet on a race or in a day or some other period.

Hand ride—Urging horse toward longer, faster, more rhythmic stride by rolling hands on its neck, lifting its head at beginning of stride.

Handy—Of a nimble, trappy, lightfooted, easily guided horse.

Hang—Of a horse unable to produce the expected finishing kick and therefore unable to improve its position in the stretch.

Hardboot—A Kentucky horseman of the old school, because of the legendary mud caked on his boots.

Hat trick—The winning, usually by a jockey, of three races on a single program.

Have one in the boot—To ride a horse whose owner or trainer has made bets, including one for the rider.

Hayburner—Horse that fails to pay it own feed bill; "oatburner."

Headed—Beaten by a head to the wire.

Head of the stretch—End of the final turn; top of the stretch.

Heat—A race.

Heavy-fronted—Of a horse with extremely wide, muscular chest. Supposedly a sign of poor quality.

Heavy-headed—Of a horse that fights the reins, responds slowly to guidance, or prefers to run with its head low.

Heavy-topped—Of a horse with an unusually large, muscular body by comparison with its legs. A sign of susceptibility to soreness and lameness.

Heavy track—A running surface drier than muddy, and often slower.

Height—Of a horse, distance from ground to withers.

Herd—To alter horse's course so as to prevent another from improving its position.

Herring-gutted—A poor doer with practically no depth of abdomen.

Hind sticker—Horseshoe similar to mud calk, except cleat is on outside edge.

Hip number—Identification number attached to horse's hip at Thoroughbred sales.

Hock—Hind elbow joint between gaskin and cannon.

Homebred—Horse foaled in state where it races.

Homestretch—Straight part of track from final turn to finish wire.

Honest—Of a kind, reliable horse.

Hood—Head covering containing blinkers.

Hop—To drug a horse illegally.

Horse—Technically, any entire male aged five or more.

Horseman—An owner or trainer.

Horseman's Benevolent and Protective Association—Trade association of owners and trainers.

Horsing—Of a mare in heat.

Hot—Of a horse expected to win; of a jockey or stable on a winning streak; of a horse overheated from exertion.

Hot-walker—Stablehand who walks horse while it cools out after a race or workout.

Hunt—Amateur racing, mainly on grass and over jumps.

Hurdle race—A race over low obstacles.

Ice—To anesthetize a horse's painful feet or legs by standing it in ice.

Impost—Weight carried by horse.

In-and-outer—Inconsistent horse that "runs hot and cold."

Index—Number that identifies a specific result chart. When printed in racing papers, directs player to chart of horse's most recent race.

Infield—The area on the inner circumference of the track, where grass and jump races are run and the tote board is found.

In hand—Of a horse running under restraint.

In light—Carrying relatively little weight.

Inquiry—Official investigation of the running of a race to see whether it was fairly won.

In shape—Of a horse ready to win.

Inside—Anything to the left of a horse during the race; position closest to the rail.

Inside rail—Fence separating racing strip from infield.

Interfere—Of a horse, to strike a leg with opposite hoof; to impede another horse in the race.

In the can—An out-of-the-money finish; "in the crapper," etc.

In the money—Technically, a finish in the first four, entitling the owner to a share of the purse; among bettors, a finish in the first three, resulting in a mutuel payoff.

In tough—Of a horse entered with animals it is unlikely to beat.

Irons—Stirrups.

Jail—Of the first month that a claimed horse is in the new barn, when racing law requires it to run at a 25 percent higher claiming price or remain idle.

Jam—Traffic jam during a race.

JBM—Of a horse that won a maiden race and no other and because it "Just Beat Maidens" is given small chance against the more experienced runners it meets in open competition.

Jockey—Race rider; to maneuver for position during a race.

Jockey agent—Person who helps rider obtain mounts in return for 20 percent or more of the rider's earnings.

Jockey Club—Name taken by organizations that operate tracks; New York organization that maintains the American Stud Book and approves Thoroughbred names and registry; the governing body of British racing.

Jockeys' Guild—National association of race riders.

Jog—Slow, easy gait, similar to a trot.

Jostle—To bump another horse during a race.

Journeyman—A full-fledged professional jockey.

Jumper—Horse that runs in steeplechase or hurdle races.

Jump up—Of a horse that wins in a surprising reversal of form.

Juvenile—Two-year-old

Kiss the eighth pole—Of a horse, to finish far behind.

Kitchen—Horsemen's restaurant in backstretch area.

Knee spavin—Bony growth behind knee, caused by blow or overstrain. More serious than hock spavin.

Laminitis—Serious inflammation of equine foot.

Lay—To occupy a certain running position deliberately, while waiting to make strategic move. "Lay fourth, off the pace."

Lead pad—Saddle pocket in which lead weights can be placed.

Lead pony—Horse on which outrider escorts Thoroughbreds to the post.

Leaky roof circuit—Minor tracks.

Leather—A whip.

Leathers—Stirrup straps.

Leg lock—When jockey illegally hooks legs with another rider, impeding the other horse.

Leg up—To build horse's speed and stamina with work; a jockey's riding assignment.

Length—Eight or nine feet.

Light over the kidney—Of a horse, slender-loined; wasp-waisted.

Line—Pedigree; male side of the pedigree as contrasted with family, or female side.

Live weight—The weight of the jockey, as contrasted with dead weight.

Loaded shoulder—Unusually thick shoulder and unimpressive withers, making for an awkward gait.

Loafer—Horse unwilling to run well without hard urging.

Lob—A cooler or stiff.

Lock—A sure thing.

Look for hole in fence—Of a quitter that acts as if it would rather run back to the barn than continue in the race.

Look of eagles—The proud look in the eyes of many good horses, as if they knew they were good.

Loose-coupled—Opposite of close-coupled; slack-coupled.

Loose mount—Horse that continues running after losing rider.

Lug in—Bear in.

Machine—Battery.

Machines—The mutuels.

Maiden—Of a horse or jockey, a non-winner; of a race, one for non-winners.

Make a run—Of a horse that turns on the speed, makes a move, makes a bid.

Marathon—A race longer than 1¼ miles.

Mare—A female horse of five or older.

Martingale—Straps attached to bit or noseband and girth, preventing horse from rearing.

Match race—A race between two horses, winner-take-all.

Maturity—A race for four-year-olds in which entries are made before their birth.

Meant—Of a horse whose stable intends to win; "well-meant."

Meat ball—Cathartic pill.

Meet—Race meeting.

Middle distance—Of a race longer than seven furlongs but less than 1⅛ miles.

Mile pole—Colored post at infield rail exactly a mile from finish wire.

Minus pool—In pari-mutuel betting, a situation in which so much money is bet on a horse (usually to show) that the pool is insufficient, after take and breakage, to pay holders of winning tickets the legal minimum odds of 1 to 10 or 20. The track is required to make up the difference from its own funds.

Monkey crouch—Riding style popularized by Tod Sloan in which jockey bends forward over horse's withers; "monkey-on-a-stick."

Morning glory—Horse that runs well in workouts but not in races.

Morning line—Forecast of probable odds.

Move up—Gain ground; run in a higher-class race.

Muck out—Clean a horse's stall.

Mudder—Horse that prefers muddy going; "mudlark."

Muddy track—Soft, wet and holding.

Mutuel pool—Total amount bet to win, place or show in a race; total amount bet on daily double, exacta, quinella, etc.

Muzzle—Straps that keep horse's mouth closed, prevent it from biting.

Name—To enter a horse in a race.

Nape—Top of horse's neck; poll.

Navicular disease—A crippling, sometimes fatal ulcer which corrodes the navicular bone of the foot. Usually found in forefoot.

Near side—Horse's left side.

Neck—About ¼ length.

Nerve—To remove a nerve, eliminating pain but not the infirmity that causes it. Illegal in major racing.

Nick—To nerve a horse; a supposedly strategic feature of a pedigree, representing a particular mating or cross-breeding worthy of repetition.

Nightcap—Last race on the program.

Nod—Lowering of head; permission to a jockey to dismount after race.

Nom de course—Stable name.

Nose—The narrowest possible winning margin.

Number ball—Numbered ball drawn from number box to assign post positions.

Nursery race—Baby race.

Oaks—Stakes race for three-year-old fillies.

Oatburner—Hayburner.

Objection—Complaint by jockey that a foul has been committed.

Odd board—Tote board.

Odds man—At tracks where electronic computers are not in use, an employee who calculates changing odds as betting progresses.

Odds on—Odds of less than even money.

Off—The start, or the time of the start; difference between track record and final clocking of a race; slowness of a horse, expressed in a time comparison or a lengths comparison between its current performance and what it should do, or what other horses have done or are likely to do. "He's off at least three lengths."

Off side—Right side of a horse.

Off the board—Of a horse so lightly bet that its odds exceed 99 to 1; failure to finish in the money.

Off the pace—To run behind the early leaders.

Off the top—Of the practice of deducting a fixed "take" percentage from the mutuel pool before paying holders of winning tickets.

Off-track—A racing surface other than fast; of betting conducted away from the track.

On edge—Nervous; sharply conditioned.

One-run—Of a horse that expends all its energy in a single burst of speed, usually in stretch.

On the bit—Of a horse eagerly straining against the bit.

On the chin strap—Winning by a wide margin.

On the ground—Of a suspended jockey.

On the nose—A bet that horse will win.

On the rail—Running close to the infield rail.

On top—In the lead.

Open race—A race with lenient eligibility conditions, permitting entry of a wide variety of horses.

Optional claimer—A race for horses entered to be claimed at a fixed price or a price within a limited range, and open also to horses that have run at such a price in the past but are not entered to be claimed today.

Osselets—Bony growths on injured membrane of ankle joint.

Ouchy—Sore.

Out of—In discussing a horse's parentage, one says that it is "by" a sire "out of" a dam.

Outrider—Mounted employee who escorts horses to post.

Over at the knee—The foreleg curves forward at the knee.

Overland—Of the course followed by a horse that runs wide on the turns, losing ground.

Overlay—Horse whose odds are high by comparison with its good winning chances.

Overnight race—One for which entries close less than three days before the start of the program.

Overnights—Tomorrow's entries, as released by the racing secretary's office.

Overreach—To strike a forefoot with a hind shoe while running.

Overweight—Pounds that a horse carries in excess of officially assigned weight, because jockey is too heavy.

Pace—The speed of the leaders at each stage of the race.

Paddock—Saddling enclosure.

Pari-mutuels—From Paris ("Paree") Mutuels, system invented by Frenchman, whereby winning bettors get all money wagered by losers, after deduction of house percentage.

Pasteboard track—Fast racing strip, so-called because thin and hard.

Pastern—Area between fetlock and coronet.

Peacocky—High-headed, flighty horse.

Periodic ophthalmia—Periodic loss of vision by horse; "moonblindness."

Pic six—Known also as pick six, five-ten and many other names, this exotic proposition challenges the player to pick the winners of six successive races. When nobody does so, a small percentage of the pool may be distributed to those who pick five, with most of the money being carried over for the next day's pic six. The prizes sometimes build into six figures, at which point betting syndicates of professional sharks invest hundreds of thousands on all plausible combinations, hoping to buy the pool. They often succeed.

Pigeye—Small equine eye, supposed sign of meanness.

Pinched back—Caught in a jam and forced back during race.

Pink—Uniformed Pinkerton guard at track.

Pipe opener—Short workout; blow out.

Plater—Horseshoer, farrier; claiming horse, because of silver plates formerly awarded to winner of such races.

Pocket—Racing predicament in which horse is surrounded by others and unable to increase speed until opening occurs.

Points—In Thoroughbred conformation, a physical feature; the lower legs of a horse, especially in describing color ("Dark brown or bay horses always have black points").

Poll—Top of horse's head.

Pony—Any workhorse at a track, such as lead pony.

Pool—Total amount bet for win, place or show, or in daily double, etc.

Post—Starting gate.

Powder—Minor physical contact between horses during race.

Preferred—Of horses given preference in entry for particular race, usually previous winners or horses bred or foaled in the local jurisdiction.

Prepotent—Of horse whose offspring breed comparatively true to type, inheriting the desired characteristics.

Prod—Illegal battery, as in cattleprod.

Produce—Offspring of mare.

Prop—Refusing to break at start; standing flat-footed.

Public stable—Enterprise of "public trainer" who handles horses on freelance basis, as contrasted with one who trains stock of only one owner.

Puett gate—Widely used brand of starting gate.

Pull—To restrain horse deliberately, preventing it from winning; to "stiff."

Pull in the weights—A weight advantage.

Pull up—To stop or slow a horse during or after race or workout.

Punter—Horseplayer.

Quarter—Quarter-mile; two furlongs; side of hoof.

Quarter crack—Separation of inner and outer walls of hoof in quarter area.

Quarter horse—Extremely speedy breed used for ranch work and racing up to a quarter-mile.

Quarter pole—Colored post at infield rail exactly two furlongs from finish wire.

Quinella (quiniela; quinela)—Form of mutuel betting in which player tries to pick first two finishers, regardless of order.

Racing plate—Shoe worn for racing purposes.

Racing secretary—Official who prescribes conditions of races at his track and usually serves as track handicapper, assigning weights to entrants in handicap races.

Racing sound—Of a horse able to race, although not necessarily in prime health.

Rack up—To interfere with several other horses so severely that they all slow down.

Rail runner—Horse that prefers to run along inside rail.

Raised bar—Bar plate which helps prevent running down.

Rank—Of a fractious horse, especially when, "running rank," it refuses to be rated early in race.

Rate—To restrain a horse early in race, conserving its energies for later challenges.

Receiving barn—Where horses stabled at other tracks are kept before they go to the paddock for their races.

Red roan—Of a horse whose coat consists of red, yellow and white hairs.

Refuse—Of a horse that fails to break at the start or, in jump races, fails to attempt one of the fences.

Ridden out—Of a horse that wins under an active but not a driving ride, and probably has racing energy left; sometimes, contradictorily, a winner whose jockey parcels out its energy so that none is left after it passes finish line.

Ride short—To ride with short stirrup leathers.

Ridgling—Partly castrated horse; "rigling."

Right price—Among players, mutuel odds high enough to warrant risking a bet on a particular animal; among horsemen, odds high enough to warrant an all-out try with horse.

Rim—Horseshoe with long cleat or grab on outer rim, sometimes helps horses with bad tendons.

Ringbone—Bony overgrowth at top of hoof or near pastern bones, found often in horses with straight pasterns. Formerly treated by nerving.

Ringer—Of a horse entered under another's name.

Roan—Striking reddish or grayish color.

Roar—Of a horse, noisy breathing like coughing.

Rogue—Chronically fractious horse.

Rogue's badge—Blinkers.

Romp—An easy race.

Roping—Training or exercising a horse by having it move in circles at end of a tether.

Route—A relatively long race.

Router—Horse that does its best in races of 1⅛ miles or longer.

Rug—Heavy horse blanket.

Rule off—To bar from racing.

Run down—Of a horse, to scrape the flesh of the heels on the track surface while racing. Associated with weak pasterns; "run down behind."

Run in—To win unexpectedly.

Runner—Messenger to and from mutuel windows for occupants of clubhouse boxes.

Run out—To finish out of the money; to run toward outside rail.

Run-out bit—Bit that gives rider extra leverage on one side, helping prevent animal from lugging in or bearing out.

Run wide—To race far from inside rail, covering extra ground.

Saddlecloth—Piece of fabric between saddle and horse.

Saliva test—Chemical analysis of horse's saliva, routinely performed on in-money finishers, in attempt to see whether animal was dosed with illegal drugs.

Salute—Of jockey who raises whip in greeting to stewards after race, in customary request to dismount.

Sand crack—Vertical crack on hoof from coronet downward.

Sanitary ride—Of a horse that did not try its best in a race, or of a jockey that took the animal wide to avoid tight spots or flying mud, harming its chances.

Savage—Of a horse, to bite.

Save ground—To cover the shortest possible distance in a race, hugging the rail

on turns, running in direct, straight line on stretches.

Scale of weights—Official tabulation of correct weights for various age groups at all distances and all times of year; "the scale."

Scale weights—Weights carried in an official weight-for-age race.

Scenic route—When a horse loses ground by running far from rail; overland.

School—To train a horse, especially at the gate, in the paddock or over jumps.

Score—To win a race or a bet; a victory.

Scratch—To withdraw an entrant from its race.

Scratch sheet—Daily publication that includes graded handicaps, tips, and scratches.

Season—The period in which racing is conducted on a particular circuit or at a particular track; of a filly or mare, the period of estrus or "heat."

Seat—The posture of a rider on a horse.

Second dam—Horse's maternal grandmother.

Second sire—Horse's paternal grandfather.

Selling plater—Claiming horse; plater.

Selling race—Claiming race; type of race that antedated claimers and no longer is run, in which rules required that winner be auctioned off afterward.

Send—To enter a horse in a race; of a horseman, to try to win with the horse.

Send away—Of an official starter, opening the gate and beginning the race.

Sesamoiditis—Bone inflammation above and behind fetlock.

Set down—To suspend horseman, rider, stablehand from racing for a period; to shake up a horse and ask it for speed in a race or workout.

Sex allowance—Weight concession that is given to female horses in races against males.

Shadow roll—Sheepskin or cloth cylinder strapped across horse's nose to bar its vision of ground, prevent it from shying at shadows.

Shake up—To hit a horse in effort to make it run.

Shank—Rope or strap attached to halter or bridle, for leading a horse by hand.

Sheath—Fleshy pocket containing genital organs of male horse.

Shed row—Racetrack barns; the backstretch community.

Ship—To transport a horse.

Shipping fever—Respiratory ailment of

horses, associated with move from one climate to another.

Shoe board—Sign that tells what kind of shoes each entrant wears.

Shoo in—A supposed cinch bet or guaranteed victor; a fixed race.

Short—Of a horse that tires in stretch after long layoff, demonstrating need for more work.

Short price—Small mutuel payoff.

Show wear—Fetlocks swollen by overwork.

Shuffle—Of jockey who hand rides, pumping his hands and moving his feet.

Shuffled back—Of a horse that loses ground or racing position because of jams.

Shut off—To cross in front of another horse during race, forcing it to take up or go around.

Shut out—What happens to the player who gets on the betting line too late and is still waiting in line when the window closes.

Silks—Nylon or other costume worn by rider in race.

Sire—Horse's father.

Sit-still—A type of riding dependent more on patience, knowledge of pace than active, "whoop-de-doo" whipping; of a jockey who loses the race through inactivity with the whip.

Sixteenth pole—Vertical post on infield rail exactly half a furlong from finish wire.

Skin—To make a track faster by rolling and hardening the surface.

Skittish—Of a nervous horse.

Slab-sided—Of a horse with flat, narrow rib cage, indicative of poor lung capacity.

Slack of rib—Of a horse whose last rib is not close to its hip, indicating a long, weak back.

Sleeper—An underrated horse that could, or does, surprise.

Sloppy track—When racing strip is covered with puddles, but is not yet muddy, the surface remaining hard.

Slot—Post position.

Slow pill—Drug that dulls horse's nervous system, preventing it from performing alertly.

Slow track—A track wetter than good, not as thick as muddy.

Smart money—Insiders' bets, insiders themselves.

Snatch—Any violent, sudden action with reins or halter; "snatch up," "snatch around."

Snip—White or flesh-colored marking on horse's nose.

Snug—To keep a tight hold on horse while rating it during race; "snug back," "snug hold."

Socks—White ankles, allegedly a sign of weakness.

Solid—Of a ready horse, suitably placed.

Sophomore—Three-year-old.

Spanish bit—Type of bit that causes pain under pressure of reins. Used as last resort in schooling rebellious horses.

Spark—To use a battery in a race.

Spavin—Bony outcropping caused by inflammation of equine joints.

Special weights—Even weights, except for sex and apprentice allowances, assigned by racing secretary without recourse to official weight scale. Used mainly in races for better maidens.

Speedy cut—Leg injury caused by blow from opposite foot while running.

Spit out the bit—When an exhausted horse "backs up" and stops pressing against the bit.

Splint—Bony growth on horse's shin.

Split race—When an oversubscribed race is divided into two.

Sponge—To insert a piece of sponge or other foreign substance in a horse's nostrils, impeding its breathing and preventing it from performing well.

Spot—To concede weight to another horse.

Spot play—Type of play in which bettor risks money only on types of races and horses which seem relatively worthwhile risks.

Spring halt—Nerve-muscle ailment causing spasmodic elevation of rear legs.

Sprint—Short race, seven furlongs or less.

Stake—Commission paid winning jockey, trainer or groom.

Stakes—A race in which purse consists of nomination, entrance and starting fees plus money added by track itself. Improperly called "stake" race.

Stale—Of a jaded, overworked horse; of a horse, to urinate.

Stall gate—Starting gate in which each horse has its own compartment.

Stallion—Entire male horse.

Stall walker—Horse that paces its stall, consuming energy.

Stand—Of a stallion, to be at stud.

Star—White marking on horse's forehead.

Starter's list—List of horses ruled out of action by official starter because of chronic misbehavior at gate and, therefore, ineligible for racing until bad habits are corrected.

Stayer—A reliable, determined router.

Steeplechase—A race over jumps higher and broader than hurdles.

Stewards—The three duly-appointed arbiters of racing law who judge human and equine conduct at a race meeting.

Stick—Whip; to whip.

Sticker—Cleat on a horseshoe.

Stick horse—Horse that runs better when whipped.

Stiff—to prevent a horse from winning by deliberately riding poorly or by drugging it or training it inappropriately; an unfit or outclassed horse; a horse that has been stiffed.

Stifle—Forward area of horse's thigh.

Sting—To use a battery in a race.

Stirrup—Where jockey's feet go when he is mounted; irons.

Stockings—White leg markings, longer than socks.

Stooper—One of several dozen Americans who make a precarious living picking up discarded mutuel tickets at tracks and cashing those that have been thrown away by mistake.

Straight—Another term for a bet to win; "straight, place and show."

Straight as a string—Of a horse going all-out; "strung out."

Straightaway—Straight part of a race course; stretch.

Stretch call—Position in stretch where call is made for charting purposes. Usually a furlong from the wire.

Stretch turn—The turn into the homestretch.

Stride—Of a horse, its way of running or the ground it covers after each foot has been in contact with the track once.

String—The horses owned by one stable or handled by one trainer.

Strip—Racing strip; narrow white marking on horse's face.

Stripe—Marking similar to strip, but longer.

Stud—Stallion; breeding farm; horses at a breeding farm.

Studbook—Official registry of Thoroughbreds; a stallion's date book.

Stud fee—What the stallion's owner gets for its breeding services.

Subscription—Fees required of owner who enters horse in stakes race.

Sulk—Of a horse that refuses to run or respond to jockey's guidance.

Surcingle—Buckled strap that holds blanket on horse.

Suspension—Punishment, usually temporary, that declares jockey, horseman or stablehand ineligible for participation in sport.

Swamp fever—Infectious equine anemia.

Sweat the brass—To overwork a horse.

Sweepstakes—Stakes race.

Tack—What goes on the horse in addition to the rider.

Tag—Claiming price.

Tail female—Horse's female ancestry on dam's side.

Tail male—Horse's male ancestry on sire's side.

Take—Money deducted from each mutuel pool for track revenue and taxes.

Take back—To restrain a horse, either to rate it or prevent running into trouble.

Take care of—Of a jockey, to give the works to another in a race.

Take down—To disqualify a horse after it has finished in the money. Its number literally is removed from the list of early finishers.

Take out—Track take.

Take up—To slow sharply in effort to avoid collision or other racing trouble.

Tea—Any illegal chemical used to drug a horse and worsen or improve its performance.

Teaser—Stallion that tests mare's readiness for mating.

Teletimer—Electronic timer that flashes the fractional and final times of races on the tote board.

Tenderfoot—Sore-footed horse.

Thief—Unreliable horse that runs worst when its chances seem best.

Third sire—Horse's paternal great-grandfather.

Thoroughbred Racing Association—Trade association of track owners and managers.

Thoroughbred Racing Protective Bureau—The TRA's FBI, an intelligence network which combats corruption by investigating suspected evildoers and exposing those it catches.

Thoroughpins—A larger version of bog spavin that often goes right through the upper hock.

Three-eighths pole—Colored pole at inside rail, exactly three furlongs from finish wire.

Three-quarters pole—Colored pole at inside rail, exactly six furlongs from finish wire.

Throat latch—Upper part of horse's throat.

Thrush—Inflammation of the frog.

Tied on—Reins knotted and crossed, for stouter hold.

Tight—Fit and ready.

Tightener—A race intended to bring a horse to its peak.

Timber—Hurdle or other obstacle in jump race.

Timber rider—Steeplechase jockey.

Timber topper—A horse that runs in jump races.

Toe plate—Horseshoe with cleat in front, prevents sliding.

Tongue strap—Leather or cloth band that holds horse's tongue down to prevent horse from swallowing it during race or workout.

Top horse—Horse listed first in program of the race.

Top line—Male side of Thoroughbred pedigree.

Top weight—Heaviest impost in race.

Totalisator—Automated pari-mutuel machine which records bets as soon as tickets are dispensed at betting windows.

Tout—To give or sell betting advice; one who does so.

Trackmaster—Employee in charge of maintaining racing strip.

Training track—Separate track where workouts are held.

Trappy—Of a nimble, kind Thoroughbred.

Travel in straw—To travel with the horses in shipping vans, as stablehands do.

Trial—A preparatory race; a workout in which horse is asked for speed.

Trifecta—In which the winning bettor picks the first three finishers in exact order. Known also as triple.

Trip—The course followed by horse and rider from starting gate to finish wire, usually described as "good" or "bad" or even more so, depending on racing luck and riding tactics.

Triple Crown—Mythical award to any three-year-old that wins Kentucky Derby, Preakness Stakes and Belmont Stakes.

Trouble line—Words at end of each past-performance line in the Eastern edition of the *Daily Racing Form,* appraising horse's effort or stating any legitimate excuse it might have had for losing.

Turf course—A grass-covered track.

Turn out—To send a horse to the farm for pasturage and rest.

Twitch—Noose that can be tightened painfully around horse's nose and upper lip, keeping it quiet in starting gate, elsewhere "tongs."

Under wraps—Of a horse showing less than its best, probably because trainer does not want to extend it.

Untrack—What a horse is said to do to itself when it finally generates momentum and shows its talent.

Unwind—To taper off a horse's training preparatory to resting it.

Up—Of a jockey's assignment ("Buckpasser, Baeza up"), or an order to jockeys ("Riders, up!").

Urine test—Chemical analysis of horse's urine in effort to tell whether animal was drugged.

Used up—Of an exhausted horse.

Valet—Employee who takes care of jockey's clothing, carries his tack.

Van—A motor truck in which horses are shipped.

Veer—Of a horse, to swerve.

Vet's list—List of ill or injured horses declared ineligible for racing by the track veterinarian.

Vice—Any undesirable habit of a horse.

Walking ring—Oval near paddock enclosure, where horses walk and riders mount before start of post parade.

Walkover—A race from which all but one horse are scratched, permitting the horse to win by walking the distance.

Walk-up start—In contrast with the standing start at the stall gate, a start in which riders walk horses toward the starting point, and begin to run at the starter's command.

Warm up—Pre-race gallop.

Washy—Of a nervously sweating horse.

Water out—To water horse while it cools out after exertion.

Weanling—A newly weaned horse.

Weave—Of a horse, to move with a swaying, rocking motion in stall, or to pursue erratic course during a race.

Webfoot—A mudder.

Weigh in—Of jockeys, to be weighed with tack after race.

Weigh out—Of jockeys, to be weighed with tack before race.

Weight-for-age race—In which horses carry weights as prescribed by the official scale of weights.

Well let down—Of a horse with long, arched ribs, long forearms and short cannon bones, signifying good lung capacity and an easy, long stride.

Well ribbed up—Of a horse whose last rib is close to its hip, signifying a short, strong back.

Well-sprung ribs—Full, arched ribs for maximum lung capacity.

Welterweights—Weights 28 pounds over the official scale of weights, to test weight-bearing ability of entrants.

Wheel—Of a horse, to turn sharply, almost pinwheeling; a form of betting in which daily-double, perfecta or quinella player makes every possible combination bet on his favored horse or horses.

Whistle—Noisy equine breathing, like a whistle, caused by overstrained respiratory system.

Whoop-de-doo—A riding style that stresses an effort to get the lead immediately and run as fast as possible, with much whip action and little effort at rating; "whoop-de-hoo."

Wind sucker—Of a horse that swallows air, often with spasmodic motions of chin.

Winter—To spend the winter away from competition.

Wound up—Of a fit, ready horse.

INDEX